Targeting Development

A new global consensus has emerged which stresses that the objective of development is to end global poverty. This consensus is accompanied by a bold new set of targets – global poverty to be halved by 2015, along with universal primary education, the removal of gender disparities in schooling, universal access to reproductive healthcare, specific reductions in infant, child and maternal mortality rates, and a reversal in the loss of environmental resources. These 'International Development Targets' were first adopted by the OECD in 1996, and have been succeeded by the yet more widely endorsed 'Millennium Development Goals' following from the UN Millennium Summit in September 2000.

The aim of this book is to provide a critical appraisal of these targets, and the progress so far towards meeting them. The book consists of six introductory chapters on how and why the International Development Targets and Millennium Development Goals (MDG's) have become incorporated into development policy, and what their overall value is. Each chapter in the second part analyses whether current trends suggest the target can be reached. Contributors assess the main constraints that exist to achieving each of these targets and the resulting implications for policy.

This impressive collection featuring an array of respected contributors and a preface from **Mark Malloch Brown** of the UNDP, will be required reading among development economists and those interested in Development Studies more generally. Perhaps more importantly, the lessons learned from this book shall need to be understood and acted upon by policy makers at both National and International levels.

Richard Black is Reader in Human Geography at the University of Sussex, UK. **Howard White** is a Fellow at the Institute of Development Studies, University of Sussex, UK. He is also a co-author of Program Aid and Development and Econometrics and Data Analysis for Developing Countries both of which are also published by Routledge.

Routledge studies in development economics

Targeting Development

Critical Perspectives on the Millennium
Development Goals

**Edited by Richard Black and
Howard White**

Routledge
Taylor & Francis Group

LONDON AND NEW YORK

First published 2004
by Routledge
2 Park Square, Milton Park, Abingdon, Oxon OX14 4RN

Simultaneously published in the USA and Canada
by Routledge
270 Madison Ave, New York, NY 10016

First published in Paperback 2006

Routledge is an imprint of the Taylor & Francis Group, an informa business

Typeset in Baskerville by Wearset Ltd, Boldon, Tyne and Wear
Printed and bound in Great Britain by Antony Rowe Ltd,
Chippenham, Wiltshire

British Library Cataloguing in Publication Data
A catalogue record for this book is available from the British Library

Library of Congress Cataloging in Publication Data
A catalog record for this book has been requested

ISBN 10: 0-415-30376-1 (hbk)
ISBN 10: 0-415-39465-1 (pbk)

ISBN 13: 978-0-415-30376-7 (hbk)
ISBN 13: 978-0-415-39465-9 (pbk)

Contents

Illustrations

Figures

Tables

Boxes

Contributors

Juliana Amadi, Research Assistant, Institute of Development Studies, University of Sussex. Juliana Amadi is an economist with an interest in agricultural issues. She has previously worked on international commodity issues, including a spell at the International Rubber Study Group. Her publications include analyses of crop-level productivity in South Africa.

Richard Black, Professor of Human Geography, University of Sussex and Co-Director of the Sussex Centre for Migration Research, University of Sussex. Richard Black's work focuses on the study of international migration, including forced migration and post-conflict return, and related social and economic transformations. He is Director of a DFID funded Development Research Centre on migration, globalisation and poverty, building on work on migration, return, and post-conflict reconstruction in the Balkans and West Africa. This work developed out of earlier work on refugees and environment in West Africa, and his book *Refugees, Environment and Development* (Longman, 1998).

David Booth, Research Fellow, Poverty and Public Policy Group, Overseas Development Institute. David Booth is a sociologist whose work focuses on policy processes surrounding poverty reduction. Recent work has addressed new aid modalities and the national policy process; process-oriented monitoring and impact assessment; and the role of political analysis in aid, especially in sub-Saharan Africa and Latin America. He led a recent study on poverty reduction strategies in African countries, the findings from which were published in a special issue of *Development Policy Review* (March 2003).

Peter Clarke, NGO field worker specialising in local democracy and development. He has worked for the last sixteen years in the small town of Estelí, Nicaragua, in a changing context of revolution, hyperinflation, structural adjustment and natural disaster. During a recent two-year leave of absence at the Institute of Development Studies he was able to develop his concerns about the lack of relation between aid practice, policy rhetoric, development research and broader social theory.

Christopher Colclough, Professorial Fellow in Development Economics, Institute of Development Studies, University of Sussex. Christopher Colclough's areas of specialisation include educational planning and reform; the costs and financing of education and training; and labour markets and structural adjustment. Recent books include *Achieving Schooling for All in Africa: Costs, Commitment and Gender* (with others), Ashgate 2003; *Public Sector Pay and Adjustment* (ed.), Routledge 1997; *Marketizing Education and Health in Developing Countries* (ed.), OUP 1997, and *Educating All the Children* (with Keith Lewin), OUP 1993. He has worked as an adviser to many governments and international agencies, particularly on questions of education and employment policy. He was a consultant to the ANC and subsequently to the Department of Education in South Africa, 1994–2000, providing advice on the problems of financing the new government's education policies. He is currently Director of the Global Monitoring Report Team on Education for All, based at UNESCO, Paris, where he is responsible for producing an independent annual report which charts progress towards the six 'Dakar' goals and the two Millennium Development goals for education.

James Fairhead, Professor of Anthropology, Department of Anthropology, University of Sussex. James Fairhead's early work focused on issues of power, knowledge and practice in African agriculture and ecology. This led to an anthropology of farming and food systems, of development, and of colonial and post-colonial sciences, policy and administration. Routledge 1998, two books (*Misreading the African Landscape*, CUP 1996 and *Reframing Deforestation*, both co-authored with Melissa Leach) use anthropological and historical methods to confront analytical traditions in African environmental sciences and to expose their political, social and economic commitments. His most recent book, *Science, Power and Society*, CUP 2003, has taken an ethnographic approach to contemporary science and policy, comparing experiences in West Africa and the Caribbean. He is now working on social dimensions to pharmaceutical trials and immunisation.

Richard Jolly, Honorary Professorial Fellow and Research Associate, Institute of Development Studies, University of Sussex. Sir Richard Jolly is a development economist whose career has combined operational involvement with research and teaching in a wide range of countries and situations. He is currently working on a history of the UN's contributions to development ideas and thinking in the economic and social arena and on long-term trends in global inequality. He has previously been Director of IDS (1972–1981), Deputy Executive Director, Programmes of UNICEF (1982–1995) and, from 1996 to 2000, Principal Coordinator of UNDP's *Human Development Report.*

Michael Lipton, Research Professor, Poverty Research Unit at Sussex, University of Sussex. Michael Lipton's research stresses poverty impacts of:

urban–rural and state–market linkages; farm technology and science; nutrition economics; land reform; aid; and population change. In the 1970s he headed a comparative analysis of village studies from developing countries, leading to books by the team on migration, labour use and nutrition. In the 1980s and 1990s he continued to work on urban bias, rural finance, small-scale farming and post-harvest grain loss. Recently he has worked mainly on demographic interactions with poverty, and contributed to UN Human Development Reports on poverty, globalisation and technology; to the World Bank's 2000/2001 World Development Report on poverty; to the Asian Development Bank's Emerging Asia (1997); as Lead Scholar to the International Fund for Agricultural Development's 2001 Rural Poverty Report; and to analyses of the impact of transgenic crops in developing countries by the Nuffield Council on Bioethics (1999 and 2003).

Henry Lucas, Fellow, Institute of Development Studies, University of Sussex. Henry Lucas is a statistician who has specialised in research methods, particularly in the area of health sector analysis and more recently for PRSP monitoring and evaluation. He has been the principal researcher in a number of recent studies involving the combination of quantitative and qualitative/participatory fieldwork methods. These have included a review of the Malawi Social Action Fund, an exploration of the links between energy, poverty and gender in poor rural areas of China, and monitoring and evaluation aspects of a major DFID health-care programme in Nigeria. He has many years of experience in China and has undertaken a number of studies on both rural and urban healthcare reforms.

Simon Maxwell, Director, Overseas Development Institute. Simon Maxwell is Director of ODI and President of the Development Studies Association of the UK and Ireland. He worked overseas for ten years, in Kenya, India and Bolivia, and then for fifteen years at the Institute of Development Studies at the University of Sussex, latterly as Programme Manager for Poverty, Food Security and the Environment. He became Director of ODI in 1997. He is an economist with research interests in development theory and policy; poverty; food security; economic, social and cultural rights; and aid. He has advised many international agencies and governments on poverty reduction issues.

Ronald Skeldon, Professorial Fellow, Department of Geography, University of Sussex, Honorary Professor, University of Hong Kong, and Adjunct Professor at the Institute for Population and Social Research at Mahidol University, Thailand. Ronald Skeldon's research is based around questions of population and development, primarily in East and Southeast Asia. Recent work has focused on the migrations of the Chinese peoples, particularly from Hong Kong, and on irregular movements of migrants in and through Southeast Asia. Other research has concentrated on population mobility and HIV/AIDS in Southeast Asia and on questions of child labour in Asia.

Hilary Standing, Fellow, Institute of Development Studies, University of Sussex. Hilary Standing is a social anthropologist specialising in health research and social development. Current interests include household level and gender aspects of health and formal and informal care systems, gender and equity in the context of health reforms, the management of organisational change in health sector restructuring, especially the changing roles of providers, and improving greater accountability within health systems. She has worked extensively in rural and urban South Asia and convenes the international Gender and Health Equity Network.

Ramya Subrahmanian, Fellow, Institute of Development Studies, University of Sussex. Ramya Subrahmanian is a development specialist with extensive experience in the areas of gender, social development and education. Her experience includes work on mainstreaming gender/social development into development policies and institutional processes in a wide range of development agencies. Current research includes work on education exclusion, policy processes, livelihoods and education, including a recently co-edited volume, *Child Labour and the Right to Education in South Asia: Needs versus Rights?*, Sage 2003.

Jan Vandemoortele, Leader, Socio-economic Development Group, United Nations Development Programme. Jan Vandemoortele is an economist whose work has focused on labour market policies, public finance, income distribution, poverty reduction and social policy. Between 1995–2001, he was head of Social Policy at UNICEF. Between 1991–1994, he served with UNDP as Senior Economist in Malawi/Zambia as well as with the Regional Bureau for Africa. Prior to that, he worked for thirteen years for the ILO, mostly in Africa.

Hugh Waddington, Research Assistant, Poverty Research Unit at Sussex, University of Sussex. Hugh Waddington is an economist with an interest in poverty issues. He is currently engaged in preparing case studies of aid effectiveness for DFID.

Kevin Watkins, Senior Policy Advisor, Oxfam, UK. Kevin Watkins has extensive experience of researching and campaigning on global and development issues. Recent publications for Oxfam include *Rigged Rules and Double Standards: Trade, Globalization, and the Fight Against Poverty* and the *Oxfam Education Report*.

Howard White, Fellow, Institute of Development Studies, University of Sussex. Howard White is an economist with interests in poverty analysis, macroeconomic debates (especially related to growth and distribution), the determinants of human development and aid effectiveness (including the recent co-authored book, *Programme Aid and Development*, Routledge 2003). He has worked in a number of African countries (most recently Ghana, Tanzania and Zambia) as well as Sri Lanka and Vietnam. He is currently on secondment to the Operations Evaluation Department of the World Bank.

Foreword

The Millennium Development Goals have had a catalytic effect on the global development debate, largely because of their simplicity and measurability – and thus accessibility. Anybody can understand them, grasp that they matter, judge whether or not his or her country and the wider world is doing enough to achieve them, and take action if they are not. They are a bottom-up, grass-roots, pocket-book development agenda, firmly focused on the bread and butter of political life everywhere.

These Millennium Development Goals did not come out of thin air. They were agreed at the historic UN Millennium Summit in 2000 and are derived from the UN conferences of the 1990s. They also lie at the heart of the Monterrey Consensus and the Johannesburg Plan agreed at the World Summit for Sustainable Development in 2002.

As United Nations Development Programme Administrator I am responsible for leading the United Nations system in developing a strategy to support the achievement of the Goals. But my involvement extends beyond this formal responsibility to my own deep commitment to the principles behind the Millennium Development Goals. Central to reaching the Goals is the task of forging partnerships: of governments of poor and rich countries, of private corporations and foundations, of multilateral agencies, of civil society organisations, and, most importantly, of the poor themselves.

From hard experience with many past initiatives, we know that ownership is indispensable to success. To ensure that ownership, the Goals need to be customised and tailored to national circumstances and built into national medium-term goals and strategies. For over seventy of the world's poorest countries, these strategies take the form of a Poverty Reduction Strategy Paper (PRSP). The Goals can be seen as both the front and the back end of the PRSPs: they represent the overarching objectives of the PRSPs and the way to monitor whether they are performing as advertised. As such, the Goals offer a real-time accountability framework – tracking what is working and what isn't, where progress is being made and thus helping drive real change in a much more timely and effective manner than the traditional five- and ten-year conference reviews.

The success or failure of this entire vision depends crucially on a global partnership between developed and developing countries, expressed in Goal 8. It is no exaggeration to say the outcome will hinge on the commitments of rich countries to help poorer nations that are undertaking economic, political and social reforms in good faith. While the reallocation of domestic resources will be instrumental – alongside strengthened governance and sound social and economic policies – these measures alone are unlikely to be sufficient to achieve the Millennium Development Goals.

Goals and targets to halve hunger and poverty will fail without a fundamental restructuring of the global trading system, particularly in agriculture and textiles. The fight against HIV/AIDS, malaria and other diseases will be lost without affordable essential drugs. Without steep and fast debt relief, macroeconomic stability will remain elusive for most of the heavily indebted poor countries. And last, but by no means least, it is important to remember that an extra $50 billion in annual official development assistance will be a minimum to meet the Goals.

Yet there is a chance the poor will get those resources – and, much more important, the political and social momentum for real change on the Millennium Development Goals as a simple but powerful idea whose time has come. Already these Goals are taking discussions about development to classrooms and coffee houses, town halls and tenements, fields and factories, showing everyone from the president or prime minister down to schoolchildren where more attention needs to be paid and where things are off track, where more resources are essential and where they are not being effectively used.

It is against this background that I warmly welcome this book. The various chapters provide thoughtful and important contributions to formulating reforms to meet the Millennium Development Goals. The contributors do not suggest that meeting the Goals or implementing the required changes will be easy – and I agree with them. But nor do they suggest that it is impossible – again, I agree with them. It is by tackling the issues they raise that we can make the dream of a world without poverty a practical reality.

Mark Malloch Brown
UNDP Administrator

Preface

A new global consensus has emerged that stresses that the objective of development is to end global poverty. This consensus is accompanied by a bold new set of targets – global poverty to be halved by 2015, along with universal primary education, the removal of gender disparities in schooling, universal access to reproductive healthcare, specific reductions in infant, child and maternal mortality rates, and a reversal in the loss of environmental resources. These International Development Targets (IDTs) were first adopted by the OECD in 1996, and have been taken up enthusiastically by the New Labour government in Britain and many international development agencies. The UN Millennium Summit in September 2000 endorsed the approach, setting its own Millennium Development Goals (MDGs), which again put the elimination of poverty at the heart of the international development agenda.

The aim of this book is to provide a critical appraisal of these targets, the progress so far towards meeting them, and obstacles to their attainment. The book consists of six introductory chapters on how and why the International Development Targets and Millennium Development Goals have become incorporated into development policy, their overall value, and an assessment of whether they are feasible, followed by a chapter addressing each goal or target (or related set of targets). Each chapter in the second part sets out the background behind the target, and analyses whether current trends suggest the target can be reached. Is even a global halving of poverty – rather than its 'eradication' – achievable? Can the world realistically move towards universal education and access to reproductive healthcare, and does it make sense to set a time limit for the achievement of these objectives?

Contributors assess the main constraints that exist to achieving each of these targets and the resulting implications for policy. They also consider the relevance of the targets that have been set in London and Washington to the problems of the poorer countries of the world, suggesting alternative approaches where appropriate. In doing this, the aim is to undertake the first comprehensive account of the International Development Targets and Millennium Development Goals and progress towards them.

The book is based on a series of 'Sussex Development Lectures' first delivered at the University of Sussex in Autumn 2001. These lectures represent a collaborative initiative between a group of Sussex institutes and centres concerned with international development, including the Institute of Development Studies (IDS), the Culture, Development and Environment Centre (CDE), the Science and Technology Policy Research Unit (SPRU), the Institute of Education (USIE) and the Economics, International Relations and Politics, Social Anthropology and Geography Subject Groups. The lecture series was delivered primarily by faculty based at Sussex, and this is reflected in the origin of the majority of contributors to this volume. However, we have also gone outside Sussex to commission a small number of additional chapters, in order to give a fully rounded view of the targets, and gain additional insights.

We would like to thank all those who have contributed to making this book a reality. Special thanks go to Hugh Waddington for his careful editing of the chapters and Julie McWilliam for producing the final versions. Part of Howard White's input to the editing of this collection has been funded by DFID support to research on poverty reduction policies and we are grateful for this funding. All royalties from the production of this book are being donated to Oxfam.

Richard Black
Howard White
Falmer, University of Sussex

Abbreviations

ACP	Africa, Caribbean and Pacific
ARDE	Annual Review of Development Effectiveness
ARROW	Asian-Pacific Resource and Research Centre for Women
ATC	Agreement of Textiles and Clothing
ATP	Aid-Trade Provision
CBN	cost of basic needs
CEDAW	Convention on the Elimination of All Forms of Discrimination against Women
CEO	Chief Executive Officer
CHANGE	Center for Health and Gender Equity
CIA	Central Intelligence Agency (USA)
CIDA	Canadian International Development Agency
CPR	contraceptive prevalence rate
CSP	Country Strategy Paper
CWIQ	Core Welfare Indicators Questionnaire
DAC	Development Assistance Committee (of the Organisation for Economic Cooperation and Development)
DFID	Department for International Development (UK)
DHS	Demographic and Health Survey
DOTS	Directly Observed Treatment Short Course
DRC	Democratic Republic of Congo
DTI	Department for Trade and Industry (UK)
EC	European Commission
EPI	Expanded Programme of Immunisation
EU	European Union
FAO	Food and Agriculture Organisation
FCO	Foreign and Commonwealth Office (UK)
FEM	food energy method
FEZ	Food Economy Zone
FY	fiscal year
GAO	General Accounting Office (USA)
GATS	General Agreement on Trade in Services
GAVI	Global Alliance for Vaccines and Immunisation

GDP	gross domestic product
GER	gross enrolment ratio
GM	genetic modification
GNI	gross national income
GNP	gross national product
GPRA	Government Performance and Results Act (USA)
HDR	*Human Development Report*
HIPC	heavily indebted poor country
ICPD	International Conference on Population and Development
IDA	International Development Agency
IFAD	International Fund for Agricultural Development
IMF	International Monetary Fund
I-PRSP	Interim Poverty Reduction Strategy Paper
ISP	Institutional Strategy Paper
LDC	least developed country
MCH	maternal and child health
MFA	Multi-Fibre Agreement
MMR	maternal mortality ratio
MoD	Ministry of Defence (UK)
MTEF	Medium Term Expenditure Framework
NAO	National Audit Office (UK)
NEPAD	New Partnership for Africa's Development
NER	net primary enrolment ratio
NGO	non-governmental organisation
NHP	National Health Programme (Oman)
NIC	newly industrialising country; National Intelligence Council (USA)
ODA	Official Development Assistance
OECD	Organisation for Economic Cooperation and Development
OED	Operations Evaluation Department
ORT	oral rehydration therapy
PAM	Poverty Aim Marker
PARIS	Partnerships in Statistics for Development in the Twenty-First Century
PEAP	Poverty Eradication Action Plan (Uganda)
PER	Public Expenditure Review
PET	public expenditure tracking
PETS	Public Expenditure Tracking Studies
PPA	Participatory Poverty Assessment
PPP	purchasing power parity
PRA	Participatory Rural Appraisal
PRSC	Poverty Reduction Strategy Credit
PRSP	Poverty Reduction Strategy Paper
PSA	Public Service Agreement
RAWOO	Netherlands Development Assistance Research Council

RBM	results-based management
ROAR	Results-Oriented Annual Report
RTI	reproductive tract infection
SDA	Service Delivery Agreement
SPA	Strategic Partnership for Africa (previously Special Partnership for Africa)
STI	sexually transmitted infection
SWAP	sector-wide approach
TRIMs	Trade-Related Investment Measures
TRIPs	Trade-Related Aspects of Intellectual Property Rights
TSP	Target Strategy Paper
UCI	universal coverage of immunisation
UN	United Nations
UNCTAD	United Nations Conference on Trade and Development
UNDP	United Nations Development Programme
UNESCO	United Nations Educational, Scientific and Cultural Organisation
UNFPA	United Nations Fund for Population Activities
UNICEF	United Nations Children's Fund
UNRISD	United Nations Research Institute for Social Development
USAID	United States Agency for International Development
VIP	ventilated improved pit latrine
WDR	*World Development Report*
WHO	World Health Organisation
WIDER	World Institute for Development Economics Research
WSSCC	Water Supply and Sanitation Collaboration Council

1 Millennium Development Goals

A drop in the ocean?

Howard White and Richard Black

Introduction

What are the development targets, such as the International Development Targets and the Millennium Development Goals, for? For supporters, they are a crystallisation of what it is that international development is supposed to be about. The Targets are seven quantifiable goals, against which the performance of donors and international development agencies can be measured. First set out in the Organisation for Economic Cooperation and Development (OECD) document *Shaping the Twenty-First Century* (OECD, 1996), they won unprecedented support and prominence. In the UK in particular, the Department for International Development (DFID), and its former Secretary of State, Clare Short, was vocal in promoting the International Development Targets. They have occupied a central position in two government White Papers, the public pronouncements of the Secretary of State, and within DFID in developing its new anti-poverty strategy. Meanwhile, agreement on the 'Millennium Development Goals' at the Millennium Summit in New York in September 2000 has extended the number of agreed targets to eighteen, although some are not precisely defined.[1]

Yet there have been many previous development goals and targets over the decades. International development agencies and donors have sought to promote economic growth, and then 'growth with equity'; in the 1980s there was then a shift towards the meeting of 'basic needs', before the rhetoric of 'sustainable development' took over in the 1990s. Why, then, is this set of goals and targets new? Do they justify analysis, or are they simply a passing fad? Clearly, our argument is that they do merit attention. As a comprehensive and measurable set of indicators, the International Development Targets and the successor Millennium Development Goals have established themselves as a major force in current development practice. They help to define both the goal of development cooperation activities, and a set of priorities to be followed within these activities. They sit alongside other international goals and targets, notably those relating to climate change that followed from the Earth Summit in 1992. International targets also stand as a basis on which development practitioners can be held accountable for their actions.

This does not mean, however, that the targets are, or should be universally accepted as, a guide and measure of international development performance. It is clear, for example, that they are more significant for some donors than for others. The World Bank and the International Monetary Fund (IMF) both adopted the International Development Targets, and they became a reference point for the World Bank's annual flagship statistical publication *World Development Indicators*. However, for most other donors they did not assume the importance they did for DFID, although the Millennium Development Goals have gained greater prominence. Both the United Nations Development Programme (UNDP) and the World Bank have Web sites dedicated to the Millennium Development Goals, with links from their home pages. The extent to which the targets have influenced strategy and programmes is of course another matter, one which is pursued throughout this volume. Whilst growing out of the OECD's Development Assistance Committee (DAC), and endorsed by the United Nations (UN), the targets have already arguably been overtaken for some, especially in the US administration, by new concerns to tie development assistance to security issues in the post-11 September 'war on terrorism'. Moreover, although quite broad in their conception of poverty, and ranging across several different sectors, the targets could still be seen as quite limited and narrow in their scope – more basic even than 'basic needs'. Some would reject the contention that the goals of international development practice can be reduced to a set of quantifiable indicators, whilst the action required to achieve these goals could be perceived as rather unambitious. In this sense, are the International Development Targets and the successor Millennium Development Goals simply a drop in the ocean?

It is the aim of this chapter to examine what the International Development Targets and Millennium Development Goals are trying to achieve, and whether it is worth achieving. Subsequent chapters then follow up specific aspects of an approach based on targets, before focusing attention on the extent to which progress is being made towards meeting various individual targets. This chapter begins with a brief introduction to the targets as measures of performance, and why they have gained in importance. We then move on to discuss the extent to which the International Development Targets and Millennium Development Goals really matter, and some of the problems that are inherent in their adoption. Finally, we provide a summary of how the argument is taken forward in subsequent chapters.

What are the International Development Targets and Millennium Development Goals?

The International Development Targets

The International Development Targets are diverse both in nature and provenance (Table 1.1). Divided into three fields – economic well-being, social development and environmental sustainability and regeneration – they collectively represent a set of goals for poverty reduction, embodying a multidimensional conception of poverty (Baulch, 1996; White, 1999). The targets demonstrate that in current development practice, poverty is about more than just a lack of income. Instead, drawing on the work of the UNDP on 'human development', and a series of UN conferences through the 1990s, they extend to include deprivation with respect to other aspects of well-being such as health and education.

The targets share a number of characteristics. First, each is designed to be quantifiable, although in some cases this causes difficulty. In particular, there is no agreed indicator for access to reproductive health services. Contraceptive prevalence is commonly used as an indicator, but is not acceptable in some cultures, whilst the United States Agency for International Development (USAID) is forbidden by law to support programmes that provide abortion services. Even where contraceptive prevalence is acceptable, there is no agreed target level, since the desired level depends on desired fertility.

Second, most of the targets define the expected outcomes of development, rather than inputs in the form of resources. This, for example, sets them apart from the best known of previous development targets – that developed nations should set aside 0.7 per cent of their gross domestic product (GDP) in development assistance. However, here too there are exceptions. Thus the target on environmental sustainability stresses the need for national-level planning, rather than any particular environmental outcome, whilst targets for reproductive health and education stress access to services rather than health or educational results.

Third, accompanying the targets as a whole is a statement recognising the importance of qualitative factors related to governance. The current consensus amongst the international community is that democratic accountability and a lack of corruption are necessary to achieve poverty reduction goals. Although there are numerical indicators for such things (such as those produced by Freedom House on political freedom and civil liberties),[2] they have not been used to monitor progress. This is because donors have been unable to reach agreement on what should go into such indicators. In this context, 'good governance' is less a goal in itself, and more a precondition for meeting the development targets.

Confusingly, the targets too have not remained fixed. An additional target was added on HIV/AIDS, namely a 25 per cent reduction in HIV

Table 1.1 The International Development Targets

Target	Where the target comes from
Economic well-being	
• The proportion of people living in extreme *poverty* in developing countries should be reduced by at least one-half by 2015	• Copenhagen Declaration and Programme of Action (1995)
Social development There should be substantial progress in primary education, gender equality, basic health care and family planning, as follows:	
• *Universal primary education* should be achieved in all countries by 2015	• Jomtien Conference on Education for All (1990), endorsed at Copenhagen Summit on Social Development (1995) and Beijing Conference on Women (1995)
• Progress toward *gender equality* and the empowerment of women shall be demonstrated by eliminating gender disparity in primary and secondary education by 2015	• Cairo Conference on Population and Development (1994), also Beijing and Copenhagen
• The *death rates for infants and children aged under 5 years* should be reduced in each developing country by two-thirds of the 1990 level by 2015	• Cairo, confirmed at Beijing
• The rate of *maternal mortality* should be reduced by three-quarters during this same period	• Cairo, confirmed at Beijing
• Access should be available through the primary health care system to *reproductive health* services for all individuals of appropriate ages, including safe and reliable family planning methods, as soon as possible and no later than the year 2015	• Cairo
Environmental sustainability and regeneration	
• There should be a current national strategy for sustainable development, in the process of implementation, in every country, by 2005, so as to ensure that current trends in the loss of environmental resources – forests, fisheries, fresh water, climate, soils, biodiversity, stratospheric ozone and the accumulation of hazardous substances and other major indicators – are effectively reversed at both global and national levels	• Rio Conference on Environment and Development (1992)

Source: Development Assistance Committee (1996).

infection rates amongst 15 to 24-year-olds in the worst-affected countries by 2005 and globally by 2010. Meanwhile, the rather general target on environmental sustainability was altered to include more specific goals, including some 'outcomes' in terms of protection, energy use and emissions. There are also more indicators that can be used to measure progress than those explicitly mentioned in the definition of each target. A list of indicators has been developed around each target (Table 1.2), many of which are also outcome indicators. In the three cases in which the target itself does not measure outcome (education, reproductive health and environment), some of the related indicators do so (e.g. literacy rates and fertility rates). In other cases, the additional indicators listed do not measure outcomes, but provide a quantifiable indicator of access to a service that critically affects the desired outcome (e.g. attended births).

The International Development Targets were formally adopted at the Thirty-Fourth High-Level Meeting of the DAC on 6–7 May 1996 in Paris. Given the recent prominence of 'participatory' approaches to

Table 1.2 Target-related indicators

Target	Indicators
Poverty reduction	Population below a dollar a day Incidence times depth of poverty Poorest fifth's share of national consumption Prevalence of underweight under 5
Universal primary education	Net primary enrolment ratio Survival to fifth grade of primary education Literacy rate of adults
Gender equality	Ratio of girls to boys in primary and secondary education Ratio of literate females to males
Infant mortality reduction	Infant mortality rate
Child mortality reduction	Under-five mortality rate
Maternal mortality reduction	Maternal mortality ratio Births attended by skilled health personnel
Reproductive health	Contraceptive prevalence rate Total fertility rate
Environment	Existence of national strategies for sustainable development
Sustainable environment	Population with access to safe water Biodiversity: land area protected Energy efficiency: GDP per unit of energy use Carbon dioxide emissions

Source: DAC 'Methodological Note', DCD/DAC (98)6/ADD, Paris: OECD/DAC (available at http://www1.oecd.org/dac/Indicators/pdf/METHOD.PDF).

development, and the fact that the targets themselves are conceived as part of the process of making development assistance more accountable to aid beneficiaries (see pp. 12–13), it is somewhat ironic that it was a developed country group such as DAC that set targets for developing countries.

There are two defences against this criticism. First, developing country governments do not have to sign up to precisely these poverty reduction goals. Rather, the idea is that donor support should be predicated upon recipient commitment to poverty reduction, measured against an appropriate target that they may choose themselves. For example, the target of the Ugandan government is to reduce the poverty head count to 10 per cent or less by 2016, in addition to meeting specific target figures for infant and child mortality. Second, the International Development Targets were based on resolutions passed at various international conferences, and in this sense they have already been endorsed by developing countries. Nonetheless, in some cases it is the principle rather than the specific target that was adopted at UN conferences. This is the case, for example, with the target set for reduction in income poverty.

The Millennium Development Goals

The discontent felt in some quarters that the International Development Targets represented an imposition by the developed country members of the Development Assistance Committee manifested itself at the Millennium Summit in New York held on 6–8 September 2000. There, an alternative set of development targets, the Millennium Development Goals, was adopted (UN, 2000). The *Millennium Declaration* contained a list of goals which overlapped with the International Development Targets but were not the same. However, a year later the UN document *Road Map towards the Implementation of the United Nations Millennium Declaration* laid out a finally agreed list of Millennium Development Goals as shown in Table 1.3. This list fully encompassed the earlier targets, whilst adding new elements of its own.[3] The most notable differences between the two sets of targets are as follows:

- There are more Millennium Development Goals than International Development Targets, comprising eight goals with eighteen separate targets (although seven of these targets relate to the new eighth goal of global partnership); there is an expanded list of forty-eight indicators to monitor the targets (which are still under development).
- The International Development Targets are embodied in the first seven Goals, but with additional aspects added, notably nutrition, shelter and diseases other than HIV/AIDS.
- Although governance indicators are still generally absent, female representation in parliament is included amongst the expanded set of indicators for gender equality.

Table 1.3 The Millennium Development Goals

Goals and targets	Indicators

Goal 1: Eradicate extreme poverty and hunger

Target 1: Halve, between 1990 and 2015, the proportion of people whose income is less than one dollar a day

1 Proportion of population below US$1 per day
2 Poverty gap ratio [incidence multiplied by depth of poverty]
3 Share of poorest quintile in national consumption

Target 2: Halve, between 1990 and 2015, the proportion of people who suffer from hunger

4 Prevalence of underweight children (under 5 years of age)
5 Proportion of population below minimum level of dietary energy consumption

Goal 2: Achieve universal primary education

Target 3: Ensure that by 2015 children everywhere, boys and girls alike, will be able to complete a full course of primary schooling

6 Net enrolment ratio in primary education
7 Proportion of pupils starting grade 1 who reach grade 5
8 Literacy rate of 15- to 24-year-olds

Goal 3: Promote gender equality and empower women

Target 4: Eliminate gender disparity in primary and secondary education preferably by 2005 and to all levels of education no later than 2015

9 Ratio of girls to boys in primary, secondary and tertiary education
10 Ratio of literate females to males of 15- to 24-year-olds
11 Share of women in wage employment in the non-agricultural sector
12 Proportion of seats held by women in national parliament

Goal 4: Reduce child mortality

Target 5: Reduce by two-thirds, between 1990 and 2015, the under-five mortality rate

13 Under-five mortality rate
14 Infant mortality rate
15 Proportion of 1-year-old children immunised against measles

Goal 5: Improve maternal health

Target 6: Reduce by three-quarters, between 1990 and 2015, the maternal mortality ratio

16 Maternal mortality ratio
17 Proportion of births attended by skilled health personnel

Goal 6: Combat HIV/AIDS, malaria and other diseases

Target 7: Have halted by 2015, and begun to reverse, the spread of HIV/AIDS

18 HIV prevalence among 15- to 24-year-old pregnant women
19 Contraceptive prevalence rate
20 Number of children orphaned by HIV/AIDS

continued

Table 1.3 continued

Goals and targets	Indicators
Target 8: Have halted by 2015, and begun to reverse, the incidence of malaria and other major diseases	21 Prevalence and death rates associated with malaria 22 Proportion of population in malaria risk areas using effective malaria prevention and treatment measures. 23 Prevalence and death rates associated with tuberculosis 24 Proportion of tuberculosis cases detected and cured under DOTS (Directly Observed Treatment Short Course)
Goal 7: Ensure environmental sustainability[a]	
Target 9: Integrate the principles of sustainable development into country policies and programmes and reverse the loss of environmental resources	25 Proportion of land area covered by forest 26 Land area protected to maintain biological diversity 27 GDP per unit of energy use (as proxy for energy efficiency) 28 Carbon dioxide emissions (per capita). [Plus two figures for global atmospheric pollution: ozone depletion and the accumulation of global warming gases.]
Target 10: Halve, by 2015, the proportion of people without sustainable access to safe drinking water	29 Proportion of population with sustainable access to an improved water source
Target 11: By 2020, to have achieved a significant improvement in the lives of at least 100 million slum-dwellers	30 Proportion of people with access to improved sanitation 31 Proportion of people with access to secure tenure. [Urban/rural disaggregation of several of the above indicators may be relevant for monitoring improvement in the lives of slum dwellers.]

continued

Table 1.3 continued

Goals and targets	Indicators
Goal 8: Develop a Global Partnership for Development[a]	

Target 12: Develop further an open, rule-based, predictable, non-discriminatory trading and financial system. Includes a commitment to good governance, development, and poverty reduction – both nationally and internationally

Target 13: Address the special deeds of the Least Developed Countries (LDCs). Includes: tariff and quota free access for LDC exports; enhanced programme of debt relief for Heavily Indebted Poor Countries (HIPC) and cancellation of official bilateral debt; and more generous Official Development Assistance (ODA) for countries committed to poverty reduction

Target 14: Address the special needs of landlocked countries and small island developing states (through Barbados Programme and Twenty-Second General Assembly provisions)

Target 15: Deal comprehensively with the debt problems of developing countries through national and international measures in order to make debt sustainable in the long term

Target 16: In co-operation with developing countries, develop and implement strategies for decent and productive work for youth

Target 17: In co-operation with pharmaceutical companies, provide access to affordable, essential drugs in developing countries

Target 18: In co-operation with the private sector, make available the benefits of new technologies, especially information and communications

Some of the indicators listed below will be monitored separately for the Least Developed Countries, Africa, landlocked countries and small island developing states

Official Development Assistance (ODA)

32 Net ODA as percentage of DAC donors' gross national income (GNI) [targets of 0.7 per cent in total and 0.15 per cent for LDCs]

33 Proportion of ODA to basic social services (basic education, primary health care, nutrition, safe water and sanitation)

34 Proportion of ODA that is untied

35 Proportion of ODA for environment in small island developing states

36 Proportion of ODA for transport sector in land-locked countries

Market access

37 Proportion of exports (by value and excluding arms) admitted free of duties and quotas

38 Average tariffs and quotas on agricultural products and textiles and clothing

39 Domestic and export agricultural subsidies in OECD countries

40 Proportion of ODA provided to help build trade capacity

Debt sustainability

41 Proportion of official bilateral HIPC debt cancelled

42 Debt service as a percentage of exports of goods and services

43 Proportion of ODA provided as debt relief

44 Number of countries reaching HIPC decision and completion points

45 Unemployment rate of 15- to 24-year-olds

46 Proportion of population with access to affordable essential drugs on a sustainable basis

47 Telephone lines per 1,000 people

48 Personal computers per 1,000 people

Source: UN (2001) www.oecd.org/DAC.

Note

a The selection of indicators for Goals 7 and 8 is subject to further refinement.

- The new eighth goal adds targets relating to the direct contribution of the developed countries to meeting the Millennium Development Goals, with mention of aid, debt relief and tariff barriers. It is significant that such actions (e.g. debt reduction, higher aid) have been added. However, the wording of most of these is vague ('address ... ', 'deal comprehensively with ... ', 'more generous ... ', etc.) compared to the precise numerical goals for developing country performance.

With the adoption of the Millennium Development Goals, the prominence of the targets has increased amongst donor agencies. The extent to which these targets represent a valuable set of measures on which to assess international development performance is considered in more depth in Chapter 3.

Why have targets gained importance?

Why have first the International Development Targets, and now the Millennium Development Goals, gained an importance that escaped previous development targets? Three reasons suggest themselves. The first is the establishment of poverty at the top of the development agenda during the 1990s. Of course, poverty has always been a concern for development agencies, though the extent to which it has received explicit attention has varied greatly across time, and between different agencies. Yet during the 1990s nearly all development agencies have reaffirmed and strengthened their commitment to poverty reduction and have been searching for ways in which to realise this commitment. The end of the Cold War in some respects released development aid from its political straitjacket, allowing greater autonomy for development agencies in the definition of their objectives. Thus in the UK, DFID was able to steer an International Development Act through Parliament in early 2002, which defined the objective of development as the eradication of poverty.[4]

Adoption of the International Development Goals, and subsequently the Millennium Development Goals, has been part of this process. For example, for DFID, the targets have been internalised into agency practice, setting out in concrete terms the general orientation towards poverty eradication. The new formulation has been designed not only to act as a guide for action, but also as a bulwark against the diversion of aid that was perceived by some in government and outside to have occurred in the past – notably incidents such as the linking of UK development aid for the Pergau Dam in Malaysia to the sale of arms. Nonetheless, there have been countervailing tendencies – notably the increased role played by humanitarian assistance, and the rise of political–military involvement in this sector both before, but especially after, 11 September 2001.

Second, the 1990s also saw an emerging emphasis on results-based management (RBM), especially in North America. For example, the

World Bank adopted this approach in 1993, whilst in 1995 the Canadian International Development Agency (CIDA) produced an overview of its experience (Brown, 1995).[5] Of course, donors have always aimed to have some sort of monitoring at the project level, albeit often with an input focus. Project monitoring is carried out both by the project management and, often drawing on that, by agency staff for their own purposes through supervision missions, mid-term reviews and the like. For example, the World Bank has 'Project Performance Reports',[6] which are completed for each project following a staff mission to the project, usually on an annual basis. These reports include an assessment of performance on several criteria and overall development impact as judged against the project objectives. However, the rise of results-based management has shifted the focus to country programmes and the agency's overall performance (DAC, 2000: 18).

Once again, results orientation has taken a particular hold in the UK. It first emerged in the 1990s, notably with the introduction of the Citizen's Charter, and league tables for schools. Since 1997, the Labour government that took office in that year has warmly embraced this approach, starting with its five pre-election pledges and continuing, for example, with the expansion of league tables to other public services.[7] A recent best-selling account of 'new' Labour's first term in office in Britain put it that 'the government had more targets – over 6,000 on one count – than Stalin' (Rawnsley, 2001: 292). Within UK government practice, what are known as 'Public Service Agreements' (PSAs) embody this approach. The Public Service Agreement and Service Delivery Agreement are written commitments of a department's objectives, related performance measures, and the activities to be undertaken in support of those objectives. In turn, the International Development Targets are an obvious set of development results for development agencies to attach themselves to, and DFID has used them as the basis for its PSA targets (see Chapter 3).

The third point is that the targets have received strong support from some key institutional actors, which has helped to propagate them elsewhere. For the International Development Targets, their origin in the DAC and subsequent championing by DFID helped them gain a foothold in the international community, their position becoming assured once they were adopted by the World Bank. The Millennium Development Goals came from an even broader institutional base, the UN, but the seriousness with which they have been taken by the international community rests with the groundwork done for the International Development Targets.

However, whilst there is no doubt that the targets have become important, questions can be raised as to whether this is a good thing or not. This question can be asked in two ways. First, are outcome targets of any sort a good guide to policy? Second, are the specific targets that have been set for development a good set of performance measures? These questions are addressed in the next two sections.

Do targets matter?

Targets can be seen as important for a number of reasons (Box 1.1). First, the identification of targets can be one way to define an organisation's purpose, since they set out what exactly is to be achieved in terms of outcomes. During the past decade, most development agencies have adopted an overall aim related to poverty reduction. For DFID, this is the 'the elimination of poverty in poorer countries', whilst for the World Bank, the aim is 'a world free of poverty'. Yet what does 'the elimination of poverty' mean in a world where it is accepted that poverty is multidimensional? Targets make what is potentially a very general statement of purpose much more specific, by outlining what development organisations aim to achieve across the different dimensions of poverty. That said, there is of course quite a gap between the aspiration to 'eliminate' poverty, and the target of reducing it by half within twenty years, leading to the possible charge that setting an exact target leads to a watering down of aspirations.

The focus on outcomes is nonetheless important. There has been a tendency, certainly amongst development agencies, to have performance measurement systems (monitoring and evaluation) with too strong a focus on inputs. In such systems, often the only question is: 'Was the money spent?' Worse, there is a tendency for budgetary units to spend money quickly towards the end of a budget year, in order to meet their financial targets. In contrast, stressing outcomes reminds us what the money is being spent for. If the outcomes are not being achieved, then having spent the money may be a bad thing rather than a good thing.

A second important point is accountability. It is increasingly recognised that public bodies need to be held accountable for their activities. With clear targets for development, international aid agencies can in principle be held to account for their performance in achieving these targets, just as companies are held accountable to shareholders, government departments to taxpayers or politicians to voters. The statement of a target represents a commitment to achieve that target, so that the agency can be judged by whether it does so or not. By stating a clear target, an organisation can also show clearly what its purpose is, so, in the case of government departments, can make a case for funding. In an age when all government budget headings are under scrutiny, and public support for

Box 1.1 Why do international targets matter?

- They define the objectives of policy in terms of outcomes.
- They provide a basis for accountability.
- They make a case for carrying out supporting activities.
- They allow comparisons of performance to be made.
- They create a sense of common purpose.

international development assistance cannot be assumed, aid programmes can arguably be defended on the basis that they help to make quantifiable progress towards reducing world poverty.

However, there are some problems with using targets to make development agencies accountable for their performance (see also Chapter 3 for an elaboration of such problems). First, there is the issue of how simple or complex the target is. A simple target – eliminating poverty, for example – is easy for the public to understand, but correspondingly difficult to achieve. Yet as soon as it is made more concrete, it also becomes more complex, such that there is no longer any single 'bottom line' on which a government or agency can be measured. This links to a second point, concerning the discrepancy between the wide range of activities across which the public wishes a government or government agency to perform, and the narrow range of remedies the public has in holding a government or one of its agencies to account.

In a company, for example, it is possible for shareholders to remove an underperforming director, or require an existing board to modify its approach in certain ways following an annual meeting. In contrast, voters have only one direct sanction against underperformance of government ministers or ministries – to sack the entire government – and even then, usually have the chance to use that sanction only once every four or five years. This begs the question of how voters (or others) might hold a government or development agency accountable for failure to meet one or more of the international development targets. It is not generally possible to vote out an international development minister whilst leaving her government in place. Nor, given the twenty-year lifespan of the international development targets, is it likely that ministers or officials responsible for setting the targets (and committing themselves to achieving them) will still be around at the time when it is clear whether or not they have been achieved.

Of course, some progress can be made in this direction. For example, it is possible to tell already whether certain individual development targets are likely to be achieved – indeed, that is one purpose of this book. Moreover, some indirect pressure could be brought to bear on development agencies, for example via the media, if progress is not being achieved. There might be calls for the resignation of a minister or senior officials who were seen as falling short of stated objectives. However, even if it were possible to hold individuals or departments accountable in this way, this still begs a number of important questions, notably the question of to *whom* such individuals or departments should be accountable. In the case of aid donors, accountability is formally to 'Northern' electorates, which are not directly affected by whether development targets are met or not. In the case of international organisations such as the UN, the lines of accountability are less clear. In neither case is there direct accountability to the beneficiaries of development aid.

However, this point does lead to a third argument for setting international development targets, which is that they can be linked to a rights-based approach. Rights-based approaches – increasingly popular with many development agencies – focus not so much on people's needs, but more on what they have a right to expect – both in terms of basic human rights such as the right to life, food, water, shelter, etc., and in terms of their right to have their views represented to agencies that have an impact on their lives (DFID, 2000; Crook, 2001). If governments sign up to the targets, this means in principle that the people whose interests they are meant to serve can lobby them to behave in the manner most consistent with meeting the targets. In this conception, 'beneficiaries' of aid have a right to expect that agencies will act fairly in pursuing stated objectives.

In the parallel field of international humanitarian assistance, a rights-based approach stresses how people's rights as defined by international humanitarian law have been violated, and sees international intervention as helping people to regain those rights. This positions the beneficiaries of aid as claimants, rather than as beggars (Slim, 2001). Nonetheless, it should be remembered that UN conference resolutions do not have legal status. In this sense, for a rights-based argument to be fully convincing in terms of the international development targets, 'Southern' governments need to reflect their commitment to the targets by passing relevant legislation (e.g. making school attendance compulsory).

A further point in favour of targets is that where it is possible to disaggregate performance either by service provider or for different areas of provision, then standardised performance targets allow comparisons to be made. One clear example of this is in the compilation of league tables for schools, universities, hospitals and social services departments in the UK. This is seen as helping those using services to make informed choices about where the best available provision can be found, as well as encouraging those using the services of 'underperforming' providers to put pressure on the school or hospital in question to improve. Such tables are also used to influence the provision of public money, whether through 'rewarding' the high achievers, or through the provision of targeted resources to turn round those that are seen as falling below the expected standard.

In the case of the International Development Targets and Millennium Development Goals, the relative performance of countries and regions can also be compared through such standardised tables. However, it is less clear what conclusion should be drawn from this comparison. Specifically, if a country is falling short of achieving the outcome target, should it receive more assistance or less? Alternatively, should failure to make progress lead to the provision of assistance of a different kind? In part, the answer depends on why the country is 'off track', which hints at the fact that outcome-based measures do not in themselves constitute an adequate basis for performance measurement. This point is argued at more length in Chapter 3. At the same time, the ranking of countries in this way reveals another confusion about targets, namely: who is responsible for achieving them?

For example, the argument so far has implied that the targets are essentially about measuring and monitoring the performance of development agencies – especially UN agencies and the development cooperation ministries of Northern governments. However, the ranking of countries in terms of their progress towards the targets implies that countries themselves, and especially the governments of (Southern) countries, are the ones expected to meet them. In this sense, although publication of 'league tables' of countries' progress towards targets might lead to the citizens of these countries questioning why they have not made more progress, there are limits on what they can do about it.

Interestingly, a similar argument can be made within the UK in relation to league tables for schools and hospitals. For example, parents or patients might question why their local school or hospital is underperforming, but they have relatively few avenues through which they can promote improved performance, not least because they do not hold the purse strings. As a result, the standard reaction is, for those who are able to do so, to choose a different school or hospital, perhaps by moving to a different area, effectively worsening the situation for those (mainly poorer households) who are unable to move. In a world of increased possibilities for mobility, it is arguably possible for wealthier individuals in developing countries to have exactly the same reaction, with their migration to the North leading to similar consequences.

Looked at in general, targets can have a positive motivational role both within and across organisations. As a prominent supporter of the International Development Targets, DFID has posters that set out each target prominently displayed in its offices worldwide. Where several development organisations are working in the same area, then targets can create a sense of common purpose across these agencies. Setting targets can be argued to have played the role of increasing the cohesiveness of the international development community, helping to focus the renewed attention to poverty in the 1990s. However, these targets are arguably much less motivating for Southern governments, especially those that are 'left behind'.

Comparison with performance targets in the UK also reveals a number of other weaknesses and limitations of the approach of targeting development. For example, focus on a single indicator can risk distorting programmes or sacrificing quality. Thus targets to reduce health service waiting lists in the UK are claimed by some to have been achieved by prioritising quicker and cheaper operations. The target set for a loan scheme in London to minimise default encouraged rescheduling of ultimately unpayable debts (Jackson, 2000). Meanwhile, targets for local government authorities to collect more recyclable waste have sometimes been met, but with the consequence that these authorities have then been forced to burn or bury the waste, as recycling capacity has been exceeded (NAO, 2001).

Similar concerns apply to some of the Millennium Development Goals. For example, with respect to the goal of universal primary education, getting more children into already overcrowded classrooms, with few materials and poorly motivated teachers, might meet the target for quantity, but only at the expense of the quality of education provided to the children. To take another example, achieving the target of having a national strategy for sustainable development does not mean that this strategy is implemented. Indeed, the resources put into developing a formal strategy may well divert resources from existing activities that are actually promoting sustainability.

Moreover, as noted above, performance targets may also tend to simplify problems, focusing on what is identifiable and measurable whilst ignoring what really matters but is more complex. This is an argument that will resound with those working in poverty analysis, where the complexity and multidimensionality of poverty is well understood (see, for example, Jodha, 1988; Chambers, 1997).[8] Even if a target is well identified, it may have adverse organisational effects by discouraging innovation. Managers are likely to rely on tried and tested methods where there is a clear target to be achieved, rather than risk missing that target by trying out a new approach. Targets may also undermine other forms of accountability. In the bid to satisfy performance criteria, particular problems or interests may be missed. Finally, the focus on outcomes may deflect attention from the costs borne in achieving those outcomes, so that the efficiency focus of traditional management systems is lost (Cummings, 1997).

Conclusion and structure of the book

This chapter has argued that International Development Targets, launched in 1996, have caught the attention of the development community, attention which has increased with the Millennium Development Goals. Unlike previous targets, they have not (as yet) fallen by the wayside, but continue to be referred to and monitored. Their dominance is explained partly by the renewed focus on poverty, partly by the rise of results-based management and partly by the support they have received from key actors including the UK government. Targets can play an important role in accountability and performance measurement, but they are not without their disadvantages.

Chief amongst these disadvantages is a continued lack of clarity about *whose* targets the International Development Targets and Millennium Development Goals actually are. The emergence of a 'rights-based' agenda for development stresses how the recipients of international aid can use clear objectives to argue for their right to be dealt with in accordance with these objectives. They, and others, can, in principle, hold development actors accountable for their actions, perhaps for the first time. But who are 'development actors', and to whom are they supposed to be accountable? Moreover, why should development actors be accountable on the basis of a series of targets that they have devised from the 'top down', rather than on the basis of criteria identified from the bottom up?

What is missing from discussion of targets for international development agencies is any theory of accountability. For real accountability, at the very least there needs to be more transparency as to who is responsible for what, and more ownership of goals by those expected to meet them. In this sense, scale is also important. Individuals and agencies need to be held accountable for targets that are realistic and achievable at the level at which they are working. It would be ridiculous for an individual development worker to be held 'accountable' for not eradicating poverty; but it is equally ridiculous to hold the North responsible for ensuring that every child in Bangladesh goes to school.

Here, it is not particularly important that a range of different actors *endorse* the principle of setting targets for development, or even the substance of what each individual target is. If endorsement of the approach is all that happens, the likelihood is that targets simply bureaucratise further the business of development, making it more remote from ordinary people in both North and South. Rather, goals and targets need to be something that can *inspire* both those working within international development agencies, and those outside who might call aid workers to account for their actions.

The remainder of this book is structured in two parts. Chapters 2–6 explore a number of issues relating to the setting of targets for development, whilst Chapters 7–14 focus on individual targets, goals or sets of targets, to assess what each target is, why it has been set, what progress has been made towards meeting it, and what the prospects are for its being achieved.

In Chapter 2, Simon Maxwell shows how the setting of international targets for development forms part of the 'new New Poverty Agenda' which emerged in the late 1990s. This agenda has five elements: the targets themselves; a revised strategy for poverty reduction as laid out in the World Bank's *World Development Report*, 2000/2001; Poverty Reduction Strategy Papers (PRSPs); new tools in the form of Medium-Term Expenditure Frameworks (MTEFs), sector-wide approaches (SWAPs) and Poverty Reduction Strategy Credits (PRSCs); and a stress on performance management. Providing a simple guide to this new maze of abbreviations, the chapter argues that the new agenda is indeed 'new' and different from what went before, but nonetheless needs to be applied flexibly. Six risks are identified in the new way in which poverty has been constructed, followed by six principles that could guide a more flexible approach: (1) the need for 'subsidiarity'; (2) the need to focus on essentials; (3) the importance of not forgetting difficult sectors and cross-cutting issues; (4) the need to recognise the political nature of poverty; (5) the importance of partnership; and (6) the need for a process-based approach, which accepts that achievements will take time to materialise.

Next, in Chapter 3, Howard White considers further the question of whether it makes sense to use global targets as a measure of development performance. The chapter sets out a number of criteria that could be used for the assessment of performance, and considers how the International Development Targets and Millennium Development Goals match up against these. To be most effective, performance measures should satisfy a number of criteria. White argues that the International Development Targets and Millennium Development Goals satisfy only some of these criteria. They are relevant, mostly well defined and correspond to existing indicators. But they are also mostly outcome oriented, with little effort made to build a consensus around an underlying logical model of how the targets are to be achieved. In the absence of such a model it is extremely difficult to say anything sensible in terms of attributing changes in target indicators to the actions of the development community.

Some donors, notably DFID, have tried to bridge this gap between development actions and desired outcomes through the preparation of 'Target Strategy Papers' (TSPs) and 'Country Strategy Papers' (CSPs). In these documents, DFID has tried to set out how it will achieve its targets, especially the reduction of poverty. In Chapter 4, Howard White and David Booth examine how CSPs analyse poverty and what the implications are for the strategies used to halve world poverty. However, Booth and White argue that the problem of the 'missing middle' remains; there continues to be a gap between the causes of poverty identified in the poverty profile and the proposed interventions.

In Chapter 5, David Booth and Henry Lucas shift attention to the question of how progress towards the Millennium Development Goals can be accurately monitored by individual countries. Again the focus is on PRSPs, and the extent to which these have involved adequate procedures and monitoring systems to assess effectively whether poverty is being reduced. A review of existing PRSPs and Interim Poverty Reduction Strategy Papers in Africa suggests that a lot remains to be done in terms of improving the quality of recording of administrative data. In response, the chapter seeks to propose some practical ways forward, and highlights areas in which further work is needed on the strategic selection of indicators.

Despite the limitations in approach and monitoring systems highlighted so far, a book on progress towards the Millennium Development Goals would hardly be complete without an overall review of whether the goals themselves are feasible. This is provided in Chapter 6 by Jan Vandermoortele, who seeks to go beyond averages and aggregates to consider the unevenness of progress towards different goals, in different places and for different groups in society. Vandermoortele argues that the Millennium

Development Goals are both technically feasible and financially affordable, and that most will be met by at least some countries. Nonetheless, much more committed leadership, stronger partnerships, extra money and deeper participation by the poor will be needed to ensure that they are met overall.

In the second half of the book, attention turns to individual targets, goals and sets of goals. In Chapter 7, Michael Lipton and Hugh Waddington address the target of reducing income poverty by half by 2015. They argue that global trends suggest considerable progress towards this target. However, a closer look at regional patterns suggests a more pessimistic view. Most of the progress at the global level has been fuelled by progress in East Asia, particularly China. This region simply cannot sustain the same contribution to the target: doing so would require more people to be brought out of poverty by 2015 than are actually poor at the moment! Elsewhere, Lipton and Waddington explore the obstacles to poverty reduction, notably the absence of growth and the persistence of inequality. They ask what factors underlie these constraints, and argue that to achieve accelerated poverty reduction, we must address the underlying fundamentals, tackling issues such as asset distribution and the spread of new technologies.

The Universal Declaration of Human Rights, adopted by the United Nations in 1948, stated that primary schooling should be free and compulsory in all nations. More than fifty years later, the world still has far to go in order to achieve this goal. Yet in Chapter 8, Christopher Colclough argues that the recent reaffirmation of the aim of achieving schooling for all by 2015, and of gender equity in schooling by 2005, again risks failure, especially in the poorest regions of the world. The challenge is greatest in the countries of sub-Saharan Africa, where scarcely half the eligible children were attending primary school at the end of the twentieth century. Across sub-Saharan Africa as a whole, the proportion of children enrolled was no higher than it had been in 1980. Girls were hardest hit, with 20 per cent fewer girls attending school than boys.

Colclough examines some of the main causes of this disappointing progress. Costs are important constraints on school participation – at both macro and household levels. But commitment is also found to be lacking in some countries, where higher levels of spending on schooling than presently exist could easily be afforded. Where household demand is low, girls tend to be last to be enrolled. Policies need to address not only supply-side changes, but also measures to support and stimulate demand.

In Chapter 9, Ramya Subrahmanian addresses progress towards gender equality, focusing her attention not only on the specific gender goals, but on how gender issues permeate other targets. She argues that feminist lobbying and activism have successfully put gender onto the international agenda through strategic advocacy at international conferences and a push for greater inter-agency collaboration. As a result, several targets and goals have a gender component – including commitments to remove gender disparities in education, reduce maternal mortality by three-quarters, and ensure reproductive health for all. But do the Millennium Development Goals really promote a discourse of gender equality and empowerment? And are the new policy instruments and approaches framed to meet the targets working in favour of gender equality? Subrahmanian argues that the ways in which concepts of gender equality and empowerment are used by different agencies and brought into the framing of targets present a double-edged sword: while gender equality is given rhetorical prominence, this is done in ways that run the risk of depoliticising what are in essence issues of rights and redistribution.

In Chapter 10, Howard White addresses what he argues is the most important development challenge embodied in the development targets: ending avoidable infant and child deaths. Although there has been progress in reducing mortality, this has slowed in recent years, especially in the worst-affected areas (notably sub-Saharan Africa). This reversal is partly because of HIV/AIDS and conflict, but also reflects the impact of long-run economic decline and the resulting deterioration in health service provision. Current trends suggest that the targets will not be met. Yet it is not clear how the international community could or should respond. Some argue that reduction in infant mortality is largely driven by growth – if only poverty can be eradicated, infant and child mortality will fall. For others, there is scope for health provision to improve things. White argues for the latter view, suggesting that it is indeed possible for the target to be met with a sufficient push and resources. Relevant policies include universal immunisation – even though immunisation rates fell in Africa in the second part of the 1990s.

In Chapter 11, Hilary Standing addresses the goal of providing access for all to reproductive health, which was included as an International Development Target but removed from the final list of Millennium Development Goals. The target is placed in the context of a range of reproductive health indicators. Discussion then focuses on how reproductive heath itself has come to prominence in international development discourses, especially following the Cairo Conference on Population and Development Goals, and what are the key obstacles to improving reproductive health. A major problem is funding, but the goal of providing reproductive health for all is often tied up with wider health reforms taking place in most low- and middle-income countries. Standing argues that it is unlikely that the original International Development Target for reproductive health will be met, but that nonetheless, the Cairo agenda for reproductive health provides an innovative and important way forward.

Like the targets for gender inequality and child and infant mortality, the target to halt and reverse the spread of HIV/AIDS can also be seen as underpinning a number of other targets embodied in the Millennium Development Goals. In Chapter 12, Ronald Skeldon considers whether the specific target of a 25 per cent reduction in HIV/AIDS amongst 15- to 24-year-olds in the worst-affected countries by 2005, and globally by 2010, might be achieved. He argues that progress has been made in many countries, but that global progress is more difficult, given the different stage of the epidemic in different countries. Recent shifts in global geopolitical concerns have made galvanising the international community on this issue more and more problematic, even though reducing HIV/AIDS has been maintained as a Millennium Development Goal after failing to achieve the initial list of International Development Targets.

The next two chapters turn attention to targets in the field of the environment and sustainable development. Whilst the International Development Targets were quite specific from the start in their objectives on poverty, health and education, the environment has provided a more difficult field to develop targets than others. Here, the UN's Millennium Development Goals are more specific than the OECD's International Development Targets: they suggest we should aim to halve the proportion of people in the world without access to safe drinking water. In Chapter 13, Richard Jolly reviews progress towards meeting this goal, stressing that much remains to be done if safe and clean drinking water for all is to become a reality. He also highlights the need for a parallel indicator on hygiene and sanitation, an issue that was a major area of debate at the Earth Summit in Johannesburg in August and September 2002.

Then, in Chapter 14, James Fairhead considers the earlier target of ensuring that each country has a national sustainable development strategy, in the process of implementation, by 2005, as well as exploring more generally the ethics of setting such a target. In an argument that could be applied more broadly to the Millennium Development Goals as a whole, Fairhead questions an approach that requires Southern countries to adjust their policies to meet a target that deals with a problem that they could be seen as having little or no responsibility for creating. He also focuses on the broader need for transparency at national and international levels if targets for 'sustainability' as well as in specific sectors are to be met.

In the final two chapters we turn to the rather complex goal of 'developing a global partnership for development'. Unlike the other Millennium Development Goals, this goal encompasses some eight individual targets, yet none of these is quantified in the same way as the majority of the other targets, making analysis of progress towards them somewhat more difficult. Rather than seeking to measure progress, we therefore include two chapters which look at how and why 'partnership' and the associated concerns of aid, trade and debt have come to be included in the Millennium Development Goals, and some of the questions raised by this inclusion. In Chapter 15, Peter Clarke draws on an analysis of the public statements of DFID to question whether a 'global partnership for development' is either possible or meaningful. Clarke uses the example of

the unequal power relations between Northern and Southern governments to illustrate how the discourse of partnership could be viewed as a
'political technology' which depoliticises development and creates a
veneer of ownership on the part of less powerful groups. Such an outcome
is not inevitable, however, with Clarke suggesting that it is at a local level
that we need to look for contestation and negotiation over a more
genuine 'partnership'.

Finally, in Chapter 16, Kevin Watkins and Juliana Amadi argues that for
a genuine global partnership for development, Northern countries need
to take more decisive action in opening trade to developing countries
(including the commodities they mainly produce), increasing development finance and reducing the burden of debt. Although aid spending
has recently risen in some countries, five of the G-7 donors have failed to
reverse a long-term decline in aid, whilst the sustainability of debt relief
can also be called into question.

Overall, the chapters of this book do not paint a rosy picture of
progress towards the International Development Targets or Millennium
Development Goals, and in some cases take a quite critical stance on the
process of their development and implementation. Nonetheless, we would
argue that the Targets and Goals do represent a valid attempt to define
the purpose of work by both international development agencies and
national governments. The UK government in particular has spearheaded
this approach in a range of international forums, and deserves recognition for its attempts to make aid more accountable. By focusing on a series
of key indicators, the targets have helped to put the fight against poverty
into the mainstream of development activity, whilst resisting the tempta-
tion to define poverty too narrowly.

Nonetheless, problems remain. First, it is clear from individual chapters
that many of the Millennium Development Goals remain quite unlikely to
be reached by their target date, if at all. Second, it is not always clear how
the activities of aid agencies might have contributed to whether they are
reached or not. Worst of all, there is a danger that the targets themselves
will not make agencies more accountable, but simply more bureaucratic.

Where should international development agencies go from here? Three
immediate options present themselves in relation to the targets themselves.
One option would be to put the best gloss possible on progress towards
reaching the targets, although this could be regarded simply as political
'spin'. A second option would be to refine the targets, so that they are
more meaningful, or more achievable, although this could be seen as
'fixing' the targets. A third option might be to scrap the targets altogether,
although this could easily be seen as defeatism.

We do not advocate any of these steps, but rather set ourselves the
more modest aim of understanding the targets – including why they have
been set, and what might need to occur if some or all of them are to be
achieved. It is also important to keep in mind that the setting of targets is

only a means to an end, rather than an end in itself. In this regard, the real goal remains much broader: the eradication of poverty, no less. The setting of a series of development goals is one step towards this goal.

Notes

1 For example, the second goal is to halve hunger but the benchmark to define hunger is not given. Goals 12 to 18 do not include a quantified target.
2 Downloadable from www.freedomhouse.org.
3 The process by which this outcome was reached has not been documented, but DFID claims to have worked toward this end, i.e. that the Millennium Development Goals should not conflict with the International Development Targets. The fact that they do not has made it relatively straightforward for donors to switch from one set of targets to the other.
4 The text of the Act is available on http://www.hmso.gov.uk/acts/acts2002/20020001.htm.
5 The US agency USAID also has extensive experience, which is drawn on in Chapter 3. A more comprehensive review is DAC (2000).
6 Formerly known as Form 590.
7 See National Audit Office (2001: appendix 2) for a chronology of performance measurement in UK central government.

References

Baulch, R. (1996) 'The New Poverty Agenda – a Disputed Consensus', *IDS Bulletin*, 27(1): 1–10.

Brown, B. (1995) *Results-Based Management: Danger or Opportunity. Lessons from the CIDA Experience*, Ottawa: CIDA.

Chambers, R. (1997) *Putting the Last First*, London: IT Publications.

Crook, R. (2001) 'Editorial Introduction', *IDS Bulletin*, 32(1), 1–7, Brighton: Institute of Development Studies.

Cummings, F.H. (1997) 'Logic Models, Logical Frameworks and Results-Based Management: Contrasts and Comparisons', *Canadian Journal of Development Studies*, 18: 587–596.

Denery, L. and Walton, M. (1999) 'Are the Poverty and Social Goals for the 21st Century Attainable?' *IDS Bulletin*, 30(2): 75–91.

Department for International Development (DFID) (2000) *Realising Human Rights for Poor People: Strategies for Achieving the International Development Targets*, London: DFID.

Development Assistance Committee (DAC) (1996) *Shaping the Twenty-first Century*, Paris: OECD.

—— (2000) 'Results Based Management in the Development Co-operation Agencies: A Review of Experience (Executive Summary)', Paris: OECD.

Jackson, A. (2000) 'An Evaluation of Evaluation: Problems with Performance Measurement in Small Business Loans and Grant Schemes', *Progress in Planning*, 55: 1–55.

Jodha, N.S. (1988) 'Poverty Debate in India: a Minority View', *Economic and Political Weekly*, 22(45–47): 2421–2428.

National Audit Office (NAO) (2001) *Measuring the Performance of Government Departments*, London: The Stationery Office.

Organisation for Economic Cooperation and Development (OECD) (1996) *Shaping the 21st Century: The Contribution of Development Co-operation*, Paris: OECD.

Rawnsley, A. (2001) *Servants of the People: The Inside Story of New Labour*, London: Penguin.

Slim, H. (2001) 'Not Philanthropy but Rights: Rights-Based Humanitarianism and the Proper Politicisation of Humanitarian Philosophy in War', Humanitarian Practice Network Conference Paper, London: Overseas Development Institute, February.

United Nations (UN) (2000) *United Nations Millennium Declaration*, Document A/RES/55/2, New York: UN (http://www.un.org/millennium/declaration/ares552e.pdf).

—— (2001) *Road Map towards the Implementation of the United Nations Millennium Declaration: Report of the Secretary-General*, Document A/56/326, New York: UN.

White, H. (1999) 'Global Poverty Reduction: Are We Heading in the Right Direction', *Journal of International Development*, 11(4): 503–519.

2 Heaven or hubris

Reflections on the new 'New Poverty Agenda'[1]

Simon Maxwell

Oh! pleasant exercise of hope and joy!
For mighty were the auxiliars which then stood
Upon our side, we who were strong in poverty reduction!
Bliss was it in that dawn to be alive
But to be a poverty planner was very heaven!
(after William Wordsworth)

Introduction

Wordsworth, above and as amended, has it absolutely right: poverty planning is on a roll. This is because a new construction has been put in place that locks together five elements of new thinking about the subject. The five elements are:

- the Millennium Development Goals, with poverty reduction at their heart;
- international consensus on how to reduce poverty, best summarised in the World Bank's *World Development Report* for 2000/2001, 'Attacking Poverty';
- a mechanism for operationalising the strategy at country level, in Poverty Reduction Strategy Papers;
- technologies for delivering aid in support of Poverty Reduction Strategy Papers, notably Medium Term Expenditure Frameworks, sector-wide approaches and Poverty Reduction Strategy Credits;
- underpinning the other four, a commitment to results-based management.

There is no doubt that this construction is superior to previous attempts at housing a new approach to poverty – for example, the initiative on poverty reduction that followed the publication in 1990 of an earlier *World Development Report* on the subject, described at the time as defining a New Poverty Agenda (Lipton and Maxwell, 1992). That had a strategy, and a degree of operationalisation (e.g. through the World Bank's *Poverty Handbook* and

Operational Directive (World Bank, 1992a, b)), but lacked the targets, the aid modalities and the emphasis on results-based management.

It is too early to say whether the current and new 'New Poverty Agenda' will deliver the expected results in terms of real poverty reduction for real people in developing countries. On present trends, as we see in this volume, many of the Millennium Development Goals will not be met. We should not, however, be churlish; as Wordsworth remarks, this is a new strategy which

> The beauty wore of promise, that which sets
> The budding rose above the rose full blown.

True enough, but there are risks associated with this budding rose, and this chapter is largely about these risks. They lie in the realms of economics, politics and public administration. They include issues to do with equity, consensus-building, partnership, and managing change by simple targets. They are not insignificant risks, but nor are they immutable, and this is the point: by being clear about the risks, we can modify strategies and take action to maximise the probability of success. Not to do so is to fall into the trap of hubris, of pride before a fall.

Poverty reduction: the new construction

There is much to commend in the new approach to poverty reduction.

The Millennium Development Goals

The Millennium Development Goals are summarised in Chapter 1. They represent the latest manifestation of the International Development Targets, agreed (mostly) at United Nations (UN) conferences in the early 1990s and codified in 1996 by the Development Assistance Committee (DAC) of the Organisation for Economic Cooperation and Development (OECD). Yet progress against the targets is uneven. For the key poverty reduction target, the data (Figure 2.1) show that developing countries taken as a whole are more or less on track to halve the proportion of those in absolute poverty by 2015, but that this is not true for Europe and Central Asia, the Middle East and North Africa, South Asia, and (most markedly) sub-Saharan Africa. In sub-Saharan Africa, the proportion of people living below an income level of one dollar a day is rising, not falling. Global success owes a great deal to rapid progress in poverty reduction in East Asia and the Pacific: here, the proportion fell sharply, and the number in absolute poverty declined during the 1990s, by 192 million people.

We will come later to some risks associated with using targets to drive policy, but their value in clarifying policy and in providing a political framework deserves to be noted. In particular, the targets have provided

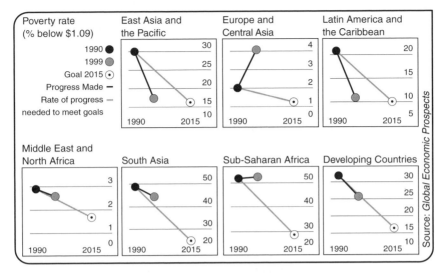

Figure 2.1 Progress towards the Millennium Development Poverty Goals.

Source: World Bank website: http://www.developmentgoals.org/Poverty.htm.

political impetus to poverty reduction efforts. As Wordsworth rightly observes,

> What temper at the prospect did not wake
> To happiness unthought of? The inert
> Were roused, and lively natures rapt away!

A strategy to reduce poverty

The *World Development Report* (WDR) 2000/2001 laid out a strategy for reducing poverty, resting on three legs: opportunity (meaning growth), empowerment and security (World Bank, 2000). Other overviews of policy to reduce poverty, such as the *DAC Poverty Guidelines* (DAC, 2001), cover similar territory. There are, as we shall see, some rough edges, but the *World Development Report* strategy comes close to capturing an international consensus. It has some notable innovations, at least for the World Bank. These have been summarised as follows (Maxwell, 2001c: 144–145):

- Methodological innovation, in the shape of participatory poverty assessments in sixty countries, collectively articulating the 'Voices of the Poor' (see Narayan *et al.*, 2000).
- Partly inspired by 'Voices', but also drawing on an extensive literature, explicit adoption of a multidimensional model of poverty, which sets

low incomes alongside access to health and education, vulnerability to shocks, and, importantly, voicelessness and powerlessness.

- Emphasis on the value of growth in reducing poverty, as one might expect, but also considerable emphasis on redistribution. This is, admittedly, largely for instrumental reasons, rather than as an end in itself. It represents a way of raising the poverty elasticity, but is also included because more equal societies grow faster.
- Predictably again, a commitment to markets and to openness, but strong statements throughout about the dislocations associated with market reform and market processes, the need for strong and prior institutional underpinning of markets, and the 'obligation' (World Bank, 2000: 76) to protect losers and those excluded from the benefits.
- Empowerment as a major theme – not just participation in a narrow sense, but a focus on making state institutions responsive to poor people and on building social institutions.
- Security promoted from being half a leg (as in the 1990 *World Development Report*) to a full leg, with a typology of risks, and a review of mitigation, coping and response strategies for natural disasters, economic crises, and many kinds of idiosyncratic risk facing individuals.
- Finally, a discussion of international actions around the core themes of opportunity, empowerment and security, which touches on well-worn themes (protectionism in the North, debt relief, more and better aid), but also recognises why countries are nervous about capital market liberalisation and calls for democratisation of global governance institutions.

It is important to say about the WDR strategy that many of its elements could be found in earlier efforts to synthesise an overall approach to poverty reduction. This includes earlier WDRs on the subject, in 1980 and 1990, but most notably a series of United Nations Development Programme (UNDP) *Human Development Reports* (HDRs) launched in 1990, especially the 1997 report, which dealt specifically with poverty (UNDP, 1997). Thus the 1990 HDR introduced the multidimensional model of poverty in its exploration of 'human development'; it also talked about the need for greater participation and greater equity, and emphasised the importance of social subsidies (UNDP, 1990). The 1997 HDR called for greater accountability in government and urged that globalisation be managed to protect and benefit the poor.

That the World Bank should assume part of UNDP's mantle on poverty reduction is, of course, a cause of wonder; but it is also cause for congratulation. The WDR strategy marks the closest we have yet come to an international consensus on poverty reduction. The recent *DAC Guidelines on Poverty Reduction* reflect this on the donor side. In an approach consistent with that of the WDR, they adopt a capabilities approach to understanding poverty, incorporating ideas about influence, freedom, status and dignity, as well as income and assets; and they cover similar policy areas, including growth, empowerment, social services and social protection (DAC, 2001: 37ff.). Certainly, international discourse has come a long way in the past decade.

Poverty Reduction Strategy Papers

Poverty Reduction Strategy Papers (PRSPs) were introduced in the context of the enhanced settlement for debt relief in heavily indebted poor countries (HIPCs) in 1999 (DFID, 2001; Gunter, 2002). Their key features are that they are:

- in principle, country owned and led;
- based on a participatory process, leading as far as possible to a national consensus;
- accepted by donors on the basis of conditionality on process rather than substance;
- designed to evolve over time, providing 'road maps' rather than blueprints for poverty reduction.

In order to qualify for relief under this process, countries must have at least an Interim Poverty Reduction Strategy Paper (I-PRSP). Full relief is dependent on having a full PRSP. By mid-2002 there were fifty-nine countries involved in the PRSP process. Of these, fourteen had completed a full PRSP that had been endorsed by the boards of the World Bank and the International Monetary Fund (IMF), six had completed a full PRSP that had yet to be submitted, twenty-nine had completed an I-PRSP, and ten were yet to complete an Interim PRSP (PRSP connections, 2002).[2]

More abbreviations: MTEFs, SWAPs and PRSCs

Various 'technologies' have been put in place to help improve the management of public expenditure and aid flows. Governments are encouraged to produce Medium Term Expenditure Frameworks (MTEFs). Donors are encouraged to work together in support of sector-wide approaches (SWAPs). And the World Bank, in particular, is expected to replace structural adjustment lending with new Poverty Reduction Strategy Credits (PRSCs).

Sector-wide approaches are a particularly important feature of the new apparatus. As described by Foster, the defining characteristic of a SWAP is that 'all significant funding for a sector supports a single sector policy and expenditure programme, under Government leadership, adopting common approaches across the sector, and progressing towards relying on

Government procedures to disburse and account for all funds' (Foster, 2000: 9). The stress on government leadership in SWAPs should reinforce partnership and accountability.

Results-based management

Results-based management (RBM) can be characterised as an approach to managing organisations and programmes by focusing on outputs and outcomes rather than inputs and activities: reduction in poverty, say, rather than expenditure on poverty reduction programmes. A good example of its use is in public expenditure management in the UK, where the Treasury negotiates output-oriented Public Service Agreements (PSAs) or contracts with individual ministries. The PSA for the DFID for the period 2002–2006 is reproduced by way of illustration in Box 2.1. It contains six objectives, mostly specifying the outcomes expected, along with specific targets for poverty reduction or other elements of the Millennium Development Goals.

It is important to note that RBM is not just used for setting targets. It can also be used to structure rewards, for individuals, teams, organisations, local government departments and the like. The way in which DFID has used the Millennium Development Goals as the basis for judging its results is discussed in Chapter 3.

Six risks with the new construction

The new construction on poverty reduction has undoubted strengths. Here, however, are six risks, which cut across the various levels of the new construction. We will come later to remedies.

Targets and performance indicators may oversimplify and distort development efforts

The use of targets is central to the new construction. They are the main feature, of course, of the Millennium Development Goals; but they also feature strongly in PRSPs, which are about how to reach goals at country level, in SWAPs, which tie public expenditure to targets, and in results-based management.

We know why targets are useful. They clarify objectives. They rally support. And they provide an instrument with which to reform public services. These are valuable benefits. But we also know why targets pose risks: they can encourage a reductionist approach to complex problems, privilege quantitative indicators at the expense of qualitative indicators, distort resource allocation, and undermine professional motivation and responsibility (Maxwell, 1998).

Many examples have been cited in the literature, in both developed

Box 2.1 Department for International Development Public Service Agreement, 2002–2006: objectives and performance targets

Objective I: Reduce poverty in sub-Saharan Africa

1 Progress towards the Millennium Development Goals in sixteen key countries demonstrated by:

- A sustainable reduction in the proportion of people living in poverty from 48 per cent across the entire region.
- An increase in primary school enrolment from 58 per cent to 72 per cent and an increase in the ratio of girls to boys enrolled in primary school from 89 per cent to 96 per cent.
- A reduction in under-five mortality rates for girls and boys from 158 per 1,000 live births to 139 per 1,000, and an increase in the proportion of births assisted by skilled birth attendants from 49 per cent to 67 per cent; and a reduction in the proportion of 15- to 24-year-old pregnant women with HIV from 16 per cent.
- Improved effectiveness of the UK contribution to conflict prevention and management as demonstrated by a reduction in the number of people whose lives are affected by violent conflict and a reduction in potential sources of future conflict, where the UK can make a significant contribution. (Joint target with Foreign and Commonwealth Office (FCO) and the Ministry of Defence (MoD.)
- Effective implementation of the G-8 Action Plan for Africa in support of enhanced partnership at the regional and country level.

Objective II: Reduce poverty in Asia

2 Progress towards the Millennium Development Goals in four key countries demonstrated by:

- A sustainable reduction in the proportion of people living in poverty from 15 per cent to 10 per cent in East Asia and the Pacific and 40 per cent to 32 per cent in South Asia.
- An increase in gross primary school enrolment from 95 per cent to 100 per cent and an increase in the ratio of girls to boys enrolled in primary school from 87 per cent to 94 per cent.
- A reduction in under-five mortality rates for girls and boys from 92 per 1,000 live births to 68 per 1,000; and an increase in proportion of births assisted by skilled birth attendants from 39 per cent to 57 per cent.
- Prevalence rates of HIV infection in vulnerable groups being below 5 per cent; and a tuberculosis case detection rate above 70 per cent and cure treatment rate greater than 85 per cent.

continued

Objective III: Reduce poverty in Europe, Central Asia, Latin America, the Caribbean, the Middle East and North Africa

Objective IV: Increase the impact of key multilateral agencies in reducing poverty and effective response to conflict and humanitarian crises

3   Improved effectiveness of the international system as demonstrated by:

- A greater impact of European Commission (EC) external programmes on poverty reduction, including through working for agreement to increase the proportion of EC official development assistance to low-income countries from 38 per cent to 70 per cent.
- Ensuring that three-quarters of all eligible heavily indebted poor countries (HIPCs) committed to poverty reduction receive irrevocable debt relief by 2006 and work with international partners to make progress towards the United Nations 2015 Millennium Development Goals. (Joint target with Her Majesty's Treasury.)

4   Secure agreement by 2005 to a significant reduction in trade barriers leading to improved trading opportunities for the UK and developing countries. (Joint target with Department for Trade and Industry (DTI) and FCO.)

Objective V: Develop evidence-based, innovative approaches to international development

Objective VI: Value for money

5   Increase the proportion of DFID's bilateral programme going to low-income countries from 78 per cent to 90 per cent and a sustained increase in the index of DFID's bilateral projects evaluated as successful.

Source: UK Treasury 2002, at http://www.hm-treasury.gov.uk/mediastore/otherfiles/psa02_ch11t.pdf

---

and developing countries. Some of the best come from the developed country literature: health targets set centrally as reduction of waiting lists, which encourage doctors to treat less urgent but easy cases and neglect more urgent but more difficult cases (Chapman, 2002); or testing regimes for schools, again set centrally, which distort teaching priorities, and provide incentives to teachers to manipulate results (Davies, 2000). In international development the main debates have been about the reductionist nature of the dollar-a-day target for poverty reduction (Maxwell, 1998), but also about the difficulty of attribution, when the phenomena with which targets are concerned are subject to many different influences (White, 2002). To take an easy example of the latter, the UK's DFID is committed in its PSA to a reduction of poverty in South Asia from 40 per cent to 32 per cent by 2006. This is a region in which aid is relatively insignificant, accounting for less than 3 per cent of public expenditure; and in which donors can have relatively little influence on the prospects for growth and poverty reduction. Hubris? Or, a cynic might argue, commitment to a target which is so likely to be achieved that there is little risk of being exposed?

It might be thought that the right reaction to these problems is to set better targets or manage them differently, but critics argue that the problems lie deeper, in the treatment of professional standards or in the nature of the organisations concerned. Thus Onora O'Neill (2002: 3) rages against the undermining of professional integrity, arguing that 'central planning may have failed in the former Soviet Union but it is alive and well in Britain today. The new accountability culture aims at ever more perfect administrative control of institutional and professional life.'

Chapman sets out the argument about organisations. He argues that public service organisations are complex, adaptive systems, which can be expected to respond poorly to centralised targets. Targets will (1) maximise the likelihood of adverse unintended consequences, (2) increase administrative overheads, (3) make institutions more fragile, (4) demotivate staff throughout the system, and (5) cause disillusion among clients. He concludes that 'the current approach to policy-making and implementation *can be expected to fail*' (2002: 52, original emphasis).

A preoccupation with poverty reduction may detract from the importance of citizenship as an intrinsic component of development

Poverty reduction is a good objective, particularly if it can be interpreted in the wider human development sense, rather than narrowly in income terms – and if the wider interpretation can be remembered when it comes to monitoring achievement of the relevant Millennium Development Goal. In addition, as is discussed in Chapter 1, poverty reduction is not the only Millennium Development Goal.

There are gaps, however. The Millennium Development Goals are strong on material aspects of deprivation, but not so strong on non-material aspects – which may therefore be neglected in PRSPs and SWAPs. This is about more than the limitations of targets.

Compare the Millennium Development Goals with the DAC framework on poverty reduction, reproduced in Figure 2.2. The boxes on economic, human and protective dimensions broadly correspond to the Millennium Development Goals (though protection issues are not well handled in the Goals). The items covered in the socio-cultural and political boxes, however, are missing from the Goals. These correspond to the empowerment theme of the WDR, and might broadly be interpreted as 'citizenship' (Gaventa et al., 2002).[3]

One interpretation might be that rights, for example, are instrumental

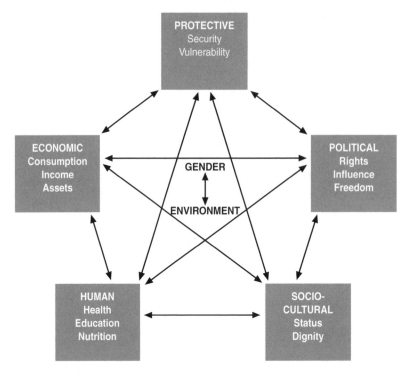

Figure 2.2 Interactive dimensions of poverty and well-being.

Source: DAC, 2001: 39.

to achieving the other aspects, and therefore of a lower priority. In this interpretation, the achievement of income, health or education is what matters, and action to secure achievement is merely the means to the end: citizen action over the right to jobs, health services or schools, for example, or initiatives to make rights available under the constitution or through the legal system.

In fact, few would take this line. As the *DAC Guidelines* make clear, rights, influence, freedom, status and dignity are all components of well-being, part of 'the good life' (Christie and Nash, 1998). They deserve attention in their own right. Moser and Norton describe this as the 'maximum' scenario and make the important point that the achievement of rights is not just about legal structures, but also about social mobilisation. Thus, in a volume entitled *To Claim Our Rights*, they argue that

> a growing culture of rights strengthens the degree to which individuals relate to state structures as citizens with rights and responsibilities. In turn, this weakens the extent to which people expect to extract benefits from the state through relations of clientilism and

patronage. The citizenship model fosters the capacity for collective action across traditional divisions of class, ethnicity and caste, thereby increasing the capacity of social mobilisation to favour (or at least include) the marginalised.

(Moser and Norton, 2001: 39)

This is not simply a theoretical perspective. As Norton and Elson (2002) make clear, there are practical implications for the design of poverty programmes and public budgets.

A more controversial question is whether equality should also feature as an objective. The treatment in the 2000/2001 *World Development Report* is, as noted above, largely instrumental: lower inequality is valued because it increases the poverty elasticity (the amount by which a given amount of growth reduces poverty), and also because unequal societies are characterised by violence and insecurity, which undermine social capital, disrupt orderly economic life, and divert resources from productive investment into consumption on security (World Bank, 2000: 52ff.). All this is true (Killick, 2002; McKay, 2002; Naschold, 2002; White, 2001), but it can also be argued that lower inequality is a necessary condition for social inclusion, an intrinsic good in its own right. As I have argued elsewhere,

Intellectual foundations for this view can be found in the literature on social exclusion (de Haan, 1998), particularly in the French variant which is based on a solidarity paradigm of social inclusion, stressing the importance of social bonds (Silver, 1994). There are connections, too, to the literature on relative deprivation, in which poverty is defined, not in absolute terms, but as a standard of living which is below that 'customary, or at least widely encouraged and/or approved, in the societies to which [people] belong' (Townsend, 1979): a certain degree of equality is implied by this definition.

(Maxwell, 2001b: 335)

If these arguments hold, should there not be an international target for inequality? Building on work by Cornia, it has been suggested that a Gini coefficient below 0.45 should be the target (ibid.: 339). On the figures given in the 2000/2001 *World Development Report*, thirty out of 105 countries would miss this target.

The desire to maximise participation and build a national consensus on poverty reduction may obscure important trade-offs and conflicts of interest

Although citizenship does not feature as prominently as it might in the Millennium Development Goals, it is certainly true that participation is a prominent thread of national poverty reduction processes. This begins with Participatory Poverty Assessments (PPAs) (Norton, 2001), but extends to discussion about the content of PRSPs, and to measures which increase the accountability of government agencies (World Bank, 2000: chapter 6). There is an increasing wealth of experience with participatory methods, measures to increase accountability, and, more generally, with democratic decentralisation (Johnson, 2001).

This is entirely admirable, but it should not be concluded that conflicts will thereby disappear. A national consensus which obscures the fact that there will be losers as well as winners, probably among the poor as well as between the poor and the non-poor, will do the poor no service.

Many examples could be chosen to illustrate this point, but here is one: the contribution of agriculture to poverty reduction. It is a frequent observation that agricultural growth helps reduce poverty, but it does this through many different pathways, with different effects on different groups of poor people, many of them contradictory. Irz *et al.* (2001) summarise the pathways, in Box 2.2: agricultural growth can reduce poverty by increasing farm income or employment, by creating jobs or livelihoods in related industries or by means of consumption linkages, by means of lower food prices, or through increased tax revenue being spent on services which benefit the poor. The interests, then, are contradictory: between food suppliers and food buyers; between the producers and consumers of industrial raw materials; and between the urban poor, who favour lower food prices, and the rural poor, many of whom will benefit as net food buyers from lower prices, but many of whom will benefit from greater employment in farm or farm-related industries if prices are high.

The implication of this example is that PRSPs and SWAPs, in particular, need to articulate choices and adjudicate between them. In the case of agricultural development, key choices are between crops, farm sizes and degrees of labour intensity, between degrees of liberalisation, and between investment in high- and low-potential areas (Maxwell, 2001a: 35). No one should pretend that these choices are not highly contested in most poor countries, and unlikely to be the subject of a national consensus. Indeed, one of the main conclusions of a recent review of the institutionalisation of PRSPs is that 'politics matters' (Booth, 2003). Politics, of course, is partly about the art of achieving change, even when there is no consensus.

A focus on public expenditure may distract attention from the importance of macroeconomic policy

The issue of choices also arises in the context of overall macroeconomic policy, a topic often neglected in countries where the management of public expenditure seems to have become the main instrument of public policy. Yet the fact is that choices made with respect to financial or monetary policy, or trade policy, can have big effects on poor people. Poverty strategies are not good, on the whole, at making these choices clear.

Box 2.2 The benefits of agricultural growth

Farm economy

- Higher incomes for farmers, including smallholders.
- More employment on-farm as labour demand rises per hectare, the area cultivated expands, or frequency of cropping increases. Rise in farm wage rates.

Rural economy

- More jobs in agriculture and food chain upstream and downstream of farm.
- More jobs or higher incomes in non-farm economy as farmers and farm labourers spend additional incomes.
- Increased jobs and incomes in rural economy allow better nutrition, better health and increased investment in education amongst rural population. Lead directly to improved welfare, and indirectly to higher labour productivity.
- More local tax revenues generated and demand for better infrastructure: roads, power supplies, communications. Leads to second-round effects promoting rural economy.
- Linkages in production chain generate trust and information, build social capital and facilitate non-farm investment.
- Reduced prices of food for rural inhabitants who buy in food net.

National economy

- Reduced prices of food and raw materials raise real wages of urban poor, reduce wage costs of non-farm sectors.
- Generation of savings and taxes from farming allows investment in non-farm sector, creating jobs and incomes in other sectors.
- Earning of foreign exchange allows import of capital goods and essential inputs for non-farm production.
- Release of farm labour allows production in other sectors.

Source: Adapted from Irz *et al.* (2001).

An example is trade policy. It hardly needs to be stated that trade policy is among the most highly contested areas of development policy. On the one hand, trade liberalisation is seen as a rapid route to growth and poverty reduction; on the other hand, it is criticised for being risky at best and often damaging to the poor (Bussolo and Solignac Lecomte, 1999; McCulloch *et al.*, 2001; Morrissey, 2002; Oxfam International, 2002). Very different prescriptions follow. Some are to do with public expenditure: investment in education and infrastructure to facilitate trade, for example, or expenditure on safety nets and other measures to compensate the losers from trade liberalisation. Many others have to do with the overall development stance of the country. The list could include the commitment to state involvement in productive sectors, the regulation of utilities, land reform, labour market issues and core labour standards – all trade related at some level. As pointed out in Oxfam's recent trade report,

> It had been hoped that the new framework for poverty reduction developed by the IMF–World Bank would help to integrate poverty reduction into all aspects of government policy.... Unfortunately ... experience to date has not been encouraging – especially in the case of trade. No national PRSPs to date have even provided a credible analysis of the potential impact of trade liberalisation on the poor, and none has reviewed existing commitments on trade reform in the light of such an analysis.
>
> In view of the enormous impact of trade liberalisation – for better or for worse – on the livelihoods of the poor, it is essential that its implications are subjected to a proper assessment in advance, rather than a retrospective justification on the basis of pre-conceived theory. The timing, sequencing, and coverage of liberalisation all need to be carefully reviewed. For example, it may make sense to liberalise imports for a particular agricultural good after the implementation of an investment programme to develop the capacity of small farmers, but not before. Above all, trade liberalisation should be made part of an informed national public debate about poverty-reduction strategies.
>
> (Oxfam International, 2002: 246)[4]

Focusing on sectors where sector-wide approaches work well may over-emphasise social sectors at the expense of growth policies and cross-cutting themes like rural development

SWAPs are proving to be a powerful instrument for improving the management of aid, delivering coordinated donor support through the budget and in pursuit of agreed targets. This is certainly a big improvement over a world where donors cherry-pick individual projects, often outside the budget. There are, however, problems in applying the approach to cross-cutting sectors such as rural development, say, or nutrition.

Early experience shows that there are conditions under which SWAPs are likely to work, and others that will be more difficult. Foster (2000: 10) lists the requirements as being the following:

- public expenditure as a major feature of the sector;
- a substantial donor contribution;
- basic agreement on strategy between government and donors;

- a supportive macro budget environment;
- manageable institutional relationships; and
- incentives such as to garner support in sectoral ministries.

Several of these present problems from the point of view of cross-cutting issues. For example, the first requirement has been cited as the reason why SWAPs work well in sectors such as health, education and roads, where the private sector is relatively small, and where expenditure (rather than, say, pricing policy) is the main determinant of outcomes, but not so well in agriculture, where public expenditure is less important and policy more important (Foster *et al.*, 2001). Nutrition is another sector where public expenditure certainly has a role to play, but also where private expenditure (not least on food) is important, and where policy decisions (e.g. on exchange rates or food safety regulation) can have a major impact.

The fifth requirement, about institutional relationships, has been interpreted to mean that SWAPs work well when an identifiable ministry controls a sector, and not so well otherwise. Foster observes that

> sector programmes have worked most effectively where they are defined in terms of the area of budget responsibility of a single sector ministry, programmes in education or health have proved more manageable than sector programmes for cross-cutting themes such as the environment.
>
> (2000: 10)

This would appear to place a multi-sectoral area at some disadvantage.

The sixth requirement, about incentives, may also be relevant to cross-cutting programmes in some circumstances, especially if large reallocations of funds between programmes (and probably between ministries) are involved. The argument is that public officials will respond well to SWAPs only if they are likely to receive increased funding as a result. Winners will support SWAPs; losers will not.

Commitment to partnership may degrade into a form of covert conditionality

'Partnership' is another term that runs through the new construction of poverty. It features centrally in the Millennium Development Goals and is especially important in the discussion about new aid modalities, for example the Comprehensive Development Framework (Wolfensohn, 1999). Key concepts include shared ideals, trust, transparency, dialogue and frequent review. The main fault lines in the debate are about how to achieve genuine, reciprocal accountability, and about the extent to which partnership arrangements should be contractual.

On reciprocal accountability, the problem arises from the inequality built into the relationship between a rich and powerful donor and a poorer, less powerful 'beneficiary'. Donor countries have expectations of their developing country partners, like good governance; but the real flow of resources and concessions, for example aid and trade access, is from the donor to the beneficiary. In these circumstances, the relationship is most easily understood as one of 'asymmetric accountability' (Maxwell and Riddell, 1998).

One way to counter this is for the partnership to be contractual, with obligations written down and procedures put in place for independent review. A prototype example is the Cotonou Convention between the European Union (EU) and seventy-seven countries of the African, Caribbean and Pacific (ACP) Group. This specifies standards with respect to human rights, democratic principles, the rule of law, and corruption. Joint institutions of the ACP, particularly the joint Council of Ministers, monitor the partnership and adjudicate disputes. The system has yet to be tested fully, and at this stage applies more to the developing countries than to the EU. But it would be perfectly possible to imagine future Conventions specifying standards to which the EU should adhere (concerning aid flows, for example, or trade access).

An alternative, though weaker, approach is that of peer review. The approach has long been used in DAC, whereby donor countries monitor each other's performance. It is now being taken up by developing countries, for example in the context of the New Partnership for Africa's Development (NEPAD, 2001). An innovation proposed by NEPAD is that peer review be reciprocal, involving review of donor policies by African governments. This is certainly a step on the road to full reciprocal accountability.

The *DAC Guidelines on Poverty Reduction* emphasise the importance of partnership, and give some indication as to what might be required on the donor side. The guidelines stress that 'working in partnership means giving serious attention to assessing agency performance in measuring up to agreed responsibilities and obligations' (DAC, 2001: 47) and suggest the indicative criteria set out in Box 2.3. The use of the word 'commitment' in respect of resource transfers suggests that the DAC has moved some way from an earlier and more cautious position, in which the term 'compact' was preferred to the idea of 'contract' (OECD, 1996).

Ways forward

We have listed problems, but the intention is not to undermine new approaches. Remember, these are risks, and the way to deal with risks is to recognise them in advance and take appropriate action.

What, then, would be appropriate? There are two alternative approaches,

Box 2.3 Assessing development agency policy reduction efforts

Working in partnership means giving serious attention to assessing agency performance in measuring up to agreed responsbilities and obligations. The following indicative criteria could be useful in this regard:

- Is the development agency's country strategy based on the partner country's own assessment and strategy for addressing poverty?
- To what extent does the agency's country strategy address the multidimensional aspects of poverty?
- To what extent have the agency's co-operation activities been carried out jointly or in co-ordination with other bilateral and multilateral development agencies (e.g. missions, appraisals, data collection, analyses)?
- Allowing for agency constraints, to what extent have agency administrative and financial requirements been adjusted to, or harmonised with, the partner country's existing procedures or with those of other external partners, where these procedures are deemed appropriate?
- To what extent has the agency implemented its support in a manner which respects and fosters partner country ownership?
- Has the agency supported and strengthened country-led planning, implementation and co-ordination processes?
- Has the agency helped to facilitate civil society's participation (at local, national and international level) in debating and deciding the contents of the country's poverty reduction strategy in ways that respect government efforts and concerns?
- Has there been a clear, serious commitment of resources to poverty reduction?
- Has a commitment been made to provide predictable resources over a medium-term planning time-frame?
- Has sufficient care been taken to avoid duplication of effort and to build on complementarities across the external development community?
- Have efforts been made to improve policy coherence within the agency and, more broadly, across the full range of Development Assistance Committee member government ministries and departments, and has progress been achieved?

Source: DAC (2001: 47).

and again Wordsworth had his finger on the button, identifying both a top-down approach:

> The playfellows of fancy, who had made
> All powers of swiftness, subtilty and strength
> Their ministers, – who in lordly wise had stirred
> Among the grandest objects of the sense,
> And dealt with whatosever they found there
> As if they had within some lurking right
> To wield it;

and a bottom-up approach:

> . . . they, too, who, of gentle mood,
> Had watched all gentle motions, and to these
> Had fitted their own thoughts, schemers more mild,
> And in the region of their peaceful selves;

A bottom-up approach seems more consonant with current approaches, which stress developing country ownership and process rather than the wielding of power by the 'Lords of Poverty' (Hancock, 1989) and other outside agencies. What might it mean in practice? There are six principles:

- *Practise subsidiarity.* Donors need to be flexible in encouraging countries to set their own targets and design their own strategies, and central governments need to be equally flexible in dealing with local government and professional bodies. Conditionality on process rather than substance needs to be maintained, in the implementation of programmes as well as in setting targets.[5] This might mean that targets and programmes set locally bear little relation to the Millennium Development Goals. So be it.
- *Focus on the essentials.* The last thing PRSPs should be is documents which touch every base, cover every point, mention every sector, design every programme, set every target, and establish every monitoring procedure. A PRSP should help to establish the big picture and adjudicate on the key choices: state or market, institutions before liberalisation, open economy or closed economy. If the big picture is right, then the sectors will begin to take care of themselves.
- *Do not forget the 'difficult' sectors and the cross-cutting issues.* Remember that the current technologies of aid delivery favour social sectors because these meet the criteria for successful SWAPs. Yet it is important to include sectors such as agriculture, which do not meet the criteria, and to tackle issues such as rural development which are not usually ministry-led sectors at all.

- *Recognise the political nature of poverty reduction.* Ownership of the process is important, and so is participation. Empowerment is rightly a major theme of the new approach. However, it would be naive to expect a national consensus on poverty reduction policy: the poor are not a homogeneous group, and will not have identical interests.
- *Build partnerships based on reciprocal accountability.* It is important not to forget that partnership is a two-sided coin. Mutual accountability is a cardinal principle.
- *Follow a process approach.* Interim and even full PRSPs are just the first step. They are being revised at regular intervals. Donors should not ask too much of the PRSPs, especially in the early stages. Partnerships take time to build.

These principles are not theoretical. They can be summarised operationally (Table 2.1), for donors, as a list of do's and don'ts. If we implement these principles, then there is no reason to worry about hubris. We can be, indeed, in very heaven:

> Not in Utopia, subterranean fields
> Or some secreted island, Heaven knows where!
> But in the very world, which is the world
> Of all of us, – the place where in the end
> We find our happiness, or not at all!

Table. 2.1 Do's and don'ts of development

Do	Don't
Reinforce government leadership	Impose rigid conditionalities
Encourage a broad-based debate	Assume consensus is possible
Expect a strategic vision which identifies and adjudicates between key macroeconomic and public expenditure choices	Expect all to agree with the vision
	Focus only on social sectors amenable to sector-wide approaches (SWAPs)
Ensure that productive sectors and cross-cutting issues are properly dealt with	Insist on international targets
	Suggest using results-based management in a narrow way
Encourage subsidiarity in setting targets	Insist on the perfect plan before starting
	Make unrealistic demands for data
Encourage process approaches to managing public services	Set performance standards for one side only
Disburse quickly	
Revise frequently	
Build two-way accountability	

Source: Adapted from Maxwell and Conway (2000a: 21).

PS: Wordsworth, of course, was not a poverty planner in the modern sense. All the quotations come from his poem of 1809, 'The French Revolution as it appeared to enthusiasts at its commencement'. The full text can be found at http://www.bartleby.com/145/ww285.html.

Notes

1 This chapter has grown out of lectures for the Netherlands Development Assistance Research Council (RAWOO) in The Hague; the Von Hugel Institute, Cambridge; the London School of Economics; the Development Studies Association, Manchester; the Royal Holloway College, University of London; and the International Training Centre, the International Labour Organisation, Turin. Thanks to participants for insights and advice. It also draws on earlier papers dealing with different aspects of the new construction (Maxwell and Riddell, 1998; Maxwell and Conway, 2000a, b; Maxwell and Ashley, 2001; Maxwell, 2001b, c; Maxwell and Christiansen, 2002). I apologise in advance for the degree of self-referencing which this entails. An earlier version of the paper appears on the RAWOO Web site at http://www.rawoo.nl/ main-5l.html. This version also appears in *Development Policy Review* 21(1). Responsibility is mine. Special thanks to David Sunderland.
2 The fourteen countries with PRSPs endorsed by the boards were Albania, Bolivia, Burkina Faso, The Gambia, Guinea, Honduras, Mauritania, Mozambique, Nicaragua, Niger, Tanzania, Uganda, Vietnam and Zambia.
3 It is notable, however, that rights did not feature in WDR 2000/2001. This was a notable gap in WDR's attempt to forge an international consensus, not least since UNDP's HDR took rights as its theme in the same year (Maxwell, 2001c: 146ff.).
4 These findings are broadly consistent with a recent World Bank/IMF review which concluded that 'None of the PRSPs has dealt systematically with part experience of trade reforms, but several PRSPs (including Albania, Honduras and Mozambique) have included specific measures in support of trade promotion and liberalization. Only in Honduras and Mozambique was there an attempt to clarify the link between these reforms, and growth and poverty reduction' (IDA and IMF, 2002: para. 43).
5 Chapman (2002) develops the idea of a 'soft systems' approach to managing public-sector organisations, building on the theory of learning organisations. See Maxwell (forthcoming) for more detail and a discussion of the application to results-based management.

References

Booth, D. (2003) 'Are PRSPs Making a Difference? The African Experience', *Development Policy Review*, 21(2), special issue, March.

Bussolo, M. and Solignac Lecomte, H.-B. (1999) *Trade Liberalisation and Poverty*, ODI Poverty Briefing 6, London, December.

Chapman, J. (2002) *System Failure: Why Governments Must Learn to Think Differently*, London: DEMOS.

Christie, I. and Nash, L. (1998) *The Good Life*, Demos Collection: 14, Demos: London.

Davies, N. (2000) 'Fiddling the Figures to Get the Right Results', *Guardian*, 11 July, UK.

de Haan, A. (1998) 'Social Exclusion: an Alternative Concept for the Study of Deprivation', *IDS Bulletin*, 29(1): 10–19, Brighton: Institute of Development Studies.

Development Assistance Committee (DAC) (2001) *The DAC Guidelines on Poverty Reduction*, OECD: Paris.

Foster, M. (2000) *New Approaches to Development Co-operation: What Can We Learn from Experience with Implementing Sector Wide Approaches?*, ODI Working Paper 140, London.

Foster, M., Brown, A. and Naschold, F. (2001) 'Sector Programme Approaches: Will They Work in Agriculture?', *Development Policy Review*, 19(3): 321–338.

Gaventa, J., Shankland, A. and Howard, J. (eds) (2002) 'Making Rights Real: Exploring Citizenship, Participation and Accountability', *IDS Bulletin*, 33(2): 1–11, Brighton: Institute of Development Studies, April.

Gunter, B. (2002) 'What's Wrong with the HIPC Initiative and What's Next?', *Development Policy Review*, 20(1): 5–24, March.

Hancock, G. (1989) *Lords of Poverty*, London: Macmillan.

International Development Agency (IDA) and International Monetary Fund (IMF) (2002) *Review of the Poverty Reduction Strategy Paper (PRSP) Approach: Main Findings*, at http://www.worldbank.org/poverty/strategies/review/findings.pdf.

Irz, X., Lin, L., Thirtle, C.G. and Wiggins, S.L. (2001) 'Agricultural Productivity Growth and Poverty Alleviation', *Development Policy Review*, 19(4): 449–466, December.

Johnson, C. (2001) 'Local Democracy, Democratic Decentralisation and Rural Development: Theories, Challenges, and Options for Policy', *Development Policy Review*, 19(4): 521–532, December.

Killick, T. (2002) *Responding to Inequality*, DFID Inequality Briefing Paper 3, London: DFID, March.

Lipton, M. and Maxwell, S. (1992) *The New Poverty Agenda: An Overview*, IDS Discussion Paper 306, August, Brighton: Institute of Development Studies.

McCulloch, N., Winters, L.A. and Cirera, X. (2001) *Trade Liberalisation and Poverty: A Handbook*, London: Centre for Economic Policy Research.

McKay, A. (2002) *Defining and Measuring Inequality*, DFID Inequality Briefing Paper 1, London: DFID, March.

Maxwell, S. (1998) 'International Targets for Poverty Reduction and Food Security: A Mildly Sceptical but Resolutely Pragmatic View with a Call for Greater Subsidiarity', *Canadian Journal of Development Studies*, Special Issue, 19: 77–96.

Maxwell, S. (2001a) 'Agricultural Issues in Food Security', in Devereux, S. and Maxwell, S. (eds) *Food Security in Sub-Saharan Africa*, London: ITDG Publishing.

—— (2001b) 'Innovative and Important, Yes, but Also Instrumental and Incomplete: The Treatment of Redistribution in the "New Poverty Agenda"', *Journal of International Development*, 13(3): 331–341.

—— (2001c) 'WDR 2000: Is There a New "New Poverty Agenda"?', *Development Policy Review*, 19(1): 143–149, London: ODI.

—— (forthcoming) 'Lost in Translation? Implementation Constraints to Results-Based Management', in UNDP/DFID (provisional title/publisher) *Enhancing Development Effectiveness: A New Focus on Managing for Results*, New York: Earthscan.

Maxwell, S. and Ashley, C. (2001) 'Rethinking Rural Development', *Development Policy Review*, 19(4): 395–425, December.

Maxwell, S. and Christiansen, K. (2002) '"Negotiation as a simultaneous equation": building a new partnership with Africa', *International Affairs*, 78(3): 477–491.

Maxwell, S. and Conway, T. (2000a) *New Approaches to Planning*, World Bank Operations Evaluation Department (OED) Working Paper series 14. Summer, Washington, DC: World Bank.

—— (2000b) *Perspectives on Partnership*, World Bank Operations Evaluation Department (OED) Working Paper series 6, Summer, Washington, DC: World Bank.

Maxwell, S. and Riddell, R. (1998) 'Conditionality or Contract? Perspectives on Partnership for Development', *Journal of International Development*, 10(2), March–April.

Morrissey, O. (ed.) (2002) 'Investment and Competition Policy: Issues for Developing Countries'. *Development Policy Review*, 20(1): 63–73, March.

Moser, C. and Norton, A. (2001) *To Claim Our Rights: Livelihood Security, Human Rights and Sustainable Development*, London: ODI.

Narayan, D. with Patel, R., Schafft, K., Rademacher, A. and Koch-Schulte, S. (2000) *Voices of the Poor: Can Anyone Hear Us?*, New York: Oxford University Press for the World Bank.

Naschold, F. (2002) *Why Inequality Matters for Poverty*, DFID: Inequality Briefing Paper 2, London: DFID, March.

NEPAD (2001) Policy Document, October 2001 (English version) at http://www.nepad.org/Documents/AA0010101.pdf.

Norton, A. (2001) *A Rough Guide to PPAs: Participatory Poverty Assessment – An Introduction to Theory and Practice*, London: ODI.

Norton, A. and Elson, D. (2002) *What's Behind the Budget? Politics, Rights and Accountability in the Budget Process*, London: ODI.

O'Neill (2002) *A Question of Trust*, Reith Lectures 2002: 3, at http://www.bbc.co.uk/radio4/reith2002/lecture3_text.shtml.

Organisation for Economic Cooperation and Development (1996) *Shaping the 21st Century: The Contribution of Development Co-operation*, Paris: OECD.

Oxfam International (2002) *Rigged Rules and Double Standards: Trade, Globalisation, and the Fight against Poverty*, Oxford: Oxfam.

PRSP Connections (2002) *PRSP Connections: Monitoring and Synthesis Project*, Issue 5, London: ODI, May.

Silver, H. (1994) *Social Exclusion and Social Solidarity: Three Paradigms*, IILS Discussion Papers 69.

Townsend, P. (1979) *Poverty in the UK*, Harmondsworth, UK: Penguin.

UNDP (1990) *Human Development Report*, New York: Oxford University Press.

—— (1997) *Human Development Report*, New York: Oxford University Press.

White, H. (2001) 'National and International Redistribution as Tools for Poverty Reduction', *Journal of International Development*, 13(3): 343–352.

—— (2002) 'A Drop in the Ocean? The International Development Targets as a Basis for Performance Measurement', appendix 2 in National Audit Office (2002) *DFID: Performance Management – Helping to Reduce World Poverty*, Report by the Controller and Auditor General, National Audit Office, April.

Wolfensohn, J. (1999) 'A Proposal for a Comprehensive Development Framework (a discussion draft)', memo to the board, management and staff of the World Bank Group, 21 January, Washington, DC: World Bank.

World Bank (1992a) *Poverty Handbook*, Washington, DC: World Bank (discussion draft).

—— (1992b) *Poverty Reduction Operational Directive*, Washington, DC: World Bank.

—— (2000) *World Development Report*, New York: Oxford University Press.

3 Using development goals and targets for donor agency performance measurement[1]

Howard White

Introduction

In Chapter 1 it is suggested that the dominance of the International Development Targets and subsequently the Millennium Development Goals in current development policy is partly a consequence of a stress on results-based measurement, which seeks to judge development agency performance against outcomes. However, whilst such an approach is intuitively appealing, there are a number of potential problems with it, which are addressed in this chapter. The chapter starts by setting out a list of the desirable properties of performance measures, and then considers how these measures can be applied using logic models. In the light of this discussion, the International Development Targets and Millennium Development Goals are assessed. It is argued that although they are reasonable measures of progress, they cannot easily be used to monitor the performance of particular agencies, as is illustrated by the attempts of UK aid agency the Department for International Development (DFID) to internalise the development targets in developing its own strategy.

Desirable properties of performance measures

The literature identifies several desirable features of performance measures (e.g. Hakes, 2001; Jackson, 2000; National Audit Office, 2001). In particular, it can be argued that measures should be:

- *Relevant and balanced.* Balance breaks down into three areas: (1) the range of measures should cover all elements of an organisation's activities – and they should not include things which are not a part of them (i.e. indicators should be relevant); (2) they should focus on both short- and long-term performance (which may correspond to the distinction between outcomes and impact); and (3) they should cover the whole process that leads to a measure being met (including inputs, activities and outputs). This last point is further discussed below. A further question of balance is the different weight given to different measures; some can be more important than others, and this fact should be explicitly recognised.

- *Known, understood and trusted.* For performance measures to have their desired organisational impact, they must be known by the members of the organisation and their meaning must be understood. But it is also necessary that they are trusted. That is, members must believe they are useful and well defined and that the quality of the underlying data is good.[2] A related issue is that of ownership. Ideally, measures should be owned by those responsible for delivering the performance, which means they are involved in developing the targets. In practice, performance measurement systems are often passed down from the top or designed by outsiders.
- *Affected and attributable.* Changes in performance measures should be affected by the activities of the organisation, and the extent of the effect should be measurable (attributable). This is also referred to as the problem of additionality. The UK Treasury defines additionality as 'the amount of output from a policy as compared with what would have occurred without intervention' (quoted in Jackson, 2000: 11) For outcome indicators, attribution can be problematic, and this is a major issue in relation to development targets, as we shall see.
- *Achievable.* Targets should be achievable, but not too easily.
- *Linked to existing management systems.* Organisations will already have in place management information systems. The rise of results-based measures was in part a response to the fact that existing systems focused on inputs and internal activities, e.g. spending and staffing, rather than achieving outcomes. But new systems should not be separate from or parallel to these existing systems. Rather, they should be integrated, hence encompassing the logic of how inputs lead to outcomes.

Using performance outcome measures

Performance outcome measures serve two main functions: accountability, and improving organisational performance. The accountability function is in principle straightforward. An organisation commits itself to achieving certain outcomes and it either does or does not deliver. For taxpayers, politicians or shareholders, this may theoretically be sufficient, since they can respond by withholding votes or funds – though problems with such an approach are highlighted in Chapter 1. Further problems arise in the use of performance measures as a management tool. Managers need to understand why outcomes have or have not been achieved. There are three questions here, but only one answer. The questions are: (1) how can performance measures help change organisational practice to enhance the likelihood that targets will be met; (2) how can measures be interpreted to understand how inputs have or have not led to the desired out-

comes; and (3) how can the organisation's activities be linked to the outcomes? The one answer is the importance of logic models.[3]

Ideally, performance measures affect organisational culture. Simply
shifting to performance-based measurement is itself a substantial change
in practice: 'the cultural change required to achieve performance-based
management in any public or non-profit agency presents an enormous
challenge' (Schemer and Newcomer, 2000: 63). But the process of planning how targets will be achieved opens up substantial possibilities for
changing working practices. This planning process should be systematic
and broadly based within the organisation. This is where logic models
come in.

Logic models and the logical framework are schemes for linking inputs
to outcomes. Terminology varies somewhat, but all capture the same basic
idea. The stages recognised in the model used by the NAO are resources,
inputs, processes (often called activities), outputs and outcomes (also
called impacts) (NAO, 2001: 2). It is a rather obvious truism that resources
should be utilised in such a way as to achieve the desired outcomes. But a
failure to do this has been commonly observed. For the government sector,
the most substantial evidence base comes from the USA, since the 1993
Government Performance and Results Act (GPRA) requires all government agencies to have outcome-based targets against which their performance is to be judged. The General Accounting Office (GAO) makes annual
assessments of plans and outcomes. Both the GPRA itself and GAO (1998)
suggest that performance measures should span inputs, outputs and outcomes. However, in practice such logic models have been applied in few
GPRA plans (Scheirer and Newcomer, 2000). The absence of indicators
reflects the fact that there is too little conscious analysis as to how plans
and programmes will affect outcomes (GAO, 1999).

The attraction of logic models is partly that they should force the
agency to examine programmes to see if they really will achieve the
desired outcomes (Millar *et al.*, 2000). However, logic models are a starting point for planning, rather than the end point. It is an easy matter to
put a poverty-related goal at the top of a log-frame as a goal, but a rather
more complex one to be clear how the inputs will help achieve that goal
and to monitor progress accordingly. For example, DFID's budget support
to Kenya in 2000, which was paid in support of the public-sector reform
programme (i.e. to finance retrenchment), included a reduction in the
maternal mortality rate as a goal indicator. It is very difficult indeed to
trace any links between this intended outcome and the activities undertaken by DFID or the Kenyan government, particularly given their short-
term nature. It is all too easy to explain away discrepancies between what
is actually achieved and the initial targets with reference to problems of
attribution or external factors. Nonetheless, if used properly, logic models
should be able to help overcome these problems, although the evidence
base for this being so in practice is quite thin.

Logic models provide a basis for understanding performance. That is, they potentially solve the problem of attribution. Various types of modelling can be undertaken to demonstrate the determinants of outcomes and thus the contribution made by an organisation's activities. Yet in practice such modelling is too costly, cumbersome and frequently contentious to provide a basis for regular performance monitoring. Instead, less rigorous strategies have been proposed to establish 'plausible association' between programme efforts and performance (Scheirer and Newcomer, 2000: 68). These should include attempts to account for the influence of external factors, which may of course be positive or negative.

Attribution becomes harder as we move along the causal chain. It is easy to attribute responsibility for delivering inputs, and usually for carrying out activities, although external factors may play a part. These activities should lead to desired outputs which deliver the target outcomes, again subject to external factors. If the underlying model is correct, then indicators should capture whether the organisation is doing what it needs to do to achieve the outcomes – which may well be the case even if the targets are not met. Conversely, targets may be met 'by accident' (i.e. because of external factors) rather than on account of the conscious efforts of the responsible agency. Whilst logic models can uncover this fact, it is unlikely to matter very much.

The International Development Targets and Millennium Development Goals as performance measures[4]

Relevance and balance

The Millennium Development Goals and International Development Targets score highly on relevance. They capture some of the main aspects of poverty in the developing world. Maxwell (1998) argues that the Goals and Targets simplify the complex phenomenon of poverty by reducing it to a dollar a day. But this argument misses the point that every one of the targets is poverty related, not just the one for income poverty. Rather, the Goals and Targets should be praised for capturing the multidimensional nature of poverty.

It can further be argued that the Goals and Targets have made themselves relevant. Their prominence has resulted in a consensus around a particular set of indicators for monitoring poverty reduction, paving the way for an unprecedented degree of co-ordination amongst donor agencies, and facilitating a harmonisation of performance monitoring which has proved difficult to achieve in the past (DAC, 2000: 21).

But criticisms may be made regarding what is excluded. First, some important dimensions of development are missed out. Neither food nor shelter appeared in the International Development Targets, though these have been added as the second and eleventh goals in the Millennium

Development Goals. A more pertinent critique may be the focus on the measurable. Although the Millennium Development Goals also mention the importance of qualitative aspects of development, such as the importance of governance, most discussion of the indicators themselves focuses on those which can be measured. However, some other agencies are active in promoting the qualitative aspects.

Nor are the Goals balanced, in that for most of them the target date is 2015, with one for 2005. Fifteen years (twenty when they were set) is definitely a long-term goal. Although progress can be measured with respect to being on track, it is preferable to set explicit short-term goals. These short-term goals may be either interim targets for the same variables, or targets for outputs that will help achieve the desired outcome. This brings us to another lack of balance in the indicators.

The Goals are also not balanced in that they are mostly outcome measures, as are most of the wider set of indicators associated with them. Some are output indicators, but not in a consistent manner of a set of indicators capturing inputs, process, outputs and outcomes for a single target, where outputs are the products of the 'investment' such as immunised or educated children, and outcomes are direct measures of welfare such as morbidity, mortality or higher expenditures. Hence, they do not provide a basis for monitoring performance or taking the steps necessary to achieve the outcomes they contain. This problem is not because such indicators are not amenable to international agreement. For example, the Copenhagen Social Summit of 1995 launched the 20:20 initiative, by which 20 per cent of government spending and 20 per cent of aid monies should be devoted to providing basic services to the poor. Data are available to monitor progress in meeting this target, and this progress has been dismal, especially on the part of donors. Another example is immunisation, an important factor for child survival, which has suffered setbacks in recent years. A further example would be the establishment of adequate food security systems. Although nutrition is not amongst the main target indicators, it is in the wider variable list and is an important determinant of some of the outcomes which are listed, most notably child survival.

Are the targets well defined and can progress be measured?

Most of the Millennium Development Goals are clearly defined. Four exceptions may be noted. First, access to reproductive health is not measured by any existing indicator and the proxy of contraceptive prevalence is problematic. Second, the targets are loose, with child survival terminology used in a way which would upset demographers. Infant mortality is the probability of dying before the first birthday, child mortality that of dying between the first and fifth birthdays and under-five mortality that between birth and fifth birthday. Under-five mortality is thus a weighted average of infant and child mortality, but is not liked by many demographers as the factors underlying the two mortality rates vary (see Chapter 10). The most appropriate indicators would therefore be infant and child mortality, but the targets are for infant and under-five mortality (although some sources give child mortality instead). Third, the environmental target speaks of reversing current trends in resource use. Taken literally, this means that the available quantity of environmental resources should begin to increase rather than decrease. Aside from being unattainable, this target does not fit with the general consensus that it is all right to use environmental resources but they must be used in a way which is consistent with overall sustainable development. DFID, which uses the expression 'managing environmental resources', recognises this fact. Finally, it may be questioned whether equality in school enrolments is an adequate proxy for gender equality. A defence of the measure is that equality of education is a necessary starting point for achieving other forms of equality.

Knowledge of the Goals and Targets amongst DFID staff is high.[5] This does not imply that they are aware of the precise technical definition of the variables. For example, understanding of the purchasing power parity (PPP) dollar a day used for income poverty is mainly restricted to economists,[6] and understanding of the relevant age groups for infant and child mortality to health advisers. But it is doubtful whether lack of this precise knowledge impedes work on the targets.

The chosen indicators are all ones for which data were already being collected. They are now published in a variety of places, notably the Development Assistance Committee (DAC) Web site, the World Bank's *World Development Indicators* and DFID's *International Development Statistics*. However, data quality varies by indicator. An issue for all the indicators is coverage, meaning for how many countries data are available. The Organisation for Economic Cooperation and Development (OECD) document *Methodological Note* reports the baseline data for the various indicators. For some indicators coverage is low (see Appendix 3.1, pp. 66–67, for a summary). For example, income-poverty data were missing for about 30 per cent of the population of the developing world, and nearly two-thirds of those in sub-Saharan Africa. For net primary enrolments there is only 12 per cent coverage for South Asia and 69 per cent globally.

A further issue is the frequency and timeliness with which data are available. Income poverty data come from income and expenditure surveys, which are not conducted annually in many developing countries but rather every three to four years. Vital registration systems and health facility-based reporting have inadequate coverage of the population in developing countries to be a reliable source of health data. Good-quality data on child health, including infant and child mortality, are provided by Demographic and Health Surveys (DHSs), but these are conducted about every four years and not in all countries. It is difficult to respond to performance data which are available only with a three-year lag.

Even where data are available, they may be of poor quality. From the targets themselves, maternal mortality data are the most problematic area. These data are notoriously unreliable (see Box 3.1), to the extent that it is surprising that the indicator was deemed suitable for inclusion amongst the targets. In measuring progress on this target, *A Better World for All* (IMF *et al.*, 2001) reported the percentage of attended births rather than maternal mortality itself.

But the setting of the Goals and Targets has in itself provided an impetus to the improving of data quality. As attention is focused on these outcomes, there is an awareness that efforts need to be made to ensure that the underlying data are sound: 'a more concerted effort by the donor community is needed to support partner countries' capacity to collect data and monitor progress towards the international goals over the coming years' (DAC, 2000: 22).

Are the targets achievable?

Whether or not the targets can be achieved has been the area of analysis that has attracted most attention. Chapter 1 reviews some of the existing evidence and Chapter 6 presents a new discussion of this issue. The main point to note is that there is common agreement that most of the targets will not be met: 'on current trends, none of the international development goals on health and education are likely to be achieved at the global level' (IMF *et al.*, 2001: 12). For example, on current trends there will still

Box 3.1 Data quality: the case of maternal mortality

Maternal mortality for Ghana jumped from 400 to 1,000 per 100,000 from one issue of the World Bank's *World Development Report* (WDR) to the next. Maudlin (1994) showed that although they both used the same source, the WDR reported data for fifty-six developing countries, whereas the UNDP's *Human Development Report* (HDR) did so for fifty-five of these fifty-six and forty-eight further countries (for which the WDR indicated that data were unavailable). The Development Assistance Committee baseline data sheets state that coverage for this indicator includes practically every country in the world.

Counting differences of less than 50 points as the same, HDR gave higher values than WDR for twenty-six countries, lower for twelve and about the same for seventeen. Some differences are substantial, for example Benin at 800 and 161 in the two sources. The correlation coefficient between the two sets of figures is only 0.7, dropping to 0.4 for high-mortality countries. A comparison of WDR and DHS data for 1997 also shows substantial discrepancies.

Source: White *et al.* (2001).

have been 100 million children of school-going age out of school in 2001. These pessimistic conclusions arise even from 'base run' predictions which are typically based on the usually rather optimistic growth forecasts produced by the World Bank and IMF. Forecasts based on historical growth performance show even greater divergence from the targets, and current economic performance suggests that growth from the 1990s may overestimate that for the new decade.

The second point is that performance varies greatly by region. The targets themselves are defined at various levels of aggregation. Some apply globally (e.g. income poverty), some are country specific (e.g. infant and child mortality) and some necessarily apply to each country (e.g. universal primary education will be achieved only when it is achieved in all countries). But even the targets stated as global figures are intended to be met at the disaggregated level – that is, for each country and region: 'while expressed in terms of their global impact, these goals must be pursued country by country' (DAC, 1996: 2). Here performance varies: 'the education and gender equality goals are likely to be achieved in some regions and many countries. And a few countries are on track to achieve large reductions in infant and under five mortality' (World Bank, 2001: 12). In general, Africa is performing worst with respect to the different targets and East Asia the best. Some of these differences are explained by continued high growth in East Asia (so that the income-poverty target has already been met) compared to low growth in Africa. But African countries also suffer from much higher rates of HIV/AIDS, which has helped reverse the long-run decline in mortality rates in several countries, and from extensive conflict, which undermines the ability of countries to attain any of the targets. Experience varies for the other regions. The transition economies of Eastern Europe and the former Soviet Union saw very sharp increases in poverty in the early 1990s so that the income-poverty target is unlikely to be met, and in some countries, notably Russia, social indicators have also worsened.

Whether or not the targets will be achieved is not the same thing as whether they are achievable. The papers reviewed offer limited advice on this point. The main argument made is the importance of a good policy environment (see Collier and Dollar, 2002; Demery and Walton, 1999; IMF *et al.*, 2001): 'whether or not poverty incidence will be halved by 2015 depends in part on how well economies are managed' (Demery and Walton, 1999: 83). The argument is that better policies promote growth, which reduces income poverty and other forms too, such as mortality rates. Most papers on the subject do not discuss an explicit role for development agencies. The exception is that by Collier and Dollar, who build on the suggestion that aid works best at promoting growth, and so reducing poverty, when the policy environment is right. Hence, the prospect of meeting the Goals and Targets is enhanced if aid is concentrated on poor countries with good policies. This piece of research has had an influence on several development agencies, though its theoretical and empirical basis is highly contestable (see Lensink and White, 2000).

Attribution

The Millennium Development Goals do least well with respect to attribution. It is impossible (or at very best, virtually impossible) for an individual agency to isolate its impact on global, or even country-level, trends in the relevant indicators. This fact is demonstrated by the experience of the United States Agency for International Development (USAID).

In 1997, USAID laid out six strategic development goals (e.g. 'broad-based economic growth and agricultural development encouraged'), and for each of these defined a set of outcome indicators at both country and global levels (e.g. 'average annual growth rates in real per capita income above one per cent'). With respect to the growth goal, the fiscal year (FY) 2000 performance report states that 'nearly 70 per cent of USAID-assisted countries were growing at positive rates in the second half of the 1990s, compared with 45 per cent in the early part of the decade' (USAID, 2001: v). However, that same performance report noted that 'one cannot reasonably attribute overall country progress to USAID programs' (ibid.: viii). Commenting on the previous year's USAID Performance Report, GAO had similarly observed that the goals were 'so broad and progress affected by many factors other than USAID programmes, [that] the indicators cannot realistically serve as measures of the agency's specific efforts' (2000: 1–2). In response to these criticisms, the FY 2000 performance report (USAID) announced that the indicators related to the strategic goals will no longer be used to measure USAID's performance (but they will be reported as being of interest in their own right, being referred to as 'Development Performance Benchmarks'). Rather, performance will be measured against the strategic objectives of the individual operating units (e.g. country programmes).

The difficulties of attribution are further illustrated by a GAO report on USAID's child survival programme, launched in the 1980s (GAO, 1996). Entitled *Contributions to Child Survival Are Significant but Challenges Remain*, it lists the uses of funds under the child survival budget line and reports progress on reducing child mortality and immunisation rates in recipient countries (an activity supported by a number of donors). It makes pertinent observations on some of the activities financed by child survival programmes (a bridge in Mozambique and a water tower in Egypt) and points out that many countries with high mortality do not get funds, whereas those with low mortality continue to do so. But no attempt is made to link the inputs described to the outputs and outcomes reported. To do so would not be an impossible task: there are models of the determinants of infant and child mortality which could be used to look at the trends in these determinants and how they have been affected by USAID's activities. But it would be a major undertaking – not one that can be accommodated within routine performance measurement. The best that performance measurement can do is have a set of indicators spanning inputs to outcomes based on such an underlying model. It is for these reasons that evaluators have turned to the logical framework and approaches such as theory-based evaluation.

Integration with existing management information systems

The DAC report on results-based management (DAC, 2000) identifies three approaches to agency-wide monitoring:

- aggregating project- and programme-level outputs;
- aggregating project- and programme-level outcomes;
- reporting country-level trends.

This classification may be simplified to 'bottom-up' versus 'top-down' systems. Bottom-up systems take individual activities as the primary unit of analysis and aggregate performance across countries, sectors and the agency as a whole. Top-down systems report on outcome indicators for a country (or at least sector in a country) and whole regions. Top-down systems suffer from attribution problems – can a link be made between the observed outcome and the agency's activities? If not, then the information is of limited, if any, value, in guiding management systems. Bottom-up systems, which are more strongly rooted in traditional management information systems, face problems of aggregation and linking to relevant outcome indicators.

All donor agencies have some sort of monitoring and evaluation system at the project and programme level, which should provide a basis for both feedback at the project level and 'feed-up' to management. For our purposes here we are interested in the two questions suggested in the previous paragraph. First, are the data that are collected of a suitable form to be aggregated to give an overall indication of agency performance (and broken down at the country, regional and sectoral levels)? Second, if there is such an aggregation, does it yield information on outcomes in relation to the development goals?

The World Bank's rating system is an example of a system which does yield agency-wide results. All activities are rated under a number of criteria on a regular basis and upon completion. These ratings include an overall rating of whether the activity has been satisfactory. Hence overall portfolio performance can be judged by the percentage of projects deemed satisfactory. Such analysis is published in the *Annual Review of Development Effectiveness* (ARDE) produced by the Operations Evaluation Department of the World Bank. This system does yield information of use to management, which has a systematised approach to identifying 'problem areas'. In the decade from 1991 the percentage of 'problem projects' rose from 11 to 20 per cent, resulting in the creation of the Portfolio Management Task Force, whose report (known as the Wapenhans Report after the lead author) advocated a number of changes and contributed to the adoption of results-based management within the World Bank.[7]

Whilst a 'satisfactory' project is defined as one which is substantially meeting its development objectives, this does not allow us to say anything about the contribution of the World Bank to the meeting of the goals. The information collected is simply not the right sort to provide that information. There is a misalignment between the data collected from the 'bottom up' and the sort of outcomes being monitored in 'top-down' International Development Target-oriented systems. The same is true of all other agencies which collect data of a form suitable for bottom-up aggregation.

There are two possible responses to this problem of misalignment. The first is to say that it is inevitable. The problem of attribution is not going to be solved for routine monitoring purposes, so no attempt should be made to link agency performance as measured by bottom-up systems with agency impact on the Millennium Development Goals and International Development Targets. That answer does not seem satisfactory for agencies, like DFID, which have pinned their performance to the International Development Target mast. So the second response to the misalignment problem is to resort to logic models. The bridge must be made between observing satisfactory activities and presumed impact on development outcomes. Whether this is feasible is an issue I return to in the next section.

Summary

The Millennium Development Goals and International Development Targets are relevant as a measure of development progress, are well defined and understood, and data are mostly available, if of variable quality. But they have two important shortcomings, and one perhaps less important one. First, the indicators themselves are output and outcome oriented. There has not been international agreement on the underlying logic model to produce the indicators required to monitor inputs and processes necessary to achieve these outcomes. The partial exception is the consensus on the need for market-led economic growth, though whether this is the best way to achieve the targets is debatable. Second, it is not possible to attribute changes in these measures to the actions of development agencies, either individually or collectively. Both these arguments point to the need for a more holistic performance measurement system, one which integrates the monitoring of inputs and process with that of outputs and outcomes. Finally, the targets seem unlikely to be attained.

Whilst the Millennium Development Goals and International Development Targets are mostly a satisfactory measure of development progress, this does not mean that they are suitable indicators with which to measure the performance of any single development agency. Indeed, a short period of reflection shows that the problem of attribution alone means that outcome indicators are by themselves unlikely ever to be suitable, especially ones of a global nature. Hence some modification is necessary. To what extent has DFID's approach to the targets tackled these problems?

The use of targets by donor agencies: the Department for International Development

DFID has embraced the International Development Targets and then the Millennium Development Goals more strongly than any other bilateral donor. The targets have been given pride of place in both the 1997 and 2000 White Papers on International Development, they have featured strongly in the public pronouncements of the former Secretary of State, Clare Short, and have been promoted in various ways such as through posters. DFID staff view them as highly relevant to their work. But more important than these changes in external presentation have been the internal efforts to accommodate the Goals and Targets, principally through strategy papers, the Public Service Agreement (PSA) and the Service Delivery Agreement (SDA).

From target to strategy

At a workshop held to discuss the first White Paper, many commentators argued that the Paper was full of good intentions but rather silent on how these intentions were to be fulfilled (see the papers in White, 1998). But since that time, DFID has put in place a process for elaborating a strategy to this end. Central to this work have been the strategy papers: Target Strategy Papers, Institutional Strategy Papers and Country Strategy Papers (see Box 3.2). The discussion here focuses on the first two, since Country Strategy Papers are the subject of Chapter 4.

Box 3.2 The Department for International Development's strategy papers

---

Target Strategy Papers (TSPs) address a single development target (e.g. income poverty) or group of targets (health).

Institutional Strategy Papers (ISPs) have been, or are being, prepared for each of DFID's main partners amongst international organisations.

Country Strategy Papers (CSPs) outline the main challenge of poverty reduction in each of the partner countries.

The intended relationship between the different documents is shown in Figure 3.1.[8] Target Strategy Papers have a central role, defining the long-term strategies to meet the development targets. These strategies should inform the content of the Institutional Strategy Papers and Country Strategy Papers. CSPs should also be informed by the relevant ISPs. Various processes have been put in place to ensure these links, starting with the collaborative way in which strategy papers were prepared. The geographical desks were asked to draw up a response to the TSPs, outlining the implications for their work. In practice, most of the 'new generation' of CSPs currently in use were prepared prior to either TSPs or ISPs being available, so that the links shown in Figure 3.1 will not have operated in practice. But the question is the extent to which CSPs prepared since the beginning of 2001 are consistent with the TSPs (and indeed the PSA, which is discussed below).

TSPs might be faulted for their sectoral bias, which can overlook cross-sectoral linkages – for example, health matters for education and vice versa, whilst lack of access to water close to home may be the main thing keeping girls from school. Hence preparing papers on each target separately misses the importance of a multidimensional approach. Examining the papers shows this criticism to be only partially justified, since several papers discuss these cross-sectoral linkages. For example, the environment TSP makes much of public health arguments.

All strategy papers have a common structure which corresponds to a logic model. The first section sketches out the challenge, e.g. the relevant International Development Target(s) in the case of a TSP, how an organisation relates to the poverty agenda for an ISP and the poverty situation in a country for a CSP. The next section lays out the strategy necessary to meet this challenge. This is a strategy for all partners, not DFID alone. The paper then reviews the role of different actors and, finally, the part that DFID can play.

However, analysis of CSPs shows that they suffer from a 'missing middle' (see Chapter 4). Figure 3.1 shows also the PSA/SDA and the annual performance plans, which are important in bringing the Millennium Development Goals and International Development Targets down to a realistic management time-frame. Fifteen years is too long for management targets. The PSA (see Box 2.1, pp. 31–32) and SDA bring these down to targets for 2006, though sometimes making them more ambitious than their longer-run counterparts. For example, the target for under-five mortality requires an annual reduction of around 6 per cent, which over twenty-five years would imply a nearly 80 per cent reduction as against the International Development Targets of two-thirds. Since most countries are not on track for the longer-run target, the chances of meeting the shorter-run one must be doubted. The PSA has five development objectives and one management one (value for money). Each objective has a number of performance targets, which are a mixture of process, output

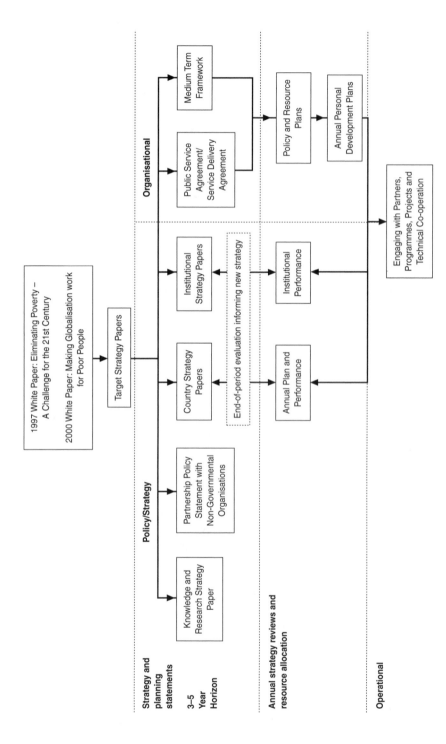

Figure 3.1 Overview of Department for International Development strategy: vision statement, fifteen-year horizon.

and outcomes. Some objectives (health and education) remain largely focused on outcome performance measures, whereas others (income poverty) are far more process oriented. The SDA is firmly focused on process issues linked to each of the PSA objectives.

The PSA and SDA deal to some extent with problems of affect and attribution in two ways. First, the targets are defined in relation to a smaller number of countries rather than all developing countries. For example, the health and education targets are set with respect to the top ten recipients of UK health and education sector support respectively. Second, the PSA and SDA, at least to some extent, provide the logic model which is missing from the Millennium Development Goals and International Development Targets taken by themselves.[9] However, there are also problems in the approach, principally that of data availability: as mentioned earlier, data of the sort required are often collected on a three- to four-year cycle at best. Hence there may well be gaps in monitoring fulfilment of many of the PSA targets. The outcome indicators given in the PSA are also not suitable for judging agency performance. But these outcomes can be observed, along with the contribution that DFID may or may not have made to their fulfilment, as judged by the input and process indicators contained in the PSA and SDA.

The PSA shown (in Appendix 3.2) is the second produced by DFID and differs from the first in that it no longer specifies targets for the top thirty recipients of the various types of aid.[10] The shift to a smaller number of targets reflects a more realistic objective in terms of attribution, though it by no means solves that problem. On the other hand, it may be thought difficult to obtain representative data for a smaller number of countries. Though the target relates to specific countries, proper monitoring requires data on all countries. As indicated above, these data are not likely to be readily available for several indicators. Moreover, it is not for DFID alone to develop the monitoring systems to collect these data. The Millennium Development Goals and International Development Targets potentially provide the basis for harmonised monitoring procedures across donors, although this has not been achieved in the past.

The PSA does solve the problem of how to judge agency performance by aggregating across the agency. And it probably will do so without creating burdensome reporting procedures which have weighed down other agencies:

> In USAID, for example, operating units and implementing partners are beginning to complain that there is no time left for implementing programs, and that much of the higher-order results data collection is not considered directly relevant or useful to them, but is only being used to 'report upward'.
>
> (Development Assistance Committee, 2000: 23)

But others might argue that the disjuncture between project- and programme-level monitoring and judging DFID's performance is a bad move. This aggregation is not based on activity-level performance. Indeed, the performance measures explicitly exclude many DFID-financed activities.

So wouldn't the Department's performance best be judged by aggregating the performance of different activities? In practice, the data do not exist to do so, and trying to collect them would indeed be onerous. In recent years a database, PRISM, has been developed to contain data on project activities, though the rules which are applied mean that only 30 per cent of projects should be included. And of the over 700 projects on which information should be held, the output to purpose review (not available for all projects, but a major part of monitoring) was available for just over fifty.[11] Even if PRISM were to have full coverage, it is not clear that it will be able to generate aggregate data on agency performance (in the manner of the World Bank described above), and certainly not to give any information relating to the Millennium Development Goals and International Development Targets.

At present, one must wonder on what data DFID management do base their decisions. There is no 'bottom-up' system to indicate overall performance. And the goal-related indicators embodied in the PSA are of little operational use.[12]

However, DFID is one of the foremost donor agencies in the related developments of increased budget support and Sector Programmes (sector-wide approaches, SWAPs, in DFID terminology). These are consistent with both harmonised procedures and monitoring based on country-wide performance indicators. To the extent that these are developed and DFID harnesses the information they provide, then there will be some sort of systematised feedback, though not in a form that can be readily aggregated.

However, important issues remain as to (1) the extent to which the PSA and SDA manifest themselves in the daily work of DFID (e.g. by being incorporated in CSPs), and (2) whether the underlying model is 'right'.

On the first of these questions, DFID staff readily point to changes brought about by the renewed focus on poverty. For example, DFID's programme to China has changed from being focused on infrastructure in the relatively affluent seaboard provinces to social sectors in poorer western provinces. It is debatable how much the change comes from adopting the International Development Targets *per se* rather than an increased poverty focus. Such a focus has already been there since 1990. And, for example, during the 1990s the Zambia programme shifted from secondary schools and support to hospitals to primary education and health clinics. Attitudes as to how important the goals themselves are to arguing for the poverty agenda vary between staff – but their effect is seen as either neutral or positive; there was no suggestion that they have detracted attention from 'main issues'. Those who see a positive role argue that stressing the Millennium Development Goals and International

Development Targets has enabled internal policy changes (abolishing Aid and Trade Provision, more aid for South Asia) and can be a useful tool in discussions with partners.

It is striking that DFID staff and outside experts stress that a major part of DFID's contribution to achieving the targets comes through its influence on partner-country policies and the actions of other actors. Yet measuring impact through influence is an under-researched area.

Whether the model is right is not a matter of objective fact. Targets do not in themselves contain the strategy as to how they should be attained, so that competing strategies may be proposed. The changes that DFID is making, e.g. towards selectivity, are in line with the consensus amongst donor agencies, if disputed by some critics (Lensink and White, 2000). Other areas of contention include the nature and depth of debt relief and cost recovery schemes for basic services.

Data quality

DFID staff are aware of data quality issues. Whilst operational staff express appropriate scepticism as to the quality of the data, various initiatives are under way to promote use of the data and improve them. Indeed, an advantage of the Millennium Development Goals and International Development Targets is said to have been to draw attention to data quality issues. The publication formerly called *British Aid Statistics* has become *International Development Statistics* and includes data on the Millennium Development Goals and International Development Targets. CSPs are required to report a country's performance with respect to the International Development Targets indicators (though this has been done in an uneven way – see Chapter 4). Staff of the DFID's statistics department are well informed on data quality and are active in supporting initiatives for them to be improved, notably DAC's PARIS initiative (Partnerships in Statistics for Development in the Twenty-First Century).[13]

DFID staff do not feel that the Millennium Development Goals or International Development Targets stress quantitative at the expense of qualitative aspects of development since they believe the importance of the latter is well understood. In addition, DFID has supported work by DAC on governance indicators to quantify the governance target. When the working group was unable to reach agreement, DFID support shifted to ongoing efforts to develop acceptable indicators by the World Bank.[14] The difficulty in selecting measures of 'governance' revolves in part around disagreements as to what constitutes 'good governance'. With respect to human rights, European countries may wish to include the absence of the death penalty, but this is still applied in other developed countries. The extent of restrictions on individual freedom for reasons of national security is another murky area. The indicators being developed by the World Bank attempt to sidestep these issues to some extent by proposing a set of process indicators – such as civil service wages and the nature of elections (e.g. whether they use proportional representation or not) – which have no normative content. Performance measures on the quality of governance – such as corruption and the predictability of policy-making – are included separately.

Summary

The PSA and SDA have potentially provided a vehicle to enable DFID to travel the road travelled in rather more time by USAID. That is, there is a move away from the outcome indicators as the measure of performance. DFID staff are indeed generally, although not universally, sceptical that the Millennium Development Goals or International Development Targets can be used to assess the DFID's performance. The PSA and SDA spell out a number of process indicators which may be used to capture DFID's contribution toward meeting the Millennium Development Goals and International Development Targets. This role is appreciated by DFID staff. One commented that the Millennium Development Goals and International Development Targets could not be used to assess DFID's performance but that DFID should 'track changes and make sure that their work is consistent with the Millennium Development Goals and International Development Targets' (adding that the PSA played this role). This scepticism also appeared in that no respondents thought that the fact that indicators are currently not on track to meet the targets called for major changes in DFID's strategy. It is also shown by the ease with which the DFID Departmental Review explains away deviations from the targets. However, the PSA also does contain outcome indicators, so it is worth emphasising that development outcome indicators of this sort are not a suitable vehicle for judging the performance of individual agencies. And there are problems of incomplete coverage of DFID's activities and misalignment with the reporting system being developed using PRISM.

Conclusions

The International Development Targets, launched in 1996, have caught the attention of the development community, which has become stronger with the successor Millennium Development Goals. Unlike previous targets, they have not fallen by the wayside, but continue to be referred to and monitored. Targets can play an important role in accountability and performance measurement, though they are not without their disadvantages. To be most effective, performance measures should satisfy a number of criteria. The Millennium Development Goals satisfy only some of these criteria. They are very relevant, are mostly well defined and correspond to existing indicators. But they are mostly outcome oriented, with little effort made to build a consensus around an underlying logic model of how the targets are to be achieved. In the absence of such a model it is extremely difficult to say anything sensible as to whether changes in target indicators can be attributed to the actions of the development community. To put it bluntly: the Millennium Development Goals are not suitable for judging the performance of individual development agencies.

Amongst bilateral donors, the UK's Department for International Development has been a prominent supporter of the targets and has made substantial steps to internalise them. Nonetheless, this chapter has not been able to assess the extent to which the model contained in the Public Service Agreement and Service Delivery Agreement has influenced DFID's work on the ground. The targets have been central to the two White Papers produced since 1997 and strategy papers have been produced that seek to show how the targets may be achieved. The PSA and SDA contain performance measures which are related to the international goals, but also include inputs, process and outputs. Hence they contain a model of how to achieve these interim targets and so, implicitly, the Millennium Development Goals themselves. To the extent that performance is judged by these intermediary indicators, the PSA and SDA represent an improvement. However, worries remain over the misalignment between these top-down targets (which have incomplete coverage of DFID's activities) and the nascent bottom-up system in PRISM. A key area of further investigation is the extent to which the SDA affects the work of the various parts of DFID.

Appendix 3.1 Data coverage of baseline data for the International Development Targets

		East Asia and Pacific	Europe and Central Asia	Latin America and Caribbean	Middle East and North Africa	South Asia	Sub-Saharan Africa	World
Number of countries		20	27	35	15	8	48	200
Poverty head count	Countries	6	9	9	5	4	11	44
	% of pop.	83	71	65	52	78	36	71
Poverty depth	Countries	4	16	10	3	4	11	48
	% of pop.	86	71	65	52	78	36	57
Poor's consumption share	Countries	8	16	15	7	5	18	69
	% of pop.	86	72	73	57	86	58	86
Underweight	Countries	12	10	25	1	8	45	120
	% of pop.	98	66	99	28	100	100	89
Net primary enrolment	Countries	9	16	24	13	2	30	127
	% of pop.	88	73	90	97	12	56	69
Completion fourth grade	Countries	11	8	17	9	4	32	100
	% of pop.	84	28	81	50	78	61	68
Literacy	Countries	8	12	25	13	7	36	120
	% of pop.	97	68	100	89	100	83	83
Girls to boys enrolments	Countries	14	25	25	13	7	42	161
	% of pop.	94	99	66	97	100	98	96
Female to male literacy	Countries	28	8	6	10	21	4	77
	% of pop.	78	95	94	63	98	3	84

Infant mortality rate	Countries	20	27	35	15	8	48	200
	% of pop.	100	100	100	100	100	100	100
Under-five mortality rate	Countries	20	27	33	15	8	48	187
	% of pop.	100	100	99	100	100	100	100
Maternal mortality rate	Countries	12	26	23	11	5	38	144
	% of pop.	100	99	99	97	98	97	100
Attended births	Countries	14	18	14	12	8	39	137
	% of pop.	42	99	62	97	100	88	86
Contraceptive prevalence	Countries	5	6	15	8	3	29	69
	% of pop.	90	43	61	76	95	84	75
Process for sustainable development	Countries	34	7	16	5	18	6	86
Access to safe water	Countries	21	9	33	13	7	45	151
	% of pop.	100	26	100	85	100	89	89
Land area protected	Countries	27	12	23	13	5	39	146
	% of pop.	100	100	99	100	98	98	100
GDP per unit of energy use	Countries	6	24	21	12	5	18	116
	% of pop.	95	97	96	100	98	76	95
Carbon dioxide emissions	Countries	20	26	35	13	9	45	..
	% of pop.	100	100	100	100	100	99	..

Source: OECD Methodological Note DCD/DAC (98) 6/ADD, Paris: OECD/DAC (available at http://www1.oecd.org/dac/Indicators/pdf/ METHOD.PDF).

Appendix 3.2 DFID Public Service Agreement and Service Delivery Agreement. Aim: the elimination of poverty in poorer countries

Objectives	Performance targets	Delivery
1 To reduce poverty through the provision of more focused and co-ordinated development assistance by the international community to low- and middle-income countries.	1 An increased focus by DFID on poor countries, particularly those with effective governments pursuing high growth and pro-poor economic and social policies, as demonstrated by: • An increase in the percentage of DFID's bilateral programme going to poor countries, particularly those with favourable policy environments; • An increase in the percentage of European Commission (EC) development assistance going to poor countries and; • Adoption and implementation of effective Poverty Reduction Strategies by 2004 in all countries accessing International Development Agency (IDA) high-impact or adjustment lending.	Successful delivery depends on DFID and multilateral institutions becoming more selective, and focused on poverty reduction. DFID will therefore: • Deliver a more effective and focused bilateral programme by: (a) working with partners in poor countries to deliver country strategies which support poverty reduction; and (b) allocating DFID support, taking account of numbers of poor people, the effectiveness of country programmes, and partners' progress in developing and implementing sound pro-poor policies. • Seek to improve the effectiveness of EC development assistance and the European Development Fund by working with other government departments (especially Foreign and Commonwealth Office, and Her Majesty's (HM) Treasury) and European Union (EU) member states to: (a) establish better organisation of EC programme delivery, by end-2001; (b) gain agreement in Council and Commission to redirect allocations and spend towards programmes which reduce poverty by 2003; (c) increase the proportion of EC country-specific Official Development Assistance (ODA) going to poor countries from 50 per cent in 1998 to 70 per cent in 2006. Where poor countries have demonstrated a clear commitment to developing and implementing comprehensive Poverty Reduction Strategies, donors should respond by supporting delivery of these Strategies. DFID will therefore:

- Provide support to at least twelve partner countries by 2004 to develop and implement Poverty Reduction Strategies in co-ordination with other donors.

II To promote sustainable development through co-ordinated UK and international action.

2 To promote the integration of developing countries into the global economy through co-ordinated UK and international action, including by:

- Relief of unsustainable debt by 2004 for all Heavily Indebted Poor Countries (HIPCs) committed to poverty reduction, building on the internationally agreed target that three-quarters of eligible HIPCs reach decision point by end-2000 (joint target with Her Majesty's Treasury); and
- Gaining international agreement on the integration of social, economic and environmental aspects of sustainable development into poverty reduction programmes.

Relief of unsustainable debt burdens is essential if poor countries are to harness the resources they need for economic growth and development, to reduce poverty and reap the benefits of globalisation. DFID will therefore:

- Work to secure faster, wider and deeper debt relief for the poorest countries, through effective implementation of the Heavily Indebted Poor Country (HIPC) Initiative. Effectiveness will be determined by the involvement of all creditors (including securing the necessary financing for multilateral creditors), the extent of front-loading (meaning that more of the benefit of debt relief is felt in the early years (including from Decision Point)), the speed of the process and the strength of the link to poverty reduction, ensuring that debt relief assists countries to implement their national poverty reduction strategies and achieve the international development targets.

To ensure that development is sustainable over the long term and benefits future as well as current generations, poor countries need to integrate sustainable development into their policies and programmes. DFID will therefore work towards:

- Developing guidance on the principles of sustainable development, securing OECD Development Assistance Committee (DAC) agreement to it by mid-2001, and work to secure wider international agreement by end-2001;

continued

Appendix 3.2 continued

Objectives	Performance targets	Delivery
		• Successful integration of these principles into government, multilateral and DFID policies and programmes in ten key DFID partner countries by early 2004, including agreed approaches to water resources management, and capacity-building for environmental management.

Successful integration of poor countries into the global economy will depend on the creation of a supportive environment in which trade and enterprise can flourish, and contribute to poverty reduction. DFID will therefore:
• Work with the public and private sectors to improve the business environment, especially access to finance and other business services for enterprises that employ or benefit the poor.
• Promote increased private-sector foreign investment in poor countries by turning the Commonwealth Development Corporation (CDC) into a public–private partnership, when business conditions are right, with majority private capital. CDC is required to make 70 per cent of its new investments in poor developing countries and seeks to make 50 per cent of its new investments in sub-Saharan Africa and South Asia.
• Work with the EU and other partners for multilateral trade negotiations to improve trading opportunities for poor countries, whilst working with other donors to deliver more effective capacity-building support for poor countries so that they are equipped to participate fully in the international trading system. |

Effective action to tackle HIV is essential if poor countries are to sustain economic growth, development and poverty reduction. DFID will therefore:

- Work with partners in countries with high, or increasing, HIV prevalence to develop and implement strategies which intensify multi-sector and co-ordinated international action on HIV/AIDS.

Successful delivery depends on governments, donors, international bodies, civil society groups, the private sector and others co-operating closely in the design and delivery of coherent, complementary policies and interventions in order to defuse tensions, reduce violence, tackle the factors that underlie armed conflict, and build governments and institutions capable of sustaining peaceful and democratic societies.

Where the UK can make a significant contribution, DFID, FCO and the Ministry of Defence (MoD) will work in partnership with others to:

- Strengthen international and regional systems and capacity for conflict prevention, early warning, crisis management, conflict resolution/peacemaking, peacekeeping and peace-building.
- Contribute to global and regional conflict prevention initiatives, such as curbing the proliferation of small arms and the diversion of resources to finance conflict.
- Promote initiatives in selected countries, including indigenous capacity building, to help avert conflict, reduce violence and build sustainable security and peace.

3 Improved effectiveness of the UK contribution to conflict prevention and management, as demonstrated by a reduction in the number of people whose lives are affected by violent conflict and by a reduction in potential sources of future conflict, where the UK can make a significant contribution (joint target with FCO and MoD).

continued

Appendix 3.2 continued

Objectives	Performance targets	Delivery
III Improved education outcomes in key countries receiving DFID education support.	4 Improved education systems in our top ten recipients of DFID education support demonstrated by: • an average increase in primary school enrolment from a baseline established in 2000 of 75 per cent to 81 per cent on the basis of data available in 2004; and • improvements in gender equality in education, particularly primary education	Successful delivery depends on donors and poor-country partners working together to design and deliver effective policies and support for education. DFID will therefore work in partnership with others to support: • Implementation of the agenda agreed by the International Community at the Dakar World Education Forum in April 2000 through the provision of focused support by relevant multilaterals, partner countries, bilateral donors and non-governmental organisations. • Successful adoption and implementation of education-sector strategies which include explicit objectives on equitable access for girls and boys by 2004, in at least eight of our top ten recipients of bilateral education assistance. • Development of basic monitoring and evaluation mechanisms and their integration into education sector strategies by 2004 in at least eight of our top ten recipients of bilateral education assistance.
IV Improvements in health outcomes in key countries receiving DFID health care assistance.	5 Improvements in child, maternal and reproductive health in our top ten recipients of DFID health care assistance demonstrated by: • a decrease in the average under-five mortality rate from 132 per 1,000 live births in 1997 to 103 on the basis of data available in 2004;	Successful delivery depends on donors and poor-country partners working together to design and deliver effective policies and support for health. DFID will therefore work in partnership with others to support: • Development and implementation of strategies focused on improving access to safe water and sanitation and reducing levels of child mortality in at least eight of the top ten recipients of bilateral health assistance by 2004.

• an increase in the proportion of births assisted by skilled attendants from a baseline established in 2000 of 43 per cent to 50 per cent on the basis of data available in 2004; and • improved access to reproductive health care.	• Development and implementation of health-sector strategies by 2004 in at least eight of the top ten recipients of bilateral health assistance which: (a) aim to improve child health outcomes and include actions to strengthen immunisation and prevention, and the treatment of childhood illnesses, including malaria where endemic; and (b) include explicit policy and operational frameworks to strengthen the capacity of health systems, improve the quality and coverage of maternal health care, and ensure universal access to reproductive health services. • Strengthened multilateral initiatives to combat HIV/AIDS in Africa (UNAIDS) and roll back malaria (WHO) demonstrated through national strategies, with jointly agreed milestones, in at least five of the top ten recipients of DFID health-care assistance.
Value for money.	
6 Improved value for money and effectiveness of projects in DFID's bilateral programme, as demonstrated by a year on year improvement in the index of their evaluated success.	Successful delivery of improved value for money will be measured by the index of evaluated success. This depends on annual project scoring and risk labelling of projects; roll-out and full use of Performance Reporting Information System for Management by 2001; effective quality control and monitoring.

Source: http://www.dfid.gov.uk

Notes

1 This chapter is based on a report prepared for the National Audit Office's (NAO's) review of performance measurement in the Department for International Development (NAO, 2002). Thanks to Robert Owen of NAO for support to that work which has informed my views. Useful comments on an earlier draft were received from Richard Black. The usual disclaimer applies.

2 For a discussion of data quality issues, see Divorski and Scheirer (2000).

3 'Logic models' is the preferred term in the literature; these are very similar to the concept of the logical framework (log-frame) familiar in development agencies. Cummings (1997) distinguishes logic models, the logical framework and results-based management only to conclude that the three are closely related.

4 This and the following sections draw on a questionnaire completed by a number of key informants within the DFID.

5 This statement is based on the assessment of the DFID staff interviewed and on the author's experience of leading a poverty training programme targeted at all DFID staff.

6 The income-poverty line is a dollar a day, but a dollar buys much more in, say, Kampala or Delhi than it does in New York. The poverty line is equal to the local cost of purchasing the goods which could be purchased for one dollar in the USA.

7 See Carvalho and White (1996: 9–17) for further discussion.

8 The figure is from the DFID Poverty Guidance, *Bridging the Gap*, at http://www.dfid.gov.uk/Pubs/files/poverty_bridgegap_guidance.pdf.

9 Sketching the logic models underlying the various objectives shows them to be somewhat patchy – that for health is the most complete. They are particularly weak on outputs.

10 Comments by NAO on an earlier version of this chapter asked what was the view of UK academics of this change. I sent an e-mail question to ten academics who 'do aid' (there are not so many who do). Of the seven replies, three had not heard of the PSA, one had but was unsure what it was, and the other three had heard of it but were unaware of the change. DFID does not generally draw on the academic community for these 'management tools' (policy documents are a different matter), and even academics with a close relationship with DFID, or a good working knowledge of aid, are usually vague on the Department's internal workings.

11 Personal communication from Michael Flint, main author of the DFID's first development effectiveness report.

12 The questionnaire sent to some DFID staff in preparing this chapter asked what the Department's response should be to the fact that *A Better World for All* showed that none of the Millennium Development Goals or International Development Targets would be met at the global level. Virtually all respondents thought no response was necessary – clearly illustrating that data on the goals do not yield information of operational significance.

13 See http://www.paris.org.

14 For a summary of this work see http://www1.worldbank.org/publicsector/indicators.htm. This site includes a discussion of available indicators including those from other sources such as Freedom House.

References

Carvalho, S. and White, H. (1996) 'Implementing Projects for the Poor: What Has Been Learned?' *Directions in Development*, Washington, DC: World Bank.

Collier, P. and Dollar, D. (2002) 'Aid Allocation and Poverty Reduction', *European Economic Review*, 26: 1475–1500.

Cummings, F.H. (1997) 'Logic Models, Logical Frameworks and Results-Based Management: Contrasts and Comparisons', *Canadian Journal of Development Studies*, 18: 587–596.

Demery, L. and Walton, M. (1999) 'Are the Poverty and Social Goals for the 21st Century Attainable?', *IDS Bulletin*, 30(2): 75–91.

Development Assistance Committee (DAC) (1996) *Shaping the Twenty-first Century*, Paris: OECD.

—— (2000) *Results Based Management in the Development Co-operation Agencies: A Review of Experience (Executive Summary)*, Paris: OECD.

Divorski, S. and Scheirer, M.A. (2000) 'Improving Data Quality for Performance Measurement: Results from a GAO Study of Verification and Validation', *Evaluation and Program Planning*, 24(1): 83–94.

General Accounting Office (GAO) (1996) *Contributions to Child Survival Are Significant but Challenges Remain*, Washington, DC: GAO.

—— (1998) *The Results Act: An Evaluator's Guide to Assessing Agency Performance*, GAO/GGD-10.1.20, Washington, DC: GAO.

—— (1999) *Managing for Results: Opportunities for Continued Improvements in Agencies' Performance Plans*, GAO/GGD/AIMD-99-215, Washington, DC: GAO.

—— (2000) *Observations on the US Agency for International Development's Fiscal Year 1999 Performance Report and Fiscal Years 2000 and 2001 Performance Plans*, Washington, DC: GAO.

Hakes, J.E. (2000) 'Can Measuring Results Produce Results: One Manager's View', *Evaluation and Program Planning*, 24: 319–327.

International Monetary Fund, Organisation for Economic Cooperation and Development, United Nations and World Bank (2001) *A Better World for All*, Washington, DC.

Jackson, A. (2000) 'An Evaluation of Evaluation: Problems with Performance Measurement in Small Business Loans and Grant Schemes', *Progress in Planning*, 55: 1–55.

Lensink, R. and White, H. (2000) 'Assessing Aid: A Manifesto for Aid in the 21st Century?', *Oxford Development Studies*, 28(1): 5–17.

Maudling, W.P. (1994) 'Maternal Mortality in Developing Countries: A Comparison of Rates from Two International Compendia', *Population and Development Review*, 20(4): 413–421.

Maxwell, S. (1998) 'International Targets for Poverty Reduction and Food Security: A Mildly Sceptical but Resolutely Pragmatic View with a Call for Greater Subsidiarity', *Canadian Journal of Development Studies*, 19, Special Issue 1998.

Millar, A., Simeone, R. and Carnevale, J. (2000) 'Logic Models: A Systems Tool for Performance Management', *Evaluation and Program Planning*, 24(1): 73–81.

National Audit Office (2001) *Measuring the Performance of Government Departments*, London: The Stationery Office.

—— (2002) *Performance Management: Helping to Reduce World Poverty*, London: The Stationery Office.

Scheirer, M.A. and Newcomer, K. (2000) 'Opportunities for Program Evaluators to Facilitate Performance-Based Management', *Evaluation and Program Planning*, 24(1): 63–71.

United States Agency for International Development (USAID) (2001) *FY 2000 Performance Review*, Washington, DC: USAID.

White, H. (ed.) (1998) *Journal of International Development: Special Issue*, on 1997 UK White Paper on International Development.

White, H., Killick, T., Kayizzi-Mugerwa, S. and Savane, M.-A. (2001) *African Poverty at the Millennium*, Washington, DC: World Bank.

World Bank (2001) 'Progress toward the International Development Targets: Submission by the World Bank to UK Select Committee on International Development', Washington, DC: World Bank.

4 Using development goals to design country strategies[1]

Howard White and David Booth

Introduction

As described in Chapter 3, the UK's Department for International Development (DFID) has embraced the International Development Targets, and subsequently the Millennium Development Goals, as central to its mission. However, if targets are to mean much in practical terms, they need to be pursued in a concrete fashion at the country level. Chapter 3 described DFID's overall strategic approach, in which strategy papers play a key part. This chapter focuses on DFID's Country Strategy Papers (CSPs) as an example of country-level priority setting. It reviews the first CSPs completed under the 'new regime' following the 1997 White Paper on International Development and the extent to which they promote a new approach to poverty reduction. Our main argument is that there appears to be a 'missing middle' in the CSPs. Whilst the poverty reduction objectives, linked to international targets, are clearly stated, and planned spending for the coming years is laid out, there is little to connect the two.

Most donor agencies define a strategy for each major partner country on a three- to five-year cycle. DFID is no exception, so that CSPs are not new to the agency. However, a new set of guidance was issued for these papers following the 1997 White Paper, which attempted to make them more strategic in nature in order to mainstream poverty reduction into DFID's activities. This chapter assesses how successfully this has been done. In the next section we review the first thirteen of the 'new CSPs', discussing the contents of their poverty analysis, what they say about partnership and how all this informs the future DFID strategy proposed for the country. In doing this we use the DFID guidance on CSPs as a benchmark for what they should contain. The subsequent section deepens the discussion, with reference to a set of particular problems that are known to pose particular challenges to country programme design and management within the current policy framework.

DFID's Country Strategy Papers

The CSP is the key document which outlines DFID's intended programme in the country concerned for the coming five years. According to the guidance for these papers, a CSP must comprise the following five sections: A) Summary; B) The Challenge (outlining the nature of poverty and the main poverty reduction objectives); C) Partnerships (other stakeholders involved in poverty reduction efforts); D) Current UK Development Portfolio; E) Future UK Development Strategy (overview of strategy); F) Implementing the New Strategy (details of programmes and projects to be supported); G) Programme Resources (table of the allocation of resources for the coming period). This structure can be labelled a logical one, embodying the logic model which Chapter 3 argues to be important to good strategy. In addition, CSPs are intended to be produced in a collaborative manner and the process of CSP preparation has to be summarised in an annexe to the paper. In this section we discuss the thirteen 'new' CSPs available at the time of our review.[2]

Before we proceed, a caveat is in order. The following analysis is based entirely on the content of the CSPs. The comments are thus not to be taken as judgements on the programmes, which may or may not have shortcomings that are suggested by the CSPs. However, the logic of the exercise being carried out here implies that if a CSP is deficient, so is the programme to which it refers. There are clearly cases when something probably has been done but was missed by us simply because the CSP does not mention the fact. We realise that there is a tight space constraint on CSPs and that the demands on what they must do in this space are high.

In this section we first look at partnerships and the process of preparing a CSP. We then turn to the adequacy of the poverty analysis and the strategy laid out in the papers.

Partnerships and process

DFID alone will not achieve the poverty reduction goals in any of these countries. It will, however, contribute to a joint effort from a variety of stakeholders. Hence partnership is central to the strategy, which implies that the process by which the strategy is developed should be a collaborative one. A note of caution should be expressed on the problem of donor proliferation. If every donor wishes to have a collaborative process on 'their' strategy for a country, this will greatly consume the time and resources of government and other stakeholders. The ideal is of course for a government-led process defining the overall strategy which allocates roles to the various partners, thus defining the strategy for each of them. In principle, this is what Poverty Reduction Strategy Papers (PRSPs) are intended to do. In practice, it is too early for most of them to have greatly influenced what is actually being done. And there are varying degrees to which donor agencies take the PRSP as their reference point. More progress is being made in at least some countries with government-led initiatives at the sector level with what are called sector programmes, or the sector-wide approach (SWAP).

The appropriate partners are those engaged in poverty reduction, with differing degrees of involvement with government depending on the seriousness of that government's anti-poverty programmes. There is no systematic basis for assessing whether a particular government is to be considered pro-poor or not, hence there is little discussion in the CSPs of the different partnership arrangements that are appropriate under different circumstances. Guidance suggests that there can be 'high' and 'low' scenarios, with the extent and nature of DFID support varying according to the government's stance. This option is adopted only in the Kenya CSP. However, the discussion of government does usually at least state whether or not the government is committed to poverty reduction (sometimes also gender equality) and whether its objectives are consistent with the International Development Targets.

The CSPs adopt a far less critical stance with respect to the donor community. The discussion of partnerships with other bilateral donors and multilateral agencies is largely a description of their areas of involvement, often with a note that more donor co-ordination would be desirable. The idea that other donors might be an important channel for influence appears only sometimes, and the issues on, and means by, which it might be desirable to influence other donors are hardly considered. There is thus no serious discussion of whether the programmes of the various agencies, of which the World Bank and International Monetary Fund (IMF) are invariably key players, are consistent with poverty reduction priorities.

Similarly, civil society is invariably seen as a good thing, whereas one can imagine possibilities for a more nuanced discussion. In the real world, organisations within civil society have strengths and weaknesses that often closely reflect those of government.

Each CSP reports on the country strategy preparation process. This is done in varying degrees of detail, ranging in length from half a page to two pages. The consultation process can be divided into the part that happens in-country and the part that takes place elsewhere. Within each part we distinguish three stages: (1) initial consultation (in-country only); (2) feedback on/formulation of the actual strategy; and (3) review of the draft CSP. Although the distinction between these different stages is not always watertight, it is clear that opportunities to influence the general nature of the programme are greater the earlier in the preparation process that consultation begins.

In general, there were initial consultations with, and limited to, government. There were, however, exceptions, where a wider range of stakeholders was involved from the start, and others (two) in which initial strategic thinking was internal to DFID and based on commissioned studies. Consultations continued and widened in most countries as the strategy evolved, though in rather fewer cases were actual drafts subject to this process. In-country consultations appear to have been most systematically and comprehensively approached in South Africa.

Consultation with the private sector and academics during strategy formulation in the UK was common,[3] and in some cases this included non-governmental organisations (NGOs) active in the country. Other donors were also consulted, though this was most usually in-country.

Poverty analysis

As discussed in previous chapters, international development goals are designed, at least in part, to focus the attention of both donor and developing country on the issue of poverty reduction. CSPs are expected to crystallise this focus at the country level: 'CSPs set out the strategy by which DFID will achieve its objectives, particularly the elimination of poverty.'[4]

The first, and most obvious, question is: do the country strategies address poverty? In practice, poverty emerges as a key issue in all the CSPs reviewed, especially in the 'Challenge' section. Explicit mention of poverty issues, or identification of links to poverty reduction targets, is less common in discussions of the future UK development strategy. In addition, and as will be clear from what follows, the extent of the poverty analysis undertaken varies quite widely between CSPs.

The foundation of the poverty analysis comes in 'The Challenge', which 'should analyse the economic, social, political and environmental situation and recipient Government policies. It should assess the causes, characteristics and consequences of poverty in the country and should review the country's progress with respect to the main International Development Targets.'[5] This is quite a demanding task, requiring both a poverty profile and identification of the main causes of poverty in a couple of pages, along with policy analysis of the recipient government's position.

A second set of questions relates to how poverty is defined in the country strategies and programmes. What concepts and indicators of poverty are used? How have poor people's own perspectives been incorporated into the analysis?

The tables in the appendices to this chapter provide the details on which our discussion is based. For example, Appendix 4.1 presents data on the definition of poverty used and incorporation of the perspectives of the poor, whilst Appendix 4.2 records which indicators are reported (characterised as International Development Target-related and others).

Although the majority of CSPs also report social indicators, it seems, despite adoption of the multidimensional International Development Targets, that the notion of income poverty as the 'real meaning' of poverty is quite resilient. A locally defined poverty line is used most frequently, sometimes accompanied by the 'dollar a day' line.[6] Of course, a head count based on a locally defined line in itself tells us little, but it does provide a benchmark against which to measure progress.

The four Southern African countries give the most comprehensive treatment. The South Africa CSP reports the current status of all the International Development Target-related indicators in a single table, whereas other papers give them section by section. But overall, less than half the countries meet the requirement to report progress in meeting the International Development Targets; in the majority of the cases even the current levels are not reported. None of the CSPs for Asian countries reports more than one or two International Development Target-related indicators. The most commonly reported non-International Development Target indicators are life expectancy and literacy, with gender disaggregation of the latter being common. Explicit mention of the results of participatory analysis is rare and only in one case does the discussion lead on participatory results.

Moving from the poverty profile to the causes of poverty, the relevant questions are: (1) how has poverty been analysed?; and (2) what balance is evident between social and economic perceptions of poverty? The causes of poverty are addressed only indirectly in many CSPs. Most commonly, a leading section on poverty pays little attention to causes. On the other hand, sections follow on the economy, human development, politics and the environment, which may be seen as indirectly discussing causes of poverty. But such links are only rarely explicit.

Although some CSPs give greater emphasis to economic causes of poverty (including the distribution of income and wealth, which is given a particularly central role in South Africa and Vietnam, but mentioned in many other cases), they all give treatment of social issues, the most commonly mentioned being gender discrimination. It is notable that the CSPs do not shy away from mentioning political constraints to poverty reduction, and problems in government (most usually corruption) may even be identified as a central constraint on reducing poverty (e.g. in the highlighting of patronage in the Nepal CSP).

That said, neither this section nor that on partnership can be seen as representing a systematic attempt to identify the extent of genuine government commitment to poverty reduction, gender equity or the achievement of the International Development Targets. Within DFID there has been work by both the Caribbean and the Africa regions in developing checklists to assist in identifying pro-poor governments (covering macro policy stance, social service provision, accountability and respect for human rights). But these still have some way to go in tackling the important conceptual issues posed by the development of such checklists.[7]

Strategy: the missing middle

Whilst poverty reduction objectives are linked to the International Development Targets, how well are these objectives followed through in the proposed strategy? A general question here is 'What is a strategy?' The CSPs themselves appear somewhat confused on this subject, and the guidance tends to tiptoe around the topic rather than confronting it directly. Thus in many CSPs it is difficult to work out what 'the strategy' is, in the sense of the intended linkage between the goals/overall objective/purpose and DFID-supported activities. The guidance requirement that explicit attention be paid to linking activities to poverty reduction is often disregarded. We found it difficult to find explicit links between the poverty analysis and the proposed future programme, partly on account of the weakness noted earlier, that explicit consideration of the *causes* of poverty is missing from the poverty analysis.

These observations lead us to identify a general problem of 'the missing middle' in CSPs. The middle that is insufficiently developed (or at least, under-reported in CSPs) includes (1) distinguishing and ranking the causes of poverty corresponding to the poverty profile in 'The Challenge', and (2) being clear and precise about how the DFID programme proposes to break into the circles of causation that have been identified, and why the activities chosen are the best from this point of view.

An important distinction can be made between enabling, inclusive and focused (or targeted) interventions (see Box 4.1 for the definition of these terms). This is partly because these are collections of activities, which individually could be more readily classified. In only one case could the classifications be quantified. However, it is clear that focused/targeted interventions are very much in the minority.[8]

In principle, this last observation does not say anything about the degree to which country programmes are rigorously constructed for maximum

Box 4.1 Poverty Aim Marker (PAM) classifications

Enabling actions which underpin pro-poor economic growth and the broader policies and context for poverty reduction and elimination, and will lead to social, environmental and/or economic benefits for poor people.

Inclusive actions (e.g. sectoral development programmes) which aim to benefit broad-based population groups, including poor people, but also address issues of equity and barriers to participation or access of poor people.

Actions *focused* predominately on the rights, interests and needs of poor people.

Source: DFID Statistics Department, *Policy Information Marker System; Policy Aim Marker; Policy Objective Marker*

impact on poverty, and are in that sense poverty focused. Logic alone does not compel any particular balance between the three types of action. However, we suspect that the actual balance reflects the fact that there has been quite a lot of 're-dressing' of current programmes that are skewed towards the enabling and inclusive approaches, a suspicion confirmed by looking at the CSPs prepared before the 1997 White Paper.

More on the missing middle

The problem of the missing middle suggests that a logical framework (log-frame) approach might usefully be applied. Indeed, a log-frame is actually required by the guidance, but it does not constitute a part of the published report (and so, we understand, has not been produced in all cases – only one has been available to us). Table 4.1 shows a log-frame based on the Malawi report.[9] The Malawi example is not being singled out as an example of bad practice. To the contrary, it is a case where such a treatment may easily be applied and where useful steps have been taken which help to illustrate the challenges facing country programme design generally.

In the Malawi case a logic does seem to flow from goal through to activities. But this is done without reference back to the causes of poverty (the goal is said to be set that way, but not the selection of activities). The main causes of poverty are seen as low growth with high inequality, poor human resource development (and the problem of AIDS), and a legal system which does not meet the needs of poor people. Questions that should thus be raised include: (1) do the planned activities conform to these priority areas?; (2) do the planned activities confront the main concerns in the priority areas?; (3) do the planned activities engage government and other actors in a way which prioritises poverty reduction?; and (4) how can the link between these activities and poverty reduction be monitored?

Underlying several of these questions is the degree to which the shape of the UK development programme is determined by inertia. Some role for inertia is inevitable, as ongoing commitments must be honoured. However, that being the case, it seems to us that it would be better to be honest about this and distinguish between the elements of the programme that are justified in strict log-frame terms, and those that will be allowed during a period of restructuring the programme.[10]

Outcomes, impacts and monitoring

It is also important to consider what the intended outcomes of the strategy are. Relevant questions are: (1) how will poverty impacts be identified?; (2) what are the indicators for assessing achievements?; and (3) how will this impact be measured?

Most CSPs do not give any explicit outcome targets (Appendix 4.3), and the goals they do have are not usually quantified. Some are explicitly

Table 4.1 Tabular presentation (modified log-frame) of future UK development strategy: Malawi

Level	Goal	Purpose	Specific objectives	Impact areas	Activities/interventions
Content	To contribute to the elimination of poverty in Malawi	To build partnerships that promote poverty elimination, equity and human rights in Malawi	Policies and actions which promote sustainable livelihoods	Rethinking the role of government, including decentralisation	Advice on restructuring; financing redundancy package; co-finance the United Nations Development Programme's (UNDP's) pilot decentralisation programmes; influence government and World Bank to protect key services during restructuring
				Economic and financial management	Budget support; debt relief; advice on public financial management (including customs); support to Poverty Policy Unit and Anti-corruption Bureau
				Human rights	Support to police force and prison service; radios to women's groups
				Sustainable rural livelihoods	Advocacy and assistance with land reform; advice and support to enhance soil fertility; rural pubic works; credit and training
			Better education, health and opportunities for poor people	Better access to and quality of basic health and education	Support health sector strategy and projects in contraceptive supply, TB care and reproductive health. Supporting Policy Investment Framework for education, and community schools project and support for teacher development
			Protection and better management of the natural and physical environment	Safeguarding the environment	Support for Forestry Action Plan and for community initiatives for biodiversity protection
Determined by:	Analysis of the challenge, and consultations with civil society and government		From White Paper	Poor people's priority needs, DFID's comparative advantage; and linkages to goal and purpose	Not stated

vague. Discussion of measuring poverty impact or of monitoring procedures is the exception rather than the rule. There is a major difficulty in monitoring DFID impact with reference to national indicators such as infant mortality or the poverty head count. Even when sound, these indicators change slowly and respond to myriad factors that are impossible to disentangle. These difficulties (which may anyhow be insoluble) are exacerbated when funds are channelled through sector programmes, or when working through partnership arrangements (so that influence is a major objective). But these difficulties should be confronted rather than ignored. Guidance has commented that CSPs tend to be rather grandiose and long term in their targets and proposed monitoring, whereas a more day-to-day set of indicators (say, on involvement with government) would be more appropriate. We agree.

Discussion

The points raised in the previous section highlight some priority problems in country programme design that call for attention. We do not think the more important of these issues are technical deficiencies arising from a particular document format. They are at the heart of what it means to be more strategic about reducing poverty and meeting DFID's other central objectives.

Several issues for further discussion flow directly from the above discussion of the CSPs. Others that we want to suggest are a selection of especially timely and difficult specific examples of the same central challenges to country programme design. Some brief additional comments are made in this section to suggest why these issues seem to call for closer attention.

Key issues concern the requirements of a strategic approach to facilitate the following:

- *Pro-poor partnerships* – by developing the criteria for a selective approach to partners and spelling out the implications for the content of country programmes.

Selectivity is a key feature of the White Paper's concept of partnership for poverty reduction. The distribution of DFID resources is supposed to reflect an assessment of the level of commitment of government and other potential partners to achieving the International Development Targets or equivalent national objectives. Government commitment is notoriously hard to assess, for both conceptual and empirical (evidence) reasons. For these and other reasons, new CSPs do not travel at all far down this road. Yet it is hard to see how it is possible to be strategic about poverty without at least some guiding principles for such an assessment (including implications for the CSP preparation process) and clear ideas about the implications of different conclusions for programme content.

- *Overall country programme design* – by filling in the missing middle between the poverty profile and the proposed activities.

As we have seen, this is a weakness in the explicit content of CSPs, if not in the country programmes themselves. There is more vagueness than there needs to be about general and country-specific causes of poverty. It is often not clear that instruments have been selected because they are judged to be the most effective way of breaking into the chain of causation. Other criteria (honouring existing commitments, etc.) are operating but are not made explicit. Potentially important instruments which are also key partnership issues, such as influencing other donors and agencies, do not seem to be taken as seriously as they might be. Monitoring of effectiveness is discussed in ways that reflect the missing middle rather than helping to solve the problem.

- *In-country arrangements for attracting and using heavily indebted poor country (HIPC) debt relief* – by articulating the form and content of DFID influence on government in this area.

Influence strategies have been identified by recent evaluations as a typically under-articulated and under-appraised component of country programmes. Yet providing clear, consistent and timely advice to a government partner is potentially one of the most powerful ways DFID can contribute to poverty reduction. The shaping of a government's arrangements for attracting and deploying new forms of external budgetary support, including debt relief, is an important current area where influence of this kind could yield important results.

But how and in what direction should influence be exercised in this case? The answers are by no means obvious. There is an ongoing debate amongst economists about whether it is strictly true that all aid is fungible – that is, impossible to tie down to particular uses because of the way external finance releases domestic funds for other uses. The idea that aid is fungible has recently gained common currency, with a push coming from the World Bank's *Assessing Aid* report. This bears on whether it is sensible to channel new money into earmarked 'poverty funds' (the 'Uganda model'). Though it may assist in the international politics of debt relief and the domestic politics of poverty reduction, earmarking also may conflict with building up a country's capacity for outcome-oriented budgeting and resource management. Public finance issues at this point merge with social development and governance questions. These include the conditions for improving morale, effectiveness and accountability in the civil service, and the likelihood of any of these problems being more readily solved under a decentralised government system.

- *Increasing the likelihood of 'pro-poor growth'* – by influencing the design of structural reforms.

This is another area in which DFID influence could have been more deliberate and carefully thought out than it has been. There is clear evidence from IMF and World Bank sources on a number of countries in Africa that the design of structural adjustment packages in the 1990s had serious shortcomings. As a result, there was less economic growth, and what there was had fewer benefits for the poor, than might otherwise have been the case. Influencing the policies of the international financial institutions in this regard does not seem to have been a priority for many DFID country programmes. Meanwhile, the downturn in Asia has brought the issue of alternative approaches to economic stabilisation and adjustment back to the forefront of the international agenda. How might country programme managers (and DFID advisers placed in the multilateral financial institutions) go about defining a new approach to these questions?

- *New sector-wide partnerships, or SWAPs* – by taking a hard look at the difficulties of reconciling the demands of partnership at this level and those of meeting the International Development Targets.

One of the commonest kinds of 'missing middle' or strategic fuzziness in country programmes is a set of loose and unchallenged assumptions about the value of social-sector spending and aid for poverty reduction. Programme components that have a fairly strong 'inertial' element are redressed to suit the requirements of a poverty-focused approach. But if a strategic approach means what it says, programme design should surely begin with what it would take to meet the relevant International Development Targets in this particular country context, working backwards to identify the most suitable modes of intervention.

The adoption of a sector-wide approach has the important potential of increasing the overall rationality of resource allocation across a sector. In health and other fields, it is a welcome departure from the tendency of donor funding to produce unsustainable islands of excellence in seas of mediocrity and deprivation. On the other hand, it has been pointed out that sector-based partnerships do not necessarily have a positive impact on the rationality of resource allocation *between* sectors. Also, it could be argued that making a prior commitment to a SWAP on partnership grounds places yet another obstacle in the way of a genuinely strategic approach to the International Development Targets, since it cannot be assumed that the interventions that are indicated by this method will have any particular sectoral location.

Last but not least, it is notorious that SWAPs do not necessarily improve services to the poor in the short term. This may be because the poor have limited access to the relevant services and because there are no resources with which to significantly improve access. It may also be because the sector has its own political economy of interest groups and patronage networks that tends to override the pro-poor policy commitments of the sector. Either way, a strategic orientation on DFID's part calls for an effort to reconcile these opposing principles within an overall approach that is driven by poverty analysis and informed by a subtle understanding of the country context.

Conclusions

The DFID Country Strategy Papers are a departure from earlier such papers, in that they have been redefined to mainstream poverty reduction in the agency's work. The papers have a logical structure flowing from an analysis of the poverty situation and the causes of poverty, laying out a strategy to address poverty and locating DFID's position within that strategy. However, in practice there is a missing middle, by which we mean that the interventions to be supported by DFID are not clearly located in the context of the main causes of poverty which have been identified. This argument has strong parallels with that made in Chapter 3. The only other similar analysis of which we are aware for another agency finds similar shortcomings: the country strategies of the World Bank in Africa were found to be strong on anti-poverty in the discussion of high-level strategy, but far less so when it came to what was actually being done on the ground (World Bank, 1997). Agencies need to develop clear ideas of how it is that they can affect poverty outcomes – that is, adopt a logical framework approach. They then need the institutional flexibility to take on board the implications of such analysis.

Appendix 4.1 Definitions and perceptions of poverty

Country	Definition of poverty/poverty indicators	Incorporation of the perspective of the poor
Bangladesh	Locally defined poverty line	Not explicitly mentioned
China	Locally defined and dollar-a-day poverty lines	Not explicitly mentioned
Ghana	Social indicators and locally defined poverty line (notes that dollar-a-day data unavailable)	Yes, leads with perceptions of poor before quantitative poverty profile
India	Locally defined poverty line and social indicators	Not explicitly mentioned
Kenya	Dollar-a-day poverty line	Mentions that Participatory Poverty Assessment (PPA) 'corroborates' quantitative results
Malawi	Income-poverty trend mentioned (no line indicated) and discussion of social indicators under International Development Target headings	Very brief mention ('Malawians feel they are getting poorer')
Mozambique	Sections on economic well-being (locally defined poverty line), human development (social indicators), environment and qualitative elements	Not explicitly mentioned
Nepal	Income poverty line and social indicators	Not explicitly mentioned
South Africa	Dollar-a-day poverty line and social indicators	Not explicitly mentioned
Tanzania	Locally defined poverty line, and education and health indicators. Also mentions that poverty is complex and discusses Participatory Rural Appraisal (PRA) results	Yes, features prominently in poverty profile to list dimension/causes of poverty
Uganda	Locally defined poverty line and social indicators	Yes
Vietnam	Income poverty line and social indicators	Not explicitly mentioned
Zimbabwe	Locally defined poverty line and minimum food requirements	Not explicitly mentioned

Appendix 4.2 Reporting of International Development Targets and other indicators

Country	Income poverty	Primary school enrolments	Ratio of male to female enrolments	Infant mortality rate	Under-five mortality	Maternal mortality rate	Reproductive health services	National strategy for sustainable development	Comment/other indicators
Bangladesh	x	*	..	..	..	..	..	..	Ratio of male to female literacy
China	x	..	..	..	..	..	..	..	Life expectancy, Human Poverty Index
Ghana	x	..	..	..	..	..	..	..	Ratio of male to female literacy, child labour
India	x	..	..	x	..	..	..	x	Literacy, life expectancy (some indicators reported at state level)
Kenya	x	*	..	..	..	..	..	..	Indicators mentioned but values not given
Malawi	..	x	x	x	x	x	x	x	Life expectancy, female literacy, secondary school enrolments; target-specific sections

Mozambique	x	x	x	x	x	x	x	Ratio male to female literacy, secondary school enrolments, access to safe water; target-specific sections
Nepal	x	:	:	:	:	:	:	:
South Africa	x	x	x	x	x	x	x	Table of International Development Targets and current status
Tanzania	x	x	x	x	x	x	x	Total fertility rate (TFR), child poverty rate (CPR), literacy
Uganda	:	:	:	x	x	:	x	Ratio male to female literacy, life expectancy, access to water, total fertility rate; list of government health targets (some overlap International Development Targets)
Vietnam	x	:	:	:	:	x	:	Life expectancy
Zimbabwe	x	x	x	x	x	x	x	Life expectancy; target-specific sections

Notes

x, current level of indicator reported; *, no level reported but trend indicated; .., indicator not mentioned.

Appendix 4.3 Intended outcomes and monitoring procedures

	Intended outcomes	How will poverty impacts be identified?	Indicators	How measured or monitored
Bangladesh	Long-term objective: help Bangladesh achieve sustainable reductions in poverty. Six thematic objectives: (1) sustainable improvements in livelihoods and basic services for the poor, extreme poor and those vulnerable to poverty; (2) sustainable, broad-based and pro-poor growth; (3) better governance and more effective institutions; (4) improved realisation of human rights; (5) improvements in the position of women in society; and (6) consistency in DFID and broader UK and Bangladeshi government policies in support of the elimination of poverty in Bangladesh	Not discussed	None listed (implicitly the International Development Targets?)	One individual in DFID Bangladesh responsible for each objective
China	Goal: poverty elimination	Not discussed	None listed	Not discussed
Ghana	Overall objective: support goals in Vision 2020 (improve quality of life, generate employment, and reduce poverty)	Not discussed	Given implicitly by support for government programmes	Not discussed
India	Goal: make progress towards the elimination of poverty. Purpose: work effectively with partners to reduce poverty significantly over next 10 years	Not discussed	Poverty target, but indicator not identified	Not discussed
Kenya	Goal: reduce proportion living in extreme poverty by 2015. Purpose: sustainable improvements in the livelihoods of poor people in Kenya over the next 5 years	Not discussed	Goal gives income-poverty target	Not discussed

Malawi	Goal: to contribute to the elimination of poverty in Malawi. Purpose: to build partnerships that promote poverty elimination, equity and human rights in Malawi. Six impact areas (see Table 4.1) are classified under DFID's specific objectives. Specific outcomes not indicated	Not discussed	Goal gives (vague) income-poverty target. No others listed	Not discussed
Mozambique	Four impact areas (see Table 4.1) are classified under the first two of DFID's specific objectives. Specific outcomes not indicated.	Not discussed	None listed	Not discussed
Nepal	Goals: significant reduction in poverty in 10–20 years; measurable improvements in key indicators, nationally and in selected areas within 5–10 years	Not discussed	Goals give (vague) references to indicators	Not discussed
South Africa	Support to government strategy (see Table 4.1)	Not discussed	Some project/activity-specific targets (e.g. water supply services)	Not discussed
Tanzania	Goal: a 50 per cent reduction in number of absolute poor by 2015. Purpose: sustainable improvements in the livelihoods of poor people in Tanzania over the next 5 years. Five impact areas (see Table 4.1) 'to make a measurable difference in partnership'	Not discussed	Goal gives income poverty target	Strengthen capacity to monitor impact of sector programmes. Increased attention to monitoring impact, using evaluations. Annual reviews considering impact

continued

Appendix 4.3 continued

	Intended outcomes	How will poverty impacts be identified	Indicators	How measured or monitored
Uganda	Goal: to reduce the proportion of Ugandans living in absolute poverty to less than 10 per cent of the total population by 2017. Purpose: to contribute to sustainable improvements in the livelihoods and conditions of poor people in Uganda. Britain seeks measurable impact in the five areas identified in Table 4.1	Not discussed	Goal gives income poverty target. Government health targets listed (infant mortality rate, under-five mortality, immunisation, malnutrition, maternal mortality; contraceptive prevalence, fertility rate). None listed for other impact areas	Monitoring mentioned but system not discussed
Vietnam	Long-term goal: reduction in extreme poverty (International Development Target-based); and immediate goal to promote pro-poor growth. Purpose: promote and support government policies for reform and provision of public services and investment	Not discussed	Goal gives income-poverty target	Not discussed
Zimbabwe	Purpose: to reduce poverty in Zimbabwe	Monitor poverty impact of programmes and progress towards International Development Targets	International Development Target-based	Annual progress review with government and civil society

Notes

1 This chapter is based on an issues paper prepared for the session 'How do CSPs address poverty?' at the joint DFID Economists'/Social Development Advisors' retreat on 23 September 1999 at Eynsham Hall, UK. We are grateful to Richard Black for comments on an earlier draft of this chapter. The usual disclaimer applies.
2 See the tables in Appendix 4.1 for a list of countries. This list includes nine of the top ten recipients of UK aid in 1999–2000. The exception is Zambia, for which a prototype 'new CSP' was prepared in advance of the White Paper and so is not covered by this review.
3 The Guidance emphasises the importance of consultation with the private sector, although it is unclear if this means the domestic private sector or UK business interests. Generally, CSPs try to cover both of these.
4 Quotations are from the various memos of guidance on CSPs unless otherwise indicated.
5 The Guidance, and this review, preceded the adoption of the Millennium Development Goals, so the International Development Targets are referred to in this chapter.
6 The Guidance suggests that both of these should be given.
7 Critical issues are whether to judge on past performance or future plans (and whether to use the level or the change in commitment), the extent to which outcome indicators can be used to measure policy stance, and how to determine acceptable threshold levels when these may vary from country to country.
8 This fact is consistent with reviews of aid programmes which generally find that the amount directly targeted to poverty reduction is low, probably somewhere in the region of 10–15 per cent (see White, 1996).
9 The Malawi log-frame is one of the few available to the authors, though the presentation here is our own modification.
10 The Guidance requirement that changes between future and current strategies be explicitly addressed is met scantily if at all in most cases; the CSP for Vietnam is a notable exception.

References

White, H. (1996) 'How Much Aid Is Used for Poverty Reduction?', *IDS Bulletin*, 27(1): January.

World Bank (1997) *Taking Action for Poverty Reduction in Sub-Saharan Africa: Report of an Africa Region Task Force*, Washington, DC: World Bank.

5 Monitoring progress towards the Millennium Development Goals at country level[1]

David Booth and Henry Lucas

Introduction

How can countries monitor progress towards meeting the Millennium Development Goals? This chapter draws lessons from a review of the process of establishing Poverty Reduction Strategy Papers (PRSPs) for the poorest countries of the world. Two main areas are covered. First, the chapter considers the progress made towards establishing effective poverty monitoring systems, drawing on evidence from Africa. We then analyse the process of choosing realistic indicators to monitor whether Poverty Reduction Strategy Papers have moved countries closer towards meeting the Millennium Development Goals.

The chapter first focuses on institutional and procedural questions about monitoring, then moves on to addresss the selection of indicators. After that there follow two sections that adopt a more forward-looking perspective, making practical suggestions about how to meet some of the biggest challenges facing those concerned with monitoring progress in reducing poverty. A final section presents conclusions.

Roles of monitoring and information in a Poverty Reduction Strategy Paper context

The PSRP is intended to put poverty at the centre of a government-led policy process. The approach taken to monitoring needs to be correspondingly innovative. There is much to be learned from the established fields of project planning and sector programming. But the point of departure needs to be a clear understanding of the change of gear that the initiative is meant to facilitate. We should start from what a PRSP is meant to be, not simply from the accumulated wisdom of the monitoring and evaluation profession, or indeed from the more recent field of poverty monitoring. We identify five aspects of the approach.

First, the advent of PRSPs means that it is no longer 'business as usual'. PRSPs have brought new concerns to the attention of policy-makers in the South. The form of conditionality of aid is changing, with emphasis shifted from traditional forms to a focus on in-country processes. Such 'process conditionality' is a means of opening up discussion among stakeholders about the ways and means of addressing poverty reduction goals. Several points are included in this new form of conditionality. For example, the processes that lead to poverty reduction are expected to be:

- more 'owned' by the country – that is, more rooted in national processes of policy dialogue and accountability;
- more comprehensive, both in terms of the sectors covered and in co-ordinating the full range of national and international resources; and
- more performance based and outcome oriented in the way they allocate resources.

Second is the need for a more realistic view of the policy process. The framework for monitoring the plans needs to be realistic about the way the different elements fit together. Attention has to be paid to the substantial literature on the nature of the policy process (involving both policy formulation and policy implementation), which may be general, or country or region specific (see, for example, Hill, 1993, and Turner and Hulme, 1997, respectively). It cannot be assumed that formal commitment to a set of objectives on the part of senior government officials implies an ability, or even a willingness, to deliver all of the consequent actions.

Third, monitoring and evaluation is not simply a technical matter, but is also about politics. Most of the conceptual vocabulary of monitoring and evaluation reflects a rationalistic model of the policy process, not the realistic one just described. This does not mean that current thinking on monitoring and evaluation is irrelevant in the real world of policy. But it does imply the need for a shift in emphasis on the role played by monitoring and evaluation. Special attention should be given to the parts of the literature that address the issue from a more realistic perspective, such as that concerned with 'process monitoring' (Mosse *et al.*, 1998).

Fourth, contrary to the impression that is sometimes given, an outcome-oriented approach to monitoring does not imply an exclusive focus on final outcomes/impacts[2] or poverty monitoring (see Chapter 3 of this volume). Improved poverty outcome data are important for several purposes, including basic analysis of the causes of poverty, which is essential to good policy design. This issue – what might be called 'poverty monitoring' as opposed to 'PRSP monitoring' – has a certain importance. But in most countries it is more important to focus on the process of implementing policy rather than on the final outcome, if learning and accountability are to be achieved. Policy is likely to improve, and/or become more outcome oriented, only if new incentives come into play. Information on the final outcomes or impacts of policy rarely has practical implications, since (1) it arrives too late, and (2) it has too many difficulties of attribution.

Paradoxically, this means that information on the performance of policy implementation may be more powerful in making policy more oriented towards outcomes than final outcome monitoring can hope to be. This is a key issue in deciding the scope and balance of monitoring systems for PRSPs. In addition, reliable data on intermediate output and outcome issues are very hard to come by in most countries, even on an untimely basis.

Fifth, the above assumes that the principal role of monitoring policy is to ensure that policy-makers learn and are held accountable to domestic stakeholders. This assumption neglects the fact that policy-makers are also held accountable to donors. The role of a monitoring system in providing for accountability to donors is not unimportant, because nothing discourages donors more from pooling their funds in sector programmes or general budget support than the perception that accountability requirements will not be satisfied. On the other hand, the best bet for enhanced accountability to donors is undoubtedly one that also enhances responsiveness to domestic stakeholders.

Five areas of interest in monitoring Poverty Reduction Strategy Papers

This section goes on to consider current documentation on PRSPs, and what it has to say about the following five areas: input monitoring; the monitoring of implementation and intermediate outputs and outcomes; the measurement of poverty outcomes and impacts; measures to make information more available; and steps to enhance the use of information.

A strong overall impression of the current situation is that thinking and practice are at quite an early stage. Some topics, such as the financing of sustainable monitoring systems, are hardly covered at all. On the range of activities and the allocation of institutional responsibilities, the details given in the PRSPs vary from thin to comprehensive but still incomplete (e.g. Uganda). For this reason, the review was largely concerned with rather elementary questions about each activity, such as, is monitoring mentioned at all, are steps being taken to initiate activity, and do these steps make sense?

Input monitoring and budget reform

Guidance and training materials for implementing PRSPs identify input monitoring as important. For example, it is usual to refer to indicators of expenditure on particular items such as primary education. However, the usefulness of this type of measure depends on the way budget line items are defined, and thus on the nature of the prevailing budget system. Other questions are the degree to which actual releases of funds are determined by initial allocations, and what percentage of funds reach their final destinations.

A key step in outcome-oriented budget reform is the establishment of a Medium Term Expenditure Framework (MTEF). In Uganda and Tanzania the MTEF has laid the basis for progress in the preparation of budgets on a programme basis in line ministries and local government. However, while the Ugandan authorities see the MTEF as providing the framework for their Poverty Eradication Action Plan,[3] Tanzania makes little of this and other improvements in public expenditure management systems in its PRSP. In Burkina Faso, significant headway has been made in linking funding to performance, providing the context for discussions about reforming the budget process. In Mauritania the introduction of programme budgeting was scheduled to start in 2002, though the country has some way to go before the gap between the budget and the bulk of targeted project expenditure on poverty begins to close.

Countries not yet in a position to prepare a PRSP have been able to submit an Interim Poverty Reduction Strategy Paper (I-PRSP), which provides an overview of a poverty reduction strategy and the process by which a full PRSP will be prepared. An I-PRSP is sufficient to qualify for HIPC funds. Most I-PRSPs in Africa mention budget reform, either confirming that it is happening (in Benin, Ghana, Guinea, Kenya, Malawi, Mali, Rwanda and Senegal) or stating it as an objective (in The Gambia, Niger and Zambia). Assessments of PRSPs frequently emphasise the impossibility of setting overall priorities in the absence of the realistic expenditure ceilings that would be provided by an MTEF. Whilst not strictly a monitoring issue, this shows how reform of public expenditure management may be a precondition for improvements in monitoring.

Public expenditure tracking

Without budget reform and the associated technical improvements in public expenditure accounting, it is not usually practical to take the step of comparing budget allocations with releases according to sectoral and sub-sectoral priorities. Moreover, even in countries where budget reform is taking place, there is little discussion of this issue in PRSPs.

Public Expenditure Tracking (PET) Studies, which report how much spending reaches the final destination (e.g. how much of the education budget is spent on items appearing in schools), have been undertaken in a number of countries. In Uganda, such exercises are now a routine part of monitoring the country's Poverty Eradication Action Plan (PEAP). Tracking exercises have been undertaken as part of Tanzania's rolling Public Expenditure Review (PER), although this fact is not highlighted in the country's PRSP. Other countries are at very different stages. Some declare an intention to undertake tracking studies (e.g. Guinea, Rwanda), but others have not completed the more basic step of systematically reviewing public expenditure, and many report nothing on the subject.

The Kenyan I-PRSP includes a summary of perhaps the ideal poverty monitoring system. It locates the national poverty reduction effort squarely within high-level arrangements for monitoring and tracking prioritised public expenditures. A stakeholder committee would meet monthly, and transmit its concerns through a committee of Permanent Secretaries to the Cabinet. In the way it integrates financial and implementation issues and guarantees a hearing for stakeholder assessments of monitoring data at the highest policy level, the Kenyan proposal provides a model of what might be done in all countries. However, few countries could achieve such an arrangement at this stage. Even in Kenya, whether this can be implemented is open to doubt.

Implementation monitoring with administrative data

A key dimension of performance monitoring is monitoring intermediate outputs, including process-based aspects of policy implementation. African PRSPs cannot be accused of neglecting this aspect of monitoring if the criterion is the volume of indicators identified for the purpose. However, this would clearly not be an appropriate criterion.

The indicators identified are numerous and rather unselective, raising doubts as to the feasibility of obtaining reliable data at reasonable cost. Do PRSPs include steps for bringing administrative data and/or sectoral management information systems closer to the required quality standards, and do they envisage alternative means of acquiring quick feedback? Overall, these concerns are very striking by their absence. PRSPs almost invariably include a commitment to make arrangements for monitoring plan implementation using official statistics. Occasionally, data deficiencies are mentioned as a problem, and the institutional and technical arrangements for co-ordinating data from different sources are frequently discussed. However, the possibility that there might be fundamental obstacles to using routine data to monitor progress on account of severe problems of unreliability is not acknowledged at all.

Alternative feedback mechanisms

In the light of the above comments, it is not surprising that the coverage of other forms of feedback on implementation is also slight. There are two reasons why methods such as participatory beneficiary assessments, implementer self-assessments using focus-group methods, 'exit polls' and simple service delivery surveys might be considered. One is that they provide a check on information reported, slowly and unreliably, through official channels. They can also provide a more dynamic type of input into the political process of the PRSP, highlighting problems while there is still time to act on them and to mobilise public interest and pressure at the same time.

There are hints of such possibilities in some Papers. In general, they are not fleshed out sufficiently to justify confidence that they will be pursued in the absence of strong donor pressure and offers of funding. But a different picture may emerge from new initiatives mooted in a number of countries, such as the regular stakeholder opinion polls that are proposed in Burkina Faso, or the participatory monitoring arrangements that have been suggested in Tanzania and The Gambia.

Where service-quality enquiries and self-assessments have been used to set benchmarks for public service reforms before the advent of PRSPs, these have not always been considered relevant by those drafting the Papers. In Senegal's PRSP a mechanism of this sort is mentioned; but the equivalent arrangements in Ghana do not figure in the initial monitoring proposals.

Measurement of final poverty outcomes/impacts

The implementation of PRSPs will produce a dramatic improvement in the quality and general availability of survey-based household consumption data. Many new surveys are currently under way. These will not overcome all the problems of data shortage and comparability that have prevented serious analysis of poverty trends in recent years. However, the coverage is set to experience the same sort of qualitative leap in household income and expenditure survey as was caused by the wave of support for the 'Social Dimensions of Adjustment' process a decade earlier.[4]

Of course, the problems of sustainability that eventually affected this earlier round of surveys will also affect this one. However, this problem is anticipated in some documents, with several countries experimenting with light surveys (using short questionnaires, perhaps with smaller samples) for more frequent use, allowing a sensible spacing of large-scale surveys and censuses.

The strengths and limitations of household survey data for understanding national poverty profiles are more widely appreciated than they were a decade ago. Many of the country plans, with firm declarations of the importance of non-income dimensions of poverty, state that Participatory Poverty Assessments (PPAs) will be undertaken, though details are generally lacking.

Increased access to information by stakeholders

PRSPs are intended to empower a range of actors to engage in a constructive debate about why poverty reduction has proved so difficult and what can be done about this. This is not an easy thing to achieve. Even in highly institutionalised democracies, governments share information with political rivals only when compelled to do so by law or convention. Nongovernmental actors often lack the expertise to make intelligent use of official statistics. In sub-Saharan Africa in particular, political and civil society is poorly equipped to engage with the PRSPs.

Regarding monitoring, a few Papers include a continuing role for the stakeholders mobilised for the design process. For example, the details of Uganda's Plan, which entails an ongoing dialogue across political and civil society on poverty reduction priorities, are quite well known in the country. This example probably represents the apex of current African achievement in this area, at least in terms of the openness of the process and the willingness of the government to make relevant information available and reasonably accessible. That said, the arrangements are much better for information concerning final outcome (whose content is generally encouraging) than for intermediate performance indicators.

The Ugandan model depends on the centralisation of the analysis and dissemination of poverty-related information in a unit within the Ministry of Finance. The leadership of this Ministry has been strongly committed to openness and is not averse to the use of official information for advocacy purposes. In other countries, however, the institutional framework may be less favourable. Nevertheless, PRSPs give some support to ongoing monitoring by stakeholders. One issue to be confronted is that in several cases the stakeholder monitoring committees that are proposed sound like bilateral forums for government and donors. Increasing bilateral dialogue alone is obviously not the point of developing a PRSP.

Use of information for policy improvement

The focus of most of the documents at this point is on improving the availability of raw data. However, discussion is needed on the analytical uses to which good data might be put. The question then arises as to which institutions in the country actually have an incentive to use the data for purposes that serve policy improvement. This has been raised as an issue in Uganda. Existing survey data would, it is claimed, support specific studies that could improve the targeting and effectiveness of the programmes of a number of line ministries. However, under prevailing conditions (an incomplete transition to performance budgets for line ministries, and an incomplete results-based public service reform), line ministries do not have strong incentives to commission the necessary analytical work. Incentives for data use are, of course, a long-standing issue in poverty monitoring in Africa. It appears that this remains a big problem that is not even recognised in most PRSPs.

Choosing indicators: rationale, credibility and realism

What are indicators for?

It is important not to detach the choice of indicators from the aims of the planning exercise of which they are a part. In even a preliminary assessment of a country's approach to indicator choice, the purpose of each of the proposed indicators needs to be a primary consideration. The quality of the indicators can be assessed only in terms of the role(s) they are expected to play. Indicators are supposed to track progress towards certain objectives. This presupposes both that the objectives are clear and that the intermediate steps necessary to achieve them have been identified. However, initial experience with PRSPs shows that whilst setting objectives is easy enough, identifying credible intermediate steps is much more difficult.

Most PRSPs have a 'missing middle' (see Chapter 4).[5] They do not spell out how the identified activities can be expected to result in the achievement of the identified goal. This is not surprising. To the extent that improvements are possible, they will arise from the social and political dynamics of the planning process in the medium term. It is unrealistic to expect PRSPs to bring immediate improvements.

The 'missing middle' problem explains a lot about current approaches to the monitoring of PRSPs, such as the focus on final outcome/impact measurement. This leads us to expect a lack of direction in selecting indicators. If the strategy for reducing poverty is weak at the 'action plan' level, the rational basis for selecting indicators will also be limited. The choices will reflect other considerations, such as the question of which targets can be met before a debt relief package is completed, and what the corresponding indicators are.

What is a 'good' indicator?

Box 5.1 summarises what is considered a 'good' indicator in the 'monitoring and evaluation' chapter of the World Bank *Poverty Reduction Strategy Sourcebook* (Tikare *et al.*, 2001). While few would disagree that the qualities mentioned are desirable, reflection on the reliability of the indicators which are 'available frequently' in much of sub-Saharan Africa suggests that data quality may be of primary importance. It is not useful to track over time variations in indicators whose margin of error is greater than the expected changes. The need to trade off between reliability and other qualities may lead to the adoption of 'second-best' indicators in many instances.

Box 5.1 What makes a 'good' indicator?

Good indicators:

- are direct and unambiguous measures of progress: more (or less) is better;
- measure factors that reflect objectives;
- vary across areas, groups, over time, and are sensitive to changes in policies, programmes, institutions;
- are not easily blown off course by unrelated developments and cannot be easily manipulated to show achievement where none exists; and
- can be tracked (better if already available), are available frequently, and are not too costly to track.

Source: Prennushi *et al.* (2001, box 2).

Alternative data sources: reliability and cost

The World Bank *Sourcebook* also promotes the need for disaggregated indicators, in terms of location, gender, income level and social group, without which 'it is hard to design good policies and programmes' (Prennushi *et al.*, 2001: 9). Such disaggregation is also essential for effective project and programme management. This requirement, coupled with those for timeliness and affordability, would seem to imply a need to focus on indicators derived from administrative sources. While surveys may in principle provide better indicators in terms of the above criteria, their use for the frequent generation of reliable estimates, at the level of disaggregation proposed, would make excessive demands on national statistical resources.

But what about the quality of administrative data? Routine data sources in most countries suffer from well-known limitations. This implies the need for expectations to be limited, and second-best options to be explored. For example, while such basic indicators as service utilisation, access and cost are not ideal, they may provide a reasonable basis for predicting beneficial final outcomes and be either usable at present, or at least susceptible to improvement in the short run at minimal resource cost.

The use of such indicators is likely to be unsatisfactory in the absence of supporting information on the quality of services available. Knowledge of satisfactory performance on both types of indicator – for example, high levels of utilisation of *good-quality* reproductive health services at low cost – would be a sound basis for expectations that programme objectives in this area would be met. Absence of any one of these indicators might give cause for concern. Regular quality assessments, using qualitative and participatory approaches, could play an important role in delivering this information. As a minimum, reliable audit indicators assessing the adequacy of supervisory activities could provide some degree of quality assurance.

The current situation

Rationale for indicator selection

A clear rationale for indicator selection is often lacking in practice. The authors of many of the PRSPs have listed a wide range of traditional indicators in a fairly undiscriminating way. Selection seems to have operated on the basis of relevance to the various projects and programmes which have been included within the Paper. As a result, it is often difficult to see how the indicators could be effectively used to consider broader strategic issues.

In many instances, the indicators cover economic growth, macro-economic stabilisation, human resource development and other general measures of development performance, alongside indicators specifically related to poverty reduction. Without denying the importance of macro-level stability and growth for sustained poverty reduction, there would be a strong case across much of sub-Saharan Africa for measures such as the growth rate in the agricultural sector, or price movements and interest rates that particularly affect poor people, to be substituted for the broader measures chosen.

One problem is that the targets set in PRSPs and the conditions set for debt relief do not coincide closely. Nevertheless, it seems that some indicators have been selected primarily because they are also conditions for debt relief. In our view, such indicators should be clearly identified and distinguished from those for the poverty reduction strategy. For every indicator, it should be standard practice to specify the intended uses and users. Such an approach would facilitate the categorisation of indicators by purpose and allow the designation of a limited number of 'core indicators' to monitor overall performance of the strategy. In Burkina Faso, donors have stated their interest in a small core set of performance indicators and agreed to limit their attention to that set. However, the degree to which this process involved wider stakeholders in a national dialogue remains an important issue.

The quality problem in administrative data

Many of the indicators proposed in PRSPs derive from routine administrative data. Given that such sources are generally agreed often to be at best highly unreliable, the PRSPs often appear to be highly optimistic as to the possibilities for measuring short-term indicator movements from such data. The problem is particularly serious where regional disaggregation is required. As a general rule, the quality of administrative data depends on the quality of administrators, and both tend to be correlated with incomes per capita. The poorest areas typically have the least reliable data. For example, rural health workers in poor areas (given that their government salaries are sometimes barely sufficient to purchase basic food and clothing) have become very adept at providing information that satisfies higher levels of administration while not limiting their alternative income-generating activities.

Variations in the quality of administrative data between regions may influence national estimates, as these are often based on partial coverage. Poorer regions not only tend to provide less reliable data, but often fail to provide data on time. As national estimates are sometimes based on 'grossing up' the information available when estimates are required, biases that tend to underestimate poverty indicators may be introduced.

The denominator problem

Many of the selected indicators relating to education, health and more general access to services require age-specific estimates, sometimes at regional level. These will reflect the well-known 'denominator problem' of indicator construction: the fact that the base populations are not known.[6] Changing population structures, particularly via migration, may need to be considered in the interpretation of trends over time. The influence of such changes on enrolment, access and utilisation measures can be substantial. Again, poor regions may be particularly affected by migration.

Community involvement in indicator choice?

The need for participatory approaches to the design of PRSPs is stressed in the *Poverty Reduction Strategy Sourcebook* (Tikare *et al.*, 2001) and by donors in general. However, it is very difficult to identify any evidence of community involvement in the list of proposed indicators. In general they follow standard guidelines, not only in the areas of economic growth and stabilisation, but in education, health and other areas of social policy. The inclusion of a number of 'client satisfaction' indicators appears to be the only diversion from this norm. Even in this case there is a tendency to suggest a simplistic 'opinion poll' approach, which may not be the most useful way of tapping the views of stakeholders. One important role for community involvement that is underexplored in the documents is identifying factors relating to the failure of programmes to deliver intended benefits.

Data improvement versus data on improvement

Almost all PRSPs for countries in sub-Saharan Africa stress the need to build statistical capacity and increase the quality of information available.

However, there is a practical problem that needs to be taken into account: it is often difficult to distinguish between the effect of improved measurement and real trends in economic and social variables. For example, a more systematic approach to determining all sources of income or non-market consumption may result in artificial increases in related indicators. Similarly, improved disease surveillance systems usually lead to higher reported prevalence rates.

What to monitor and why

Monitoring designs cannot be expected to solve the problems of weak planning. PRSPs should contain decisions about what needs to be done in order to achieve poverty-reduction goals. Deciding what to monitor and how to do it should be a next step, rather than being defined in advance. At best, thinking about monitoring can provide a way back into an unfinished debate about strategy.[7] This is particularly feasible if stakeholders who have been mobilised in the design of Papers remain active within the institutional arrangements for monitoring and see this as part of their job. However, that only means that monitoring processes may prompt some revisiting of the substance of poverty reduction strategies. It does not imply that monitoring is the same as planning, or can be a substitute for it.

It follows that our discussion in this section has to touch on what ought to be included in the Papers themselves, as well as on what should be monitored. We need to set some definite limits, otherwise the task would become impossibly broad. We do this by largely limiting the discussion to the challenges facing the most promising strategy, the Ugandan Poverty Eradication Action Plan.

What kinds of final outcomes/impacts?

Handling multidimensionality

Most PRSPs have some commitment to goals additional to a reduction in the percentages under the poverty line. With respect to the monitoring of Papers, this implies paying attention to Demographic and Health Surveys (DHSs) and national *Human Development Reports* as well as household expenditure surveys. There is also normally mention of the need for a participatory poverty assessment exercise.

However, despite frequent references to multidimensionality, income poverty is invariably a central focus in the Papers. In spite of the frequently stated concern to move away from income poverty measures and give greater weight to participatory assessments and qualitative information, the traditional poverty line-based head count, poverty gap and intensity indicators predominate. As Thin *et al.* (2001) point out, income is typically presented in Papers not as a means to improve welfare but as an end in itself: 'paradoxically ... lack of education and lack of adequate nutrition are seen as less basic to the definition of poverty than lack of income' (p. 8). This would be of less concern if the level of expenditure per capita were a good predictor of nutritional status, social condition, empowerment, or other factors. However, the tendency in the literature is increasingly to find relatively low associations between different measures of deprivation (e.g. Sahn, 2001).

Experience of monitoring the final outcomes of PRSPs in a balanced multidimensional fashion is as yet limited. However, for a number of years Uganda's Poverty Monitoring and Analysis Unit has been working on Poverty Status Reports, and frequent briefings weave different qualitative and quantitative poverty information into a single fabric. Although the activity of the Unit did not, until recently, draw the Uganda Bureau of Statistics and those conducting participatory assessments into a close relationship with each other, it has the capacity to move across the relevant areas of expertise, and this has ensured that these different actors have not inhabited completely different worlds. Poverty monitoring units or *Observatoires* in a number of other countries, including Rwanda, may develop a similar capability.

Why collect final outcome data?

An excessive focus on the final outcome/impact level may downgrade the essential role of input and intermediate output and outcome indicators. As we have said, final outcome data are largely useless for providing the sort of quick feedback on performance that is most needed for learning and accountability purposes. The speed with which survey data become available is improving fast (data from the Rwanda survey were incorporated in the PRSP within months). However, results are likely to remain relatively slow to appear in generally usable form, and problems in attributing trends or patterns to specific policy measures will remain.

Knowledge of final outcomes/impacts is less necessary than imagined from the point of view of impact evaluation. Theory-based evaluation (Weiss, 1998) requires the specification of a chain of theoretical 'cause and effect' linkages, which allows the likelihood of beneficial outcomes and impacts and sustainability to be assessed. For example, it is very difficult and expensive to demonstrate the impact, or even the outcome, of a given health project or programme. Even in the simplest case, that of immunisation, because both morbidity and 'cause of death' statistics are so difficult to obtain, it is usually impossible to infer in a particular instance that a given expenditure on measles vaccination has led to an identifiable decline in under-five morbidity or mortality. However, it is often perfectly reasonable to rely on past evidence of such a causal link. Effective use of donor and government resources (measured in terms of output indicators), on activities mutually agreed (based on previous experience) to be causally linked to increased welfare of the poor, would seem to be a rational basis on which to assess performance.

Final outcome or impact indicators retain an important strategic role, either as confirmatory or as warning signals. In the latter case, they may indicate either that assumed causal links were not as expected or that previously unconsidered external factors needed to be taken into account. The key quality of such indicators would be an ability reliably to determine trends over time and differences between localities and groups.

Expenditure surveys, DHSs and PPAs will remain essential in providing:

- information on who the poor are, and what their priority concerns seem to be; and
- policy learning of a deeper sort: a better understanding of how poverty sometimes gets reduced, why it very often does not and, thus, what the entry points are for reducing poverty.

The construction of 'poverty profiles' (cross-tabulations of poverty and other household characteristics) is likely to remain the principal focus in most countries. In some cases more ambitious diagnostic work may be appropriate. However, it is the *quality* of analysis and interpretation that must be paramount, not the *quantity* or apparent sophistication. Closer integration of the Integrated Household Survey and participatory appraisals as currently being attempted in Uganda may be of more value than advanced econometric analysis.

What kinds of intermediate variable? Learning from Uganda

One of the features of Uganda's Plan, especially in its revised (2001–2003) form (Uganda, 2001), is its serious effort to fill in the 'missing middle'. For each of the plan's overarching goals, the document discusses relevant evidence on what is working (and what is not). There is a recognisable effort to diagnose policy failures and identify corresponding actions. Suggestions on how progress might be monitored follow immediately, and are reproduced in a summary matrix. Particular attention is devoted to the middle columns of the matrix, headed respectively 'Outcomes' and 'Outputs/access/proximate determinants of outcomes'.

The Ugandan document is a model in terms of intentions. The institutional arrangements are also encouraging. But the intentions are not entirely realised, and some quite significant gaps still need to be filled. This is a central claim in one study of Uganda's monitoring and evaluation: Hauge (2001) argues that a gap remains at the level of expected intermediate results. For example, in the Budget Framework Paper for Education,

Goals are expressed as increases in the pupil:teacher/classroom/book ratios. There is little discussion, and no targets, pertaining to the critical dimensions of the quality issue: such as drop-out rates, years of educational completion or examination attainment standards. One is left with no answer to the question: what difference would we like improvements in [these] ratios to make, in terms of educational quality?

(ibid.: 9)

Hauge notes the danger that, with output-based performance orientation,

managers become motivated to establish goals they know they can attain, with little regard for whether they make a difference on the ground or contribute to longer-term goals.... Without a clear and common set of first order goals and targets cascading through a national development management system, it is not given that there is congruence between planning and management activity or that everybody is pulling in the same direction.

(ibid.: 9, 17)

Hauge concludes: 'emphasis must be placed on distillation of clear and consistent poverty goals, targets and performance indicators pertaining to the reach and outcome levels of change – covering a medium term time-frame such as 2, 5 and 10 years' (ibid.: 24).

These conclusions were reached before the last revision of the Plan. However, they reflect a reality that has certainly not gone away, even if some headway has been made in some sectors. Uganda, like many other countries, is in the middle of a reform of public management that includes an outcome-oriented or programme-based approach to budgeting, and a results-oriented reform of human resource management in the civil service. The country has its share of slow or stalled implementation in these areas. However, it is distinguished by an unusually vigorous use of existing instruments by the Ministry of Finance, Planning and Economic Development to challenge line ministries and local government. Currently, these focus on the medium-term Budget Framework Papers, and a number of carrots and sticks connected with the operation of the Poverty Action Fund (Bevan and Palomba, 2000; Foster and Mujimbi, 2001). Under these arrangements, line ministries are offered better *de facto* access to resources if they can demonstrate plausible linkages between proposed programmes and the goal of poverty eradication.

Input monitoring: its scope and importance

An outcome-oriented approach should not imply neglecting improvements in input monitoring. One danger is that this will be regarded too narrowly, as limited to budget allocations and financial inputs only. Experience suggests a number of issues that need tracking on the financial side, and also that some non-financial inputs are worth watching closely. Monitoring the effectiveness with which inputs are delivered to different levels of government, and to service-providing institutions, has an extremely important place in monitoring systems. Areas that need to be covered include:

- the execution, as distinct from the formulation, of the budget; and
- the extent to which funds reach their specific intended destinations, such as schools or clinics.

Uganda provides a classic example of what can be gained from tracking inputs more effectively. A series of surveys of 250 public primary schools carried out during 1991–1995 found that as little as 13 per cent of the central government's contributions to the schools' non-wage expenditure was reaching them. As a result of these surveys, a campaign to publicise the funds sent to districts for schools led to over 90 per cent of an increased allocation reaching its destination in subsequent years (Reinikka and Svensson, 2001). Moreover, it is not only financial inputs that can be missing. In the regional consultations around the PRSP in Benin, Ministry of Finance officials were surprised to be told that teacher absences represent a serious and chronic problem in rural schools (Bierschenk *et al.*, 2001). Similarly, many studies of rural health care have highlighted the widespread practice whereby trained staff use untrained 'assistants' to provide clinic services while they engage in more remunerative private-sector activities (see, for example, Assiimwe *et al.*, 1997).

How to monitor: obtaining valid and reliable information

Deciding *what* to monitor has some immediate implications for *how* to do it; some instruments are inherently unsuitable for obtaining the desired information. For example, if the reach of essential services is the key question, it is important to survey whole populations rather than particular facilities. Even if appropriate sources exist, there is also the question of how well they perform, and whether that performance can be improved.

Emphasis on the monitoring of intermediate outputs and outcomes suggests a large role for administrative data and management information systems. However, these are subject to well-known problems of reliability. What to do about such problems is as important as getting the right combination of different instruments. These form the two major concerns of this section.

Snags and new developments in the monitoring of final outcomes

Comparative reliability of participatory assessments and surveys

The battle to get the multidimensional concept of poverty accepted for operational planning purposes is not entirely won. The status that tends to be given to the traditional, survey-based approach is well illustrated by the discussion by McGee and Brock (2001: 25–26) of the controversy in Uganda about 'contradictions' between the findings of a PPA and household survey results. A principal finding from the former was that the poor saw themselves as getting poorer while the rich were getting richer. The survey results, on the other hand, were said to demonstrate that 'if anything, growth in living standards has been strongest among the poorest households'. For many, the immediate reaction was to ask, 'Why does the PPA not reflect the *true* situation?'

The subsequent analysis and discussion focused mainly on the participatory assessment findings, pointing out that they should not be treated as directly comparable with the survey results. Changing levels of consumption expenditure should not be expected to coincide with perceptions of changing levels of poverty. The two methods of assessment should rather be seen as complementary, offering alternative perspectives that could jointly provide greater insight.

While this point is well taken, it is also relevant to question the implicit assumption that the use of poverty lines to assess changes in income poverty is always reliable and robust. If great care is not taken about methods and assumptions, household surveys can get it badly wrong, as a recent example from The Gambia illustrates. Three supposedly comparable household surveys suggested that the proportion of the population falling below a food poverty line halved over one three-year period, and then trebled over the following six years. But these apparent trends turned out to be largely explained by technical issues in the definition and measurement of poverty.

Divisions of labour between surveys and participatory assessments

PPAs raise questions that lead to a re-examination of the methods used in survey analysis. But the comparative advantage of these assessments is not in challenging surveys on their own ground. Although there is some scope for methodological triangulation between the two methods – that is, for using data from the one to check those from the other – the areas of direct comparability have been exaggerated. That being the case, it is more important to develop other kinds of complementarity between the two approaches. This implies an iterative, puzzle-solving relationship, focused less on 'what?' and more on 'why?' (Appleton and Booth, 2001).

The second PPA in Uganda has taken up these conclusions in its design. The fieldwork is being prepared to ensure that questions arising from the panel element in the survey are pursued in the Participatory Assessment study sites, and that any findings feed back into the design and analysis of the survey. It has also been agreed that PPA will become less focused on exploring poverty perceptions and other final-outcome issues, and more on investigating known problems in implementing the PEAP.

Household surveys and participatory poverty assessments have come to symbolise the 'quantitative' and 'qualitative' approaches to poverty monitoring. However, this traditional distinction has proved problematic.[8] Booth *et al.* (1998) suggest that it may be more useful to think in terms of 'contextual' and 'non-contextual' information. The former must be treated as requiring interpretation within its 'social, economic and cultural context', the latter as 'untainted by the particularities of the context in which it is collected'. For example, an observation that households below the poverty line in a given country tend to have high dependency ratios might be an example of the latter; complaints that a corrupt local official was disrupting access to health services, of the former.

In purely practical terms, stressing the importance of 'context' has proved useful in advocating the value of participatory techniques in poverty assessment and monitoring, as it is more readily accessible to senior policy-makers than the quantitative/qualitative dichotomy. It also has a natural affinity with the focus on geographical locality in poverty monitoring.

Geographical information systems and poverty targeting

In most countries, geographical targeting is a key policy instrument in the poverty reduction strategy. The motivation is often self-evident. Remote, inaccessible areas with limited access to markets and public services are associated with high rates of poverty. At the same time, programmes designed to reduce poverty can be relatively easily targeted at 'poor areas', particularly if these have well-defined administrative boundaries.

Such policies have been criticised in terms of both their low 'sensitivity' – failure to identify poor households living outside these areas – and their low 'specificity' – leakage of benefits to the non-poor living in them.[9] These problems obviously increase with the size of the targeted areas. Geographical targeting would be much more cost-effective if it could be undertaken at the level of local districts or even individual villages (Bigman and Fofack, 2000). Unfortunately, the information required to work at this level is rarely available. If income poverty lines are used for resource allocation, for example, the expenditure surveys used for area classification will typically be based on sample sizes of around 2,000–4,000 households. This will usually not allow disaggregation below the level of very broad regions, which may be above the primary administrative divisions of the country (Hentschel *et al.*, 2000). A possible way round this problem is to combine household survey and census data, as is being done to generate estimates of poverty incidence for each of Vietnam's sixty-one provinces (Minot and Baulch, 2001).

Geographical targeting is traditionally based on administrative areas, given that national data-collection systems are organised on this basis. However, as Devereux (2001) points out, disaggregation by administrative area may not be very useful in terms of identifying vulnerable population sub-groups. A district, for example, though it may be the lowest administrative level in a given country, may still contain a highly heterogeneous population, particularly in terms of the range of livelihood systems adopted. A number of agencies have addressed this problem. For example, the food economy approach developed by Save the Children Fund–United Kingdom divides a country into 'Food Economy Zones' (FEZs), based on dominant livelihood systems. These zones can be characterised using both secondary data sources, for example by mapping census or survey enumeration areas onto the zones, or primary data collection, for example using participatory techniques with communities within the zones. In statistical terms this technique can be seen as an attempt to define strata that are homogeneous in terms of livelihood strategies and thus likely to display homogeneity in terms of policy impact.

Combining Geographical Information Systems and Participatory Poverty Assessments?

Geographical Information Systems may have a role to play in combining the results from participatory assessments and household surveys. For example, in The Gambia, wet- and dry-season participatory assessments are being undertaken as part of a three-year Canadian-funded project. The areas included were selected from the enumeration areas sampled for the 1998 National Health and Population Survey, and the PPA gathered qualitative information relating to income sources and expenditure items from households included in that survey. There are thus possibilities for combining data at various geographical levels: providing basic survey information on specific poverty target groups in particular regions, and supporting this with qualitative information on those same populations from participatory work.

Process monitoring: reforming and challenging administrative systems

The practical need for intermediate process monitoring

Poverty monitoring in the narrow sense is not only of limited use for accountability and immediate learning purposes, but also in some respects unnecessary. A case in point is the enormous difficulty and expense of accurately measuring short-run declines in maternal mortality, one of the primary Millennium Development Goals. The health non-governmental organisation (NGO) Options is among those stressing the value of 'process indicators' based on routinely collected facility data to monitor the situation of pregnant women. This example illustrates the wider challenge posed by the tracking of the key intermediate steps in implementing a PRSP.

Such indicators have been found potentially useful in areas of health monitoring. In an analysis of trends in infant mortality rates in Zambia, Simms *et al.* (1998) found that the most highly correlated variable was attendances at antenatal clinics. This probably simply indicated the existence of a reasonably functional local health service. The ratio of clinic births to antenatal clinic visits is also a useful local indicator of women's ability to afford maternal health services (whilst visits may be free or very low cost, giving birth at a clinic is expensive compared to having a traditional birth attendant).

Whatever their merits, 'For process indicators to be successfully used, projects need to invest time and resources in building the capacity of facility staff to understand, collect and use routine data' (Options, 2001: 1). Similar sentiments have been expressed repeatedly over the years, not only in relation to health staff, but with reference to teachers, extension workers, local government administrators and other actors in local service delivery. It is difficult to find much evidence of the considerable 'time and resources' which have indeed been allocated to this task.

Confronting incentive issues in administrative systems

The response to incentive problems should clearly not be to abandon the attempt to measure progress. Process indicators are central to monitoring poverty reduction strategies, and relatively low-level service delivery and administrative staff will be key actors in delivering the required data. However, more innovative strategies are required, beyond the established approaches based on information systems design and training programmes.

One seldom-addressed issue in poverty monitoring is that many of those charged with gathering data and reporting on the poor are themselves living very close to the poverty line. A qualified nurse in a public village health station in Nigeria has a salary equivalent to US$1 per day. A graduate teacher in The Gambia earns around 80 US cents. Less qualified staff, for example agricultural or health extension workers, may have incomes below the poverty line. Moreover, the lowest-paid staff are commonly found in precisely those areas that have the highest concentration of poor households.

What are the implications for monitoring? Two key issues are relevant. First, making additional demands on those who perceive themselves as inadequately rewarded is unlikely to be met with much enthusiasm. Second, poorly paid staff typically look for 'livelihood strategies' to increase their incomes. Such strategies usually involve at least non-observance of their working codes of conduct, and often illicit use of the resources or status provided by their position. In many countries, central administrations have limited capacity to regulate such behaviour. Those behaving in this fashion will tend to regard improved monitoring with considerable suspicion, if not open hostility. Control over information – for example, about fee rates or official opening hours of health facilities – may be a valuable 'livelihood asset', and one not willingly surrendered.

One of the few projects to directly address this issue has recently been started in Cambodia by *Médecins sans Frontières* (van Damme and Meessen, 2001). This scheme is heavily subsidised, but is not without wider interest. It offers a 'new deal' to local health workers and administrators, as a way of breaking a downward spiral linking low basic salaries with poor service quality, low utilisation and minimal fee income from which to pay bonuses. A related example of the effective use of contracting was observed in recent evaluation work in poor rural areas of China (Yu *et al.*, 1998). Service providers ('village doctors') were contracted under a limited pre-payment scheme. Claims for payment from the village health care fund required that the provider return a simple patient diagnosis and treatment record to the fund manager. The file of such records provided a basic but effective information system that could in principle be used to monitor both health service utilisation and quality of care. The simple existence of this system appears to have been sufficient to improve provider behaviour.

Communities versus providers?

In recent years there has been increased emphasis on community partici-pation in the design and implementation of development projects. It might therefore seem reasonable that actual and potential users of services should be encouraged to play a larger role in monitoring the delivery of those services. However, detailed consideration of possible mechanisms raises many difficult questions. Why should communities take on such activities? What benefits might they gain? Do suitable community groups exist, or could they be created? How should such groups be consti-tuted and what training and resources would they need? What should they monitor and how could monitoring be undertaken? What relationship would they have with providers and how would providers respond? How should they relate to existing service managers, to other local government officials and to NGOs?

The 'balance of power' between providers and users must be taken into account. Contracts work best when the services to be delivered are relat-ively easy to measure and monitor. There is a need for effective penalties for default and for both parties to have equal recourse to enforcement. Qualified staff are in short supply, particularly in poor areas. This fact gives them considerable status and may allow them to dictate conditions of service. Even when community monitoring identifies inappropriate or even illegal behaviour, local administrators may side with extension workers, teachers or health providers, to avoid losing them.

Monitoring strategies that fail to address the concerns and interests of providers stand little chance of success. An alternative is the development of 'partnership' models – supporting providers and user communities to negotiate jointly determined priorities, establish common objectives and agree how best to use their joint resources to pursue those objectives. In Bolivia the community health information system pools data collected by community health promoters and health service providers. These are presented in accessible graphical format and are used to stimulate joint decision-making, progress monitoring and advocacy to higher levels of government (Howard-Grabman, 2000). Other examples of providing information to communities on education outcomes in Cambodia, The Gambia and Ghana demonstrate how both local officials and parents can become more actively involved through obtaining even incomplete data on performance.

Beyond administrative data: parallel systems, special surveys and non-survey instruments

There are sound reasons not to rely on the reform of routine systems but to develop information sources that run parallel to them. One reason is that such reforms may take some time. The other is the problem of inherent limitations mentioned above. We need sources of information that are not facility based because reach is a crucial issue, and facility-based data cannot tell us much about reach. Not relying on administrative data does not necessarily mean creating new structures. In many countries there are relatively cheap and simple, yet reasonably reliable, data collection instruments such as those set up for famine early warning purposes. Four specific kinds of instrument merit special attention: service delivery surveys (and household surveys collecting data on service use and quality); integrity and business climate surveys; commissioned studies; and qualitative impact monitoring or participatory process monitoring.

Service delivery surveys have been used to good effect in a number of countries, including Bangladesh, Tanzania and Uganda (Foster, 2001). A typical survey combines interviews with representative samples of households, interviews with service providers and key informants, schedules completed by enumerators giving details of facilities and services, and, in some cases, user 'exit polls'. The information generated includes the proportion of the population using government and other services, differences in patterns of use across social categories, and reasons for use and non-use. Such surveys cover the key gap in administrative data, namely, the reach of official provision and the factors responsible for limiting access. Whilst no doubt subject to some methodological imperfections, these surveys effectively sidestep the problem of motivating service providers to report on themselves. Other standard surveys contain underexploited information on service use, including integrated household surveys and, in a more focused way, Core Welfare Indicators Questionnaires (CWIQs). These sources should be used more intensively as means of tracking the performance of PRSPs.

Integrity surveys and surveys that investigate the climate of business confidence in a country are also worthy of attention. For example, official corruption is often ignored in PRSPs. However, this may change as national dialogue on the Paper develops through the review and revision phases. The same goes for a somewhat broader range of issues in governance and the rule of law. Existing examples include Uganda, where use has been made of both Integrity Surveys and business climate surveys in the biennial Poverty Status Reports. Although they combine focus-group work and exit poll surveys, these studies are subject to the well-known weaknesses of 'attitude' surveys and could no doubt be strengthened with research with a more 'behavioural' emphasis (Appleton and Booth, 2001: sec. 2.4). Nonetheless, they provide a very useful complement to other survey-based and administrative information.

Commissioned studies may take the form of surveys, or be based on one-off participatory assessment exercises. There are also studies commissioned to investigate a specific 'missing middle' issue, such as the pros and cons of alternative approaches to meeting final outcome goals. Thus Foster and Macintosh-Walker (2001: 5) report:

> In the face of a disappointing public response to the expansion of primary health services, Ghana and Bangladesh have researched the causes of unequal access and are developing more specific strategies for reaching the poor. Zambia and Cambodia have focused basic education interventions on understanding the barriers to enrolment by the poor and introducing specific policies to address them. The problem of cost to parents was identified as a major barrier in all but one of our education cases (most dramatically in Uganda), and a key intervention has been to reduce costs to parents.

Qualitative impact monitoring and participatory process monitoring cover a rather broad category including a range of technically different but substantially similar traditions and techniques. In several countries there are long-established arrangements for conducting regular participatory 'beneficiary assessments' in connection with social funds and other large projects. In Zambia the group originally set up for this purpose was subsequently involved in the World Bank PPA, and has since contributed to a range of commissioned sectoral policy studies. In Kenya, Malawi and Benin, poverty monitoring arrangements are being upgraded and mainstreamed within the Papers (Bierschenk *et al.*, 2001; Gomonda, 2001; GTZ-SPAS, 2001).

There are a number of challenges. What is needed is to draw fully on the extensive experience of official and NGO project monitoring and impact assessment using learning-process and participatory methods (e.g. Brown *et al.*, 2001; Estrella, 2000; Mosse *et al.*, 1998; Roche, 1999), while adjusting for the very different purpose and scope of PRSPs. Another is to achieve the same balancing act with respect to the recorded experience of traditional participatory assessments and their linkage to policy processes (e.g. Holland with Blackburn, 1998; Norton *et al.*, 2001; Robb, 1999).

Conclusions

This chapter has explored existing Poverty Reduction Strategy Papers in sub-Saharan Africa from a particular angle. It has deliberately taken a robustly realist approach in two respects. First, the criteria applied to describing and assessing the documents in respect of monitoring systems reflect not just established monitoring and evaluation principles, but a vision of the policy process that is more realistic and less rationalistic than the norm in this field. Second, our discussion of indicators and data sources is equally stringent in not ignoring what is known about the real condition of African countries' information systems. In our view, anything less than this would do poor service to the cause of more effective anti-poverty action in the region. The thinking reflected in the PRSPs on the topic of monitoring is very patchy. This is partly because most countries only have Interim Papers that are designed in part to get access to debt relief and further international loans. However, our purpose is not to criticise, but to identify topics on which action might be taken, or further inquiries justified.

All concerned are turning a blind eye to the poor quality of administrative data. This matters in that intermediate output/outcome monitoring (in addition to input monitoring and tracking) is likely to be the most fruitful for generating information capable of changing behaviour and procedures. The enthusiasm for household surveys, and monitoring final outcomes/impacts, is in many ways justified. But it will be a pity if it provides an excuse for not tackling the issue of quick feedback on implementation.

Two key questions arise: how can improvement of administrative reporting and management information systems be addressed, given the limited achievements of numerous previous attempts; and how should this activity be balanced against development of other monitoring procedures? There are various alternatives to the management information systems approach, some already fairly well institutionalised within the better public service reform programmes, others reflecting a decade of work by participation specialists at the World Bank and elsewhere, and yet others pioneered by non-governmental organisations. NGO experience on impact assessment may have additional clues as to worthwhile shortcuts in monitoring. Further systematic reviews of these alternatives would be worthwhile.

More strategic selection of indicators is an obvious topic for further work. However, this cannot be pursued as a mere monitoring question. The appearance of randomness in current indicator listings arises in good part from the 'missing middle' in poverty reduction strategies. Most Papers developed to date fail to identify which critical changes need to occur for the identified actions to produce the desired results. Ideally, a monitoring system should focus on detecting quickly whether such key changes are occurring.

A point of entry into this topic from the perspective of good practice in the development of monitoring systems is the question of the continuing involvement of a range of stakeholders in monitoring activities. If non-governmental stakeholders remain mobilised after debt relief has been secured and can receive feedback on implementation issues, fresh thinking on strategic bottlenecks and priority actions may be stimulated. Further work to document the lessons of early experience on this point would be justified.

Notes

1 This chapter derives from a report commissioned by the Department for International Development (DFID) (Booth and Lucas, 2001a, b) on behalf of the Strategic Partnership with Africa's (SPA's) Poverty Monitoring Task Team. Its description of the content of PRSPs refers to the situation in 2001.
2 The language conventions in this field are a mess. The main issue is that different meanings are given in different contexts to the words 'outcome' and 'impact'. The Development Assistance Committee (DAC) and the monitoring and evaluation profession convention, in the field of poverty reduction policy, is that outcomes are 'specific results and the utilisation of means/services by beneficiaries'. Movements in measures of poverty are referred to as 'impacts'. However, in the broader social science fields concerned with poverty reduction strategies and poverty information, it has been conventional to speak of the final goal of policy as to influence poverty 'outcomes', or 'outcomes for the poor'. There is also a tendency to associate 'impact' with the activity of evaluation, implying that an impact is not just a final result, but one that can be attributed to a specific intervention. We have tried to avoid misunderstanding by qualifying everything. Thus we distinguish intermediate outcomes, closely linked to intermediate outputs, and final outcomes or poverty outcomes. In deference to the DAC convention, we often write 'final outcomes/impacts'.
3 This is the Ugandan equivalent of a Poverty Reduction Strategy Paper.
4 The perhaps misleadingly named 'Social Dimensions of Adjustment' was a joint World Bank–United Nations Development Programme (UNDP) initiative, supported by several bilateral agencies, primarily aimed at improving data collection.
5 Uganda is a partial exception.
6 Population estimates in years removed from that in which the census is taken are derived from demographic models, often based on parameters estimated from Demographic and Health Surveys (DHSs). The procedure is reasonably

reliable at the national level, but the estimates are not intended for sub-national estimation and provide little evidence on internal migration. Adjusting such demographic models to allow for the unprecedented impact of the AIDS pandemic is also a relatively new and uncertain methodological exercise.

7 See the PRSP Institutionalisation Study (Booth and associates, 2001: chapter 1).

8 For example, PPAs have been widely used to generate 'quantitative' findings on specific communities.

9 These concepts are used in a number of areas including medicine and engineering. They also relate to the traditional Type I and Type II errors of hypothesis-testing.

References

Appleton, S. and Booth, D. (2001) 'Combining Participatory and Survey-Based Approaches to Poverty Monitoring and Analysis', Uganda Workshop Background Paper, second draft, 27 May.

Assiimwe, D., Mwesigye, F., McPake, B. and Streetland, P. (1997) 'The Private-Sector Activities of Public-Sector Health Workers in Uganda', in Bennett, S. and McPake, B. (eds) *Private Health Providers in Developing Countries: Serving the Public Interest?* London: Zed Books.

Bevan, D. and Palomba, G. (2000) 'Uganda: The Budget and Medium Term Expenditure Framework Set in a Wider Context', background paper for Poverty Reduction Support Credit with DFID finance, October.

Bierschenk, T., Thioléron, E. and Bako-Arifari, N. (2001) 'Institutionalising the PRSP Approach in Benin', chapter 2 in Booth D. and associates, *PRSP Institutionalisation Study: Final Report*, submitted to the SPA, October.

Bigman, D. and Fofack, H. (2000) *Geographical Targeting for Policy Alleviation: Methodology and Applications*, Washington: World Bank Regional and Sectoral Studies.

Booth, D., Holland, J., Hentschel, J., Lanjouw, P. and Herbert, A. (1998) *Participation and Combined Methods in African Poverty Assessment: Renewing the Agenda*, London: DFID, Social Development Division, February.

Booth, D. and Lucas, H. (2001a) *Desk Study of Good Practice in the Development of PRSP Indicators and Monitoring Systems: Initial Review of PRSP Documentation*, report commissioned by DFID for the SPA, May.

Booth, D. and Lucas, H. (2001b) *Desk Study of Good Practice in the Development of PRSP Indicators and Monitoring Systems: Final Report*, report commissioned by DFID for the SPA, November.

Booth, D. and associates (2001) *PRSP Institutionalisation Study: Final Report*, submitted to the SPA, October.

Brown, D., Hussein, K. and Longley, C. with Howes, M. (2001) *Review of Participatory Rural Appraisal in The Gambia*, London: ODI.

Devereux, S. (2001) 'Food Security Information Systems', in Devereux, S. and Maxwell, S. (eds) *Food Security in Sub-Saharan Africa*, ITDG.

Estrella, M. (ed.) (2000) *Learning from Change: Issues and Experiences in Participatory Monitoring and Evaluation*, London: Intermediate Technology Publications/ IDRC.

Foster, M. (2001) *Use of Surveys to Improve Public Expenditure Management*, London: CAPE/ODI, June.

Foster, M. and Mackintosh-Walker, S. (2001) *Sector Wide Programmes and Poverty Reduction*, London: CAPE/ODI.

Foster, M. and Mujimbi, P. (2001) *How, When and Why Does Poverty Get Budget Priority? Uganda Case Study*, London: Overseas Development Institute, April.

Gomonda, N. (2001) 'Qualitative Impact Monitoring of the Poverty Alleviation Policies and Programmes in Malawi', Second Forum of Poverty Reduction Strategies, Dakar, 10–13 September.

GTZ-SPAS (2001) *An Introduction to KePIM: Kenya's Participatory Impact Monitoring Exercise*, Nairobi: Ministry of Finance and Planning and Poverty Eradication Unit, Office of the President.

Hauge, A. (2001) *Strengthening Capacity for Monitoring and Evaluation in Uganda: A Results Based Management Perspective*, Washington, DC: World Bank OED, Evaluation Capacity Development Working Paper 8, January.

Hentschel, J., Lanjouw, J., Lanjouw, P. and Poggi, J. (2000) 'Combining Census and Survey Data to Trace the Spatial Dimensions of Poverty: A Case Study of Ecuador', *World Bank Economic Review*, 14(1): 147–165.

Hill, M. (ed.) (1993) *The Policy Process: A Reader*, New York: Harvester Wheatsheaf.

Holland, J. with Blackburn, J. (1998) *Whose Voice? Participatory Research and Policy Change*, London: Intermediate Technology Publications.

Howard-Grabman, L. (2000) 'Bridging the Gap between Communities and Service Providers', in Cornwall, A., Lucas, H. and Pasteur, K. (eds) Accountability through Participation: Developing Workable Partnership Models in the Health Sector, *IDS Bulletin*, 31(1): 88–96.

McGee, R. and Brock, K. (2001) 'From Poverty Assessment to Poverty Change: Processes, Actors and Data', *IDS Working Paper* 133, Brighton: Institute of Development Studies, July.

Minot, N. and Baulch, B. (2001) 'The Spatial Distribution of Poverty in Vietnam and the Potential for Targeting', research funded by DFID Poverty Analysis and Poverty Support Trust Fund and World Bank Development Economics Research Group, mimeo, August.

Mosse, D., Farrington, J. and Rew, A. (eds) (1998) *Development as Process: Concepts and Methods for Working with Complexity*, London: Routledge/ODI.

Norton, A. with Bird, B., Brock, K., Kakande, M. and Turk, C. (2001) *A Rough Guide to PPAs*, London: Overseas Development Institute.

Options (2001) *Options News*, newsletter no. 7, July 2001.

Prennushi, G., Rubio, G. and Subbarao, K. (2001) 'Monitoring and Evaluation', *World Bank Poverty Reduction Strategy Paper Sourcebook* (draft for comments, April 2001) (www.worldbank.org/poverty).

Reinikka, R. and Svensson, J. (2001) 'Explaining Leakage of Public Funds', paper prepared for the World Institute for Development Economics Research (WIDER) Development Conference on Debt Relief, Helsinki, 17–18 August.

Robb, C. (1999) *Can the Poor Influence Policy? Participatory Poverty Assessments in the Developing World*, Washington, DC: The World Bank.

Roche, C. (1999) *Impact Assessment for Development Agencies: Learning to Value Change*, Oxford: Oxfam/Novib.

Sahn, D.E. (2001) 'Strengthening Quantitative Methods Through Incorporating Qualitative Information', in Kanbur, R. (ed.) *Qualitative and Quantitative Poverty Appraisal: Complementarities, Tensions and the Way Forward*, Cornell University Workshop, 15–16 March.

Simms, C., Milimo, J.T. and Bloom, G. (1998) 'Reasons for the Rise in Childhood Mortality during the 1980s in Zambia', IDS Working Paper 76.

Thin, N., Underwood, M. and Gilling, J. (2001) *Sub-Saharan Africa's Poverty Reduction Strategy Papers from Social Policy and Sustainable Livelihoods Perspectives*, Report for DFID, Oxford: Oxford Policy Management, March.

Tikare, S., Youssef, D., Donnelly-Roark, P. and Shah, P. (2001) 'Organizing Participatory Processes in the PRSP', World Bank *Poverty Reduction Strategy Sourcebook* (draft, April 2001) (www.worldbank.org/poverty).

Turner, M. and Hulme, D. (1997) *Governance, Administration and Development: Making the State Work*, London: Macmillan.

Uganda (2001) *Poverty Eradication Action Plan (2001–2003)*, vol. 1, Kampala: Ministry of Finance, Planning and Economic Development.

van Damme, W. and Meessen, D. (2001) 'Sotnikum New Deal, the First Year: Better Income for Hospital Staff; Better Service to the Population', mimeo, Cambodia: *Médecins sans Frontières.*

Weiss, C. (1998) *Evaluation*, second edition, Englewood Cliffs, NJ: Prentice Hall.

Yu, H., Lucas, H., Gu, X.-Y. and Shu, B.-G. (1998) 'Financing Health Care in Poor Rural Counties in China: Experience from a Township-Based Co-operative Medical Scheme', IDS Working Paper no. 66, Brighton: Institute of Development Studies.

6 Are the Millennium Development Goals feasible?[1]

Jan Vandemoortele

As long as you travel to a goal, you can hold on to a dream.

(Anthony de Mello)

Introduction

The Millennium Development Goals are a set of numerical and time-bound targets that express key elements of human development. They include halving income poverty and hunger; achieving universal primary education and gender equality; reducing under-five mortality by two-thirds and maternal mortality by three-quarters; reversing the spread of HIV/AIDS; and halving the proportion of people without access to safe water. These targets are to be achieved by 2015, from their level in 1990 (United Nations, 2000).

It is often said that global targets are easily set but seldom met, which poses the question as to whether the Millennium Development Goals are feasible. Progress in over 130 developing countries regarding the many dimensions of human development – such as education, health, nutrition and income – is difficult to summarise. The 1990s saw many success stories, including those relating to education in Guinea and Malawi; HIV/AIDS in Senegal, Thailand and Uganda; child mortality in Bangladesh and the Gambia; nutrition in Indonesia, Mexico and Tunisia; and income poverty in China. Globally, the number of polio cases dropped from nearly 250,000 in 1990 to less than 3,000 in 2000, making eradication of the disease by 2005 a realistic goal.

But for each success story there have been setbacks. The under-five mortality rate increased in Cambodia, Kenya, Malawi and Zambia – an unprecedented trend after decades of steady decline. The primary school enrolment ratio dropped in Cameroon, Lesotho, Mozambique and Tanzania. The gender gap in primary education widened in Eritrea, Ethiopia and Namibia. Instead of decreasing, malnutrition increased in Burkina Faso and Yemen. Access to water became more difficult for millions of people; Bangladesh faced a major problem with arsenic water poisoning. In the 1990s, countless countries saw their HIV prevalence rate double, triple, quadruple, even increase tenfold – severely undermining the feasibility of most Millennium Development Goals, in health and beyond.

Monitoring can be done at different levels, from the global to the local. The level of assessment will influence the outcome regarding the feasibility of the Millennium Development Goals. If Millennium Development Goals appear feasible at the global level, it does not necessarily imply that they will be feasible in all nations or at all locations. Averages are commonly used at each level to measure Millennium Development Goal progress. While they give a good sense of overall progress, averages can be misleading. The failure to understand that the average is an abstraction from reality can lead to unwarranted conclusions that are based on deduction from abstractions, not on real observations.

A good assessment of progress towards the Millennium Development Goals must, therefore, go beyond averages and aggregates. The failure to disaggregate according to gender, for instance, easily leads to the fallacy of 'misplaced concreteness' (Daly and Cobb, 1994). Average household income is very much an abstraction for women who have little or no control over how it is spent; it may exist in the mind of economists but it does not necessarily correspond with the reality faced by millions of poor women.[2]

This chapter reviews global progress towards the Millennium Development Goals during the 1990s. The picture that emerges shows a very uneven pattern across regions and countries and between different socioeconomic groups within the same country. Although the picture is mixed, the overall conclusion is that none of the agreed targets for 2000 were met at the global level. If the 1980s were the 'lost decade for development', the 1990s should go down in history as the 'decade of broken promises'. If current trends prevail, only one Millennium Development Goal will be reached by 2015.

Is progress on track?

This review is based on the best data that are currently available. It focuses on indicators for which global information is reasonably reliable, comparable and up to date.[3] However, it must be kept in mind that global trends are estimates; they are never precise or actual values. Therefore, different sources often give different estimates, without necessarily being inconsistent. Indicators without trend data or with inconsistent data have been omitted, hence the review does not include all Millennium Development Goals. Subsequent chapters fill some of these gaps, as well as amplifying the argument for particular indicators.

Income poverty

In developing countries the average proportion of people living on less than $1 per day[4] decreased from 32 per cent in 1990 to 25 per cent in

1999, according to the latest estimates (World Bank, 2002).[5] The simple extrapolation of this trend suggests that the world is on track to halving income poverty by 2015. Unfortunately, the reality is more complicated and decidedly less satisfactory. Most of the global progress was due to a rapid decline in Asia, particularly in China. Progress in Latin America and the Caribbean, sub-Saharan Africa, and the Middle East and North Africa, combined, was merely a tenth of what was required to meet the agreed target.

In addition, poverty estimates for China show large discrepancies, which seriously undermine the reliability of global poverty data (see also Chapter 7). Figure 6.1 shows a steep decline in China's income poverty between 1993 and 1996, when the head-count index reportedly declined from 29 per cent to 17 per cent. This implies that the number of people in China struggling to survive on less than a $1 per day dropped by a staggering 125,000 people per day for three years running. This remarkable achievement came to a sudden – and mysterious – end in 1996. Actually, the number of poor people reportedly increased slightly between 1996 and 1999.

National poverty estimates, on the other hand, show a less dramatic decline in China's poverty level. Poverty estimates reported by the Ministry of Agriculture show a decrease by less than one percentage point per year between 1993 and 1996 (Khan and Riskin, 2000), considerably less than the four percentage points suggested by the World Bank estimates.[6] More-

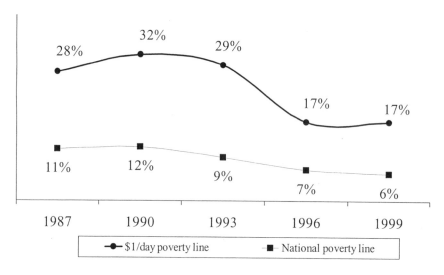

Figure 6.1 Incidence of income-poverty in China, 1987–1999 (percentage of the population below the poverty line).

Source: Based on data from the World Bank (2002) and data supplied by the Ministry of Agriculture, China.

over, if demographic change has been a major force behind China's success in reducing income poverty – as some analysts have documented (Gustafsson and Zhong, 2000) – then it would be unwise to assume that its rapid decline will continue until 2015.

In short, global poverty trends cannot be taken at face value. Given the inherent weaknesses associated with the fixed and static poverty line of $1 per day and given the inaccuracy of purchasing power parity (PPP) conversion rates, global poverty estimates are not a reliable source of information. Global poverty data are not robust; therefore, it cannot be argued that the world is on track to reach the target for halving income poverty by 2015. Dozens of countries experienced a decline in average living standards in the past decade. Moreover, the simple extrapolation of global poverty trends to 2015 is invalid because large countries – such as China and Indonesia – will gradually become less powerful in pulling global poverty down as they reach lower levels of poverty. Global poverty projections will be meaningful only if they are based on country-specific projections.

Education

In 1990 the goal was set to provide basic education for all children by 2000. The sad truth is that the 1990s saw only about a fifth of the global progress needed. For developing countries, the average net enrolment ratio for primary education increased from 78 per cent in 1990 to 83 in 2000. Not surprisingly, the goalpost was moved to 2015; but this promise will not be kept either if progress does not accelerate twofold between 2000 and 2015. At the current rate, the global education target will not be reached until 2030 (see also Chapter 8).

Figure 6.2 shows that progress was significantly slower in the 1990s than in the preceding three decades, when the average enrolment ratio increased by approximately ten percentage points per decade – compared with only five percentage points in the 1990s.[7] In 2000, an estimated 120 million school-age children were not enrolled – about the same as a decade earlier. They joined the ranks of the nearly 1 billion adults who cannot read or write – most of them women. Globally, the world is not on track to meeting the education target.

Failure to meet the education target will reduce the chances of reaching other Millennium Development Goals because basic education is key to unlocking positive externalities and synergies. Basic education empowers a young woman and enhances her self-confidence; an educated mother is likely to marry later, space her pregnancies better, and seek medical care for her child and herself when needed (see also Chapter 11). Evidence shows that babies born to mothers without formal education are at least twice as likely to suffer from malnutrition or die before the age of 5 than are babies born to mothers who completed primary school (Bicego and Ahmad, 1996). An educated girl is also the best guarantor that her

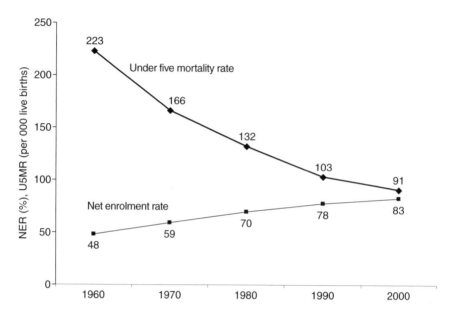

Figure 6.2 Average net primary enrolment ratio (NER) and under-five mortality rate (U5MR) in developing countries.

Source: Based on UNICEF (2001) and data supplied by United Nations Education, Scientific and Cultural Organisation (UNESCO).

children attend school – thereby ending the inter-generational transmission of poverty. Health investments are more efficient when the people are better educated, in large part as a result of the adoption of good hygienic behaviour. In short, girls' education is key to achieving the Millennium Development Goals.

The good news is that the gender gap in primary enrolment narrowed in the 1990s. For developing countries, the number of girls per 100 boys enrolled in primary school increased from 83 in 1990 to 88 in 2000. However, this will be insufficient to reach gender equality by 2005, as agreed in the Millennium Development Goals. Progress would have to accelerate more than fourfold in the period 2000–2005 if this target were to be achieved. Globally, the world is not on track to reaching gender equality in primary education by 2005.[8] At the current rate, the target will not be met until 2025. Gender discrimination in primary school enrolment remains a concern in several countries, particularly in sub-Saharan Africa, South Asia and the Middle East and North Africa (see also Chapter 9).

Child mortality

In 2000, more than 10 million children under the age of 5 died, mostly from preventable causes such as pneumonia, diarrhoea, measles, malaria, HIV/AIDS and malnutrition. For developing countries, the average under-five mortality rate decreased from 103 to 91 deaths per 1,000 live births between 1990 and 2000. The rate of progress was less than half that achieved in the previous three decades, as shown in Figure 6.2 (see also Chapter 10). For several countries, slow progress was due to the mother-to-child transmission of HIV, which is contributing to an unprecedented increase in infant and child mortality. In Zimbabwe, for example, some 70 per cent of deaths among children under the age of 5 are due to AIDS (see also Chapter 12).

There is no marked difference between girls and boys when it comes to the average under-five mortality rate but Demographic and Health Surveys (DHSs) show that in virtually all countries, baby boys experience higher levels of infant mortality – sometimes 50 per cent higher – than baby girls, mostly because of biological factors. After infancy, however, the gender gap in terms of mortality gradually reverses, switching from being pro-female in infancy to being pro-male in childhood (ages 1–4). Such a reversal is observed in Bangladesh, Bolivia, Brazil, Cameroon, the Dominican Republic, Gabon, Guatemala, Haiti, India, Kenya, the Kyrgyz Republic, Nepal, Niger, Nigeria, Peru and Vietnam.

In the absence of a biological explanation, environmental factors must be examined to understand the causes for this reversal. DHS surveys consistently show that baby boys are more likely to be vaccinated and breast-fed than baby girls.[9] Both indicators suggest a greater commitment on the part of parents and service providers to the health and development of boys *vis-à-vis* girls.

If the global trend of the 1990s were to continue at the same rate until 2015, the reduction in the under-five mortality rate would be about one-quarter – far less than the agreed target of a two-thirds reduction. Meeting the global target will require that the rate of reduction increases more than fivefold between 2000 and 2015 – an extremely unlikely scenario. Almost half of the under-five deaths occur in sub-Saharan Africa, so that a sudden and dramatic improvement in child mortality in that region must come about if the global target is to be achieved. Globally, the world is not on track to reach the target for child mortality.

Immunisation is essential to reducing child mortality. Measles is among the leading causes of child mortality that are vaccine-preventable; but immunisation coverage stagnated in the 1990s at about 70 per cent. The coverage has to reach at least 90 per cent to reduce measles deaths effectively. That level was reached only in Latin America and the Caribbean and in East Asia, whereas coverage actually decreased in sub-Saharan Africa to about 50 per cent in 2000, down from over 60 per cent in 1990.

Child malnutrition

Deaths among children under the age of 5 are often associated with malnutrition, mostly with moderate malnutrition; only one-quarter of the deaths result from severe malnutrition. The crisis is, therefore, largely invisible as the young victims seldom show outward signs of under-nourishment.

In 1990 the target was set to halve the proportion of children suffering from malnutrition by 2000. Data show that the proportion of moderately and severely underweight children in developing countries declined from 32 per cent to 28 per cent, respectively. Thus only one-quarter of the promise was kept. As part of the Millennium Development Goals, the goalpost was pushed to 2015; but the current rate of progress will have to increase threefold if malnutrition in developing countries in 2015 is to be half the level that prevailed in 1990. Globally, the world is not on track to meet the nutrition target.

The largest decline was observed in East Asia, especially in China; substantial improvements were made in Latin America and the Caribbean. Less progress was made in South Asia, where underweight prevalence remains very high. Sub-Saharan Africa saw little or no change over the decade. Overall, the number of malnourished children in developing countries fell by approximately 25 million – or 15 per cent – decreasing from 174 million to 150 million. However, their numbers increased in sub-Saharan Africa and South Asia.

Data from over 100 countries do not suggest that girls are more likely to be malnourished than boys. Except for South Asia, most regions actually show a slightly higher rate of malnutrition for boys. However, gender gradually becomes a greater liability as girls grow older, and by the time they reach reproductive age, many suffer from anaemia. In almost all countries, rural children are more at risk of malnutrition than their urban counterparts. In some countries the percentage of rural children who are underweight is more than 50 per cent higher than that for urban children.

HIV/AIDS

Two decades after it was first reported, AIDS is the most serious threat to human development in a growing number of countries. It is the leading cause of death in sub-Saharan Africa; worldwide it is number 4 in the league of major killers. The pandemic – raging in Africa and spreading fast in other regions – is perhaps the greatest impediment to achieving the Millennium Development Goals by 2015 (see also Chapter 12). Even countries with a relatively low national HIV prevalence rate can have clusters of people or specific locations where the prevalence rate is as high as 20 per cent or more; but these pockets of crises are hidden in national statistics owing to the relatively small populations affected.

About one-third of those currently living with HIV/AIDS are aged between 15 and 24 years. Adolescent girls are at particularly high risk, owing to a mix of biological and social factors. HIV/AIDS is a disease for which gender could not be more central: women represent a growing proportion of people living with HIV/AIDS. In countries with high HIV prevalence, young women with little or no education – that is, those without much power in society – are at the greatest risk of infection (Vandemoortele and Delamonica, 2000). Studies in Africa show that teenage girls are five to six times more likely to be infected by the HIV virus than boys their age (UNAIDS, 2000). New HIV infections are disproportionately concentrated among poor and illiterate adolescent women.

After a strong public information campaign, Uganda saw the number of new cases of HIV/AIDS drop from 239,000 in 1987 to 57,000 in 1997. But even in this exceptional case, the impact on the poor – that is, those with little or no education – was the least. The HIV infection rate amongst educated women dropped by almost half in the 1990s, whereas it did not show a significant decrease for women without formal schooling.

Millions of young people do not know how to protect themselves against HIV. In the late 1990s, surveys in sub-Saharan African countries found that half the teenagers did not know that a healthy-looking person can be HIV-positive. The proportion of young people who do not know that HIV/AIDS cannot be transmitted by mosquitoes is over 80 per cent in Albania, Azerbaijan, Chad, Niger, Somalia, Tajikistan and Uzbekistan. Out of a sample of twenty-three countries, that proportion is less than half in only two: Cuba (35 per cent) and Kenya (45 per cent). In many countries, open and frank discussions about HIV transmission face a wall of silence. Four allies make the virus so prevalent in many societies: silence, shame, stigma and superstition. These four Ss thrive in a climate of ignorance and illiteracy, making education a key to defeating this deadly alliance.

But several countries face a Catch-22: education is important to reverse the pandemic but HIV/AIDS undermines the education system. Absenteeism among teachers is high, owing to AIDS-related illness and deaths, care for sick family members, attendance at funerals, and increased moonlighting. In Zambia, for instance, 1,300 teachers died in the first ten months of 1998 – twice the number of deaths reported in the previous year. In the Central African Republic, 300 teachers died in 2000, 85 per cent as a result of AIDS. Several African countries are reportedly losing more teachers than the number of new recruits. HIV/AIDS also reduces the demand for basic education, because of the family's inability to pay for schooling, concerns about sexual activity at school as they are not always sanctuaries and safe havens for children, and the declining quality of education that makes many children and parents lose interest in school. Globally, no progress has been made towards the target of reducing the HIV prevalence among young people.

Maternal mortality

Complications during pregnancy and childbirth cause the death of approximately 500,000 women each year – about one every minute. But measuring maternal mortality is notoriously difficult, owing to under-reporting and incorrect diagnoses. Countries with a comprehensive vital registration system represent less than one-quarter of the world population.

Together with income poverty, the maternal mortality ratio is among the most difficult indicators to monitor. But there is consensus that the proportion of births attended by skilled health personnel – a doctor, nurse or midwife – is very closely correlated with maternal mortality. Access to care by a skilled health provider at childbirth – when obstetric complications are most likely to occur – greatly reduces maternal mortality.

In 1990 the target was set to cut maternal mortality in half by 2000. In developing countries the proportion of births attended by skilled health personnel increased from 42 per cent to 53 per cent between those two dates. This was just over a third of the agreed target.[10] Not surprisingly, the goalpost was changed to reducing the maternal mortality ratio by three-quarters by 2015, which is slightly less ambitious. But the current rate of progress will have to increase more than threefold if the target is to be met by 2015. Globally, the world is not on track to reach the target for maternal mortality.

Progress differed across regions. Sub-Saharan Africa and the Middle East saw little or no change, whereas North Africa and East and South Asia observed considerable progress. Latin America and the Caribbean, with the highest percentage of births attended by skilled health workers, saw moderate progress. High fertility, combined with high maternal mortality risk, make a woman in sub-Saharan Africa face a one in thirteen chance of dying in childbirth over her lifetime, compared with one in 160 in Latin America and the Caribbean, and one in 280 in East Asia. In industrialised countries the risk is one in 4,100.

Safe water

Safe sources of drinking water include piped water in the house, public standpipe, borehole, protected dug well, protected spring, and rainwater collection. In developing countries, coverage of improved drinking water sources rose from 71 per cent in 1990 to 78 per cent in 2000 – leaving an estimated 1.1 billion people without access to safe water.

Progress fell far short of the goal set in 1990 to reach universal access to safe water by 2000. Not only was the goalpost moved to 2015, but the new Millennium Development Goal target was lowered from universal coverage to halving the proportion of people without access to safe water. Thus the new target is nearly five times less ambitious than the initial one. At the current rate of progress, the world is on track to reach the new target for safe water by 2015, but far from reaching its initial goal.

The fastest progress was made in South Asia; little or no progress was made in the world's poorest nations – the least developed countries. Rural areas lag far behind; the rural–urban gap in terms of access to safe water is greatest in sub-Saharan Africa, where only 45 per cent of the rural population have access – against 83 per cent for their urban counterparts (see also Chapter 13).

Do the poor benefit from 'average' progress?

There are different ways of reaching a global or national target. At one extreme, it can be achieved by improving the situation of the already better-off segments of society – that is, a top-down approach. At the other extreme, a target can be achieved by improving the situation of the worse-off population – that is, a bottom-up approach. Many combinations are possible in between. The evidence suggests that most countries come closer to following the top-down rather than the bottom-up approach. Frequently, the poor are not fully taking part in national progress; evidence suggests that disadvantaged groups are often bypassed by 'average' progress.

Different groups in society usually have very different levels of social and economic well-being, based on characteristics such as gender, age, rural/urban location, region, ethnicity, religion, wealth, and any combination thereof.[11] Disaggregated data confirm that social indicators vary enormously across groups within the same country. Thus national indicators hide wide disparities.

Data from over forty DHSs show that a child from a poor family is invariably more likely to die before age 5 than her counterpart from a rich family – on average about twice as likely. Similarly, children from poor families are less likely to complete primary education than children from rich families. Data for twelve countries in Latin America show that over 90 per cent of the children in the top income decile complete primary education. The share falls to two-thirds for children in the middle decile and drops below 40 per cent for children in the bottom decile (Inter-American Development Bank, 1998).

Given these significant differences in the absolute value of social indicators across groups, progress too is likely to be very different for different groups. Indeed, an increase in a national indicator does not necessarily mean that all groups will see their situation improve at the same rate.

DHSs for 1994 and 1997 in Bangladesh, for instance, show that improvements in access to basic education benefited foremost the children from better-off families; while children from poor families saw little or no improvement.[12] In Peru, where access to primary education worsened in the 1990s, only the poor bore the consequences; the non-poor were not

affected. Data for over forty countries indicate that poor children represent a growing proportion of the 'education queue' as the national indicator for education improves, suggesting that the poor often find themselves
at the end of the queue and do not always benefit from 'average' progress.

There are twenty-four countries with at least two DHSs between the late
1980s and the late 1990s, which makes it possible to track progress in child
mortality across different groups in the same country. They show that disparities across wealth groups widened in the majority of them. The gap
between the bottom and top quintiles increased most significantly in
Brazil, Colombia, the Dominican Republic, Ghana, Indonesia, Kazakhstan,
the Philippines and Zimbabwe (Figure 6.3).[13]

In Indonesia, for instance, children in the bottom quintile witnessed a
reduction in under-five mortality rate by one-fifth between 1987 and 1997;
those in the top quintile saw a reduction by one-half. Thus the ratio
between the bottom quintile and the top quintile rose from 2.3 to 3.8. The
trend in Zimbabwe was even starker: a decline in average under-five mortality masked a rise in the number of deaths of children in the poorest
fifth of the population. Between 1988 and 1999 the national under-five
mortality rate decreased by a modest four percentage points, but that for
the bottom quintile actually increased by some twenty percentage points.
By 1999, children in the poorest quintile had an under-five mortality rate
that was four times higher than that for their counterparts in the richest
quintile. Thus the average trend had little to do with the reality faced by

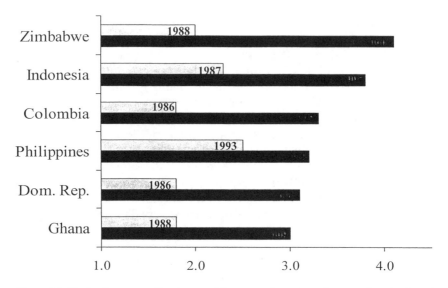

Figure 6.3 Under-five mortality by wealth group in selected countries (ratio of
average under-five mortality rate for bottom/top quintile).

Source: Based on Minujin and Delamonica (2002), using DHS data.

poor Zimbabwean children during the 1990s. Indeed, averages can be deceiving.

On the income front, disparities are also on the rise. A growing body of data suggests that income disparities are widening, both between and within countries (see Cornia, 1999; Galbraith *et al.*, 1998; Milanovic, 1999; United Nations Conference on Trade and Development, 1997; United Nations Development Programme, 1997). No matter how it is measured, it is increasingly difficult to dismiss the evidence that inequality is on the rise. Disparities are increasing not only between the rich and the poor, but also among the poor. Nigeria, for instance, saw the poverty head-count index decline by nine percentage points between 1985 and 1992; but the incidence of extreme poverty increased by three percentage points (Demery and Squire, 1996). This led to a paradoxical situation in which the number of poor declined, yet the number of destitute people increased. A similar story emerges for rural Kenya and rural Tanzania.

In sum, averages do not tell the full story. Groups for which social progress has been fastest seldom represent the disadvantaged people. Some countries appear to be on track to reach a particular target on the basis of 'average' progress; yet the situation for disadvantaged groups in those countries is stagnant or deteriorating. As disparities are widening for a range of indicators, such as income, mortality and education, the informational value of national averages is gradually decreasing, thereby augmenting their potential to induce misleading conclusions.[14]

Are the Millennium Development Goals affordable?

Why are the promises not being kept? Why are hundreds of millions of people struggling to overcome the daily grind of hunger, disease and ignorance when the global economy is experiencing unprecedented prosperity? Many reasons account for this apparent paradox, and they are often country specific. However, two reasons stand out in virtually all countries: (1) under-investment in basic social services; and (2) public action that frequently fails to take advantage of cross-sectoral synergies.[15]

Recognising the fact that global goals will require extra money as well as new approaches, the United Nations proposed the 20/20 Initiative (UNDP *et al.*, 1998). It embodies the principle of shared responsibility for the Millennium Development Goals by encouraging developing countries to allocate about 20 per cent of their national budget to basic social services; and developed countries to devote about 20 per cent of their development assistance to the same services. Experience shows that once access to an integrated package of basic social services of good quality becomes universal, social progress can be dramatic and economic growth can be sustainable and equitable.

But instead of a '20/20' deal, the reality comes closer to a '12/12' ratio (Figure 6.4) (UNICEF and UNDP, 1998). Governments in developing

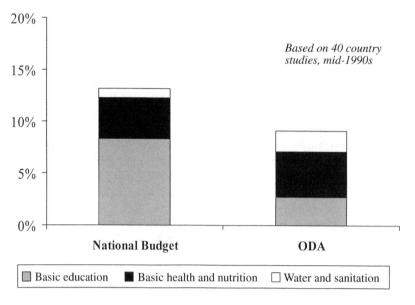

Figure 6.4 Underinvestment in basic social services (spending on basic social services as a percentage of national budget and Official Development Assistance). Based on forty country studies, mid-1990s.

Source: Based on UNICEF and UNDP (1998).

countries spend, on average, between 12 and 14 per cent of the national
budget on basic social services. Donor countries allocate, on average,
about 10–12 per cent of their aid budget on these services. Both shares
have shown an upward trend in recent years, but they fall far short of the
share of 20 per cent that is accepted as a minimum – based on the
experience of high-achieving countries such as Botswana, Costa Rica and
the Republic of Korea.

Reaching the Millennium Development Goals will require universal
access to basic social services of good quality. The financial cost of reaching universal coverage is modest, whereas the benefits that beckon are
enormous. Global public spending on basic social services falls short by
about US$80 billion per year (at 1995 prices) of the level required to
ensure universal coverage (UNDP *et al.*, 1998).[16] The full implementation
of the 20/20 initiative would generate enough resources to close this
financial gap. Although large in absolute terms, US$80 billion represents
about one-third of one per cent of global annual income. Indeed, achieving the Millennium Development Goals is more about setting priorities
than about mobilising extra resources or making technological breakthroughs.[17]

Although the Millennium Development Goals appear affordable at the
global level, many governments will be hard-pressed to meet the financial

requirements for achieving the targets by 2015. Sub-Saharan African and South Asian countries, in particular, will need to expand their budgetary outlays on basic social services at a rate that will not be sustainable without additional assistance, in terms of aid, debt relief and trade. It would be unrealistic to expect that low-income countries can meet the Millennium Development Goals without additional and concerted international support.

Official development assistance and debt relief will be indispensable, especially for the least developed and low-income countries. A steady decline in ODA characterised the 1990s, when the relative aid effort fell by one-third – dropping from 0.33 per cent of the combined gross national income (GNI) of developed countries in 1990 to 0.22 per cent in 2000 (Figure 6.5) (OECD and DAC, 2001). It now stands at less than one-third of the agreed target of 0.7 per cent. The total shortfall *vis-à-vis* that target amounts to about US$125 billion per year. Aid efforts vary considerably among donor countries,[18] and none of the G-7 countries is a member of the 'G-0.7' group, which comprises Denmark, the Netherlands, Norway and Sweden, and more recently Luxembourg. An extra US$50 billion per year in donor resources, as called for by the UK Chancellor of the Exchequer (Brown, 2001), would go a long way towards reaching the Millennium Development Goals at the global level.

A study of budgetary spending in thirty developing countries found that two-thirds of them spend more on debt servicing than on basic social services (UNICEF and UNDP, 1998), with some spending three to five times more on debt. In sub-Saharan Africa, governments spend about

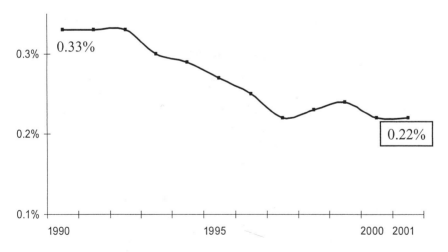

Figure 6.5 Decline of Official Development Assistance (total Official Development Assistance as percentage of combined gross national income of donor countries).

Source: Based on OECD and DAC (2000).

twice as much to comply with their financial commitment *vis-à-vis* external creditors than to comply with their social obligation *vis-à-vis* the people. Debt servicing often absorbs between one-third and one-half of the national budget, making macroeconomic stability an elusive goal. To spend more on external debt than on basic social services, when tens of millions of people see their fundamental human rights denied, is ethically wrong and makes no economic sense. The Heavily Indebted Poor Countries (HIPC) Initiative is a first attempt to resolve the debt problem comprehensively but its implementation is painfully slow, while declining commodity prices are making it increasingly ineffective.[19] For many countries, slow debt relief will mean slow Millennium Development Goal progress.

Conclusion

The Millennium Development Goals are technically feasible and financially affordable. Yet the world is off track to meet them by 2015. The Millennium Development Goals are ambitious, but each and every target will be met by some countries, including a few low-income countries. If these countries can achieve the Millennium Development Goals, there is no reason why others cannot.

Figure 6.6 summarises global Millennium Development Goal progress so far. Of the eight targets listed, only one is on track. Monitoring income

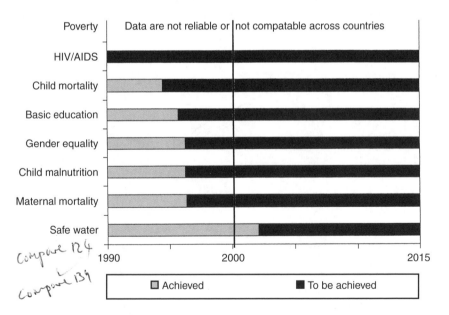

Figure 6.6 Broken promises of the 1990s (share of the target covered in the 1990s, unfinished agenda for 2000–2015).

poverty at the global level is subject to serious conceptual and measurement constraints. Global estimates based on the norm of US$1 per day tend to underestimate global poverty and overstate poverty reduction (Reddy and Pogge, 2002). Current data on global poverty are simply not robust enough to make an informed judgement as to whether the world is on track towards the 2015 target.[20]

Little or no progress was achieved in reversing the HIV/AIDS pandemic; HIV prevalence rates continue to rise in numerous countries. Only a few succeeded in reducing the spread of HIV, including Cambodia and Uganda. The HIV/AIDS pandemic is a major obstacle on the road towards the Millennium Development Goals.

Progress was slow for child mortality, basic education, malnutrition, maternal mortality and gender discrimination in primary school enrolment. They all recorded about one-quarter or less of the agreed target, leaving three-quarters or more to be covered in the next fifteen years. Since the Millennium Development Goals are to be achieved between 1990 and 2015, 40 per cent of the road should have been covered by 2000. Instead, just over half that level was recorded.

Only a fifth of the education target was achieved in the first ten years, leaving 80 per cent to be covered in 60 per cent of the time period (between 2000 and 2015). No matter what the challenge is – HIV/AIDS, child mortality, malnutrition, income poverty, maternal health, gender discrimination or environmental degradation – basic education is invariably at the centre of the solution. Failure to keep the promise to give every child a good basic education will undermine the chances of reaching the other Millennium Development Goals.

There is no good reason why universal primary education should not yet be a practical reality. Progress toward that goal is truly discouraging: its global cost is perfectly affordable (Delamonica *et al.*, 2001); no new technology breakthroughs are needed to get all children in school; there is consensus that it makes good economic sense;[21] and basic education is a fundamental human right that must not be denied to any child.[22] If these conditions are not enough to ensure success, then the question arises as to what it will take to meet the other Millennium Development Goals.

Only one Millennium Development Goal is on track, the one of halving the proportion of people without access to safe water by 2015. However, the current rate of progress may not be sustainable: countless countries face acute water shortages in the near future if no swift and decisive action is taken soon. Wastage, population growth, urbanisation and desertification are gradually leading to looming water scarcity in many parts of the world; industrialisation and modern agriculture are adding to the risk of more water pollution. Future conflicts over the allocation of fresh-water resources are likely to slow down progress in the years to come.

Not only was global progress inadequate in the 1990s, but much of it bypassed the poor. Slow 'average' progress was compounded by limited progress for the poorest and most disadvantaged groups within countries. Global goals are primarily meant to help improve the situation of the poor and the disadvantaged, not only that of better-off and privileged people. Unfortunately, the poor have benefited proportionately little from 'average' progress, as evidenced by widening disparities in terms of income, education and mortality.

In sum, the world is not on track to meeting the Millennium Development Goals by 2015. In 2001, Nelson Mandela asked, 'Will the legacy of our generation be more than a series of broken promises?' In opening the Children's Summit in May 2002, Kofi Annan, UN Secretary-General, stated, 'We the grown-ups must reverse this list of failures.' In 1993 the late James Grant, then UNICEF Executive Director, said, 'The problem is not that we have tried to eradicate global poverty and failed; the problem is that no serious and concerted attempt has ever been made.' Sadly, these words still ring true today.

But while the Millennium Development Goals remain unfulfilled, they also remain feasible and affordable. Committed leadership, stronger partnerships, extra money and deeper participation by the poor can bring the world back on track towards the Millennium Development Goals. It is not too late to realise the dream by 2015.

Notes

1 The views expressed in this chapter do not necessarily reflect those of the United Nations Development Programme. The usual disclaimers apply.

2 Cost recovery in a water project in western Kenya, for example, was low despite seemingly high average household income. The cause was traced to the fact that women were responsible for this expense but had little or no control over household income. Affordability studies often target the wrong group and frequently produce misleading policy advice.

3 Based on the latest information from a variety of sources, mostly from within the United Nations system, and particularly the United Nations Children's Fund (UNICEF) (2001).

4 That is, US$1.08 per day purchasing power parity 1993 prices.

5 Global poverty estimates are often presented with a decimal point, which may give a false sense of sophistication and accuracy. Given their approximate nature, rounded figures are more appropriate.

6 The data of the Ministry of Agriculture relate to rural poverty, whereas World Bank data refer to total poverty. Since poverty in China is overwhelmingly rural, the discrepancy cannot be explained by the difference in geographical coverage. The national poverty line is lower than the international one based on $1 per day. Therefore, the national poverty estimate falls below the $1 poverty trend. It should be noted, however, that the difference between the two poverty trends was halved, narrowing from 20 percentage points in the early 1990s to about 10 percentage points in the late 1990s.

7 Another way of assessing progress is by measuring it against the remaining gap; but this interpretation of the data also shows that progress slowed down in the 1990s. It should be noted that global targets set for reducing under-five mortal-

ity and net primary enrolment rate by 2015 are not out of line with historic trends.

8 Faster progress was made towards gender equality in secondary and tertiary education, but here too it will not be enough to close the gender gap by the agreed date.

9 Lower levels of vaccination among baby girls explain, in part, their increased child mortality rate *vis-à-vis* that of boys. Countries where a significant shift occurs from a pro-female bias in infant mortality to a pro-male bias in child mortality are often those with the largest gender gap in terms of immunisation. Another factor that is likely to add to explaining the reversal in gender-specific mortality rates is nutrition. Food allocation within the family is frequently determined by gender, and disparities in feeding practices between girls and boys appear early in life. Data on breastfeeding reveal that in most countries a baby boy is more likely to be breastfed than a baby girl.

10 Assuming a proportionate change in the maternal mortality ratio and the percentage of births attended by skilled health personnel.

11 Therefore, generalisations about the feminisation of poverty should be used with caution. Statements such as '70 per cent of the poor are women' are not always backed by hard evidence. Aggregates and averages can be used – and abused – to back either side of an argument. The 1997 *Human Development Report* points out that not all evidence supports different poverty levels between male- and female-headed households (United Nations Development Programme, 1997). A recent World Bank report on rural poverty in China states that 'available evidence does not suggest that women are greatly over-represented among the poor' (World Bank, 2001). Gender discrimination does not occur indiscriminately, but is often mediated through a multitude of factors. Gender, for instance, is more a liability to a poor girl than to her non-poor counterparts, to a girl from an ethnic minority than to one from the majority, to a rural girl than to an urban one.

12 DHSs do not collect income or consumption data, but the information on household assets such as a bicycle, radio, size of the dwelling, type of construction materials, and source of drinking water makes it possible to cross-tabulate social indicators by socio-economic groups, as has been done by Filmer and Pritchett (1999) and Gwatkin *et al.* (1999).

13 Only two countries – Guatemala and Togo – reported a significant improvement over time in child mortality for the poorest quintile *vis-à-vis* the richest quintile.

14 An example of 'misplaced concreteness' is the well-publicised finding that income of the poor rises one-for-one with overall income per capita (Dollar and Kraay, 2001). Although the finding may be statistically correct, it is not necessarily true. When the same statistical analysis is applied to random values, the same results are obtained. The argument that a one-for-one relationship exists between the income of the poor and average income per capita is more the result of using aggregates and averages, than of actual behavioural relationships. It is striking how a simple analysis based on a set of aggregate averages can exert so much influence on so many people: policy-makers, researchers and journalists alike.

15 Too often, health goals are pursued through health interventions alone; education goals are pursued through education programmes alone. Basic social services comprise an integrated package of basic education, primary health care, nutrition, reproductive health, water and sanitation.

16 Estimating the cost for reaching the Millennium Development Goals is a complex task which is beset by serious methodological problems. Unit costs in absolute terms vary greatly from country to country because salaries dominate the cost structure, which relate to the level of economic development. In

addition, expressing them in a common currency, such as the US dollar, introduces more inaccuracies. Unit costs vary much less when expressed in relative terms (as a percentage of income per capita). Using average regional unit costs unduly inflates the cost of reaching the target; relative country-by-country unit costs are preferable. However, average costs may lead to considerable underestimation because reaching the last 10 or 20 per cent of the population with basic social services is likely to be more costly (i.e. marginal costs will exceed average costs). On the other hand, efficiency gains can reduce overall costs, but improving quality may offset these gains. HIV/AIDS has significant cost implications but its quantification is virtually impossible, given current knowledge and available data (see also Chapter 12). Furthermore, calculating the costs of the each Millennium Development Goal separately will unduly inflate the total cost because synergies and complementarities will be missed. Last, but not least, dividing total cost between domestic sources and Official Development Assistance (ODA) flows is subject to judgement, and can always be challenged. Thus, costing the Millennium Development Goals is not as straightforward as it seems at first glance. Approximating it by using the 20/20 rule is unlikely to be less 'scientific' than other approaches.

17 Reaching the Millennium Development Goals will require not only extra spending, but also better spending. Money alone will not solve the problem; human and institutional capacities need improvement too. However, the argument that existing resources must be used more efficiently first before investing extra money in basic social services misses the point that insufficiencies often create inefficiencies. For example, when teacher salaries absorb 98 per cent of the budget for primary education but fail to provide a living wage, there is little scope for improving the quality of education. Indeed, inefficiencies and insufficiencies are not independent but very much interdependent.

18 In 2000 they ranged from a high of 1.06 per cent of GNI for Denmark to a low of 0.10 per cent for the USA. The aid effort of G-7 members is considerably lower than that of non-G-7 countries. In 2000 the respective averages were 0.19 per cent and 0.45 per cent of their combined income.

19 The criteria for eligibility under the HIPC initiative are mostly trade related, despite the obvious fact that it is government, not exporters, that repays external debt. The 'enhanced' HIPC initiative does not take into account the fiscal burden of debt servicing in determining a country's external debt sustainability.

20 Progress towards the poverty target is best measured on the basis of national poverty lines; although this will not readily produce internationally comparable poverty data. However, the quest for comparable data in this area has been rather elusive so far.

21 Numerous empirical studies have documented the critical role of basic education in the economic and social development in Europe, North America, Japan and, more recently, East Asia (e.g. World Bank, 1993).

22 Perhaps it is the most 'human' of all human rights since it is reading and writing that sets *Homo sapiens* most apart from all other species.

References

Bicego, G. and Ahmad, O. (1996) *Infant and Child Mortality*, Demographic and Health Surveys Comparative Studies 20, Calverton, MD: Macro International.

Brown, G. (2001) 'Globalisation', address to Press Club in Washington, DC on 17 December, at www.hm-treasury.gov.uk/Newsroom_and_Speeches/Press/2001/press_146_01.cfm.

Cornia, A. (1999) 'Liberalization, Globalization and Income Distribution', World Institute for Development Economics and Research (WIDER/UNU), Working Paper 157. Helsinki: WIDER.

Daly, H. and Cobb, J. Jr (1994) *For the Common Good: Redirecting the Economy Towards Community, the Environment and a Sustainable Future,* Boston: Beacon Press.

Delamonica, E., Malhotra, S. and Vandemoortele, J. (2001) 'Is EFA Affordable? Estimating the Global Minimum Cost of "Education for All"', Division of Evaluation, Policy and Planning, Staff Working Paper 01–01, New York: UNICEF.

Demery, L. and Squire, L. (1996) 'Macroeconomic Adjustment in Africa: An Emerging Picture', *World Bank Research Observer,* 11: 39–59.

Dollar, D. and Kraay, A. (2000) *Growth Is Good for the Poor,* Washington, DC: World Bank, Development Research Group.

Filmer, D. and Pritchett, L. (1999) 'The Effect of Household Wealth on Educational Attainment: Evidence from 35 Countries', *Population And Development Review,* 25(1): 85–120.

Galbraith, J., Darity, W. and Jiaqing, L. (1998) 'Measuring the Evolution of Inequality in the Global Economy', mimeo, Austin: University of Texas at Austin.

Gustafsson, B. and Zhong, W. (2000) 'How and Why Has Poverty in China Changed? A Study Based on Microdata for 1988 and 1995', *China Quarterly,* 164(1): 983–1006.

Gwatkin, D., Rustein, S., Johnson, K., Pande, R. and Wagstaff, A. (1999) *Socio-economic Differences in Health, Nutrition and Population,* Country Notes, Health, Nutrition and Population Department, Washington, DC: World Bank.

Inter-American Development Bank (1998) *Facing Up to Inequality in Latin America,* Washington, DC: Inter-American Development Bank.

Khan, A. and Riskin, D. (2000) *Inequality and Poverty in China in the Age of Globalisation,* New York: Oxford University Press.

Milanovic, B. (1999) *True World Income Distribution, 1988 and 1993: First Calculation Based on Household Surveys Alone,* Washington, DC: World Bank, Development Research Group.

Minujin, A. and Delamonica, E. (2002) 'Socio-economic Inequalities in Mortality and Health in the Developing World', mimeo, New York: UNICEF.

Organisation for Economic Cooperation and Development (OECD) and Development Assistance Committee (DAC) (2001) *Development Co-operation Report 2000,* Paris: OECD.

Reddy, S. and Pogge, T. (2002) *How Not to Count the Poor,* New York: Columbia University, at www.socialanalysis.org.

UNAIDS (2000) *Aids Epidemic Update: December 2000,* Geneva: UNAIDS.

United Nations (2000) *Millennium Declaration,* New York: United Nations.

United Nations Children's Fund (2001) *Progress since the World Summit for Children: A Statistical Review,* New York: UNICEF.

United Nations Children's Fund and United Nations Development Programme with contributions from the World Bank and the United Nations Fund for Population Activities (1998) 'Country Experiences in Assessing the Adequacy, Equity and Efficiency of Public Spending on Basic Social Services', document prepared for the Hanoi meeting on the 20/20 Initiative, New York: UNICEF.

United Nations Conference on Trade and Development (1997) *Trade and Development Report, 1997: Globalization, Distribution and Growth,* Geneva: UNCTAD.

United Nations Development Programme (1997) *Human Development Report 1997: Eradicating Human Poverty*, New York: Oxford University Press.

—— (1999) *Human Development Report 1999: Globalisation with a Human Face*, New York: Oxford University Press.

United Nations Development Programme, UNESCO, UNFPA, UNICEF, WHO and the World Bank (1998) *Implementing the 20/20 Initiative: Achieving Universal Access to Basic Social Services*, New York: UNICEF.

Vandemoortele, J. and Delamonica, E. (2000) 'The "education vaccine" against HIV'. *Current Issues in Comparative Education* (online), 3(1), at www.tc.columbia.edu/cice/vol03nr1.

World Bank (1993) *The East Asian Miracle: Economic Growth and Public Policy*, New York: Oxford University Press.

—— (2001) *China: Overcoming Rural Poverty*, a Country Study, Washington, DC: World Bank.

—— (2002) *World Development Indicators*, Washington, DC: World Bank.

7 Halving world poverty[1]

Michael Lipton with Hugh Waddington

Introduction

There has been considerable disagreement about whether, or to what extent, the world is on track to meet the United Nations (UN) Social Summit target of halving 'incidence of dollar-a-day (1993 purchasing-power parity or PPP) poverty in developing and transitional countries' (hereafter called 'world' or 'global' poverty) in 1990–2015. The International Fund for Agricultural Development's (IFAD's) *Rural Poverty Report* (2001) argued that big changes were needed to do so. However, far from arguing that this target was 'doomed to failure', the *Rural Poverty Report* showed that sufficient poverty reduction to meet the target had been achieved in many places and at many times – when, and where, there was rapid, poverty-oriented, employment-intensive rural development, usually based on rising yields of staple foods. Unfortunately, progress in yields of staple foods and land reform slowed right down between the 1970s and the 1990s, as did poverty reduction. Between the late 1980s and the late 1990s, the real value of aid to agriculture fell by almost two-thirds.

Many people are fairly cynical about UN targets. There have been so many declarations with no enforcement mechanisms, no visible means of support and little or no result. However, some people are rather enthusiastic about the world poverty targets and the process put into place to meet them. Certainly there are plenty of issues that the targets and the process do not address. Some of the serious concerns are explained in this chapter. However, it is something to have a set of internationally agreed targets, not only with a policy commitment by developing countries at the UN Social Summit in Copenhagen in 1996, but also endorsed as the guiding principle of aid by the Organisation for Economic Co-operation and Development (OECD) donors in 1996 and by the G-7 finance ministers in 2001. Country-specific Poverty Reduction Strategy Papers (PRSPs) (while unfortunately linked to flawed Heavily Indebted Poor Country (HIPC) procedures) nevertheless are intended to embody government programmes, discussed through civil society procedures, to achieve and monitor progress towards the target of halving 1990 levels of dollar-a-day poverty by 2015 – and, increasingly, to act as a gateway to, and a structuring device for, concessional financial flows from the World Bank. In other words, the country-specific poverty-halving target has standing, a body of knowledge and support, some implementing and monitoring procedures, and a considerable amount of supportive international aid. It is increasingly possible for critics to hold both developing-country governments and aid donors to poverty targets, and to implementing procedures, to which they are publicly committed.

This chapter analyses progress towards meeting the world poverty target. The definition of the target is discussed in the next section. It is argued that, whilst there are several objections to reviewing progress in reducing the proportion of persons below purchasing power parity poverty lines, and quite substantial ways of improving this definition, it is manageable. The section after that discusses the process through which the targets are to become realities. Several important principles have been recognised in this respect: not only is the process 'country-led', but it recognises specifically that it is both essential for effectiveness and morally right that decisions about how to reach a particular target, such as poverty reduction, have to involve participation by the people affected by it.

There then follows an assessment of the feasibility of the target. Much past evidence suggests that it can be met: very large parts of the world in recent history have reduced poverty for quite long periods and at rates sufficiently fast to reach the target of halving world poverty by 2015. However, despite some assertions to the contrary, we are very far below the rate of progress needed to achieve the target. If the regions of the world continue to reduce poverty in 1998–2015 no faster than in 1990–1998 (the longest period after 1990 with a wide spread of evidence globally), then we shall achieve only 40 per cent of the target. In other words, we shall underachieve by 60 per cent.

Getting poverty reduction back on track – the subject of the final section – needs changes in policy both in developing countries and in developed countries. The most important change is to reverse the collapse of support for labour-intensive farming of staples in smallholdings, and to help revive the performance of smallholders in the developing world, in particular in the area of food production for local consumption.

Definition

Although this chapter is entitled 'Halving world poverty', we discuss something cruder: halving, between 1990 and 2015, the proportion of the population in developing and transitional economies in 'dollar poverty', i.e. with daily consumption per person below US$1 in 1993 purchasing power parity (PPP).[2]

In 1990, 29 per cent of the population of the 'world' consumed less than US$1 1993 PPP per day – purchasing power, that is, over a global average

1993 bundle of goods.[3] Thus the target is to bring that percentage down to 14.5 in 2015. This is narrow private consumption. It is not participatory, as advocated by Robert Chambers (1997), who argued persuasively for letting people define their own needs and translating those into policy (even at the unavoidable cost that it is hard to track or compare self-assessed poverty: one cannot discriminate between the effect of changes in the values received by the poor, and changes in their standards or expectations). Nor is it multidimensional. The PPP bundle of goods is the average bundle consumed by an average citizen of the world; the PPP exchange rate measures how much people have got to spend to purchase this basket of goods in some real purchasing power equivalent sense – a dollar is simply used as the unit of account, what economists call a '*numéraire*'.[4]

Why review progress in reducing the proportion of persons below PPP poverty lines? There are four main objections, elaborated on here.[5]

First, broader poverty measures, taking account of other determinants of welfare or capabilities than private consumption, may be desirable. However, there is a case for having a simple, readily measurable, narrow conventional definition of poverty, because targets can be set and monitored; governments, civil societies and donors can check progress for a country, or a region (or group or gender) within it, and can compare countries with one another and with past performance. Additionally, 95 per cent of the population of the developing and transitional countries of the world is now covered by representative surveys, and in most cases several surveys, allowing measurements of dollar PPP poverty to be tracked across time.

Second, however, even if a fixed absolute measure of private consumption poverty is used, a nutrition-linked measure is preferable to a dollar PPP line. 'A dollar per person per day of command over a PPP bundle for a given year', while much better than nothing as a poverty line permitting international comparisons of poverty and of progress towards targets, is highly problematic technically,[6] not intuitive, and above all, unlike nutrition-based measures, not linked to human capabilities. Among nutrition-based measures, a '*cost of basic needs*' (CBN) indicator is often used; this estimates the cost of a basic or 'typical poor person's' diet, adds either a percentage allowance or a similarly costed bundle of commodities to meet other basic needs, and defines the outcome as the poverty line (given household size and composition). The CBN approach, however, ignores differences among persons, even of a given age and activity level, in their needs for calories, other nutrients, shelter and other basic needs; CBN simply imposes standard requirements from without. Better in this and other respects is a poverty line for private consumption per equivalent adult (allowing for age-specific needs and more modest economies of scale within the household) set by the food energy method (FEM). FEM sets the poverty line at the level of consumption at which the *expectation* is that persons just fulfil minimum calorie requirements.

A further benefit of hooking a narrow consumption measure on to food poverty by FEM relates to the different environments in which people live. For example, food needs are larger in cold places than in hot ones. Also, the level of total consumption necessary to ensure that food needs are met is higher if other needs such as housing are very expensive. A purchasing power parity dollar-a-day measure will thus underestimate poverty in cold climates relative to hot ones, as food requirements, as well as shelter and heating costs, are greater in the former. Great differences amongst places in the cost of meeting food and other needs are taken into account indirectly if a food-based poverty line is used.[7]

Third, even if we use poverty comparisons based on PPP measures, there is compelling reason to doubt some important country-specific estimates and trends[8] based on the currently available data sets. For example, the risk of poverty in Bangladesh in the late 1990s is estimated as well below two-thirds of the risk in India, which is out of touch with both nutritional data and most observers' judgements.

Fourth, it would be very much better to use a measure that takes account of how far below the poverty line people are. Two things have been suggested which are preferable to the commonly used measure of *incidence:* (1) a measure of poverty *intensity* (e.g. the poverty gap index; that is, incidence multiplied by 'depth' – the shortfall of the average poor person behind the poverty line – as a proportion of that line); (2) a measure of the *severity* of poverty, which accords greater weight to those further below the poverty line. Poverty intensity is fairly intuitive because there is a very close relationship between the intensity of poverty and what it would cost to rid society of poverty if society could target resources accurately on its poor. There are various standard ways of measuring severity (e.g. the squared poverty gap index; see Foster *et al.*, 1984), and although in principle it would be a good idea to find a measure that is intuitive, it is difficult to do so. Certainly, a widening of poverty measures from incidence to intensity is entirely desirable.

All four objections have force. They should be used to develop improved measures of poverty and its reduction. However, except for the poverty gap index of intensity,[9] such measures are not widely available. Furthermore, the UN targets for progress in 1990–2015 were set and accepted using the 'dollar poverty' measure. It would be confusing and perhaps evasive to change the measure in the middle of the implementation and monitoring period. Some widening of the definition is strongly desirable from a 2015 base, however. Work to agree, measure and monitor a widened definition should commence now.

On the other hand, the popularly advocated widening to multidimensional poverty is misguided. It is infeasible to get everyone to agree on the exact indicators that should be used to measure poverty multidimensionally, or on how to value (weight) them against each other. Further, factors such as low access to health or education, low self-esteem and low esteem from others, and vulnerability to very high downward fluctuations and risks affecting standards of living, are all extremely important and are separate elements of policy, but to lump them together with consumption poverty as a single policy objective will not assist rational policy-making. These different dimensions may be causes, one of the other, or mutually reinforcing, and they may interact in complex ways, but they are not the same. Nor is it operational to take a multidimensional indicator, which is some arbitrary mix of, for example, literacy, longevity and lack of consumption poverty, and to try to monitor that; there are all sorts of different reasons why that indicator might be moving in any direction. It is not possible to make sensible policy, or apply sensible pressure from below, on the basis of such an indicator.

In sum, a narrow definition has advantages, for both intellectual and operational reasons. The narrow definition used now is not the best that could be used. We have suggested ways in which it could be improved, but monitoring of the Millennium Development Goal for poverty (halving country-by-country 1993 dollar poverty incidence in 1990–2015) should continue on the present consistent track. A shift to an FEM intensity target (perhaps with supplementary poverty-linked measures) should be put in place in 2015. The work needed to make the improvements needs to start soon. However, we should not shift to a multidimensional index of poverty, which is inevitably arbitrary in its exclusions, inclusions, weights and hence interpretations. Instead we should monitor, and analyse separately, progress against the main policy-related components of human misery and impaired functioning – notably, but not only, infant mortality, malnutrition and illness; illiteracy and educational deprivation; FEM consumption poverty; vulnerability; and lack of esteem and self-esteem.[10]

Process

The internationally agreed process for meeting the poverty target is in principle good. Each developing and transitional economy is asked to work out its own Poverty Reduction Strategy and to incorporate this into a Poverty Reduction Strategy Paper (PRSP), which sets a series of goals aimed at the halving of poverty over the period 1990–2015. Those targets are arrived at not by government in isolation, but by interplay between each government and its own civil society. Subsequently, each PRSP is assessed by the international donors who are supposed to support it in two ways: (1) by shifting aid to countries that have a serious strategy and away from countries that do not; and (2) by attempting to support sector-level or national-level activities within the 'serious' countries rather than tying aid to projects and specific activities.

In practice, although there is progress, much has gone wrong. For instance, in practice the PRSP process has been tied up with the procedure of giving debt relief through the Heavily Indebted Poor Country

(HIPC) Initiative; in fact, the great majority of PRSPs, though not all, are for HIPCs. The aim of forgiving debt for countries which will use that money for extra, cost-effective efforts to cut poverty is sensible, but the process as implemented is doing little to reduce world poverty: despite the panoply of conditions for HIPC-related debt relief, not all the countries receiving, or scheduled for, HIPC relief are giving priority to poverty or can be persuaded to do so.

Furthermore, poor countries that have not become highly indebted do not, by definition, qualify for HIPC assistance. India and China together still contain over 40 per cent of the world's PPP dollar-poor, despite large reductions due in part to the world's most substantial and serious (albeit, of course, flawed) anti-poverty programmes. They have met their international debt, and are duly punished by exclusion of their cash-strapped anti-poverty programmes from the formal PRSP procedures and aid benefits. Indeed, they together received only 9.2 per cent of 1999 net aid disbursements (UNDP, 2001: 192–194). In theory, all HIPC flows are additional to other official aid and thus cost India's and China's poor nothing, but in practice this is not the case. Additionally, substantial aid donors – possibly the International Development Agency (IDA) (the division of the World Bank giving concessional aid to so-called low-income countries) and almost certainly the International Fund for Agricultural Development (IFAD) – are finding that their low-interest loans are being effectively, or in part, written off, and the rich countries have not responded by paying those aid donors back the full amount that they lose as a result of HIPC relief.

Even more worryingly, the PRSPs contain very few sector policies. The Papers follow the prevailing development 'dialogue' (perhaps more accurately termed 'narrative') that whether a country develops depends on its macroeconomic policy, particularly on determined liberalisation and globalisation. Whether or not that is *part* of the story – and, on the whole, evidence suggests that countries which liberalise do enjoy faster subsequent growth and poverty reduction – it is not the whole story; yet the design of the HIPC process and its PRSPs is so heavily concentrated on macroeconomic policies that it suggests the contrary. There are some PRSPs in which the words 'agriculture' and 'rural' (and indeed 'industry' and 'urban') cannot be found from cover to cover. There is little hard content in many PRSPs apart from trade, macroeconomic policy, and perhaps social sectors and safety nets. Especially if, as is usually the case, these emphases require retrenchment ('cuts') in public infrastructural spending in the short term, they may well conflict with any commitment to increase public resources, or improve private incentives, for activities and areas likely to benefit poor people. Anyway, the PRSPs seldom have much detail on the *production* implications of this – that is, on efficient means of shifting scarce public resources, or private incentives, to underpin sectors employing or feeding the poor. In short, most PRSPs need to be far more production sector specific if they are to have much poverty-reducing impact. (This in no way implies large-scale state involvement in production or regulation.)

Given these criticisms, however, the process contains three big steps towards making the world poverty target more feasible:

- The first is the consensus that the success or failure of the development process is going to be assessed through poverty reduction. That does not imply that nothing else matters – not that economic growth does not matter, because you cannot reduce poverty if you do not grow, not for very long anyway; nor that environmental sustainability does not matter. What *is* implied is that poverty reduction is the main thing to be monitored when we assess the cost-effectiveness of planned economic progress, or claims that it has been achieved.
- The second is that there is a country-led presence – it is the developing country itself that prepares the PRSP; its needs assessment does not come from outside. In practice, sometimes in the first round the country will bring in a consultant to write the Paper, but this is rarely the case. Even if it is, and a PRSP genuinely affects policy or mobilises resources, domestic politics make it unlikely to happen thereafter!
- The third is that civil society is recognised. In practice, 'civil society' is usually reduced to 'non-governmental organisations', which, excellent though they often are, are seldom directly accountable downwards, especially when they are not domestic but foreign or international. 'Citizen-based organisations' *are* accountable downwards, but in many countries they are thin, weak, or hamstrung by authority.

Feasibility

To determine whether the halving of world poverty by 2015 is feasible, we must look back to where we thought we were, and what has been achieved in the past. In 1990, the base year for the target, there were about 1.3 billion dollar-poor in the world, mainly residing in China (370 million), South Asia (495 million, mostly in India) and sub-Saharan Africa (240 million). Of the remaining, 70 million were in Latin America and rather small numbers were in transitional economies and in the Middle East (see Table 7.1, p. 152).

There is a huge concentration of poverty in rural areas – worldwide, 70 per cent of the dollar-poor are rural, and the percentage is much higher in sub-Saharan Africa (Ravallion, 2000). Of the dollar-poor's consumption (in cash and kind), some 65–75 per cent by value comprises food. Indeed, about half comprises staple foods (mostly rice, wheat and maize; also, especially in Africa, sorghum, millets, cassava and yams). Over 60 per cent of the dollar-poor in the world are still either smallholders or farmworkers in their main occupation, though most of them obtain additional income from other non-farm sources.

Table 7.1 Incidence of poverty in developing regions, 1990–2015 (assuming regional rate of change in 1990–1998 and 1998–2015 is identical)

	Incidence of poverty			*Change in incidence of poverty, 1990–1998*	*Population*
	1990	*1998*	*2015**	*R(1990–1998)***	*2015*
China	31.6	17.2	4.7	0.9268	1417.7
Other East Asia and Pacific	18.5	11.3	4.0	0.9402	717.5
India	45.7	44.2	41.2	0.9958	1211.7
Other South Asia	**	**	15.5	**	473.8
Europe and Central Asia	1.6	5.1	59.9	1.1559	478.3
Latin America and Caribbean	16.8	15.6	13.3	0.9908	624.9
Middle East and North Africa	5.7	5.5	5.1	0.9955	402.5
Sub-Saharan Africa	47.7	46.3	43.5	0.9963	873.8
Total developing and transitional countries	29	24	23.2		6200.3

Sources: World Bank (2000: 23, 334–335); UNDP (2000: 223–226, 285–286); South Asian data, pers. comm., Shaohua Chen and Martin Ravallion.

Notes

*   Projection of poverty incidence to 2015 if each country or region changes its annual incidence of dollar poverty at the same rate in 1998–2015 as in 1990–1998. As explained in the text, if instead the global level changes in dollar poverty 1990–1998 were used for the projections, it would understate global poverty in 2015 at 16.1% (rather than the 23.2% reported here).

** r(1990–1998): ratio, to its level in previous year in 1990–1998 assuming steady change, of proportion of people consuming below \$1.08 in 1993 constant purchasing power per day. This proportion is 'incidence of dollar-a-day private consumption poverty' (\$1.08 in 1993 purchasing power is approximately equal to \$1.00 in 1985 constant purchasing power). This was calculated separately for Bangladesh (incidence in 1990, 33.7%; in 1998, 21.7%; in 2015, 13.7%; 2015 population, 161.5 million), Nepal (42.2%, 31.0%, 16.0%; 32.7 million), Pakistan (47.8%, 32.5%, 14.4%; 222.6 million), Sri Lanka (3.8%, 5.4%, 11.5%; 21.9 million) and Afghanistan plus Bhutan (assuming 'South Asian poverty incidence' for 1990 and 1998; 32.7% of 35.1 million in 2015).

Therefore, big reductions in poverty are likely to be achieved by addressing rural poverty, in large part by reducing local food deprivation. Experience in many parts of the world has shown that rapid success in poverty reduction proceeds through employment-intensive rural development, usually based on rising yields of staple foods, and commonly associated either with initially not-too-unequal access to farmland or with land reform (IFAD, 2001). The urban poor benefit from this type of progress as well as the rural sector, since increases in food production lead to reductions in the price of food for urban food consumers, the share of whose income spent on food is also large. The pressure of migrants on urban labour markets is also less because it pays people to stay in rural areas,[11] and therefore the rate of increase in urban real wages rises in the formal as well as the informal sectors.

Moreover, rapid falls in poverty have been achieved, principally on the basis of rural agricultural growth, in large parts of Asia – notably the great river valleys of China, the deltas of India and the irrigated areas of Punjab and some other states in India – and in large parts of Latin America. In these areas between 1975 and 1990 there was very fast growth in the yields of staple foods, particularly rice, wheat and maize, and associated with that was very fast growth in the income and consumption of smallholders and farmworkers; the rural poor in affected areas enjoyed much higher incomes, for both small farmers and landless labourers, and the urban and the rural poor had cheaper food. Dollar poverty fell at the target rate in South Asia in 1975–1990; it fell faster in East and South-East Asia. In China in particular, extensive evidence suggests that over the period 1977–1985, large areas of the country experienced the fastest period of poverty reduction ever seen over such a large population of the world. Food production grew every year for six years by more than 6 per cent. At the same time there was massive land redistribution from formerly state- or commune-held land to family farmers under the Household Responsibility System; reduced price extraction by food quotas; and, as a result, a big shift in incentives towards food production, first for own and local consumption, later for the towns. This was not simple liberalisation: irrigation and irrigation management was provided by an effective state system, as were research-improved varieties, principally of rice and wheat. In contrast, poverty incidence has stagnated in sub-Saharan Africa, where there is little research in staple foods and only around 5 per cent of total crop land is irrigated (most of that being for wealthier farms in a few selected locations).

However, since 1990 there has been a sharp slowing-down in the rates of growth of production and yields of staple foods, of research inputs, and of irrigation facilities in the developing world. For instance, since the 1970s the rate of growth in output per hectare of staple foods has been 3 per cent per year; through the 1990s it was only 1.3 per cent (Lipton, 1999). To revive the unprecedented poverty reduction of 1975–1990, and to spread it to neglected areas, its basis in the growth of yields of labour-intensive staples needs revival also.

One very important development in agricultural technology in 2001 was the announcement by Dr Gurder Singh Khush, the great plant breeder at the International Rice Research Institute, of the New Plant Type, which has the potential to make a substantial difference to rice yields. However, getting progress comparable to that during the Green Revolution will require a substantial amount of work on water control and water management – both on pricing and technology – as well as a revival of the rate of improvement of seed development, particularly in semi-arid and non-water-secure areas (IFAD, 2001). It is difficult to see how that can be done without genetic modification (GM), which will require refocusing of the GM industry away from products (and traits such as herbicide resistance) of interest mainly to capital-intensive large farmers and food processors, towards staple foods (and traits enhancing yield and robustness to moisture stress) of interest mainly to the world's poor (see Lipton, 1999).

So what progress has been made in halving world poverty in 1990–2025 so far and, given these trends, are we on target? The agreed method of checking progress on world poverty reduction is from the 1990 and 1998 estimates of 'share of developing and transitional population living on less than $1 a day'[12] poverty in World Bank (2000: 23), derived from Chen and Ravallion (2000). This section reports these rates and asks: what progress towards the target of halving poverty by 2015 will be made *not* if the world changes substantially, but if 1990–1998 rates of poverty reduction continue in 1998–2015? It might be thought better to use information about distribution of consumption per person below the poverty line, at least in major countries or regions, and to estimate how a continuation of 1990–1998 country/region-specific growth rates of mean GDP would affect mean consumption and hence, assuming unchanged distribution, the proportions of persons below the dollar PPP poverty line.[13] Also, some sort of global or regional/national economic modelling might be attempted, seeking to estimate likely changes in rates of economic growth, income distribution, and hence dollar PPP poverty incidence. These methods have been tried by others; Hanmer and Naschold (2000) and Collier and Dollar (2001) use similar methods to estimate 2015 poverty incidence of developing regions on the basis of existing forecasts of annual GDP growth of these regions. However, such methods require heroic assumptions and/or pose forbidding requirements for information – and for understanding of quantified, durable, multi-country growth and distribution changes and transmission mechanisms. The results of these methods often produce projections of poverty considerably lower than those given here. However, it would seem unduly optimistic to assume that without substantial changes in policy, the climate for poverty reduction – in regard to global economic growth, trade liberalisation for developing-country exports, changes in labour intensity of production methods, etc. – will be much more favourable for the poor in 1998–2015 than was the case in 1990–1998. Will global growth be faster? Will its impact on global poverty incidence be systematically more? One could hardly rely on either, without substantial policy changes.

So, this section tries only to answer the question: if (1993 PPP dollar) poverty incidence changes in 1998–2015, in main countries and regions, at the same rate as in 1990–1998, what will the incidence be in 2015, and, therefore, how will the fall in 1990–2015 compare with the world poverty target? This is not a silly question, since it is not obvious that poverty trends in 1990–1998 globally were somehow 'special', distorted or misreported, in ways that invalidate the naive assumption that the global path of poverty reduction in 1998–2015 will be much the same as in 1990–1998, barring major policy shifts. The 1990–1998 national surveys used, which cover more than 90 per cent of the exposed population (i.e. that of developing and transitional economies), were carefully screened for coverage and method. The 1990–1998 trends do, however, contain two cases where extrapolation is more than usually questionable:

- The estimated decline of poverty in China to 17.2 per cent in 1998 depends almost entirely on a reported fall in incidence from 29.3 per cent in 1993 to 17.1 per cent in 1996,[14] as compared with a significant rise in incidence in 1987–1990, a slight rise (if any at all) in 1996–1998 and a much slower fall in 1990–1993. Other sources (UNDP, 2001: 149; World Bank, 2000: 280) give a higher estimate of China's 1998 dollar poverty incidence, at 18.5 per cent. This implies two things: first, that dollar poverty incidence in China rose in 1996–1998 by significantly more than our estimate suggests; and second, that if the rate of change in 1990–1998 is extrapolated to 2015 using this new evidence, this would mean slower poverty reduction than given in Table 7.1 – dollar poverty incidence in China would fall to 5.9 per cent in 2015 and global poverty would be estimated at 23.5 per cent in 2015; in other words, only 38 per cent of the poverty target would be met.
- In Eastern Europe and Central Asia, poverty incidence more than tripled, from 1.6 per cent in 1990 to 5.1 per cent in 1998 – this, too, largely happened in three years, 1990–1993.

As in all other cases, we crudely extrapolate that the annual rates of change in incidence in 1990–1998 will continue in 1998–2015. This adds a projected 270 million dollar-poor to the world's projected total in 1998–2015 from Eastern Europe and Central Asia, but deducts a projected 170 million for China. Of course, these numbers tell us only what will happen if past trends continue. Things will go better in some countries and worse in others, but the global picture of poverty reduction expectations, if 1998–2015 policies remain the same as those in 1990–1998, could be about right. There is no obviously better alternative projection – and no reason to believe the global rate of poverty change will 'bend' after 1998, for example that populations whose 1990–1998 poverty-reducing performance improves in 1998–2015 will sharply outweigh those whose performance deteriorates.

The first step is to estimate the 1990–1998 rate of reduction in poverty incidence, for populations of developing and transitional economies, from World Bank (2000: 23). If we do this for the *total* population, we would derive a rate of change that is useless for estimating future global rates of poverty change, even if the future is 'like the past'. By assuming that the global 1990–1998 rate of poverty incidence reduction will prevail globally after 1998, we imply that the whole world tends towards that rate. Why is this implication unacceptable?

- First, suppose China's reduction of poverty eventually takes incidence in China to almost zero; thereafter, there is unfortunately nothing to sustain the global rate of poverty reduction by causing China's fast (but now completed) rate of improvement to 'infect' very slowly improving regions such as sub-Saharan Africa. Similarly, suppose the sharp rise in poverty incidence in 1990–1998 in the transitional economies continues in 1998–2015: applying a global rate of change of poverty to all regions would assume that this somehow 'infects' other regions.

- Second, we need to allow for differential population growth among regions.

Some optimistic forecasts of global dollar poverty incidence based on the scenario that 'past trends are continued' may derive from erroneously extrapolating the *global* poverty reduction rate, instead of (as is correct) using each *regional* rate of poverty reduction to estimate that region's expected 2015 incidence, applying it to the region's projected 2015 population, and then calculating, as a weighted sum, 2015 global dollar poverty incidence. Global dollar poverty incidence was 29.0 per cent in 1990 and 24.0 per cent in 1998 (World Bank, 2000: 23). Incorrect 'global extrapolation' to 2015 would give an incidence of 16.1 per cent – close to the UN target of halving incidence to 14.5 per cent (in fact, going 90 per cent of the distance). Furthermore, incorporating the alternative estimates for China as well as more recent ones for India (see below) gives an estimate of 1998 global poverty incidence at 22.0 per cent, which extrapolates to 12.2 per cent by 2015 – implying that not only would the target of halving incidence be met, it would be exceeded by 16 per cent.

Ideally, we would estimate the 1990–1998 rates of change of each *country's* poverty incidence, and project this to 2015. This would assume not independence among countries, but that each country's dollar poverty incidence change affected each other country's incidence similarly before and after 1998. The information for this is not available except for South Asia. We otherwise project changes for each main World Bank region, but showing China and South Asian countries separately.

Having projected each region's poverty incidence to 2015, we estimate the 2015 population to which it applies from the UNDP *Human Development Report* (2000: 223–226).[15] We then estimate Indian, Chinese and regional poverty incidences and finally global incidence for 2015, all assuming that future incidence changes are at the same annual rate as past ones for India, China and each region. These projections are presented in Table 7.1. World poverty, instead of falling from 29 per cent in

1990 to 14.5 per cent in 2015, which is the target, falls to only 23.2 per cent, which in fact is only 40 per cent of the target. In other words, if each developing and transitional region (with China and each South Asian country treated as a separate region) is projected to change poverty incidence at the same annual rate in 1998–2015 as reported by the World Bank for 1990–1998, poverty incidence in developing and transitional countries in 1990–2015 will fall not by 14.5 per cent (from 29 per cent to half that) but only by 5.8 per cent (from 29 per cent to 23.2 per cent) – that is, achieving 40 per cent (or underachieving by 60 per cent) of the target. Some countries will be able to do better by 2015 and some worse. But we have no reason to believe that things are going to get so dramatically better that we go to 14.5 per cent in 1990. In order to go past 23.2 per cent poverty in the world by 2015 and reach the 14.5 per cent target, one of two things, or some combination of them, must be achieved: (1) the rate of 'world' economic growth must be 2.5 times faster between 1998 and 2015 than it was in 1990–1998; or (2) the rate of transmission of economic growth to poverty reduction must be 2.5 times better.

More recent provisional estimates for post-reform India (Datt and Ravallion, 2002; see also Sundaram, 2001; Deaton and Tarozzi, 2000), if confirmed, improve past performance, and hence the projection for 2015, somewhat: 'incidence of [dollar] poverty in India falls from 39.1 percent in 1993–1994 to 34.3 percent in 1999–2000' (Datt and Ravallion, 2002: 14). Using the same extrapolation techniques as above, this gives a trend rate that if maintained until 2015 would cut Indian poverty incidence to 24.7 per cent. The implication of this is to reduce the above estimate of 2015 global poverty by about a further three percentage points, contributing to an achievement of 62 per cent of the 'halving global poverty' objective – better than 40 per cent, as implied in World Bank (2000), but still far below target.

Getting back on track

Reviving progress on halving dollar poverty incidence by 2015 requires changes in policy both in developing and in developed countries. Several changes are needed to get back on track; they relate to process, to aid, to agriculture, and to rural development.

Process

The process needs to ensure that underperformance is recognised where it is happening. That does not just mean the *countries*, particularly in sub-Saharan Africa, which have (at best) been reducing poverty slowly, but also the groups within countries that have remained poor. Making monitoring serious at country level is a very important part of improvement of the process. Each recipient country needs timely information not only about who are the poor, but about where the poor are getting poorer and where they are getting less poor. This cannot be done with household income-and-expenditure surveys that happen once every ten years; nor with surveys, even if frequent, requiring several years of processing time; nor with national samples too small to permit reliable disaggregation. A few countries, including India, China and Indonesia, are in a position to provide data of the frequency and quality needed for serious poverty monitoring; most are not, and some of the poorest countries will not be for many years. Participatory poverty assessment can help, especially in such cases. What is needed is a comprehensive survey, for one year, of *both* household expenditure *and* a range of other, more quickly obtainable measures, known to be correlated with well-being, probably mostly gathered in a participatory fashion. The latter measures can then be calibrated into a 'best estimator' of measured narrow consumption poverty – now mainly incidence below a currency poverty line; increasingly, one hopes, intensity below a FEM poverty line – for that year.

In Ghana the Core Welfare Indicators Questionnaire (CWIQ) – a short questionnaire (it does not collect income or consumption data) administered to a sample large enough for reliable estimation at regional level – provides ten 'poverty predictors' that have been validated against the more comprehensive Ghana Living Standards Survey. Ravallion (1996) tests the predictive powers of such 'rapid appraisal' welfare questions against consumption data and concludes that, assuming a relationship holds between the two types, rapid appraisal proxies for poverty can be useful for monitoring of poverty when survey data are unavailable or inaccurate. But, he cautions, credibility is undermined by the problems of selecting weights for multiple indicators, particularly when actual consumption data do not exist, of potential sampling biases introduced where sampling methods are not rigorous, and, most importantly, of identifying a (large enough) set of variables that can explain a significant proportion of variation in consumption. However, until there is enough statistical capacity for frequent household expenditure surveys, carefully selected, quickly obtainable measures for various regions and groups should be gathered every year or two and used to estimate consumption poverty. The calibration between the measures and consumption poverty can change, and needs to be rechecked every five to ten years. Further, *carefully supervised* participatory methods can be applied to understanding whose poverty in many senses – not just measuring whose consumption poverty – is changing, how fast and why.

Even with perfect information about poverty trends, published swiftly, it does not follow that public action, by domestic or aid authorities, will be taken to reallocate resources, or to change policies. Nor is appropriate action always obvious. Suppose group or region A is cutting poverty at well above the target rate, and group or region B well below it. Should anti-poverty policy refocus on B (in greater need) or on A (where policy is better at reducing need)? Is it much costlier to reduce poverty by the same amount for B than for A? Was B's (or A's) poverty reduced by public action (or inaction) benefiting its poor people, or by their emigration from region, or group, B (or A)? For some groups or regions, poverty may be most cost-effectively reduced by easing migration controls, not by infrastructure, institutions or even policy improvements *in situ*. But reasonably reliable poverty data that are rapidly available and publicly discussed allow these questions to be asked, and appropriate pressures on the polity applied. Decent data can supplement 'peer pressure' from officials, academics or donors with poor pressure in civil society.

Aid

The value of aid in real terms (i.e. net aid disbursements as a proportion of OECD gross domestic product) is now 5–10 per cent less than in the late 1980s, and has fallen much faster in agriculture. The real value of aid to agriculture was almost two-thirds less in 1998 than 1988 (IFAD, 2001: 41). The main reason for this collapse in aid to agriculture, over and above the decline in total aid, is the fact that agriculture's share of project and sector aid has fallen sharply – from 20.2 per cent in 1987–1989 to 12.5 per cent in 1996–1998 (ibid.). Moreover, neither the public sector in the recipient countries, nor private investors, have anything like fully replaced the lost agricultural support that was formerly coming from aid.

Arguments for getting out of agriculture

Since aid to agriculture is falling so substantially, what are the reasons for reducing support to agriculture? Two main arguments are advanced. The first is fungibility: that aid supports government spending at the margin, the part of spending that government least wants to do. So, the argument goes, why aid agriculture if governments will only do less of it? This may be reasonable in some cases and in an international cross-section, but it is not a reasonable argument for some of the poorest countries of the world. In sub-Saharan Africa, as well as Bangladesh, where aid is more than public investment – indeed, a very large part of public expenditure, sometimes exceeding it – one cannot claim that aid to a sector simply displaces public investment in it. Furthermore, fungibility can be dealt with by sector agreements with the governments of the countries concerned, proceeding from the country's own PRSP, which, as argued already, should have sector policies in it. For two decades, some World Bank 'hybrid loans' to a sector have been tied to agreed expansions in publicly financed expenditure, providing infrastructure (including training and research) for that sector.

The second main argument is that falling world prices damage rates of return to some projects and sector spending in agriculture. This is less of a problem if the aid to this sector benefits principally smallholders and (via extra work on labour-intensive small farms and activities) farm labourers: if that is the case, there will be far less effect in glutting world agricultural markets, since quite a large proportion, though by no means all, of that extra income will be spent on food. Most of the evidence which has come in recently through the World Bank comparisons does not suggest a sharply falling rate of return on agriculture projects; the rate of return to agricultural research, in particular, has not come down between the 1970s and the 1990s (Alston *et al.*, 2000). That of course may be in part because there are fewer agriculture projects nowadays, and if old levels of spending were suddenly resumed, the rates would indeed fall. But these arguments need to be seen as problems to be solved, not as excuses to allow support to rural agriculture in aid programmes to collapse. It is hard to see how such a collapse is consistent with anti-poverty priorities, since it is on this sector that the bulk of the world's poor still depend for their livelihoods (IFAD, 2001).

Emphasis on rural development

We have said that rapid and significant reductions in global poverty of the order of magnitude necessary to reach the halving world poverty target by 2015 can realistically be achieved by supporting the rural poor and rural income-generating activities. The most important change is to reverse the collapse of support for labour-intensive staples farming in smallholdings, and to help revive the performance of smallholders in the developing world, in particular in the area of food production for local consumption. There is, however, a serious counter-argument against this view that agriculture, particularly local food production, is the way forward. This originates from the rationale of liberalisation – the outcome of which is that each producer specialises in what they are relatively good at producing and exchanges it with the 'rest of the world' – and the observation that there is generally more rapid growth outside agriculture than inside. However, in the early stages of transition out of extreme poverty, rapid progress has almost always started with a breakthrough in food production for local, or nearby, consumption. There is no reason why it should stop with that – cash crops, the non-farm sector, industrialisation are the paths to development that work – but they do not work usually before that initial breakthrough in food production has happened.

The appropriate policies to support rural development will differ from place to place. However, the *Rural Poverty Report* (IFAD, 2001) emphasised several key strategies for rural development:

- Reverse urban bias in public service provision and support rural education and health. Supporting education will help break the inherited cycle of poverty and lack of education.

- Increase access to physical assets such as improved farm technology, water and land. This will reinforce the long-term poverty-reducing aspects of 'human asset' policies such as health and education. Land reform (which, incidentally, can be achieved consensually with a supporting land fund that enables the poor to buy from large farmers) may be the best way to provide protection for those without physical assets against the risk of falling into extreme poverty.
- Improve communications and transport infrastructures and access to marketing and extension services for rural communities, particularly in sub-Saharan Africa. This will improve poor people's access to markets to sell goods and acquire production inputs (including credit), and, through greater access to information, their bargaining power. Better infrastructure will also improve access to public services.
- Complement such infrastructure policies (which can be regarded as emphasising incentives to increase/diversify production) with policies that enable yield increases and diversification, such as irrigation projects and agricultural research into staple foods. Agricultural research must favour technologies that are labour-intensive if the impact on poverty reduction is to be maximised.

Conclusion

This chapter has assessed the definition, process and feasibility of the UN target of halving the incidence of dollar poverty in developing and transitional countries in 1990–2015. If China, each country in South Asia, and each other region changes incidence in 1998–2015 at the same rate as in 1990–1998, then overall dollar poverty incidence will fall from 29.0 per cent in 1990 to 23.2 per cent in 2015. This is only 40 per cent of the UN target reduction of halving world poverty to 14.5 per cent incidence. More recent estimates for India and China provide a slightly brighter picture, suggesting that we will reach around 60 per cent of the target, but this is still well below what should and, with the right policies, could be achieved globally. The halving of poverty does remain feasible in Asia and Latin America over the 1990–2015 horizon, and, with suitable agricultural technology and other policies, in sub-Saharan Africa too. However, we are not at present on track; we are quite a long way behind it. That is not because the process or the definitions are inherently flawed, but because we have not fully recognised the effort needed in agriculture and the rural sector. Re-emphasising employment-intensive agricultural and rural growth, especially of staple foods, and asset distribution can revive faltering progress towards the targeted halving of world poverty.

Notes

1 Thanks to Howard White for useful comments. All remaining errors are ours.
2 About 95 per cent of people in developing and transitional economies are covered by household income-and-expenditure surveys permitting periodic estimation of the proportion in dollar poverty. The so-called 'developed' world is not included; absolute dollar poverty hardly exists in those countries.
3 This oversimplifies: (1) there is a complex chain-linking procedure among national, regional and global bundles; (2) national pricing is not (as would be ideal) of the consumption bundle typical below each nation's dollar-poverty line, but of its mean gross domestic product (GDP); (3) rankings of countries by dollar poverty, and its rate of change, are significantly affected by whether the base date for PPP estimations is, say, 1985 or 1993. For an account of the difficulties and possible routes to progress, see the May–August 2002 debate at www.socialanalysis.org between Sanjay Reddy and Thomas Pogge (see the summary of their 'How Not to Count the Poor'), and Martin Ravallion of the World Bank.
4 Most countries in Africa and South Asia, where there are a lot of poor people, look much poorer than they are if we estimate dollar poverty as the proportion with below US$1 a day *at official exchange rates*. That is because US$1, exchanged into (say) rupees or renmimbi, buys more (four to six times in most low-income countries) of the world consumption bundle than does US$1 in the USA.
5 Other minor amendments could be suggested. In principle, private consumption of public and subsidised goods and common property should be included; this is seldom done in household surveys, from which measures of those in dollar-a-day private consumption poverty are now derived.
6 See Reddy and Pogge (2002). Even the shift from 1985 to 1993 as the base-year for selecting the PPP consumption bundle makes a big difference to the numbers counted as dollar-poor in some countries, notably China.
7 There are three main objections to the food energy method (FEM)-based poverty line:

   (a) 'People do not live by calories alone.' FEM does not assume that they do, but assumes that – at the level of consumption at which a person decides to 'just about meet' calorie requirement – he or she also decides to allocate resources so as to 'just about meet' other basic needs. The assumption is, in effect, that *consumers' decisions normally reveal preferences, which are first directed towards meeting 'basic needs', balanced among types (food, shelter, etc.) appropriately for each particular person's survival and functioning.* This 'needs-oriented revealed preference' assumption is likely to be close to reality for people near the margin of poverty. To survive at all, they have to use resources reasonably rationally. There are of course diversions due to addiction, debt, unpredicted change in needs or income, waste or error; but for poor and near-poor people, such diversion is less tolerable, since it constrains their already tight expendable resources. FEM, unlike PPP, selects poverty lines that respond to a basic need for functioning (the need for food, occupying some 65–75 per cent of the budget of the poor) in the context of the need to spend on other basic needs for functioning. And FEM, unlike the cost of basic needs (CBN) approach, avoids assumptions about the 'correct' mix of consumption goods – assumptions that are paternalistic, unlikely to be similarly applicable to all persons, and unresponsive to the fluctuating needs of a family near the margin of survival.

   (b) 'FEM ignores within-household allocation of resources for food (and other basic needs).' In some countries, many households discriminate against girls aged 2–4, providing them (relative to need) with less food than other household members. An 'FEM poverty line' could, in such countries, understate the consumption per equivalent adult at which *all* household members achieve food adequacy. However, this objection (assumed fair division of consumption among household members) applies to all consumption-based fixed poverty lines. FEM at least allows the problem to be measured: in 'gender-discriminatory' populations, caloric adequacy for all household members is achieved at higher household consumption than elsewhere, so the FEM line (properly measured) is also higher. This allows the costing of socially determined gender misallocation – as, indeed, that of addiction, or of interest on debt.

(c) 'FEM-based lines privilege consumer decisions, e.g. about food, that reflect not need but choice, maybe luxury choice.' Using FEM instead of CBN recognises revealed preference, but the flip side is that the 'FEM-poor' in some areas – but not others – include those habituated to costly diets and thus calorie-underfed even at high consumption levels. Even poor people can be pushed (e.g. by convenience of prepared snacks for male casual workers, pressures on women's cooking time, or peer pressure on children) to buy costly calories. This has sometimes led to 'necessary consumption levels for caloric minima' – FEM poverty lines – set absurdly higher (over 70 per cent at one stage in Indonesia) in urban than in rural areas, leading to gross underestimation of rural, relative to urban, poverty. However, such grossly food-inflated FEM estimates are unusual, fall when urban survey techniques improve, and in part reflect genuine needs (e.g. urban snacks at work, when work is far from home).

8 See the discussion of China on p. 155.

9 In 1990–1998 the poverty gap index fell by 19.7 per cent for the total population of developing and transitional countries (10.7 per cent excluding China), as against 17.3 per cent (6.7 per cent) for incidence (Chen and Ravallion, 2000: tables 2, 4).

10 All this leaves open the issue of participatory versus top-down ways of assessing poverty. However poverty is measured, the role of participatory methods is an important but separate issue (see Chapter 5).

11 Successful farm growth first absorbs labour but eventually releases it, raising townward migration. However, this is not the desperate pressure of rural workless on urban labour markets; it is the migration of hope, not of despair.

12 In fact, US$1.08 in constant 1993 purchasing power. Globally, this poverty line corresponds roughly to US$1 a day in constant 1985 purchasing power, used in many earlier estimates. However, for some countries, the change of PPP base may significantly alter poverty estimates or even trends.

13 An apparently obvious point, appearing to justify or even to demand this procedure, is fallacious. It might be thought that growth of mean consumption must, of itself, increase the responsiveness (elasticity) of PPP dollar poverty to *future* growth of mean consumption – because earlier growth normally pulls the poor nearer and nearer to the dollar poverty line, so that a given amount of extra mean consumption pulls more people above the line (this would be even more the case for each successive 1 per cent of steadily rising mean consumption). However, this ignores the facts that a large proportion of the poor become so (or become even poorer) in any given year, and that those left in poverty by growth are likely to be those with most difficulty in escaping poverty through growth. Certainly, though there is no systematic link between growth and overall distribution, there is also no tendency for dollar poverty incidence to become more elastic to mean growth of consumption or of GDP; for example, these elasticities appear to have fallen somewhat in India as between 1975–1989 and 1992–1997.

14 This would have reduced the number of Chinese poor by 138.4 million – 40 per cent of the 1993 number, and over 10 per cent of the *world's* poor – in just three years.

15 To estimate the populations of *World Development Report* (WDR) regions, we adjust the populations of *Human Development Report* (HDR) regions where they have different membership (UNDP, 2000: 285–286; World Bank, 2000: 334–335). The main differences are the following: 'Developing East Asia and Pacific' (WDR) excludes Singapore and Hong Kong but includes Korea (Democratic Republic); the opposite is true of the (otherwise almost identical) HDR 'developing countries in East Asia, South-East Asia and the Pacific'. WDR's 'Developing South Asia' includes Afghanistan but not Iran; HDR reverses this. WDR's 'Developing Middle East and North Africa' differs from HDR's 'developing Arab States' by including Iran and Malta, and excluding Kuwait, Qatar, the United Arab Emirates and Sudan (the latter counted in 'developing sub-Saharan Africa' by WDR, whose sub-Saharan Africa definition otherwise matches HDR's). WDR's 'developing and transitional Europe and Central Asia' include Bosnia and Herzegovina, the Yugoslav Federal Republic (Serbia and Montenegro) and Turkey, but exclude Slovenia; HDR's 'developing Eastern Europe and the Commonwealth of Independent States' reverses this. In each case we use the HDR projection for the 2015 population of the WDR region (UNDP, 2000: 223–226), since WDR regions are used in poverty projections (World Bank, 2000: 23).

References

Alston, J., Chan-Kang, C., Marra, M.C., Pardey, P.G. and Wyatt, T.J. (2000) *A Meta-analysis of Rates of Return to Agricultural R&D: Ex Pede Herculem?*, International Food Policy Research Institute (IFPRI) Research Report 113, Washington, DC: IFPRI.

Chambers, R. (1997) *Whose Reality Counts? Putting the Last First*, London: Intermediate Technology Publications.

Chen, S. and Ravallion, M. (2000) 'How Did the World's Poorest Fare in the 1990s?', Policy Research Working Paper 2409, Washington, DC: World Bank.

Collier, P. and Dollar, D. (2001) 'Can the World Cut Poverty in Half? How Policy Reform and Effective Aid Can Meet International Development Goals', *World Development*, 29(11): 1787–1802.

Datt, G. and Ravallion, M. (2002) 'Is India's Economic Growth Leaving the Poorest Behind?', Policy Research Working Paper 2846, Washington, DC: World Bank, 11 February.

Deaton, A. and Tarozzi, A. (2000) 'Prices and Poverty in India', Research Program in Development Studies, Princeton University, Version 4, mimeo, 29 July.

Foster, J., Greer, J. and Thorbecke, E. (1984) 'A Class of Decomposable Poverty Measures', *Econometrica*, 52: 761–765.

Hanmer, L. and Naschold, F. (2000) 'Attaining the International Development Targets: Will Growth Be Enough?', *Development Policy Review*, 18: 11–36.

International Fund for Agricultural Development (IFAD) (2001) *Rural Poverty Report 2001: The Challenge of Ending Rural Poverty*, Oxford: Oxford University Press.

Lipton, M. (1999) 'Reviving Global Poverty Reduction: What Role for Genetically Modified Plants?' Sir John Crawford Memorial Lecture, Washington, DC: Consultative Group on International Agricultural Research.

Ravallion, M. (1996) 'How Well Can Method Substitute for Data? Five Experiments in Poverty Analysis', *World Bank Research Observer*, 11(2): 199–221, August.

—— (2000) 'On the Urbanisation of Poverty', Université des Sciences Sociales (Toulouse) and World Bank, mimeo, 6 February.

Reddy, S. and Pogge, T. (2002) 'How *Not* to Count the Poor', mimeo, Columbia University, at http://www.socialanalysis.org.

Sundaram, K. (2001) 'Employment and Poverty in the 1990s: Further Results from NSS 55th Round Employment–Unemployment Survey, 1999–2000', *Economic and Political Weekly*, 112 (11 August): 3046.

United Nations Development Programme (UNDP) (2000) *Human Development Report 2000*, New York: Oxford University Press.

—— (2001) *Human Development Report 2001*, New York: Oxford University Press.

World Bank (2000) *World Development Report 2000/2001*, New York: Oxford University Press.

8 Towards universal primary education[1]

Christopher Colclough

Introduction

The Universal Declaration of Human Rights, adopted by the United Nations (UN) in 1948, stated that primary schooling should be free and compulsory in all nations. More than fifty years later, the world still has far to go in order to achieve this goal. The Millennium Development Goals' reaffirmation of the aim of achieving schooling for all by 2015, and of gender equality in schooling by 2005, again risks failure, particularly in the poorest regions of the world. The challenge is greatest in the countries of sub-Saharan Africa, where scarcely half the eligible children attended primary school at the turn of the century. This chapter examines some of the main causes of this disappointing progress, and indicates the main policy changes needed if the development goals for education are to be met.

Why should societies seek to educate everybody?

At the outset it is worth recalling the very many ways in which education underpins the development process. Its impact is strong, particularly for the lower levels of schooling. The following generalisations are broadly supported by a large body of research:

- *Education is productive.* It more than repays its costs to society. Social returns are high, particularly at primary and junior secondary levels, and particularly if estimates for externalities are included. It provides one necessary ingredient for economic growth.
- *Primary education can directly help to alleviate poverty.* Literacy and numeracy are key instruments with which to help the self-employed, including those who are farmers, to increase their incomes. Providing the poor with human capital can represent a very targeted form of spending: once created, the enhanced human capacity cannot be taken away (except, perhaps, over the very long run, via obsolescence).
- *Primary education also brings important gendered benefits.* Better-educated

women incur larger costs if they have children, and have greater incentives to have smaller families. They are also better able to control their own fertility. World fertility surveys in thirty-eight countries show a decreased number of children born, lower total fertility rates and smaller desired family size for one to three years, four to six years and seven-plus years of schooling compared with none. This relationship is strong and widely documented at both macro and micro levels.

- *There are other palpable social benefits primarily arising from educating girls and women.* The possession of more years of schooling by the female population is associated with lower infant and child mortality. Child nutrition is higher and school attendance itself is more strongly related to the education of mothers than of fathers. Thus at the margin, the education of girls can be said to have an even higher social priority than that of boys.
- *People also want education for its own sake.* It increases their choices, both in work and leisure, and is thus an important consumption good. Thus notions of justice and equality underpin its status as a human right.

Accordingly, on grounds of consumption, production, distribution and rights, the Millennium Development Goals in education – achieving universal primary enrolment by 2015 and gender equality in enrolments by 2005 – can be given a strong and well-defended endorsement as important targets for all countries.[2] The above generalisations imply that they are also fundamental to the achievement of the other Millennium Development Goals. Poverty alleviation, infant and child mortality, fertility and sustainable development are all crucially influenced by the skills delivered by schooling being widely held.[3] Thus the education goals, in the long term, are important to achieving all the others.

What do the targets mean – and what would count as success?

The criteria for meeting the two education goals were set out, in some detail, by the Organisation for Economic Cooperation and Development (OECD) in 1996. As the following summary indicates, they are specific and demanding.

Conditions for achieving universal primary education by 2015

- Net enrolment rates (i.e. the percentage of children of primary school age actually enrolled in school) of 99 per cent by 2015. We should note that even in industrialised countries there are reasons why not all eligible children can go to school. Some are prevented from doing so by illness, some are educated at home and some are absent for other reasons. Accordingly, typical net ratios at primary level for the USA and European countries are 96–98 per cent. Thus a target of 99 per cent for all countries looks ambitious.

- Completion rates (i.e. the percentage of Grade 1 pupils who subsequently complete four years' schooling and who proceed to year 5) of 99 per cent by 2015. This is also highly ambitious, and, in combination with the first criterion, would seem to require universal Grade 1 enrolment by 2011.
- Literacy rates of 100 per cent amongst 15- to 24-year-olds by 2015. This indicator is included as a measure of the quality of schooling. Although, strictly speaking, literacy does not have to be delivered by schooling, in practice primary education is the only viable instrument for achieving widespread and permanent literacy in the younger age groups. Yet if this is so, the criterion becomes even more demanding than the first two, requiring universal Grade 1 enrolment and continuation by 2005 for it to be achieved.

Conditions for achieving gender equality

The following are the conditions for achieving gender equality:

- A ratio of girls to boys in primary and secondary schooling of 1:1 by 2005. Given the high levels of existing inequality between the enrolment of males and females, this target will almost certainly not be achieved in many countries by 2005.
- A ratio of literate females to males, over the ages of 15–24 years, of 1:1 by 2015. This requires both parity in Grade 1 enrolments and in subsequent continuation rates by 2005, which, as indicated above, looks impossibly ambitious.

What progress has been made so far?

All discussions of progress to date are hampered by a lack of data. The data are not only weak, but often severely delayed in becoming available. The United Nations Educational, Scientific and Cultural Organisation (UNESCO) has the task of collecting and publishing data on education systems world-wide. But many countries take several years to provide the statistics; when they do, they are incomplete, and those that are provided are often erroneous. These problems are greater in the poorer countries, where the gaps between targets and outcomes are greatest. Thus in Africa the most recent pupil enrolment data available in mid-2002 related to the position in 1997. Even for that year, 15 per cent of countries were unable to provide estimates for their gross enrolment ratios (GERs) for primary schooling, and one-quarter could not provide net ratios (UNESCO, 1999).[4] Many more could not provide information on intakes to school, on public expenditures or on efficiency measures. No recent data of any reliable kind exist for Nigeria, which accounts for 20 per cent of the population of sub-Saharan Africa. So, the data published by UNESCO are based upon samples of countries reporting, which are not necessarily representative of those that do not. The picture, then, is almost certainly worse than it seems. What does it tell us?

Table 8.1 shows trends in GERs by region. These data give an indication of the capacity of school systems. Traditionally, universal primary enrolment has been taken to be achieved when the GER has reached 100. But because systems are so inefficient, late enrolment and high rates of repetition result in about 20 per cent of pupils in developing countries being outside school age. So, GERs of 100 are consistent with 20 per cent of children being out of school. There is a need, therefore, to move to using net ratio data, but these are not yet reliably available on a trend basis.

The years 1965–1980 were a 'golden age' for the expansion of primary enrolments. The table shows that GERs for all developing countries taken together increased from 78 to 95 over those years, and it looked as though universal primary education was within reach. In sub-Saharan Africa, expansion was remarkable – almost doubling from 41 per cent to 77 per cent of the age group, catching up with South Asia over those years. Things changed, however, in the 1980s and 1990s. Latin America and East Asia experienced steady enrolment increases from an already high base. South Asian enrolments grew strongly. The Arab states, on the other hand, made only small progress. But sub-Saharan Africa experienced a decline in GERs, which re-attained their 1980 level only in 1997. For much of the last two decades of the century, both the proportion and the number of African children out of school increased, with their numbers being around 80 per cent higher in 2000 than they had been two decades earlier.

As regards gender equality, Table 8.2 shows that this has not been achieved in any developing region. The countries of Latin America, the Caribbean and East Asia have a 10 per cent excess of boys enrolled. The difference in other regions, however, is between 20 and 30 per cent. In

Table 8.1 Trends in primary gross enrolment ratio (GER) by region and gender, 1965–1997

	1965	1980	1990	1997
Sub-Saharan Africa	41	77	73	77
Arab States	n.a.	80	84	85
Latin America and Caribbean	98	105	107	114
East Asia and Oceania	n.a.	110	118	118
South Asia	68	77	91	95
Developing countries	78	95	99	102

Source: UNESCO (1998, 2000a).

Note
n.a., not available.

Table 8.2 Female enrolments at primary level in developing countries, relative to male enrolments (per cent), 1980 and 1997

	1980	*1997*
Sub-Saharan Africa	78	82
Arab States	73	80
Latin America and Caribbean	87	91
East Asia and Oceania	83	92
South Asia	66	73
All developing countries	79	84

Source: UNESCO (1998, 2000a).

South Asia, girls' enrolments have been growing quickly. Although the gender differential remains highest in this region, female GERs increased rapidly after 1980. Male GERs in South Asia are over 100, and some narrowing of gender differentials can be expected if policy reforms are continued. The countries of sub-Saharan Africa saw only a slight improvement towards gender equality of enrolments over the period 1980–1997 – and even then for the 'wrong' reasons: throughout the period the average female GER in sub-Saharan Africa remained roughly unchanged at around 68 per cent of the age group. Thus the gender gap narrowed because boys were withdrawn from school faster than girls over the two decades.

As a result, at the turn of the century sub-Saharan Africa had the lowest ratios of both girls and boys in school of all the developing regions, and there had been little or no progress in sub-Saharan Africa towards meeting the education Millennium Development Goals over the previous twenty years. It should be recalled that these data refer to gross enrolments. Net ratios in Africa are scarcely higher than 50 per cent, so about half of the primary-aged children in sub-Saharan Africa remained out of school. Projections of the trends implied by Table 8.1 suggest that, with no change in current rates of population growth, by 2015 the total number of children out of primary school by 2015 would fall from around 125 million to around 80 million – that is, numbers would be absolutely reduced by one-third, and schooling for all would not be achieved. Moreover, there would be a tremendous change in the regional composition of underenrolment. In particular, the number of children out of school in South Asia would be dramatically reduced – from around 60 million to about 7 million children. By contrast, those out of school in sub-Saharan Africa would increase absolutely (by about 25 per cent) and they would account for almost three-quarters of all children out of school. Thus on present trends, three out of four out-of-school children will be African by 2015 (Watkins, 1999).

Accordingly, whether or not the Millennium Development Goals for education will be achieved is likely to depend to a significant extent upon what happens in Africa. Whether, in turn, Africa can achieve the targets depends upon whether the causes of past trends can be removed or changed. We therefore need to try to understand how it is that sub-Saharan Africa has had such a dismal record in the recent past. What has caused these outcomes, can they change and, if so, how?

Causes of enrolment outcomes in sub-Saharan Africa

Supply issues

We know that at a macro level, a number of economic variables jointly determine both the number and the proportion of children attending school. These comprise society's expenditures on schooling, the average cost per student and the size of the school-age population. The greater the first of these and the smaller the last two, the greater the proportion of children who will be enrolled in school. What has been happening to these variables in sub-Saharan Africa?

Public spending on education rose to more than 5 per cent of gross national product (GNP) during the 1990s. This was high in comparison with other developing regions, and similar as a proportion of GNP to levels in the countries of Europe and North America (UNESCO, 2000a: 118). Spending on primary schooling was also high, receiving 2 per cent of GNP in sub-Saharan Africa, compared to 1–1.5 per cent in Latin America and Asia during the 1990s.

However, although commitment to public spending on education, on average, was strong, the region's capacity to generate increased resources for education was weakened by economic decline. Total education spending in current dollars increased by only 40 per cent in sub-Saharan Africa from 1980 to 1997. By contrast, in India it increased by 150 per cent, in Latin America it almost tripled and in East Asia it quadrupled over those same years. Thus a reduced relative commitment to public spending on education in South Asia still allowed increases in the value of real public spending per pupil. In sub-Saharan Africa, on the other hand, economic decline meant that it fell sharply and perilously – partly explaining the dismal enrolment progress of the region in recent years.

Furthermore, although sub-Saharan African countries, on average, can be said to have made greater efforts to achieve schooling for all children in recent years, this is by no means true of all of them taken individually. To demonstrate that this is so, Table 8.3 shows aspects of the costs of, and expenditures upon, primary schooling for a group of sub-Saharan African countries with GERs less than 100. All those having the relevant data are shown in the table, for the most recent available year. As indicated, according to UNESCO regional data, countries in sub-Saharan Africa were allocating, on average, about 2.0 per cent of GNP to public expenditures on primary schooling during the early 1990s. The (unweighted) average value for this variable, for the sub-set of countries and years shown in Table 8.3, was 1.9 per cent, indicating that they were not atypical of the

Table 8.3 Sub-Saharan African countries with gross enrolment ratios (GERs) less than 100: public expenditures on primary schooling and related characteristics

	Year of data	GER	Female GER as percentage of male GER	GNP per capita 1995 (US$)	Expenditure as percentage GNP	Unit costs	Population size	Expenditure required for GER = 100
	(1)	(2)	(3)	(4)	(5)	(6)	(7)	(8)
Low commitment – low cost								
Eritrea	1996	54	83	180	0.6	8.5	13.6	1.2
Guinea	1995	48	54	540	0.7	8.9	16.6	1.5
Madagascar	1990	84	98	240	0.7	5.9	14.8	0.9
Ghana	1990	77	83	370	0.8	6.3	16.8	1.1
Chad	1996	65	52	210	0.9	8.3	16.1	1.3
Zambia	1995	89	99	350	0.9	4.7	20.9	1.0
Central African Republic	1990	66	64	350	1.2	11.0	16.0	1.8
Senegal	1996	69	82	550	1.2	10.4	16.2	1.7
Comoros	1995	74	n.a.	440	1.4	11.1	17.3	1.9
Mauritania	1996	83	90	450	1.5	10.9	16.1	1.8
Low commitment – high cost								
Burkina Faso	1985	27	59	220	0.7	16.2	16.5	2.7
Mali	1995	34	66	250	1.0	16.9	16.5	2.8
Ethiopia	1996	37	57	110	1.2	20.8	16.2	3.4
Gambia	1990	64	68	350	1.3	14.2	14.6	2.1
Burundi	1990	73	84	150	1.5	13.4	15.8	2.1

Moderate commitment – high cost

Mozambique	1990	67	75	140	1.9	21.3	13.3	2.8
Djibouti	1990	38	71		2.0	32.2	16.1	5.2
Côte d'Ivoire	1996	71	74	670	2.1	17.7	16.7	3.0
Tanzania	1985	75	97	160	2.1	14.6	19.4	2.8
Benin	1995	72	57	350	2.5	19.5	18.0	3.5
Lesotho	1994	99	114	670	2.6	14.2	18.7	2.7
Kenya	1990	95	97	260	3.2	14.0	24.2	3.4
Average		66	77	334	1.5	13.7	16.8	2.3
Francophone average		62	71	368	1.3	14.0	16.4	2.3
Anglophone average		83	93	360	1.7	11.3	15.9	1.8
Sub-Saharan Africa Average		83	83	777	1.9	13.6	17.0	n.a.

Source: GNP per capita 1995, Atlas method World Development Indicators 2000 CD-ROM. All other data, *UNESCO Statistical Yearbooks* (1998, 1997, 1996, 1994), Paris.

Notes

n.a. not available.

Low Commitment = GER <100 in years shown *and* where public spending on primary <1.9 per cent of GNP.

Col. 5 = public spending on primary as a percentage of GNP.

Col. 6 = publicly funded costs per primary child expressed as a percentage of income per capita.

The calculated averages for sub-Saharan Africa, and for the francophone and anglophone groups, use all countries that have the relevant data, not just those in the table.

region as a whole. However, each of the first fifteen countries in the table was allocating, in the early to mid-1990s, substantially less public spending to its primary-school system than this sub-Saharan Africa average (column 5). Thus, as a group, they can be considered to have been demonstrating only a low commitment to its provision.

Many of these 'low-commitment' countries also had extremely low primary enrolments, with nine of them having GERs less than 70 (column 2). Furthermore, many of them were also spending very modest sums per pupil (column 6). In six of them, this was equivalent to less than one-tenth of income per capita (compared to an unweighted average value of 13.6 per cent for sub-Saharan Africa as a whole). Such low average per-pupil expenditures imply that for the first 'low-commitment, low-cost' group of ten countries shown in Table 8.3, universal provision of schooling (as proxied by GERs of 100) would have been easily affordable. The last column of the table indicates the amount of public spending on primary schooling, expressed as a proportion of GNP, which would have been required to achieve GERs of 100 in each country (assuming the mainte-nance of the average schooling costs and population sizes prevailing in the base year, and no demand constraints). It can be seen that the 'required' expenditure value for universal primary education in this first group, under these assumptions, would in no case have exceeded 1.9 per cent of GNP – the amount spent by the 'average' country in sub-Saharan Africa on primary schooling. Furthermore, in many cases the required financial allocation would have been much lower. It can be seen that the governments of Eritrea, Madagascar, Ghana, Chad and Zambia would have needed to allocate little more than 1 per cent of GNP for universal provision of schooling to have been achieved. This was equivalent to only about one-half of the average public expenditure allocations made by other sub-Saharan Africa countries at that time.

Unit costs

These comparisons indicate that the level of primary enrolments attain-able with a given aggregate expenditure depends upon the costs per student at primary level. Although on average in sub-Saharan Africa, public expenditures per student amounted to the equivalent of about 14 per cent of income per capita in the early 1990s, its variance was substan-tial across countries – from about 5 per cent of income per capita in Zambia to over 20 per cent in Ethiopia, Mozambique and Djibouti. In some countries, high unit costs can act as a severe constraint, preventing the achievement of universal school enrolment. For example, the middle group of five countries shown in Table 8.3 would have been unable to reach GERs of 100 even if public spending had increased to its regional average value, because all of them had relatively high unit costs. These 'low-commitment, high-cost' countries mainly spent considerably more, per primary pupil, than the average across sub-Saharan Africa. Although universal primary education was still financially practicable for them, a higher proportion of GNP would need to have been allocated for this purpose than the average for sub-Saharan Africa. Burkina Faso, Mali and Ethiopia were particularly affected by high costs: if per-pupil expenditures were to have remained unchanged, between 2.7 and 3.4 per cent of GNP would have been needed to secure universal provision. Accordingly, for these countries, some combination of increased public spending on primary schooling and reduced unit costs would probably be necessary if schooling for all were to be achieved in the near future.

A further group of the low-enrolment countries were spending more on primary schooling than the others, yet were still heavily constrained by high costs of school provision. Enrolments in this third group of 'moderate-commitment, high-cost' countries were not mainly limited by an unwillingness to commit public resources to primary schooling: each of them was allocating 2–3 per cent of GNP for these purposes in the years shown. Rather, enrolment growth was constrained by their primary systems being relatively expensive, in comparison with their levels of economic development. In a majority of these countries – Kenya, Benin, Côte d'Ivoire and Djibouti – between 3 and 5 per cent of GNP would have been needed in order to achieve universal provision of the system (column 8). Here again, strategies to reduce unit costs would be critically important if affordable expansion were to be secured.

The main determinants of the unit costs of primary schooling are teachers' salaries and pupil:teacher ratios. This is particularly so in Africa, where only a small proportion of recurrent spending is typically available for non-salary items. Accordingly, the substantial differences in costs shown in Table 8.3 are the result of country diversity in the values for these two elements. For example, where teacher earnings are high and pupil:teacher ratios are relatively low (as in Ethiopia), both need adjustment so as to allow costs to fall. By contrast, where teacher earnings are low and pupil:teacher ratios are high (as in Zambia), unit expenditures may need to increase so as to achieve a better quality of primary provision.[5] A wide range of values for each of these elements exists, requiring different policy responses in each case.

We can conclude that a good number of sub-Saharan African countries have not allocated sufficient resources to primary schooling: their commitment has been insufficient to secure universal provision. More than half of these countries could reach universal primary education by such spending changes (assuming that average and marginal costs did not differ sharply). Others would need additional resources or reduced costs. A final group has been constrained by both costs and resources, and would find the shift to universal primary education very difficult to achieve in the absence of much greater levels of external support.

Demand issues

Much of the international attention given to achieving universal primary schooling has been focused upon ways of increasing the supply of schools and teachers so as to provide the opportunities for all to attend. However, it is clear that this is often an insufficiently nuanced approach because it tends to ignore the problems of demand. This has a number of dimensions.

First, the objective of securing universal primary education needs to embrace the notion of school quality. Schools where classes are over-crowded, and where provision for desks, teaching aids and textbooks are each inadequate, are unlikely to be able to meet the learning needs of most children. The achievement of primary schooling for all would require both net enrolment ratios in the high 90s (implying GERs greater than 100 over the medium term) and an acceptable and evenly distributed level of school quality. This objective needs to replace the easy but over-simplified emphasis on the attainment of GERs of 100, which has been widely used in the literature to indicate the attainment of universal primary education.[6]

Second, as suggested earlier, the effort to reduce the costs of schooling, so as to make universal provision more affordable, can endanger school quality. In that context, it is noteworthy that the first six countries shown in Table 8.3, all of which were demonstrating low levels of commitment to public spending on primary schooling in the early 1990s, also had very low unit costs of school provision at that time. Whilst, as indicated earlier, this means that the costs of universalising the system were modest, it also suggests that the quality of primary school provision in those countries may have been much too low.[7]

Under these circumstances it is likely that the present level of average costs sharply underestimates those required to secure universal enrol-ment. In other words, there may be a significant difference between average and marginal unit costs, particularly where school quality is cur-rently very low. There are, in any case, good reasons to suppose that the costs of enrolling the final 10 per cent of an age group will be higher than the average for the rest of the population. Often the people concerned live in small or isolated settlements, in regions with difficult communica-tions, or include minority or migrant populations who cannot be catered for in the same way as other groups. But an additional, and often over-looked, problem is that those who are out of school may prove difficult to enrol because they do not believe that school attendance – at current levels of school quality – would be in their interests. Although it is a mistake to assume that public expenditures per pupil automatically provide a proxy for school quality, in practice, and in the short run, it is often very difficult to secure improvements in quality without some increase in expenditures. This generates a dilemma. Although universal provision may seem affordable at current cost levels, it may well actually require a significant increase in both total and unit expenditures. In the absence of the latter, a demand response may not appear. For example, in Malawi there was initially a massive expansion of enrolments in the mid-1990s associated with a shift to fee-free primary schooling. However, there have been recent sharp falls in enrolment, which appear to be related to reductions in unit expenditures by government and resulting low, and declining, quality of provision (Kadzamira and Chibwana, 2000: 16ff.; Rose, 2002).

As the above discussion implies, demand issues, as well as those of supply, are important in determining enrolment outcomes. In countries where households face substantial direct and indirect costs in sending children to school, policies that seek to reduce such costs can be expected to have a positive impact on demand. Experience shows that at the macro level the price elasticity of demand for schooling is quite high. Those countries that have reduced or abolished fees at primary level have witnessed significant increases in demand for places – particularly where school quality has been maintained. However, it remains the case that poverty can still be decisive: poor households need their children to contribute to the household economy, and these opportunity costs can often be significantly higher than the direct costs of school attendance. In such circumstances the benefits of schooling to households need to be palpable if the costs are to be overcome and the children are to be sent to school.

Nevertheless, the opportunities for policy to affect outcomes are substantial. One way of considering its potential impact is to look at the variance of enrolment outcomes amongst countries at different levels of income per capita. As we would expect, primary GERs tend to be lower for poorer countries. However, even at rather low incomes, some countries achieve high enrolments (Figure 8.1). Most of the sub-Saharan Africa countries are concentrated in the US$300–500 per capita range, where GERs range between 30 and well over 100 for countries at similar levels of income. Thus countries with low incomes per capita need not necessarily have to have low school enrolments: policy, or country history and circumstances appear to make a difference.

A further critical demand-side issue is that of gender. It is well established that low primary-school enrolments are associated with large gender gaps, and that gender inequality reduces as gross and net enrolments grow (Colclough *et al.*, 2000, forthcoming). In one sense they have to do so: for net enrolment rates to be sustained at over 50 per cent, female enrolment has to be higher than zero. But the range again is large. Tanzania and Benin, for example, have had similar GERs (around 70), yet the ratio between female and male enrolments in Tanzania has been close to 1, compared with only 0.45 for Benin. The difference is not accounted for by poverty, since income levels per capita in Tanzania have been considerably lower than in Benin. Rather, Tanzania has had a long-standing

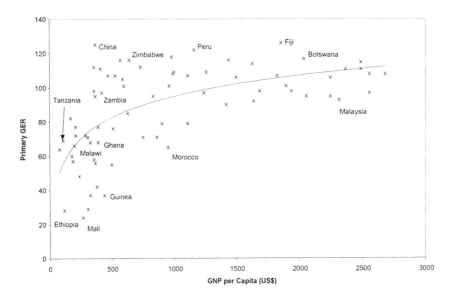

Figure 8.1 Scatter plot of primary gross enrolment ratio (GER) against GNP per capita, 1990: low- and middle-income countries.

social policy which has asserted the equality of men and women, advocated their equal need to have attended school, and established incentives to encourage that result (Peasgood *et al.*, 1997).

Evidence from nine African countries indicates the central importance of gender-focused reforms if the demand for schooling is to be maintained during the move towards schooling for all. These cannot be properly discussed in a chapter of this length. However, they would need to encompass reforms focused on the household – where the gendered division of labour is the major source of differential opportunity costs, and where parents have less direct incentive to educate girls if future material support comes mainly from sons. Reforms aimed at improving school conditions are also required – where inadequate facilities, inadequate toilets, harassment (both in school and *en route*), teacher male-bias, and the allocation of school tasks all disadvantage girls. The labour market, too, is an important site of discrimination – where formal or informal job reservation for males is widespread, where wages are lower for girls and where there are few female role models. Finally, reforms focused on changing broader traditions in society – where women's roles are expected to be centred on the family, and where early marriage robs many girls of incentives to stay in school, or even the possibility of doing so – will also be required. It can be shown that many of the relevant gender-focused, demand-side reforms cost little. But they are as central to the success of policies to achieve schooling for all as are those which focus on the supply side.[8]

The national reform process and the role of aid

The needs to increase public expenditures to finance the expansion and qualitative improvement of primary school systems, to remove school fees and to increase the incentives for the attendance of girls provide a demanding agenda for many of the poorer developing nations. Many of them will require the implementation of substantial reforms to improve the utilisation of existing resources, and to reduce costs in ways that do not compromise quality. Most analyses suggest that the potential for reducing costs and for increasing domestic resources is substantial. Efficiency savings appear capable of reducing the expenditures required for primary schooling for all by between 10 and 20 per cent, whilst in some countries the potential savings are very much greater (Colclough with Lewin, 1993: 205–241; World Bank, 2002). Equally, many countries would be capable of increasing their expenditures on primary schooling substantially. Nevertheless, even if feasible policy reforms were fully implemented, and if expenditure priorities were reassessed, financing gaps would remain, particularly in much of sub-Saharan Africa.

A wide range of estimates of the costs of achieving universal enrolment have been made. They vary from US$2.5 billion per year for forty-seven 'most at risk' countries (World Bank, 2002) to US$4.5 billion (Colclough with Lewin, 1993), $9 billion (Delamonica *et al.*, 2002) and as high as $10–15 billion (World Bank, 2001) for all developing countries taken together.[9] However, these magnitudes are not strictly comparable, since all estimates of additional costs have to make assumptions concerning the amount of policy reform to be undertaken by each country. Some estimates adopt a 'no change' scenario by calculating the additional resource costs of enrolling all of the (growing) primary age group, over a determinate number of years, at present levels of unit costs. Others build in sets of policy reforms affecting both costs and expenditures, which substantially change the implications for net additional resources required. Where governments did not implement reforms affecting revenue sources, efficiency gains and expenditure priorities, the requirements for external financing would often be two or three times as large as those estimated.

This means that the search for a single estimate of the additional resources required from external sources to achieve primary schooling for all is probably misplaced. Recent work, for example, shows that annual aid to education in eight African countries would need to increase by around 2.5 times recent levels, depending upon the assumptions made for national revenue and expenditure growth over the next fifteen years (Colclough *et al.*, forthcoming). Thus the amount of additional aid required to achieve universal primary education will be substantial, but its precise dimensions are very sensitive both to the particular countries included in the calculation, and to the extent of policy reform each of them can be expected to achieve. The search for agreement on one global estimate may be useful for purposes of advocacy – to raise expectations in the North about the scale of desirable resource transfers needed to enable the education targets to be achieved. But all estimates have to be premised upon a particular amount of policy change occurring. How much will or can happen for each country is impossible to predict, and we are left with a financing range, from aid sources, which is uncomfortably large.

The first communiqué from the 'High Level Group on Education for All' – a group of national and agency representatives convened by UNESCO – reaffirmed that 'no countries seriously committed to education for all will be thwarted by a lack of resources' (UNESCO, 2001). Yet the experience of aid to education in the first decade since the 1999 Jomtien Conference on Education, where the 'Education for All' initiative was launched, leaves room for scepticism: the hopes raised by the promises of increased support made at that time have not been realised. At the end of the decade, educational aid from all sources amounted to about US\$8 billion – roughly in the middle of existing estimates for the additional costs of achieving primary schooling for all. Thus total aid to education may need to double in real terms, to focus entirely upon the primary system, to be refocused upon a sub-set of countries mainly in Africa, and to support primarily recurrent costs. Notwithstanding recent commitments, these are strong demands. They occur at the end of a decade when aid to education from bilateral and multilateral sources actually fell by more than 30 per cent from 1990 levels. Particularly hard hit was sub-Saharan Africa, where, for example, World Bank International Development Agency (IDA) loans to education in 1999 were running at half their real value at the start of the decade. Suggested reasons include the presence of political turmoil in some of the larger countries; the weak absorptive capacity of key institutions; the reluctance of some governments to introduce policy reforms; and too much aid focus having been placed on basic education (which, it was implied, does not easily absorb large amounts of money) (World Bank, 2001). It is not clear that these factors are quickly disappearing in sub-Saharan Africa – the region facing the greatest challenges to achieving universal participation in primary schooling.

Conclusion

The ways in which the Millennium Development Goals for education are formulated, and the particular criteria established to indicate their successful implementation, need to be adjusted. The most obvious problem is that the gender target for achieving equality of enrolments by 2005 is simply impossible to achieve. Because gender inequalities in schooling have roots going well beyond the education sector, the possibilities of achieving substantial reform, in the many countries affected, so as to quickly facilitate this objective are remote. At best, most countries will move towards gender equality only with their achievement of universal primary education, and the likelihood that the gender parity targets will be able to be achieved much before 2015 is low.

The quantitative targets for universal enrolment by 2015 are achievable, but a 99 per cent net enrolment rate is higher than many rich countries achieve. Targets for completion rates of 99 per cent and for universal literacy amongst 15- to 24-year-olds actually imply the need for universal enrolment at much earlier dates than 2015. These too need to be softened, to enable realistic interim targets for progress towards primary schooling for all to be employed.

The agenda for reform, however, remains substantial. National governments will need to implement new efficiency measures, together with quality, demand-side and, particularly, gender-focused reforms. A substantially increased spending commitment will also be needed on the part of many governments. This will need supplementation by clearly targeted and increased aid from the North. Broad sectoral support will be required, flexibly delivered on a recurrent basis, and conditional not only upon stated intention to reform, but also upon actual implementation. The political economy of these changes is complex, and it is by no means clear that their net implications will be supportive. Nevertheless, the dimensions of the problem are clearer than in the past, and the mechanisms for implementation are more articulated than in the past decade. These factors, at least, present some opportunity for success.

Notes

1 This chapter has benefited from comments from Samer Al-Samarrai and Howard White. The author is responsible for remaining errors.
2 A further, rather topical reason for ensuring the provision of schooling for all has recently been suggested by a leading UN staff member: 'Across the Muslim World from West Africa to Asia, Islamic schools moved in as the state primary education system failed. This set in chain a process which resulted in the fundamentalist groups replacing governments as the focus for popular loyalty, and gave the terrorists their support structure' (Malloch-Brown, 2001). This suggests the importance of filling the educational space that may otherwise be captured by fundamentalism.
3 The perceived usefulness of education to individuals is importantly influenced by the opportunities available to them. Thus whereas in the 1960s the possession of a primary education still influenced a person's chances of getting a formal-sector job – particularly in sub-Saharan Africa – this is no longer the case. It is secondary and higher levels which now provide that access. Furthermore, many people may be unaware of the other non-wage private benefits of primary schooling, mentioned above. For these reasons, the possibility of influencing the demand for primary education may turn out to be just as important a factor in achieving the Millennium Development Goals as policies to influence its supply. These topics are discussed separately later in this chapter.
4 Gross enrolment ratios express total enrolments as a percentage of the number of children in the eligible age group. Net ratios exclude those pupils from the numerator who are outside the official school age range.

5 For further detail on these and other countries in sub-Saharan Africa, see Colclough *et al.* (forthcoming).
6 This notion of the importance of school quality, though absent from the wording of the Millennium Development Goals, is present in the six 'Dakar' Goals for achieving 'Education for All'. There, the second goal explicitly states that 'by 2015 all children ... should have access to, and complete, free and compulsory primary education of good quality'. Moreover, the sixth goal focuses upon 'improving all aspects of the quality of education and ensuring excellence so that recognized and measurable learning outcomes are achieved by all' (UNESCO, 2000b: 8). To judge by these stated intentions, then, quality issues will not be overlooked by the Education for All movement, notwithstanding their more summary interpretation by the Millennium Development Goals.
7 Separate evidence demonstrates that this was so in Zambia, Ghana and Guinea (Colclough *et al.*, forthcoming).
8 Full discussion and evidence can be found in Colclough *et al.* (forthcoming).
9 Colclough with Lewin estimated the external requirements for primary schooling for all as US$2.5 billion in 1990 prices. This is roughly equivalent to US$4.5 billion at 2000 prices.

References

Colclough, C., Rose, P. and Tembon, M. (2000) 'Gender Inequalities in Primary Schooling: The Roles of Poverty and Adverse Cultural Practice', *International Journal of Educational Development*, 20: 5–27.

Colclough, C., Al-Samarrai, S., Rose, P. and Tembon, M. (forthcoming) *Achieving Schooling for All in Africa: Costs, Commitment and Gender*, Aldershot: Ashgate.

Colclough, C. with Lewin, K. (1993) *Educating All the Children: Strategies for Primary Schooling in the South*, Oxford: Clarendon Press.

Delamonica, E., Mehrotra, S. and Vandermoortele, J. (2002) 'Is EFA Affordable? Estimating the Minimum Cost of Education for All', mimeo, New York: UNICEF.

Kadzamira, E. and Chibwana, M. (2000) *Gender and Primary Schooling in Malawi*, Brighton: Institute of Development Studies.

Malloch-Brown, M. (2001) Speech reported in *The Independent on Sunday*, 11 November.

Organisation for Economic Cooperation and Development (OECD) (1996) *Shaping the 21st Century: The Contribution of Development Cooperation*, Paris: DAC.

Peasgood, T., Bendera, S., Abrahams, N. and Kisanga, M. (1997) *Gender and Primary Schooling in Tanzania*, Brighton: Institute of Development Studies.

Rose, P. (2002) 'Cost-Sharing in Malawian Primary Schooling: From the Washington to the Post-Washington consensus', DPhil thesis, University of Sussex.

United Nations Educational, Scientific and Cultural Organisation (UNESCO) (1998) *Statistical Yearbook 1998*, Paris.

—— (1999) *Statistical Yearbook 1999*, Paris.

—— (2000a) *World Education Report 2000*, Paris.

—— (2000b) *The Dakar Framework for Action*, World Education Forum (Dakar, Senegal, 26–28 April 2000), Paris.

—— (2001) Communiqué from the first meeting of the High Level Group on Education for All, Paris, mimeo, October.

Watkins, K. (1999) *Education Now: Break the Cycle of Poverty*, Oxford: Oxfam International.

World Bank(2001) 'A Chance to Learn: Knowledge and Finance for Education in Sub-Saharan Africa', Africa Region Human Development Working Paper Series, Washington, DC.

—— (2002) 'Achieving Education for All by 2015: Simulation Results for 47 Low-Income Countries', mimeo (processed), Washington, DC: World Bank, Human Development Network.

9 Promoting gender equality

Ramya Subrahmanian

Introduction

What do the Millennium Development Goals represent for advocates of gender equality in development? 'Gender' features explicitly in the Millennium Development Goals in two ways: in relation to improvements in maternal health, and to the elimination of gender disparity in education. Education is doubly emphasised, as it is also viewed as a vehicle for promoting gender equality and empowerment. Improved educational status, increased share of women in wage employment in the non-agricultural sector, and the proportion of seats held by women in national parliaments are represented as indicators of the increased gender equality and empowerment of women. The goals of poverty and hunger eradication and reduced child mortality, however, are framed with no specific reference to gender, although some agencies report gender-disaggregated indicators.

That gender equality and the empowerment of women figure as a specific goal in the Millennium Development Goals can be celebrated as symbolic of the significant impact of feminist advocacy over many years in making the case for gender-aware development. However, at the same time, much cautionary evidence exists of the often rhetorical value of statements on gender: language has often changed without significant commensurate changes in institutional practices or financial commitments, and policies targeted at redistributing opportunities to women have not expanded to the extent necessary to address gender discrimination in development. The reduction of a form of differentiation and inequality that cuts across sectors to one goal in a list is problematic for the conceptual purist. It suggests a false and misleading separation between 'gender', on the one hand, and development processes and outcomes in a range of arenas on the other, when in fact the two intersect to perpetuate patterns of inequality between women and men across the range of development goals. To the pragmatist, however, the specification of gender equality in any global statement represents a step forward, further imprinting gender equality as a non-negotiable component of development. It offers more, and perhaps new, spaces to continue manoeuvring for greater financial and programme attention to gender equitable outcomes, and serves as a lever for demanding greater accountability from governments and agencies.

This chapter seeks to locate an analysis of gender in the Millennium Development Goals within a broader assessment of the use of such targets in international development. Current literature on the Millennium Development Goals indicates that there is much awareness of their limitations, stemming partly from the fact that these goals crystallise the commitments of donor agencies, and thus serve primarily as shorthand for inter- and intra-donor communications. As a pithy summary of the chief concerns facing the development agenda, the Millennium Development Goals signal two significant features of the new consensus: the acceptance of a multidimensional approach to poverty reduction (White, 2001), and the importance of basic human well-being and good-quality basic social services as a non-negotiable goal of development intervention.[1]

Some cynicism arises from the fact that targets have been set before, but never met (White, 2001). Goals and targets flag destinations or the finishing line, but not the route. They emphasise outcomes, but yield no insight into the processes that are necessary to ensure that these outcomes are achieved. The Millennium Development Goals are a selective prioritisation of some goals over others. In some cases they specify inputs and outputs; in others they tell us about desired outcomes (McGee, 2000). They sketch assumed pathways and causalities between ends (desired outcomes) and means (inputs and outputs) but are not helpful in illuminating the complexities and multiple dimensions of lived poverty that often obstruct efforts to reduce poverty. These limitations can be viewed as benign, outweighed by the importance of having clearly defined goals governing international development co-operation, or they can be viewed as significant, representing a weakly developed agenda with the associated danger of deflecting attention from promoting the types of pro-poor reforms that are really necessary to make a substantial dent in world poverty.

However, the Millennium Development Goals may be somewhat different from other 'target'-based approaches. Although it is quite obvious already that most of the Millennium Development Goals are unlikely to be reached within their specified time-frames (Hanmer and Naschold, 2000; Hanmer and Wilmshurst, 2000; McGee, 2000; White, 2001; and Chapter 6 of this volume), they provide a strategic talking-point for assessing what the barriers to the achievement of goals are, and provide a tool with which to hold both donor agencies and governments accountable (White, 2001, 2002).

Millennium Development Goals also need to be discussed within the context of enhanced efforts towards increasing donor collaboration. As is argued in Chapter 3 of this volume, the UK's Department for International Development (DFID) has internalised these goals to the extent that organisational restructuring is taking place around the attainment of the goals. New policy instruments such as Poverty Reduction Strategy Papers (PRSPs) and sector-wide approaches also represent efforts to pool donor resources for which a prior agreed common framework of goals is essential to avoid the fragmentation of earlier project-based management approaches (Mehrotra, 2001; White, 2002). Again, however, these approaches and instruments have strengths and limitations that need to be assessed carefully. While on the surface these priorities may be viewed as international commitments of both donors *and* governments, arising as they do from a range of conferences and meetings, there is the danger that they will be imposed as a fixed set of priorities on national governments as part of new aid agreement processes and frameworks. If the Millennium Development Goals dictate in a standardised fashion what aid is spent on, without contextualised priorities negotiated at national and sub-national level, then they provide an insufficient analytical map for enabling appropriate gender-aware means to be identified for poverty reduction. Thus means and ends, and goals and institutional processes need to be looked at as intersecting and hence inseparable for the purposes of assessing the usefulness of the Millennium Development Goals in development co-operation.

There are many levels on which the Millennium Development Goals can be assessed from a gender perspective: the *political value* of such international statements; the *substantive value* of the ways in which goals and targets have been set and identified; the *institutional contexts* within which they are likely to be implemented; and the *wider social, political and economic contexts* within which these identified global problems arise and are perpetuated. This is a huge terrain for assessment, but this chapter will touch on aspects of all these levels. The approach followed is to focus on the current context within which these goals are being promoted within development co-operation.

A central concern is whether the way in which gender equality is articulated in the Millennium Development Goals is sufficient to ensure translation into concrete strategies that benefit women and address discriminatory barriers to greater equality in the distribution of benefits and outcomes across the range of goals. Gender awareness and gender equality are both important means *and* ends in development. Specifying gender equality as an end is important, but cannot be achieved without ensuring that the means used in development are gender aware and address equity and equality considerations at every step of the way. Thus the conceptual frame of gender within the Millennium Development Goals provides an entry point for raising questions about what kinds of interventions are best placed to achieve these rather ambitious and broad goals. The next section lays out the ways in which gender equality is articulated and defined in the goals. The adequacy of these goals is reviewed in the light of recent evidence of the challenges that remain in securing gender equality. The analytical sufficiency of the target approach in addressing the multidimensional characteristics of poverty and the social complexities of gender relations is assessed against the backdrop of broad trends in achieving progress towards gender equality. In the subsequent section, attention is focused on the changes in aid management approaches and practices that are aimed at addressing the limitations of earlier project-based funding. The prospects for integrating gender into these new approaches need to be especially assessed in the light of the considerable experience of what we may call first-generation approaches to gender mainstreaming.

Gender in the Millennium Development Goals: an assessment

The substance of gender

The presence of gender within the Millennium Development Goals reflects the impact of long-standing efforts to mainstream gender into development thinking and planning. Feminist advocacy efforts have long 'questioned the presumed gender-neutrality of formal institutions' (Razavi and Miller, 1995: 2) and have fought for the inclusion of gender equality on grounds of justice and merit, not just need (Kabeer, 1999b). The shift towards justice as a primary rationale is yet to take root, but the arguments against viewing women merely as instruments of development have been made persistently, and have succeeded in some measure in transforming the ways in which gender is now promoted by development agencies. Early integrationist approaches had tended to 'add' women to development projects in sex-specific ways,[2] not questioning the division of labour and resources that systematically keep women in a position of relative dependence upon men in a wide range of aspects of life. The influence of efforts to 'mainstream' gender into the mandates, structures, routine practices and procedures of development organisations is somewhat evident in the Millennium Development Goals: clearly it is now acceptable for donor agencies to commit themselves to gender equality and women's well-being as goals with intrinsic value for achieving development.[3] This marks a transition, in rhetoric at least, from the earlier focus on investing in women solely in terms of the returns it would bring to development – gender equality appears as both means and ends of development in the Millennium Development Goals, albeit in very particular and rather limited ways. As Kabeer notes, the persuasiveness of claims that investing in women has policy pay-offs has made major agencies, most notably the World Bank, unlikely champions of women's empowerment (2001: 17). However, as Jackson (1998) reminds us, gender has been assimilated into development thinking in particular ways, and the assimilation has not always reflected the richness and diversity of gender analysis.

'Gender' enters the Millennium Development Goals in two ways: goals that are gender aware, and those that are gender specific (see Table 9.1).[4] It is important to distinguish between these as ways of assessing how gender is addressed, both to pinpoint the analysis that underpins gender within the Millennium Development Goals, and to indicate the potential for transforming unequal gender relations within efforts aimed at achieving the goals. The goal of universal primary education is gender aware to the extent that it explicitly mentions both boys and girls, signalling that closing the gender gap is a key means to achieving full universal primary education. In addition, the Millennium Development Goals include goals that are gender specific – that is, they specifically promote the interests of women, in ways that transform unequal access to political and economic opportunities. The choice of access to non-agricultural wage employment, and representation in national parliaments, as indicators of women's empowerment and enhanced gender equality appears, at one level, a relatively random selection out of the range of possible indicators for measuring equality and empowerment. However, their inclusion in this list merits closer attention. A positive interpretation suggests the recognition of the importance of promoting non-traditional opportunities for women that challenge ideologies that restrict women to traditional, often sex-specific, roles in society. In the case of women's economic participation, this is indeed a crucial indicator signalling the extent to which women have equal opportunities with men, and can move out of labour-intensive and often unpaid forms of employment. The improved representation of women in national parliaments, on the other hand, can be seen as a truly international choice of indicator, as the representation of women in parliaments is relatively low world-wide, and does not follow any of the usual divides: North/South; developed/developing.[5] The choice of maternal health is perhaps significant too; it suggests an intrinsic value placed on women's health (albeit the health of women in their maternal role), as opposed to merely seeing them as the means for improved child welfare.[6] However, a more realistic interpretation that suggests itself is also that the

Table 9.1 How gender enters the Millennium Development Goals

Gender-aware goals	Gender-specific goals
Achieve universal primary education, for boys and girls alike	Promote gender equality and empower women (through education, increased labour force participation of women in non-agricultural sectors; improved representation of women in national parliament)
	Improved maternal health

Source: Adapted from Kabeer (1999b).

emphasis on quantifiable indicators in the Millennium Development Goals limits the choice of indicators to those that are measurable.

To translate goals into results, however, requires more than the adoption of the right language. The *content* of agencies' understanding of development issues remains critical (Jackson, 1998). While the term 'empowerment' may embody the most noble results for women that can be desired, debates on how to promote this outcome have emphasised the inextricable connections between a wide range of resources and entitlements and the importance of processes to enable women to exert agency and exercise voice.[7] Kabeer (1999a, 2001) has been influential in pointing out the limitations of efforts to define empowerment in ways that are amenable to measurement and quantification. While it has clearly become desirable for agencies to claim that they are 'empowering' women, efforts to show results in this regard have led to methodologically flawed and reductionist approaches to both defining what empowerment means and claiming success.

A notable, and disappointing, feature of the Millennium Development Goals is the gender blindness of the goal of eradicating income poverty in particular. The poverty goal aims at reducing the poverty and hunger of populations at large without either specifying the target group or indicating that these phenomena may be differentially experienced by men and women across ages. The goals and indicators are framed in aggregate terms, neither necessitating nor reflecting gender-disaggregated analysis. However, as much of the literature on gender and poverty has discussed, poverty remains a highly gendered phenomenon, and in ways that are not captured by income or head-count measures. As Cagatay (1998: 3) notes, the concern with gender in poverty throws up three possible hypotheses, not necessarily mutually exclusive: the suggestion that women have a higher incidence of poverty than men; and/or that the incidence of poverty among women is increasing compared to men; and/or that women's poverty is more severe than that of men. These indicate that poverty can be assessed in terms of individual capabilities[8] as well as outcomes that are fostered through gender relations, and played out through processes and practices of households and other institutions. In other words, outcomes of poverty are embedded in processes and relations, and attempts to measure or address them must do the same.

The additional value of separating out these three elements is to point to the importance of evidence-based analysis in identifying whether women are indeed poorer than men, as the term 'feminisation of poverty', used widely as shorthand for discussion of gender and poverty issues, seems to imply. As Jackson (1998) argues, development agencies have been keen to collapse gender concerns within the wider category of poverty, as doing so enables the use of a fairly depoliticised and needs-based discourse as requiring focus on women *within* poor households, rather than gender disadvantage *per se*. However, analysis of the intersections between gender and poverty remains challenging, as they do not conform to broad generalisations.[9] At one extreme, measures of poverty focused on the household as a unit have obscured the intensified and differential experience of poverty by women within poor households (Kabeer, 1997); at the other extreme, awareness of gender asymmetries in access to resources has been expanded into the generalisation that all households headed by women must inevitably be poorer than those headed by men (Jackson, 1998; Whitehead and Lockwood, 1999). Seeking simple conflations of women with poverty, either through assuming they are affected as much as are their male kin by processes of impoverishment, or through assuming they are always more negatively affected, is unsatisfying and analytically potentially misleading. The variations in the correlations between female headship and poverty within and between countries indicate the need for nuanced, context-specific research.[10] Feminist scholars argue that gender ideologies permeate structures of economic and social reproduction and hence are an intrinsic feature of processes of impoverishment; this in turn will differentially impact the ways in which women and men experience poverty, and may or may not increase the likelihood of individual women being poorer than individual men. Thus while gender disadvantage may not determine economic status, poverty often intensifies gender disadvantage (World Bank, 2001a). Further, generalised statements about gender and poverty serve to demonstrate the rhetoric of commitment to gender, while at the same time obscuring from policy attention the continued forms of disadvantage that women in *non-poor* households face (Cagatay, 1998).

The above discussion seeks not to diminish the importance of focusing on poverty reduction in the Millennium Development Goals, but to emphasise the importance of including gender awareness within the framing of this particular goal. Gender-aware poverty reduction entails not just counting how many women are income-poor relative to men, but taking account of the multidimensionality of poverty and the embeddedness of poverty in gender relations. Feminist advocates have significantly influenced emphasis on the multiple dimensions of poverty and made forceful arguments against relying purely on income and head-count measures. They have long argued for approaches that recognise that poverty is reproduced through inequitable distribution practices within the family and other institutional domains, and have pointed out consistently that social norms and customs underpin economic processes. Yet approaches that are developed continue to fall short of the complexity required to understand gender in its relational sense, rather than as a characteristic of individuals. Despite appearing to build on a multidimensional approach to poverty, the Millennium Development Goals fall short in terms of mapping out a sufficiently coherent approach to poverty reduction. Again here, the emphasis on measurable indicators is likely to continue to limit the possibilities for the Goals to deal more comprehensively with complexities. The danger is, however, that these limitations will spill over into interventions that cite the Millennium Development Goals as their guiding light.

Elson (1998) articulates this problem in relation to the introduction of gender into the basic growth model, pointing to the tendency to conflate gender analysis purely with gender disaggregation. While gender disaggregation is important, for us to get a sense of relative deprivations and differences, analysis needs to go far beyond:

> The basic problem with disaggregation is that it focuses on the separate characteristics of men or women (whether individuals or groups) rather than the social institutions of gender as a power relation.... The danger is that it does not draw sufficient attention to the reciprocal determination of the characteristics of women and men as economic agents.... It would be useful to consider strategies which pose the issue of economy itself as a gendered structure, rather than as a gender-neutral structure within which men and women undertake different activities.
>
> (Elson, 1998: 160)

Further, gender disaggregation may highlight divisions of roles, but remain uninsightful in respect of the variations in configurations of power, authority and entitlements that arise in different geographical and socio-cultural contexts. The danger of standardisation of analysis of the factors that give rise to gender inequalities must be avoided, and it can be done only if management systems are responsive and open to learning and absorbing lessons about what causes change. However, the development of guidelines, checklists and measures seems to indicate a tendency towards standardisation and reduction, rather than encouragement of analytical diversity and expansion of categories.

Thus while gender equality and women's empowerment find room in the Millennium Development Goals, it is striking that the means to achieving these are identified specifically in the area of maternal mortality and education. This indicates that the key pathways that donors are pursuing towards gender equality and empowerment of women are in relation to health and education. In some senses this is a hangover from the past – a continuation of the association of women with social sectors, and with issues of reproduction.[11] This bias is not just a feature of the Millennium Development Goals; Rodenberg (2002: 2) notes that the World Bank's comparative evaluation study of PRSPs discusses gender aspects only in relation to 'the classic sectors of education and health, while the study sees no relevance for these aspects in central sectors like agriculture, the environment, transportation and urban development'. The World Bank evaluation report (2002) notes that the Bank's assistance for poor women in economic development[12] has been minimal, restricted to one-quarter of projects outside health and education. Social funds were also found to have lacked a gender strategy.

One measure of change, however, is the extent to which the shift from instrumental rationales to recognition of the intrinsic worth of gender equality as benefiting both men *and* women has taken place. The brief overview of the way in which gender is framed within the Millennium Development Goals indicates some movement away from instrumentalist goals, but also points to a persistent fallacy or error that is made in relation to the rationales and methods through which gender is addressed in development. The shift from 'women in development' to 'gender and development' was fought for precisely on the grounds that being concerned about 'gender' was not just about recognising the disadvantages that women faced relative to men in gaining access to resources, benefiting from investments and allocations of resources, and participating equitably, but also about recognising the ways in which gendered ideologies shaped the ways in which a range of institutions reproduce inequalities and asymmetries. While the rhetoric of 'engendering development' has spread widely within development institutions, whether the practice has remains to be seen, and is an issue that will be taken up in greater detail on p. 198.

Evaluating progress

Other chapters in this book provide assessments of the progress made in achieving the specific targets relating to education, maternal mortality and reproductive health (see Chapters 8 and 11). In this sub-section the focus will be on providing the wider context of progress in achieving gender equality. The selective focus of the Millennium Development Goals contrasts sharply with the wider agenda elaborated at the Fourth World Conference on Women in Beijing in 1995, which was influenced by the advocacy of women's movements around the world. The latter contains twelve areas of action[13] cutting across all aspects of development. It is this broader agenda that merits reporting on, as an indicator of the areas in which change has taken place, and where the status quo remains the most entrenched.

The question of 'progress' depends very much on what it is that is being valued. For example, the human capabilities approach, outlined in the work of Amartya Sen, but most notably in relation to gender inequalities in the work of Martha Nussbaum, sets out an approach towards identifying the universal basic social minimum that allows for 'a life that is worthy of the dignity of the human being', arrived at by focusing on central human capabilities – that is, 'what people are actually able to do and to be' (Nussbaum, 2000: 5). Such an approach entails evaluating the opportunities and liberties available to people in the widest sense of the terms.

A brief 'report card' is presented in Table 9.2, drawn from the Humana World Human Rights Guides of 1986 and 1992, which construct indicators of changes in gender equality in terms of three sets of interlinked arenas:

Table 9.2 Regional achievements in gender equality

Region	Political and legal rights		Social and economic rights		Rights in marriage and divorce proceedings	
	Ranking 1985	Relative change in 1990 over 1985	Ranking 1985	Relative change in 1990 over 1985	Ranking 1985	Relative change in 1990 over 1985
OECD	1	No change	2	No change	1	No change
Europe and Central Asia	2	Decline	1	Decline	2	Decline
South Asia	3	No change	7	Slight improvement	5	Slight improvement
Latin America and the Caribbean	4	Improvement	4	Slight improvement	4	Substantial improvement
Middle East and North Africa	5	Slight decline	5	Slight decline	7	Improvement
Sub-Saharan Africa	6	Improvement	6	No change	6	Improvement
East Asia and the Pacific	7	Slight improvement	3	Slight improvement	3	No change

Source: Adapted from Humana Index as presented in World Bank (2001a).

political and legal equality; social and economic equality; and equality of men and women in marriage and divorce proceedings.[14] Although there are many serious limitations associated with an index of this kind[15] (see Elson, forthcoming), the World Bank (2001a) report uses the data to show changing patterns over time, thus providing a synoptic view of the pressing challenges remaining in achieving gender equality. Here too it is being used as a device to raise a series of issues about the correlations between different kinds of freedoms and the types of achievement on which the Millennium Development Goals are focused. Importantly, gender equality is defined here in terms of the political and social, and in terms of civil liberties: the right to choose to marry and the right to leave the institution of marriage. As the report highlights, asymmetries in rights and privileges persist in many societies, fundamentally constraining choices available to women and 'often profoundly limiting the opportunities they have in the economy and in society' (World Bank, 2001a: 37).

In Table 9.2 I have assimilated the data from World Bank (2001a) to demonstrate the relative performance of different countries in each of the areas of concern. What the figures indicate broadly is that in general, progress has been made in women's rights in most regions of the world, although the scores achieved by different regions in these different dimensions shows that 'in no region of the developing world do women have equal rights with men in any of these dimensions' (World Bank, 2001a: 37). Three points in particular from the analysis seem striking, with implications for our discussion of the Millennium Development Goals, and are elaborated on in the World Bank report. First, gains made in one dimension are not necessarily correlated with gains in others. East Asia and the Pacific demonstrate a higher achievement in gender equality in socio-economic rights, and the provision of rights in marriage and divorce, but not in political and legal rights. Second, gains are also reversible. The case of Europe and Central Asia, where slight declines are noted across all types of rights, is particularly striking. These declines are noted in the context particularly of East European political and economic transition, where many of the earlier securities provided for women have been withdrawn. This cautions us against taking formal or *de jure* rights as sufficient indicators of *de facto* enjoyment of rights. Macroeconomic environments have a range of impacts on people's ability to exercise choices and claim rights, with potentially negative implications for impoverished and socially excluded groups. Negative impacts under neo-liberal policy environments on social development in particular have been well documented (see Molyneux and Razavi, 2002). Third, some indicators do not necessarily reveal the quality of rights enjoyed: for instance, even though women's participation in the labour force has increased, particularly in manufacturing and services and particularly in countries which have reoriented their economies for participation in the world market, wage gaps between women and men persist. Further, such indicators can be misleading where the formal sector is only a small share of the economy, with the bulk of employment opportunities, and women workers, in the informal sector.

Pathways and causalities

Despite its level of generality, the data from the Humana Index show the vulnerability of gains for women in the quest for gender equality, and how changes in any one of the four dimensions – political, economic, social and cultural – can have repercussions for the others. This illustrates the difficulties entailed in attempting to chalk out very specific pathways as measures of progress towards gender equality. It also illustrates the difficulty of trying to view broader processes of social change in terms of selected indicators and targets, even if these chosen markers are merely intended as beacons along the route.

Education is a clear example of these difficulties. Female education is widely believed to constitute an indicator of progress towards decreasing gender inequality. Whilst this may well be the case, as any reversal of restrictions placed on access to human resources can only bring positive change, claims made for the multiple positive externalities associated with education often have a hollow ring to them, especially when viewed from the vantage point of the conditions under which women participate in the economy, in society and in politics. The 'silver bullet' (Jeffery and Jeffery, 1998) approach to female education has been criticised for the burden of expectations placed on this one resource in resolving a range of goals relating to population and health, amongst others, but also because of the lack of real interest that it suggests in testing the implicit assumption that education translates into enhanced autonomy for women. The laziness of this assumption is exposed by research which focuses on what Jeffery and Jeffery (1998) refer to as the 'education for what?' question, which shows that in some contexts education serves as a means to entrench, not challenge, women's unequal position within conventional marriage and labour markets, and indeed may or may not challenge structures of inequality (Subrahmanian, forthcoming). Further, as Whitehead and Lockwood note, there is the danger of 'spurious' causality drawn between education and household income, when in fact, 'both ... may be affected by underlying patterns of wealth organized through families' (1999: 548).

The point is certainly not to suggest a counter-argument that investing in women's education is *bad* for women, but to highlight that getting females into school may not necessarily improve the quality of their lives, if the basis for evaluation is drawing on the notion of 'capabilities', referred to earlier (Subrahmanian, 2002). Biases against girls within the classroom and within the curriculum, and limited economic and political opportunities outside the school, all conspire often to reduce the transformative potential of education in women's lives. Instrumentalist arguments which suggest that reducing gender inequality in education means enhanced autonomy for women often do a disservice to efforts to challenge the gender biases within education systems, by making it all appear far simpler to achieve than it really is. They also perpetuate reliance on quantitative measures and statistical correlations to justify funding (Baden and Green, 1994). This is dangerous, particularly given the methodological flaws of many of the techniques used to assess returns to education in general, and female education in particular (Bennell, 1996; see Subrahmanian, 2001, for a discussion).[16]

The other indicators of decreasing gender inequalities also need unpacking to avoid making sweeping generalisations about their relationship with women's relative lack of participation and access to resources. Changes in women's representation in national parliaments may mean a range of things, not all necessarily positively correlated with women's empowerment. If the process by which women get to parliament does not reflect any agency on the part of women to contest and represent their chosen constituencies,[17] then it will not tell us much. Alternatively, it may reflect reductions in inequality between certain classes of women and men, rather than representing a gain for all women. Similarly, women's participation in non-agricultural employment will have limited meaning as an indicator if applied to agrarian societies, which tend to be characteristic of poor countries.

Statistical correlations often become the basis for expanded statements of explanation about complex social decisions and processes. Thus correlations between greater levels of education and smaller family sizes are interpreted as indications of changes in the *desires* of women, as opposed to exploring the possibility of other changes in the policy environment or in incentives for changing family size. Policy efforts aimed at redressing gender inequalities faced by women, and many theoretical approaches to analysing gender inequality, are littered with assumptions about causality that research tends to disprove (see Jeffery and Jeffery, 1998; Pearson, 1998). These include the assumptions that there is a direct causal connection between, *inter alia,* women's wages and empowerment; and between female education and increased autonomy. These in turn indicate that social change is conceived of in these narrow policy discourses in terms of changes made in the characteristics of individuals, rather than its being viewed as combinations of change within individuals as well as the wider societies in which they live.[18] The ways in which individuals make trade-offs between potential individual gain and the well-being and social coherence of the wider societies to which they belong, however defined, suggest that processes of social change are mutually constituted by changes in individual circumstances and changes in the norms and ideologies of their chosen or imposed groups of association. Importantly, they also suggest that these processes of change may be read off shifts in a range of variables, and also at various moments of time.

The challenge of indicators: no pain, no gain

If social change in relation to eliminating inequality and empowering people is a value-based process, subjective and defined differently by different development actors, then how can indicators be identified that reflect this complexity, whilst at the same time setting benchmarks for evaluating the extent to which desired change is taking place? The exercise of finding indicators to match such broad yet important goals seems doomed at the outset. Certainly, top-down indicators find no place within such a conceptual terrain. Yet efforts to produce indicators have long consumed efforts towards mainstreaming gender, part of the arsenal of methods aimed at persuading gender-blind development actors to grasp the importance of promoting change from a gender perspective.

Kabeer's (1999a, 2001) schema for measuring interlocking dimensions of change that transform women's capabilities provides an extremely useful way of thinking about indicators of change that are sensitive to this complexity. An essential component of any attempt to measure empowerment is a definition that frames the scope of change that is associated with the concept and the measures. Kabeer's definition of empowerment unpacks the central notion of 'power' in terms of the 'ability to make choices: to be disempowered, therefore implies to be denied choice' (2001: 18): 'Empowerment thus refers to the expansion in people's ability to make strategic life choices in a context where this ability was previously denied to them' (ibid.: 19). Thus, measuring empowerment means measuring the extent to which people are able to make new choices. Choice in turn has three inter-related dimensions:

- resources or the conditions under which choices are made;
- agency or 'the ability to define one's goals and act upon them'; and
- achievements – or the outcomes of choices.

Thus Kabeer argues for measures of change that grasp the conditions, the processes and the outcomes of choices made.

Such a schema, if applied to the case of education, discussed on p. 195, would help locate education as one resource amongst many with the *potential* to transform women's lives. Thus access to this resource would fulfil only one condition of the indicator before claims could be made about its empowering effects; the other conditions would be the extent to which access helped strengthen women's agency, and whether women's agency in addition to access to the resource would actually lead to beneficial outcomes in terms of women's capabilities. With such an approach, imputed pathways are automatically subject to scrutiny to verify how access to education enables women's 'empowerment'.

Resources and achievements are generally thought to be easier to measure, but all depends on what achievements are being valued. It is not the fact of change that is being sought to be measured, but the nature of the change. Many definitions of empowerment are unclear or opaque in their specification of what it is precisely that is being sought to be changed, and whose perspective is being reflected. Further, as Kabeer notes, it is the *process* by which resources translate into achievements that is central to establish before claims can be made about 'empowerment'. Any new resource will filter through existing webs of gender relations, but the potential to transform these existing gender relations will depend to a great extent on whether an enabling environment is created for women to exercise some agency, defined as their ability to determine what choices to make.

But agencies need performance measures, and that essentially is what the Millennium Development Goals represent to international development agencies (White, 2001). A broad analytical approach as suggested by Kabeer poses challenges both for methods that can be used and for attribution, which are clearly at odds with the purposes for which quantifiable measures are developed. Attribution remains a problem with all indicators, particularly those that operate at the level of aggregation of the Millennium Development Goal indicators, as discussed in Chapter 3. However, if agencies genuinely wish to occupy the high ground of women's empowerment, then they have no choice but to embrace complexity and show conceptual sophistication in their discourses and approaches to gender equality.

Mainstreaming gender in development: lessons learned

There is a vast literature documenting the difficulties development agencies find in translating commitment to gender equality into reality (Goetz, 2003; Razavi and Miller, 1995). Many agencies have embraced the importance of tackling gender inequality, but the record of efforts to institutionalise such change remains uneven. The World Bank's Policy Research Report *Engendering Development* (2001a) is an example of a concerted attempt to take a multidimensional approach to gender inequality. However, the contrast with other reports on the extent to which gender issues are integrated into guidelines, assessments, projects and other mechanisms of policy design and delivery indicates the wide gulf that remains between discourse and practice. Institutional issues still remain critical determinants of the achievement of goals.

The Millennium Development Goals represent one attempt to change donor approaches and practices in the disbursement and delivery of aid, and need to be understood in the context of accompanying changes in the instruments of aid and policy delivery. The shift to budgetary support in the form of sector-wide approaches in key poverty-relevant sectors such as agriculture, health and education, and to Poverty Reduction Strategies for heavily indebted countries, provides the institutional context in which resources for the achievement of goals are allocated. Thus efforts to assess the achievability of goals with reference to gender in particular need to be located within an assessment of the success of 'mainstreaming' efforts in general, both within donor agencies and within national governments, and also, crucially, at the intersection of the two, with particular reference to the processes of building national ownership of donor-initiated policy approaches.

Preliminary assessments of the success of mainstreaming gender into the new policy instruments indicate that many of the old methods of 'mainstreaming' need to be recast to meet new challenges (Standing, 2001). The focus on budgetary support (rather than projects) has put macroeconomic frameworks at centre stage of efforts to tackle poverty and inequality. Thus skills in inserting gender into these budgetary and macro-economic frameworks have become paramount,[19] and gender advocacy has now to refocus its efforts on discussion and negotiation with enormously powerful *and* historically gender-blind ministries of finance and planning (Rodenberg, 2002).

A review of what we may now call 'first-generation' approaches to mainstreaming gender within development institutions reveals a wide range of lessons about the political and institutional challenges that need to be surmounted for meaningful progress on gender equality to be achieved. These first-generation mainstreaming approaches focused on the *bureaucratic and technocratic dimensions of agenda management*, and included the establishment of special desks, officers and posts relating to gender expertise which were to be the technical and political nerve centres within development agencies, whether donor, government or non-government organisations (NGOs). Assessments of the performance and achievement of these forms of bureaucratised gender mainstreaming approaches throw up mixed results – in some cases, they have succeeded in creating spaces for women's advocacy to infiltrate the state (Goetz, 2003), but in others, they have served to limit the range of institutional actors involved in the 'negotiating frame' (Standing, 2001). The substance of the analysis of these approaches has been focused, however, on the mismatch between the resources provided to these bodies and the giant tasks of gender redistribution and transformation that they were ostensibly created to promote. In particular, Razavi and Miller (1995) note that understaffed and under-resourced units of women in development/gender and development staff were charged with tasks that actually cut across all departments of organisations, including advocacy, technical support in the form of staff training and developing guidelines and checklists, as well as oversight and monitoring functions, leaving little time for research, policy and strategy development.[20] The task of mainstreaming became displaced onto units that did not have the resources or the power to influence agendas, and prevented responsibility and accountability on gender issues from becoming part of the mandate of every department and all personnel, as originally intended.

What prospects, then, for the second generation of mainstreaming approaches, which now focus on the more political and financial dimensions of agenda-setting in development? A desk review of nineteen Interim Poverty Reduction Strategy Papers (I-PRSPs) and four full PRSPs conducted by the World Bank (2001b: 3) reveals that relatively little attention is paid to gender issues in any of their core elements or sectors. The report qualifies this further by noting that all the documents reviewed had failed to meet the rather low standard that was being applied in the review: 'making passing reference to gender in diagnosis and indicating vague intention to include men and women in their actions and indicators in each of the eight sectoral areas' (ibid.: 3). Although there are regional variations within this overall poor performance on gender, the report firmly concludes that 'the low scores ... do not reflect a lack of sophistication. Rather they reflect a failure to address gender issues, even with simple approaches' (ibid.: 5). Within the overall low attention to gender, it was found that health and education sector discussions dealt with gender issues with a greater degree of elaboration than the other 'non-traditional' sectors such as labour markets, infrastructure, governance and safety nets. It is widely noted that the addressing of gender concerns within education, health, nutrition, population and social protection is far easier to promote[21] – in fact, female education is the one policy issue on which actors at different levels of the World Bank agree (Whitehead and Lockwood, 1999).

The low attention paid to gender in PRSPs is not just a matter of poor government capacity or will. The World Bank (2001b) review examined the Joint Bank and Fund Staff Assessments, which are meant to assess the strengths and weaknesses of the PRSPs with a view both to strengthening them and also to determining the levels of funding assistance that will then flow. It found that fewer than one-quarter of Joint Staff Assessments recommended further steps relating to gender, and when they did, the nature of the comments was vague and general, and did not pick up on the glaring omissions such as the failure to consult or consider consulting women or women's organisations (p. 8). However, there were also significant differences in capacity and commitment *within* the Bank. The review found that the weakness of the Joint Staff Assessments focus on gender contrasted sharply with the comments of the World Bank's Executive Board on the full PRSPs, which identified gender as an issue requiring greater attention and provided specific comments on each of the four full PRSPs.

In their review of six World Bank Poverty Assessments from four sub-Saharan African countries (Ghana, Zambia, Tanzania and Uganda), Whitehead and Lockwood (1999) note a range of limitations in gender analysis, including variations in the way in which the language of 'gender and development' is used and the different methodologies used to measure and define poverty (see also World Bank, 2002). Their analysis and findings are not dissimilar to the findings of the review of PRSPs cited above. However, and importantly, they link the poverty of the gender analysis to overall weaknesses in the commitment and capacities of the World Bank with respect to gender issues.[22] By perpetuating the long-institutionalised association of women with 'human resources' alone, the Bank's central mandate and concern with economic growth issues have remained worryingly ungendered. The diversity of methodologies and approaches used could partly be explained by the weak operational guidelines prepared by the Bank in helping national teams develop their assessments (Whitehead and Lockwood, 1999).

A further element is the fit, or the perceived lack of it, between the issues raised by gender analysis, on the one hand, and the policy mandates within which these analyses are commissioned, on the other, revealing the selectivity and partial nature of policy recommendations. This is a crucial aspect explaining the analysis–policy gap. Gender analyses, where done satisfactorily, are contained within reports as annexes, and are not integrated into the overall analysis (World Bank, 2002). Whitehead and Lockwood's review of the Poverty Assessments found that much of the analysis was diluted or not taken into account in the drafting of the policy sections, particularly analysis drawn from the Participatory Poverty Assessments (PPAs), which record the voices of poor women and men. They note that despite the variety of methods and approaches employed in the different Assessments,

> there is a remarkable consistency of views expressed on how to reduce poverty, with usually implicit, but occasionally explicit, implications for the treatment of gender. These consistent views can be traced to an orthodoxy in the World Bank regarding the nature of poverty and policy on poverty reduction.
>
> (1999: 545)

In particular, they note the probability of the standardising effects of peer reviews on the policy sections on poverty reduction, and the implications of the standardisation for the 'filtering out' of gender issues from the assessments. Processes of dilution are evident across the different stages of production of the Assessments – from the PPAs to the Poverty Assessments; and from the empirically derived analysis sections to the policy sections (ibid.). This fits in well with Longwe's famous discussion of 'policy evaporation' (1997).

The lack of consensus within organisations such as the World Bank on the operational definitions and perspectives, as well as approaches in research and policy associated with gender analysis, is only likely to increase as several agencies come together to combine their resources towards the achievement of the Millennium Development Goals. It is not the institutional capacities of the Bank alone that are at the root of the uneven analyses of gender disadvantage. Whitehead and Lockwood (1999) note the difficulties of co-ordinated approaches between national teams, consultants, different donors involved and task managers who all bring different understandings of gender to bear on their work, which only serve to compound the weakness of the operational guidelines discussed above. The struggle for consensus is likely to be the hardest challenge to surmount. While the Millennium Development Goals represent one attempt to fashion a consensus on priorities, managing co-ordination is another challenge.[23]

New mechanisms for aid delivery have emerged out of a concern with the limited effectiveness of project approaches and the belief in the greater efficiency of resource pooling between donors and strengthened processes of debate and dialogue about key areas of priorities with governments. Bringing the state back into the picture has meant that issues of national ownership have been framed as central objectives of these new policy tools. However, many commentators note that objectives of national ownership, and – within national contexts – consultations with stakeholders, particularly the traditionally voiceless, have scarcely been met, belying the claim that these approaches constitute new participatory methods for building sustainable development (Christian Aid, 2001; Rodenberg, 2002; Standing, 2001). The World Bank (2001b) notes that consultation with organisations within civil society, particularly women's organisations, in the I-PRSPs and PRSPs reviewed revealed low levels of consultation, with only two of the nineteen I-PRSPs showing specific plans to consult poor women or women's organisations and only three in total showing any indication of incorporating better gender analysis in their plans. A Christian Aid report comments that the involvement of poor people in PRSP-related processes has been 'minimal and superficial' (2001: 2), noting particularly the selectivity of issues on which consultation is invited and the lack of support provided by international agencies to local groups whose views contradict the policy directions of the PRSPs. Given the complexity of gender issues, and the difficulties of organising and representing the voices of women, it is clear that gender issues are likely to be excluded to a greater extent from processes of negotiation and discussion.[24] Even in sectors such as health and education, which appear to engage more with gender issues, stakeholder participation is traditionally very weak, given that the nature of knowledge within those sectors is largely seen as technocratic and expert-led (Standing, 2001).

Conclusion

For gender to make the transition from rhetoric to reality requires concerted attention at all levels of policy processes, from agenda-setting to planning of all aspects, to accountability through transparent monitoring and evaluation. Half-hearted or token measures result in uneven analytical approaches and inadequate operational frameworks. Agencies appear to be several steps behind the ever-increasing conceptual sophistication of thinking on 'gender' in development scholarship, and continual processes of learning are essential. There is a danger of 'analysis fatigue' concerning gender, fuelled by reliance on particular kinds of checklists and tools which demand little attention to nuance and contextual detail.

Further, 'gender equity interests' (Goetz, 2003) need to be addressed within bureaucratic *and* political spaces to ensure that the content of policy is informed by the voices of those most likely to be affected by policies. Given the constraints operating on women's effective representation and participation in policy processes, particular attention has to be paid to ensuring that women are listened to, and enabled to influence policy agendas. While a long wish-list has been established, and the conditions under which gender interests are likely to flourish with broader developmental benefits have been well documented, the implications for taking the Millennium Development Goals forward in a meaningful way are clear. Greater transparency around the *means* through which broadly defined gender empowerment and equality goals is critical. This involves greater transparency on the part of development agencies about the processes by which they implement policies, the ways in which resources are distributed and allocated, and the outcomes to which they give rise. The World Bank evaluations cited in this chapter are a step in the right direction, acknowledging as they do their failures to realise their claims and objectives. The next steps entail meaningful action to address these failures.

Notes

1 Mehrotra notes that almost all the International Development Targets relate to basic social service provisioning (2001: 4).
2 Razavi and Miller (1995) note, for example, that the tendency has been to focus on women as mothers only, especially in arenas linked to reproduction, such as population services, nutrition education and child-related services, whereas women have been absent figures in mainstream employment schemes and land reform programmes.
3 In fact, it is argued that donor agencies have driven the gender and development agenda, raising questions about the ownership of the agenda at the level of national governments (Razavi and Miller, 1995). Razavi and Miller note that financial resources for women-in-development (WID)/gender projects within donor agencies have often come from particular donor governments through the practice of 'multi-bi' funding, and thus the 'feminist agenda has remained excessively donor-driven' (ibid.: 4).
4 The terms are used here as an adaptation from Kabeer (1999b). Kabeer defines gender-aware policies as those that recognise that development actors are both women and men, and that they are constrained in different and unequal ways from participating and benefiting from development processes. Gender-specific policies refer to those that are targeted to benefit a specific sex, based on the recognition of differing gendered needs and constraints. If

they are designed to redress disadvantage and achieve gender justice, then these policies can be considered to be transformative. Gender-specific approaches, as Kabeer argues, can serve to integrate women in sex-specific ways that do not challenge asymmetries in divisions of labour and resources; if, however, they were based on an understanding of, and commitment to challenging, these asymmetries, then they would have the potential to transform gender relations in the direction of greater equality.

5 World-wide, women's presence is less than 14 per cent in lower houses of parliament, a 'share that is growing at slower than snail's pace' (UNDP, 2002: 70).

6 It is also striking to note, though, that this gender-specific goal is the one least likely to be achieved of all the Millennium Development Goals, which points to the difficulty of seeing results in areas where women need to be targeted for themselves (Chapter 11 of this volume).

7 For instance, the World Bank's recent policy research report discusses gender equality in terms of 'rights, resources and voice' (2001a).

8 Capabilities refer to the potential that people have for achieving valued ways of 'being and doing' (Sen, 1985). The influence of Amartya Sen's work on poverty and gender has been critical for feminist analysis in development (Jackson and Pearson, 1998), particularly for shaping the focus on the links between the relations of gender and outcomes of gender inequality, and for allowing focus on processes of negotiation and bargaining as part of understanding how resources translate into outcomes.

9 Whitehead and Kabeer (2001) argue for the importance of locating understanding of intra-household gender inequalities within analysis of wider livelihoods to obtain a fuller account of the nuances of the intersections between gender and poverty.

10 See Cagatay (1998), Chant (1997), Jackson (1997, 1998) and Kabeer (1997) for detailed discussions of concepts, approaches and debates relating to gender and poverty in general, and on female headship in particular.

11 See note 4 above. The focus on education in recent times and the stress on women's education has similar roots in the concern with women's role in reproduction and child-rearing, emphasising as it does the role education, particularly primary education, plays in bringing down fertility rates and improving child health.

12 It includes increased opportunities for income generation; increased access to credit or other relevant economic services; and increased participation in training or skills upgrading activities.

13 The twelve areas of action highlighted in the Beijing Conference's Platform for Action include poverty; education and training; access to health care and related services; violence against women; effects of armed or other kinds of conflict, including effects on those living under foreign occupation; economic structures and policies, in all forms of productive activities and in access to resources; sharing of power and decision-making at all levels; mechanisms to promote the advancement of women; human rights; women's access to, and participation in, all communication systems, especially in the media; the management of natural resources and the environment; and violation of the rights of the girl child.

14 The results reported here are taken from World Bank (2001a). In this chapter, the Humana scale is replaced with a 1–4 scale (whereas the Humana Index used a 0–3 scale), with 1 representing consistent pattern of rights violations and 4 representing unqualified respect for freedoms and rights (World Bank, 2001a: 37).

15 The level of regional aggregation is deeply problematic, as is the definition of what each of these means. For instance, statutory rights are likely to vary depend-

ing on the legal system in place. Where, however, it is useful is that it looks at relative equality for women *vis-à-vis* the rights enjoyed by men in each of those dimensions.

16 Using education as an entry point to justify funding on gender raises the further danger of obscuring from policy attention a range of inequalities and disparities relating to the economic, political and social spheres. Participants from East Asia at a Regional Gender Workshop organised by the World Bank note that the Bank has 'ignored gender issues' in that region 'because there is no typical gender disparity in education enrolments' (World Bank, 2002: 27).

17 For example, situations where parties may nominate wives of male politicians as a way of strengthening the party presence, regardless of the mechanism in place to promote women's participation (party quotas; reservations of seats for women; open competition). Political parties may co-opt spaces designed to promote women's participation, which would limit the potential for claiming 'empowerment' as well as dilute the terms of apparently reduced 'inequality'. However, as Goetz (2003) demonstrates, some mechanisms are more successful in promoting women's political participation and presence than others (see also UNDP, 2002, for a discussion).

18 For instance, Croll (2000) documents evidence of the increasing scale of daughter discrimination in East and South Asia, *despite* rising levels of economic development *and* dramatic levels of fertility decline in South Asia and China in particular. In fact, economic development has seen the entrenchment of son preference in these regions, and 'son-support has been incorporated into most national strategies for economic development' (p. 9).

19 'Gender budgets' are fast emerging as a key approach to placing gender concerns at the heart of development agenda-setting and resource allocation. See Elson (1999) and Budlender (1999) for detailed discussions.

20 See Razavi and Miller (1995) and Goetz (1995) for studies of gender mainstreaming within multilateral, bilateral and government agencies.

21 See also World Bank (2002) for a report on the analysis of gender within the Bank's Sector Strategy Papers, Poverty Assessments and projects.

22 See Gender and Development Network (2000) for a brief introduction to the ways in which gender is mainstreamed within the World Bank. While there are high-powered gender bodies within the Bank, it is clear that capacity is unevenly distributed. Recent publications of the Bank, like those cited in this chapter, indicate, however, that there is an increasingly high level of awareness of the importance of gender, but like other agencies, there are institutional difficulties in translating this into a more coherent strategy.

23 See Sedere (2000) for a more general discussion of the problems of donor coordination in education sector funding in Bangladesh.

24 See Goetz (2003) for a more general discussion of issues relating to the representation of women's interests through political processes. In addition, the complexity of gender interests, given the heterogeneity of the category 'women', conflicts with the need for civil society advocates to speak with one voice, which often means 'subordinating women's gender interests to men's' (Geraldine Terry, cited in Christian Aid, 2001: 14).

References

Baden, S. and Green, C. (1994) *Gender and Education in Asia and the Pacific*, BRIDGE Report 25, Brighton: Institute of Development Studies.

Bennell, P. (1996) 'Rates of Return to Education: Does the Conventional Pattern Prevail in Sub-Saharan Africa?', *World Development*, 24(1): 183–199.

Booth, D. and Lucas, H. (2001) *Desk Study of Good Practice in the Development of PRSP Indicators and Monitoring Systems: Initial Review of PRSP Documentation*, London: Overseas Development Institute.

Budlender, D. (1999) 'The South African Women's Budget Initiative', Background Paper 2, Meeting on Women and Political Participation: 21st Century Challenges, 24–26 March, New Delhi: UNDP.

Cagatay, N. (1998) 'Gender and Poverty', Working Paper 5, New York: UNDP, Social Development and Poverty Elimination Division.

Chant, S. (1997) 'Women-Headed Households: Poorest of the Poor? Perspectives from Mexico, Costa Rica and the Philippines', *IDS Bulletin*, (28)3: 26–48, Brighton: Institute of Development Studies.

Christian Aid (2001) 'Ignoring the Experts: Poor People's Exclusion from Poverty Reduction Strategies', Policy Briefing, London: Christian Aid.

Croll, E. (2000) *Endangered Daughters: Discrimination and Development in Asia*, London and New York: Routledge.

Elson, D. (1998) 'Talking to the Boys: Gender and Economic Growth Models', in Jackson, C. and Pearson, R. (eds) *Feminist Visions of Development: Gender Analysis and Policy*, London: Routledge.

—— (1999) 'Gender-Neutral, Gender-Blind, or Gender-Sensitive Budgets? Changing the Conceptual Framework to Include Women's Empowerment and the Economy of Care', Gender Budget Initiative Background Papers, London: Commonwealth Secretariat.

—— (2002) 'Gender Justice, Human Rights and Neo-liberal Economic Policies', in Molyneux, M. and Razavi, S. (eds) *Gender Justice, Development and Rights*, Oxford: Oxford University Press.

Gender and Development Network (2000) *How to Challenge a Colossus: Engaging with the World Bank and the International Monetary Fund*, London: Womankind.

Goetz, A.M (1995) 'The Politics of Integrating Gender to State Development Processes: Trends, Opportunities, and Constraints in Bangladesh, Chile, Jamaica, Mali, Morocco, and Uganda', Occasional Paper 2, Geneva: UNRISD.

—— (2003) 'Women's Political Effectiveness: A Conceptual Paper', in *No Shortcuts to Power: African Women in Politics and Policy-Making*, London: Zed Press.

Hanmer, L. and Naschold, F. (2000) 'Attaining the International Development Targets: Will Growth Be Enough?', *Development Policy Review* 18(1): 11–36.

Hanmer, L and Wilmshurst, J. (2000) 'Are the International Development Targets Attainable? An Overview, *Development Policy Review*, 18(1): 5–10.

Jackson, C. (1997) 'Post Poverty, Gender and Development', *IDS Bulletin*, 28(3): 145–155, Brighton: Institute of Development Studies.

—— (1998) 'Rescuing Gender from the Poverty Trap', in Jackson, C. and Pearson, R. (eds) *Feminist Visions of Development: Gender Analysis and Policy*, London: Routledge.

Jackson, C. and Pearson, R. (eds) (1998) *Feminist Visions of Development: Gender Analysis and Policy*, London: Routledge.

Jeffery, R. and Jeffery, P. (1998) 'Silver Bullet or Passing Fancy? Girls' Schooling and Population Policy', in Jackson, C. and Pearson, R. (eds) *Feminist Visions of Development: Gender Analysis and Policy*, London: Routledge.

Kabeer, N. (1997) 'Tactics and Trade-Offs: Revisiting the Links between Gender and Poverty', *IDS Bulletin*, 28(3): 1–13, Brighton: Institute of Development Studies.

—— (1999a) 'The Conditions and Consequences of Choice: Reflections on the Measurement of Women's Empowerment', Discussion Paper 108, Geneva: UNRISD.

—— (1999b) 'From Feminist Insights to an Analytical Framework: An Institutional Perspective on Gender Inequality', in Kabeer, N and Subrahmanian, R. (eds) *Institutions, Relations and Outcomes: A Framework and Tools for Gender-Aware Planning*, New Delhi: Kali for Women.

—— (2001) 'Resources, Agency, Achievements: Reflections on the Measurement of Women's Empowerment', in *Discussing Women's Empowerment: Theory and Practice*, Sida Studies 3, Stockholm: Swedish International Development Agency.

Longwe, S. (1997) 'The Evaporation of Gender Policies in the Patriarchal Cooking Pot', *Development in Practice*, 7(2): 148–156.

McGee, R. (2000) 'Meeting the International Poverty Targets in Uganda: Halving Poverty and Achieving Universal Primary Education', *Development Policy Review*, 18(1): 85–106.

Mehrotra, S. (2001) 'The Rhetoric of International Development Targets and the Reality of Official Development Assistance', Innocenti Working Paper 85, Florence: UNICEF Innocenti Research Centre.

Molyneux, M. and Razavi, S. (eds) (2002) *Gender Justice, Development and Rights*, Oxford: Oxford University Press.

Nussbaum, M. (2000) *Women and Human Development: The Capabilities Approach*, Cambridge: Cambridge University Press.

Pearson, R. (1998) ' "Nimble Fingers" Revisited: Reflections on Women and Third World Industrialisation in the Late Twentieth Century', in Jackson, C. and Pearson, R. (eds) *Feminist Visions of Development: Gender Analysis and Policy*, London: Routledge.

Razavi, S. and Miller, D. (1995) 'Gender Mainstreaming: A Study of Efforts by the UNDP, the World Bank and the ILO to Institutionalise Gender Issues', Occasional Paper 4, Geneva: UNRISD.

Rodenberg, B. (2002) 'Integrating Gender into Poverty Reduction Strategies: From the Declaration of Intent to Development Policy in Practice?' Briefing Paper 2/2002, Bonn: German Development Institute.

Sedere, U. (2000) 'Rethinking Educational Aid: Sector Support Approach to Financing Basic Education: Lessons from Bangladesh', *Prospects: Quarterly Review of Education*, 116(4): 451–460, Paris: UNESCO.

Sen, A. (1985) *Commodities and Capabilities*, vol. 7 of *Professor Dr. P. Hennipman Lectures in Economics: Theory, Institutions, Policy*, Amsterdam: North-Holland.

Standing, H. (2001) 'Institutionalising Gender at a Sectoral Level: What Does It Mean and Who Does It?', paper given at the Dutch Aid Gender and Sector-Wide Approaches Workshop, The Hague, 21–23 February, Brighton: Institute of Development Studies.

Subrahmanian, R. (2001) *Gender and Education: A Review of Directions for Social Policy*, report prepared for UNRISD.

—— (2002) 'Engendering Education: Prospects for a Rights-Based Approach to Female Education Deprivation in India', in Molyneux, M. and Razavi, S. (eds) *Gender Justice: Development and Rights*, Oxford: Oxford University Press.

UNDP (2002) 'Deepening Democracy in a Fragmented World', *Human Development Report 2002*, New York: UNDP.

White, H. (2001) 'Will the New Aid Agenda Help Promote Poverty Reduction?', *Journal of International Development* 13: 1057–1070.

—— (2002) 'Using the Millennium Development Goals as a Basis for Agency-Level Performance Measurement' in Black, R. and White, H. (eds) *Targeting Development: Critical Perspectives on the Millenium Development Goals*, London: Routledge.

Whitehead, A. and Kabeer, N. (2001) 'Living with Uncertainty: Gender, Livelihoods and Pro-Poor Growth in Rural Sub-Saharan Africa', Working Paper 134, Brighton: Institute of Development Studies.

Whitehead, A. and Lockwood, M. (1999) 'Gendering Poverty: A Review of Six World Bank African Poverty Assessments', *Development and Change*, 30(3): 525–555.

World Bank (2001a) *Engendering Development through Gender Equality in Rights, Resources, and Voice*, Policy Research Report, Washington, DC: World Bank and Oxford: Oxford University Press.

—— (2001b) *Gender in the PRSPs: A Stocktaking*, Poverty Reduction and Economic Management Network, Washington, DC: World Bank, Gender and Development Group.

—— (2002) *The Gender Dimension of Bank Assistance: An Evaluation of Results*, Report 23119, Washington, DC: World Bank, Operations Evaluation Department.

10 Reducing infant and child death

Howard White

Ten thousand African children died today

Fifty years ago, close to two of every ten children born in East Asia died during their first year of life, and another one of their sisters or brothers did not reach their fifth birthday. The dramatic reductions in the rates of infant and child death achieved in the second half of the last century are a testament to the success of development efforts. Today, fewer than one in twenty East Asian children die in the first five years of life. But there is still far to go. Despite reduced mortality rates, a staggering number of children still die. Two million African infants die each year, and as many again before they reach 5. They would make a line of dead children that would stretch the entire length of the United Kingdom. This figure has not changed in over two decades. That is 10,000 avoidable deaths every day of every week of every month for over twenty years. Every single child death is a personal tragedy. In the words of a father who lost two children, 'Can you tell me why this had to happen?' (quoted in Howard and Millard, 1997: 1). There is no answer to that question. It did not have to happen. Yet, another 10,000 African children will die tomorrow, another 10,000 the day after and so on. What needs to change to stop the bodies from piling up?

The Millennium Development Goal is for a two-thirds reduction in infant and under-five mortality by 2015. The history of missed goals shows that the existence of a goal is not enough to ensure that it is met. And, as is argued in Chapter 3, the existence of a goal does not give any indication of a strategy that might be employed to achieve that goal. Historical trends, reviewed in the next section, show that progress in reducing mortality has been very uneven. The current rate of reduction is insufficient to meet the target. Yet in certain times and places, dramatic reductions in mortality have taken place. What are the lessons from these different experiences? In particular, what can be done to bring about more rapid mortality decline amongst poor performers?

There has been a debate over the sources of mortality decline in the now developed countries, most notably England (see p. 220), and this debate has been echoed in the literature on developing countries. The opposing positions are held by those who attribute the decline more to rising incomes and consequent improvements in nutrition, versus those assigning a larger role to public health and other interventions. Straw men are highly inflammable, and so should be avoided if we want sensible policy advice rather than heated debate. No one denies that economic growth matters for sustained improvements in social welfare. Few also deny at least some role for government in health service provision. The question is one of balance between the two.[1] The position taken here, developed in the section 'Reasons for mortality decline', p. 214, is that health services and other public actions do play a key role. And substantial improvements can be achieved independently of income growth, such as through the promotion of breastfeeding, which is a vital aspect of child survival chances. But the exhortation is not simply for more money; it is also for better prioritisation of expenditure, including expenditure on preventive measures (such as the promotion of breastfeeding), public campaigns and an emphasis on female education. These policy implications are laid out in the concluding section.

The uneven record of mortality decline

Figure 10.1 shows trends in infant and child mortality, the former being the probability of death in the first year of life and the latter that between first and fifth birthdays. Under-five mortality, which is the subject of the Millennium Development Goal, combines these two measures.[2] The most striking feature of the graphs is the secular decline in child and infant mortality rates in all regions,[3] with only two recent exceptions. The two recent exceptions are child mortality in sub-Saharan Africa and infant mortality in the transition economies of the former Soviet Union. But these are exceptions, and should not detract from the very marked success in reducing mortality, most notably in East Asia, but also the Middle East and North Africa. Except in sub-Saharan Africa, where the rate is 65 deaths per 1,000 live births, child mortality is now at very low levels of 10 or fewer deaths per 1,000 live births in all other regions except South Asia. In South Asia the rate is slightly higher at 15 deaths per 1,000 live births, though this figure shows a suspicious kink in the trend and is probably unreliable.

Lying behind these strong performances have been a range of social measures, which are discussed in more detail for some specific cases below. These measures, promoted by UNICEF and supported by a number of international agencies, focused around GOBI: growth monitoring of children under 2, spread of knowledge about oral rehydration therapy (ORT), breastfeeding and improved early child feeding, and immunisation. The success of these initiatives can be seen both through intermediate indicators – such as raising average immunisation coverage in

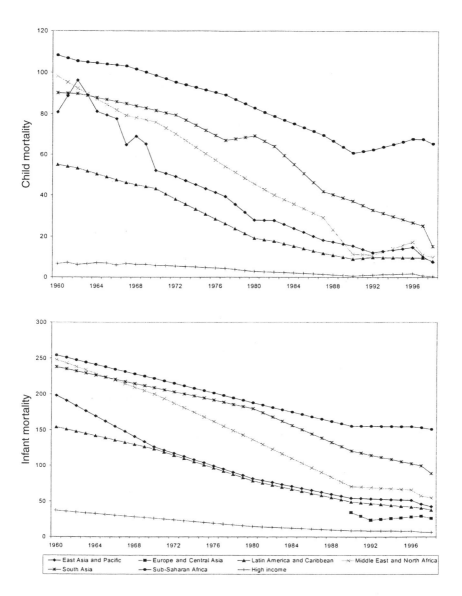

Figure 10.1 Trends in (a) child and (b) infant mortality by region (per 1,000 live births).

Source: World Bank *World Development Indicators* CD-Rom, 2001.

developing countries from 20 to 80 per cent during the course of the 1980s – and in the outcome of falling mortality. One estimate is that by 1995 these programmes had prevented some 25 million child deaths (Jolly, 2001).

The second observation from Figure 10.1 is the difference in regional performance, in terms of both levels and changes over time. The more successful developing countries are reducing their mortality rates to approach those in developed countries, although the rates in the latter countries also continue to decline. The infant mortality rate in Cuba is the same as that for the United States (8 per 1,000 live births). So a gap is opening up between good and poor performers, with sub-Saharan African countries mostly doing least well, particularly with respect to child mortality. Brief reflection on the different regional experiences yields some initial insights into the factors underlying mortality reductions:

- East Asia has been a region of strong economic growth. Whilst the East Asian newly industrialising countries (NICs) have done well on social indicators, over 80 per cent of the region's population live in China, which must therefore dominate the trend towards lower mortality. Mortality reduction in China was strongest prior to the introduction of market-based reforms in the mid-1970s, and evidence reviewed below points to the key role of health services in this good performance.
- North Africa and the Middle East includes countries which have benefited from oil wealth. There has been a tendency in the past to suggest that this wealth was not turned into general improvements in the population's welfare. The data shown here suggest that this is not so, though it can be argued that these improvements came about with a lag.[4] Table 10.2 reports data for Oman, which has reduced mortality by nearly 90 per cent since 1950. Such a decline does not come about automatically from the presence of oil but is the result of deliberate government policy to utilise the income from oil wealth for the common good. Oman's National Health Programme (NHP) has had seven separate components, including the Expanded Programme of Immunisation (EPI),[5] Mother and Child Health and Control of Tuberculosis (Skeet, 1992: 115). The programme has been implemented with a massive increase in health infrastructure: in the 1980s the number of hospitals nearly doubled, health clinics increased in number by 75 per cent and nursing staff fourfold (ibid: 112).
- Mortality started to rise in Eastern Europe and countries of the former Soviet Union. This trend can be linked to income declines but also to the associated collapse in health services as government revenue dried up, resulting in falling immunisation coverage in some countries (White *et al.*, 2000). As documented elsewhere, the more significant shift has been the rise in adult mortality (see Cornia and Paniccià, 2000).

- Infant and child mortality have declined in Africa despite deteriorating economic performance since the 1970s. The recent reversal of the decline in child mortality in Africa is in part a consequence of HIV/AIDS. But even before the effects of the epidemic were felt in the 1990s, there was a marked relative deterioration, indicating a failure to get infectious diseases under control. However, mortality rates were falling in countries in which income per capita was also falling (e.g. Zambia), showing that there is not a necessary link between economic growth and reducing mortality.

To pick up on this last point, previous studies have identified an 'exogenous component' in mortality decline. That is, if we look at the relationship between life expectancy and income (Preston, 1975) or infant mortality and income (Hanmer *et al.*, 2003), welfare is better (life expectancy higher, infant mortality lower) in more recent periods than in earlier ones for countries at the same level of real income.[6] Hanmer *et al.* calculate that this exogenous component has reduced mortality in low-income countries by about 20 per 1,000 in the past thirty years. This exogenous decline can be attributed to factors such as improved medical technology (e.g. the development of heat-stable vaccines in the 1980s, and measures to improve the monitoring of the cold chain)[7] and the greater availability of health services, as well as clean water in low-income countries. These improvements can be attributed at least in part to flows of development aid.

The third observation from Figure 10.1 is that rates of mortality decline are still generally insufficient to meet the target set by the Millennium Development Goal. A two-thirds reduction in twenty-five years (from 1990 to 2015) requires an annual reduction of 4.3 per cent. As it happens, only high-income countries have achieved this figure for infant mortality in the past twenty-five years. On the other hand, all regions other than sub-Saharan Africa have achieved sufficient progress in reducing child mortality to reach the target (Table 10.1). There may be some questions as to

Table 10.1 Annual mortality reductions over 25 years (1973–1998) by region (per cent)

	Infant mortality	Child mortality	Under-five mortality
East Asia and Pacific	−2.6	−7.1	−3.8
Latin America and Caribbean	−3.7	−5.9	−4.2
Middle East and North Africa	−3.9	−7.4	−4.7
South Asia*	−2.3	−4.5	−3.2
Sub-Saharan Africa	−1.4	−1.4	−1.3
High income	−4.3	−9.0	−5.0

Source: Calculated from World Bank *World Development Indicators* CD-ROM, 2001.

Note
*Calculated over 24 years, and 1998 data point seems suspect.

whether this rate of reduction can be sustained at lower mortality levels, though it should be possible, since it has been done in developed countries. But the target is not for child mortality but for under-five mortality, of which the largest part is now accounted for by infant deaths. Since under-five mortality is dominated by infant mortality, only two regions, the Middle East and North Africa, and Latin America and the Caribbean, appear to be achieving sufficiently high rates of reduction.

Understanding why some regions are doing better than others is the key to identifying the policies required to generalise rapid mortality decline. But regional differences hide substantial variations in country performance, so the next section begins with some country data.

Reasons for mortality decline

Table 10.2 shows infant mortality rates for selected countries since 1950 and the annual rate of change over the first twenty-five years and the next twenty.[8] Other than Oman, which was discussed above, in the countries shown there have been high rates of mortality reduction in China, Cuba and the Russian Federation (the data mostly referring to the latter region whilst it was still part of the Soviet Union). What these three countries have in common is that they all are or were centrally planned economies. They have all done markedly better in reducing mortality than countries that have followed a more market-oriented development strategy, such as Brazil, India and Kenya. For example, prior to 1975, Vietnam achieved a reasonable rate of reduction for a country at war, and since then it has accelerated the rate of improvement after unification. Although moves towards a market economy were made in the 1980s, the Vietnamese government continues to exert strong control, including control over the delivery of state-controlled health services. By contrast, the health service

Table 10.2 Infant mortality rates for selected countries (deaths per 1,000 live births)

	1950– 1955	*1960– 1965*	*1975– 1980*	*1995– 2000*	*Annual change, 1950–1975 (%)*	*Annual change, 1975–1995 (%)*
Brazil	135	109	79	42	−2.1	−3.1
China	195	212	52	41	−5.1	−1.2
Cuba	81	59	22	8	−5.1	−4.9
India	190	157	129	73	−1.5	−2.8
Kenya	155	127	93	65	−2.0	−1.8
Oman	231	207	95	27	−3.5	−6.1
Russian Federation	97	40	30	17	−4.6	−2.8
Vietnam	158	130	83	40	−2.5	−3.6

Source: UN *World Population Prospects: The 2000 Revision*, vol. 1.

has deteriorated markedly in China in the past two decades, corresponding to a considerable slowing in the rate of mortality reduction.

Contemporary wisdom has it that centrally planned economies perform badly economically. If so, then improvements in economic well-being cannot be the source of these countries' success in lowering mortality. Indeed, as just mentioned, the period of China's rapid economic growth has seen a slowing of mortality decline, hence the success of these countries seems more likely to rest with state provision of health services, as is more thoroughly documented later in the chapter.

In this section the view that public health and other government interventions matter is supported by three arguments: (1) regression analysis finds a robust effect of various measures of health service provision on infant and child mortality; (2) case studies from both developed and developing countries almost invariably report a significant role for a range of policy measures; and (3) as mortality rates fall, the structure of death changes, becoming focused on infants, whose survival is more dependent on interventions than on general environmental conditions.

Evidence from robust regression analysis

There is a substantial literature analysing the determinants of infant mortality using cross-country regressions. Infant or child mortality is taken as the dependent variable, and is regressed on a range of factors such as income per capita, maternal education and health expenditure. These studies are reviewed by Hanmer and White (1999), who report that well over thirty variables have been used as determinants of mortality. Under such circumstances it is quite possible to come up with a regression in which all coefficients are significant; but someone else could come up with quite a different set of significant determinants. There are two responses to this situation. The first is to abandon cross-country analysis in favour of case studies, and that is a route I pursue on pp. 219–233. The other is to adopt a robust regression approach.

Robust regression involves estimating all possible combinations of the proposed explanatory variables. Hanmer *et al.* (2002) used twenty-four independent variables to estimate 420,000 equations for infant and child mortality. These found income to be a robust determinant of mortality, but so were measures of health service provision, notably immunisation coverage and the number of doctors per person. Measures of education and gender inequality are also found to be robust. Claims, based on cross-country regression analysis, that health expenditure is unimportant in explaining country differences in mortality (Filmer and Pritchett, 1999) are not borne out by the robust regression approach. Money spent on health does indeed matter – though of course so does how it is spent (see pp. 226–231).

With a variable selection justified by the robust regression analysis, Table 10.3 shows some illustrative cross-country regression results for

Table 10.3 Regression results for infant mortality

	(1)	(2)	(3)	(4)	(5)	(6)	(7)	(8)	(9)
GNP per capita (logged)	-0.52 (-46.4)	–	–	-0.49 (-36.9)	-0.51 (-39.0)	-0.45 (-29.4)	-0.46 (-30.0)	-0.10 (-1.45)	-0.09 (-1.23)
DPT immunisation (logged)	–	-0.70 (-15.4)	–	-0.26 (-8.1)	–	-0.06 (-2.2)	–	0.46 (4.51)	–
Measles immunisation (logged)	–	–	-0.67 (-12.3)	–	-0.24 (-7.3)	–	-0.06 (-1.9)		0.51 (4.35)
Interactive term for income and measles	–	–	–	–	–	–	–	-0.08 (-5.44)	-0.09 (-5.07)
Interactive term for income and DPT	–	–	–	–	–	–	–	–	–
Sub-Saharan Africa	–	–	–	–	–	0.67 (9.5)	0.66 (9.3)	0.68 (9.80)	0.68 (9.77)
South Asia	–	–	–	–	–	0.22 (2.1)	0.23 (2.2)	0.25 (2.52)	0.27 (2.61)
East Asia and Pacific	–	–	–	–	–	0.19 (2.9)	0.17 (2.6)	0.60 (9.48)	0.58 (9.27)
Middle East and North Africa	–	–	–	–	–	0.61 (9.5)	0.59 (9.1)	0.18 (2.83)	0.16 (2.52)
Eastern Europe and Central Asia	–	–	–	–	–	-0.25 (-3.5)	-0.25 (-3.5)	-0.26 (-3.76)	-0.24 (-3.49)

	(1)	(2)	(3)	(4)	(5)	(6)	(7)	(8)	(9)
Latin America and Caribbean	—	—	—	—	—	0.35 (6.2)	0.36 (6.2)	0.33 (6.02)	0.36 (6.36)
1975–1979	—	—	—	—	—	−0.44 (−1.6)	—	−0.52 (−1.89)	—
1980–1984	—	—	—	—	—	−0.55 (−2.0)	−0.35 (−2.6)	−0.55 (−2.09)	−0.32 (−2.38)
1985–1989	—	—	—	—	—	−0.69 (−2.5)	−0.48 (−3.5)	−0.68 (−2.54)	−0.41 (−3.03)
1990–1994	—	—	—	—	—	−0.79 (−2.9)	−0.57 (−4.2)	−0.77 (−2.89)	−0.50 (−3.67)
1995–1997	—	—	—	—	—	−0.94 (−3.5)	−0.73 (−5.3)	−0.93 (−3.48)	−0.65 (−4.81)
Constant	—	6.37 (34.2)	6.25 (28.0)	8.29 (64.0)	8.34 (59.7)	7.61 (24.4)	7.44 (35.4)	5.38 (10.55)	4.99 (9.49)
R squared	0.67	0.25	0.18	0.76	0.72	0.85	0.86	0.87	0.86
N	1,066	716	671	645	645	606	645	606	645

infant mortality. The data are five-year period averages for 191 countries. The variables have been logged so that the coefficients are elasticities, showing that a 1 per cent rise in income per capita results in a reduction in infant mortality of about 0.5 per cent. Two immunisation variables are shown. The high correlation between the two immunisation variables (the simple correlation coefficient is 0.8) means they are put into separate equations, each having very similar coefficients (of −0.7 in the simple regression, reduced to −0.25 when income is introduced and −0.06 when time and region dummies are used). A 1 per cent increase in immunisation coverage has a significant impact on infant mortality. The size of the elasticity is much less than that for income – but increasing immunisation coverage by 1 per cent costs much less than does increasing growth by 1 per cent.

These regressions make a simple point: infant mortality is strongly related to income. Income is a means to many things which make lower mortality possible – including immunisation (the correlation between income and immunisation, both logged, is about 0.4). But the fit between infant mortality and income is not perfect; equation (1) has an R squared value of 0.67. Adding additional variables both weakens the significance of income (as will be seen in a moment, it is possible to produce regressions in which income is insignificant) as these additional variables pick up the channels through which income affects mortality. Yet it is important that a variable such as immunisation is significant when included with income, since this shows that immunisation has an impact over and above that from income – that is, health delivery makes a difference which operates independently from income.

Equations (8) and (9) introduce an interactive term, this term being the product of income and immunisation coverage. This term allows the elasticity of mortality with respect to income to vary according to the level of immunisation, or the elasticity for immunisation to vary according to income. In these equations, income is no longer significant, which might be interpreted as showing that higher income alone is no use in the absence of immunisation. But not too much importance should be attached to such an interpretation, and none should be attached to the positive coefficient which now appears for immunisation. The correct approach is to calculate the elasticities over the range of the data. That for income varies between −0.35 (immunisation coverage at 20 per cent) and −0.48 (full coverage). The elasticity for immunisation varies from −0.10 in the lowest-income countries to over −0.4 in high-income ones. Allowing for this interactive effect thus gives two important results: (1) the elasticity of immunisation is much higher than appears from regressions that ignore the interactive term, and (2) both elasticities are higher the higher the value of the other variable, a finding which is easy to explain (see the beginning of the next section on p. 219).

Equations (6)–(9) include time and region dummies. For the regional dummies, the reference group is developed countries, so the coefficient shows how much higher or lower infant mortality is in that region once the other variables are taken into account. Eastern Europe and Central Asia have a negative coefficient, indicating that (despite the relative decline in recent years) these countries enjoy low mortality relative to their income (with their high immunisation rates also being allowed for). For the time dummies, the reference period is the first five years, 1970–1975. The negative coefficients on these variables represent the 'exogenous shift' mentioned on p. 213. The size of the coefficient continuously increases from one period to the next, indicating that the shift has been present throughout the period.

Evidence from case studies

Much of the literature of the determinants of mortality is concerned with attributing primary cause either to economic factors, including nutritional status, or to public health and medical interventions. As suggested in the introduction to this chapter, this debate should be seen as a false dichotomy. More realistic is to utilise the Mosley–Chen framework, shown as Figure 10.2. According to this framework, both sets of factors matter, and neither one can operate independently of the other. Several channels exist for this inter-relationship. Sustainable provision of health services depends on their being financed, either directly by consumers or from government revenues. The effectiveness of medical interventions also depends on other risk factors. There is little point in immunising a child who has no prospect of eating (hence the significance of the interactive term in Table 10.3), or indeed one who faces too adverse a home environ-

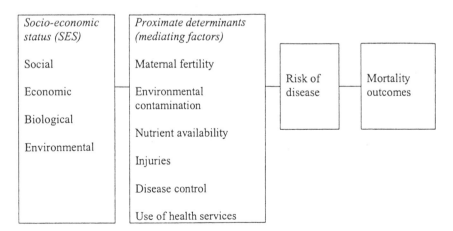

Figure 10.2 The Mosley–Chen framework for analysing mortality (modified).
Source: After Mosley and Chen (1984).

ment and a mother ignorant of good child-rearing practices such as the importance of breastfeeding. For this reason, reducing mortality requires a good domestic environment and non-hazardous working conditions. Maternal education has been identified as a crucial mediating variable, making it more likely that families will avail themselves of improved health technologies and be open to preventive health practices. The implication is that rising incomes will not be turned into reduced mortality unless the mediating factors come into play. Moreover, there is scope to enhance the 'productivity' of a given level of income by policies aimed at mediating factors (though in the end some improvement in socio-economic status is necessary for further reductions).

Cross-country regressions tend to focus too much on the left-hand box in Figure 10.2, ignoring the importance of mediating factors which may be amenable to policy intervention, and which might also contribute to lower mortality. On the other hand, much of the demographic literature has focused unduly on the two right-hand boxes of Figure 10.2, documenting the immediate causes of death without tracing these back to their proximate and underlying causes. The aim here is to look at the middle ground, drawing on case-study evidence of the effectiveness of public interventions in reducing mortality.

For developed countries the debate on the sources of mortality decline has revolved around England's experience in the late nineteenth and early twentieth centuries and the contribution of McKeown. In England, infant mortality began to decline around 1900 and that for older children somewhat earlier. Having initially written of the importance of medical advances, McKeown (1976) later reversed his position, arguing that better nutrition was mainly responsible. This argument was hotly contested, and one authority has concluded that whilst 'specific therapeutic medical treatments have played a minor role in mortality reductions in Western countries ... relatively little else of the McKeown thesis has survived' (Preston, 1996: 532). Examination of more recent work bears this out. Whilst McKeown is invariably mentioned in studies of European mortality, his position is dismissed as simplistic. To take two recent examples, Woods points to the role of the 'health of towns' movement, especially in ensuring a supply of uncontaminated water, improved milk supply and food quality, as well as the rise of female education (Woods, 2000: chapter 7). Riley (2001) argues that success in reducing mortality cannot be reduced to a single factor, but rather results from a multiplicity of factors which have varied across time and between countries, and goes on to discuss public health, medicine, income and nutrition.

Vögele's (1998) analysis of towns in the UK and Germany provides a good summary of the most accepted position that emerges from this literature.[9] Mortality increased during the nineteenth century, and this increase was largely associated with urbanisation. Vögele calls this the 'urban penalty' of higher mortality in urban areas on account of their squalid living conditions. At the beginning of the last century this penalty began to be eliminated as conditions improved, most notably sanitation. He is explicit that specific medical interventions played only a small role, although others do point out that perinatal death declined with improved delivery practices.

Mortality decline in Europe took place over a long period, with the initial stages of industrialisation being associated with increased mortality due to poor urban living conditions. The situation in developing countries has been rather different. Where long-run data are available, they suggest that mortality declines began somewhere around the 1930s, and there has been no period of increasing mortality with urbanisation. This difference in experience is due to the availability of immunisation, better access to water and sanitation, and general availability of health services. Indeed, in developing countries today there is arguably a 'rural penalty' which derives partly from the worse access to health services of those in rural areas (see p. 226 and p. 230).

Of particular interest is the situation in countries that have achieved rapid mortality reduction in a very short time. Two cases are considered here, China and the Soviet Union. Campbell presents a detailed analysis of mortality in Beijing since the seventeenth century. The period of interest here is immediately after the Communist Party came to power, from 1949 to 1955. In just six years, child mortality rate fell from 61 to 15 per 1,000 live births, and infant mortality fell from 115 to 56 per 1,000 live births, with annual rates of reduction of 21 per cent and 11 per cent respectively (Campbell, 2001: 231). Such rapid declines cannot plausibly be attributed to economic growth, but rather must result from the attention paid to the development of health services:

> [B]etween 1949 and 1955 the national government focused its attention on establishing an organisational infrastructure to implement health policies and control certain infectious diseases. . . . Attention was focused on pulmonary tuberculosis, parasites, sexually transmitted diseases and certain other acute infectious diseases. To improve maternal and child welfare, midwives were re-trained and new delivery assistants were educated.
>
> (Campbell, 2001: 233)

Measures included the greatly expanded production of vaccine, increased numbers of clinics and free treatment for all those suffering infectious diseases.

A similar story can be told about the Soviet Union after the Second World War. Until the 1940s, infant mortality was still high at over 200 per 1,000 live births, with life expectancy at birth little more than 40. Within twenty years, life expectancy had increased to close to 70 (65 for men and 74 for women), largely on account of reductions in under-five mortality.

By 1965, infant mortality was 40 per 1,000 live births, an annual reduction of close to 8 per cent. These improvements are mainly attributable to the success of the health system in controlling infectious diseases (Shkolnikov and Cornia, 2000: 254). China and the Soviet Union (and Cuba, not discussed here but shown in Table 10.2) are not isolated cases. For example, infant mortality in Czechoslovakia was more than halved between 1950 and 1960, an annual reduction of close to 8 per cent (Blazek and Dzúrová, 2002: 309).

Cases of rapid mortality decline have taken place outside centrally planned economies, and studies of these cases also highlight the role of health services. The case of Oman was mentioned above. Another example is Senegal, which had extremely high mortality rates of around 400 per 1,000 live births in the 1940s. By 1990 this had fallen to 130 per 1,000 live births, with the decrease accelerating at the end of the 1970s. A study of Senegalese mortality attributes this accelerated decline to

> a new health policy, which emphasised primary health care and was implemented during this period. . . . The proliferation of health infrastructures (which had previously been highly concentrated in Dakar) in the various regions and the implementation of the Expanded Programme of Immunisation (EPI) probably contributed significantly. . . . Continued mortality decreases in the coming years will depend substantially on the continuation of health programmes, in particular of the sustained vaccination initiative, improved pregnancy monitoring, and enhanced conditions of delivery.
>
> (Pison *et al.*, 1995: 155–157)

Studies of less dramatic mortality reductions also identify health services as being of importance. For example, in their analysis of Ovamboland in Namibia, Notkola and Siiskonen write that

> the child mortality decline happened during the 1950s and this mortality decline can be supposed to have been mainly caused by the improved health care system. The health care system was based mainly on the idea of preventing the disease epidemics. With the help of the missionary health care system the Government was also able to carry out the vaccination programme. . . . It is clear that the improved level of education of mothers influenced infant mortality and the threshold of using health services was lower due to improved education.
>
> (2000: 110–111)

Finally, studies of specific interventions point to the effectiveness of immunisation and other public health measures. For example, Kaseje (1992) reports falls in infant mortality of as much as two-thirds as a result of anti-malaria campaigns in Kenya and Nigeria (these falls being much greater than those in control communities). He also cites studies that find the decline to be much less than would have been expected from the number of malaria deaths prior to the intervention. He argues that these are cases in which mortality would be high even in the absence of malaria, so that infants die of something else once malaria is controlled. In such cases, the elimination of malaria is a necessary step to reducing mortality, but is not by itself sufficient. In the case of Sri Lanka, Preston says that the 'best estimate' is that close to half the reduction in mortality from 1930 to 1960 can be attributed to the anti-malaria programme (1996: 533).

Case-study evidence thus almost overwhelmingly points to the importance of public health measures, especially those against infectious diseases. This is not to claim that these are all that matter. As shown by Figure 10.2, there are a number of mediating factors, of which two are mentioned here. Caldwell's frequently cited 1986 paper 'Routes to Low Mortality in Developing Countries' argues strongly that women's position in society plays a critical role, and that female education is an important determining factor. Educated women are more likely, and better able, to take advantage of clean water, health services, and so on. They are also better placed to influence the allocation of household resources towards child health. Second, there is a well-documented simultaneous (i.e. two-way) relationship between fertility and infant mortality. Policies to reduce fertility, which certainly include measures to promote economic growth and other means of reducing insecurity, are undoubtedly important for reducing mortality.

The changing pattern of death

The left-hand panel of Figure 10.3 shows that there is a strong relationship between the under-five mortality rate and the proportion of under-five deaths occurring before the first birthday, using data from Demographic and Health Surveys (DHSs) from the late 1980s to 2000. For the countries

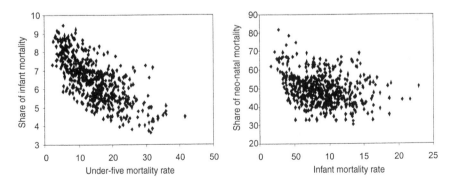

Figure 10.3 Relationship between structure and level of mortality.

Source: Based on data from www.measuredhs.com.

with the highest mortality, over half of under-five deaths occur to those aged 1 to 4. But for the countries with the lowest mortality rates, fewer than one in ten of under-five deaths take place amongst older children. In China, for example, the share of infant deaths in under-five mortality was 68 per cent in 1949, had risen to 80 per cent by 1955 and stood at 95 per cent by 1990 (Campbell, 2001: 231). The right-hand panel shows infant mortality and neo-natal deaths. Although the relationship is less strong, it is the case that amongst countries with the lowest rates of infant death, the majority of these deaths occur within the first month, whereas for countries with higher mortality at least half occur between 1 and 11 months of age.

The same point can be made by looking at the experience of individual countries. Figure 10.4 shows the neo-natal, post-neo-natal and child

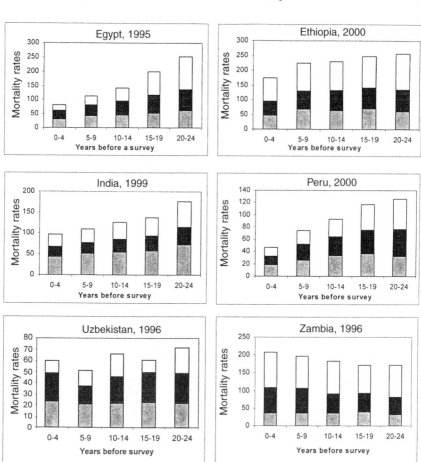

Figure 10.4 Trends in mortality rates for selected countries.

Source: Calculated from data from www.measuredhs.com.

mortality rates for six countries for five time periods (at a five-year interval). Reading the columns from right to left shows how rates have changed over time, with the height of the column being approximately equal to the under-five mortality rate.[10] The first four countries – Egypt, Ethiopia, India and Peru – all illustrate a clear trend of reduction in under-five mortality. It is notable that the bulk of the reduction comes from lower child mortality, with the least change in neo-natal mortality. For example, in Egypt, which most clearly illustrates the pattern, child mortality fell from 120 per 1,000 live births twenty to twenty-five years before the survey, to 19 per 1,000 live births in the most recent five years. Over the same period, neo-natal mortality fell from 63 to 30 per 1,000 live births, and its share of under-five deaths rose from 27 to 38 per cent.

The exceptions really are exceptions. In Zambia, mortality has been rising, in large part owing to HIV/AIDS (see Chapter 12 of this volume), though the decline of health services has also been said to have played a role (see Hanmer and White, 1999). Children born to mothers who are HIV positive have an 80 per cent chance of being HIV positive themselves, in which case they have virtually no chance of living to see their fifth birthday. This helps explain the rise in child mortality in that country. The situation of Uzbekistan exemplifies the social and economic collapse that took place in the former Soviet Union in the 1990s. Indeed, Uzbekistan fared better than most of its neighbours, experiencing the least fall in income (White *et al.*, 2000).[11] Nonetheless, the data for the 1990s show a reversal of the previous downward trend in mortality, with the largest increase being for infant deaths.

The changing age at which death is likely to occur has implications for the most appropriate policies to further reduce mortality, since the cause of death varies by age group. Writing of Africa, Tarver (1996: 66–67) lays this out as follows:

> Most neo-natal deaths are due to congenital abnormalities and injuries occurring during parturition.... In the post-neonatal period of one to 11 months, malnutrition, respiratory, and diarrheal diseases claim about 30 to 40 per cent of infant lives. After age one infectious and parasitic diseases, such as measles and diphtheria, account for about 25 per cent of all early childhood deaths.

So, child deaths are commonly linked to environmental factors and can be brought down by campaigns to control diseases such as malaria and by ensuring good immunisation coverage. Post-natal infants are also amenable to improvements in environmental conditions, especially the provision of clean water, though this can matter less if they are breast-fed, and the other factors related to GOBI-type interventions. But neo-natal deaths are very closely related to the conditions surrounding birth. In a country such as India, child mortality is low, so most under-five deaths occur amongst infants. A growing percentage of these infant deaths are neo-natal: between 1972 and 1995, this share grew from 51 to 65 per cent (Claeson *et al.*, 1999: 33). Antenatal care and attended births thus become increasingly important in bringing about further reductions in mortality.

The high proportion of child deaths in high-mortality countries (most of which are in Africa) reflects not only generally poor environmental conditions but also weak delivery of health services, including immunisation. The result is a far higher level of communicable diseases than elsewhere (Table 10.4). Infectious and parasitic diseases account for 40 per cent of all deaths in sub-Saharan Africa, compared to just 3 per cent in China, which is not much more than in developed countries. African countries have the lowest levels of immunisation overall, with particularly low rates amongst the income poor. Table 10.5 shows data on child mortality and immunisation coverage for five countries. The population are divided into asset quintiles, based on ownership of consumer durables and housing quality. In four of the five cases the percentage of children having no immunisation coverage is far greater in the poorest quintile than it is in the top quintile, with a corresponding differential in mortality rates (Chad is the exception to this). It does not have to be this way, as the case of Zimbabwe, a country with a well-developed primary health-care system, shows. However, the mortality differential is also evident for Zimbabwe, showing that high immunisation coverage alone does not reduce these differences – but overall mortality is much lower in Zimbabwe than in the other countries.

These differences between income groups reflect in part rural–urban differentials. In Ghana, for example, infant mortality in rural areas is 81 per 1,000 live births compared to 54 per 1,000 live births in urban areas. For child mortality these figures are 69 and 34 respectively – that is, child mortality is twice as high in rural areas as in urban ones. Such figures are not atypical. Greater income poverty in rural areas is one factor here, but so is worse access to health services. Nearly one-fifth of rural children are not immunised, compared to only one-twentieth of urban children. Seventy-three per cent of urban births in Ghana were attended by trained medical personnel, compared to only 37 per cent in rural areas.

Policies required to achieve the infant and child mortality Millennium Development Goal

Historical experience shows that it is possible to achieve the rate of mortality reduction required to meet the Millennium Development Goals, but that this will happen only with substantial public interventions for health and related areas, notably water and sanitation, and good education coverage, especially for women. Will economic growth alone be sufficient to bring this about? Higher incomes allow people to afford better health care. But there are economic grounds for the public sector assuming at

Table 10.4 Causes of death for selected regions, 2000

	Sub-Saharan Africa		Latin America and Caribbean		China		Developed countries	
	Male	Female	Male	Female	Male	Female	Male	Female
Number of deaths (000s)								
All causes	4,997	4,208	1,967	1,551	5,820	4,497	4,147	3,784
I. Communicable, maternal, perinatal and nutritional conditions	2,853	2,653	491	345	449	407	300	232
A. Infectious and parasitic diseases	1,986	1,798	296	176	203	144	125	48
B. Respiratory infections	534	444	81	70	158	157	146	156
C. Maternal conditions	–	111	–	11	–	9	–	9
D. Perinatal conditions	262	234	83	57	69	71	20	14
E. Nutritional deficiencies	71	66	31	31	18	27	9	13
II. Non-communicable	1,200	1,152	1,138	1,086	4,665	3,584	3,547	3,395
III. Injuries	944	402	358	120	707	505	301	157
o/w War	210	154	12	9	1	–	–	–
Percentage of total deaths								
All causes	100.0	100.0	100.0	100.0	100.0	100.0	100.0	100.0
I. Communicable, maternal, perinatal and nutritional conditions	57.1	63.0	25.0	22.2	7.7	9.1	7.2	6.1
A. Infectious and parasitic diseases	39.7	42.7	15.0	11.3	3.5	3.2	3.0	1.3
B. Respiratory infections	10.7	10.6	4.1	4.5	2.7	3.5	3.5	4.1
C. Maternal conditions	0.0	2.6	0.0	0.7	0.0	0.2	0.0	0.0
D. Perinatal conditions	5.2	5.6	4.2	3.7	1.2	1.6	0.5	0.0
E. Nutritional deficiencies	1.4	1.6	1.6	2.0	0.3	0.6	0.2	0.3
II. Non-communicable	24.0	27.4	57.9	70.0	80.2	79.7	85.5	89.7
III. Injuries	18.9	9.6	18.2	7.7	12.1	11.2	7.3	4.1
o/w War	4.2	3.7	0.6	0.6	0.0	0.0	0.0	0.0
Memo item: total population (millions)	324	327	257	262	656	619	580	612

Sources: World Bank Web site and UN *World Population Prospects: The 2000 Revision.*

Table 10.5 Child mortality and immunisation by asset quintile in selected African countries

Quintile	Chad	Ghana	Mozambique	Niger	Zimbabwe
Child mortality rate (per 1,000)					
Poorest	99	86	111	173	34
Second	106	86	90	239	37
Third	119	62	84	227	16
Fourth	100	41	61	202	25
Fifth	91	30	55	107	15
Whole population	103	61	80	190	26
No immunisation (per cent)					
Poorest	65	31	36	57	84
Second	51	18	27	45	85
Third	49	9	26	54	89
Fourth	33	14	5	37	85
Fifth	19	3	1	8	90
Whole population	43	15	19	40	86

Source: Data from World Bank Web site, calculated from DHS data.

least some of the responsibility. Arguing the case for public goods is not currently fashionable, but there are good reasons to consider public health investments as falling into this category.

Infectious diseases are, unsurprisingly, infectious, so their prevalence is a clear case of an externality (something I do, or, in this case, have, that affects you). Where externalities exist, markets will not bring about the most socially desirable outcome as there will be under-investment in the good, in this case actions required to reduce the risk of disease. Immunisation has a threshold effect, with about 80 per cent coverage required to remove the possibility of an epidemic.[12] There is a strong case for a greater emphasis on preventive health care, and it makes little or no sense to attempt cost recovery for such services. Similar arguments apply to improved water and sanitation. The current fashion is for cost recovery in this area, partly based on the failure of centralised government services to maintain facilities. However, other participatory mechanisms, such as those used in some social funds, have shown that it is possible to get communities to take responsibility for facility maintenance without requiring full cost recovery (Carvalho *et al.*, 2002). And the economics suggest that if there are increasing returns to scale, which is likely with infrastructure investments, a subsidy is required to support the optimal level of production (based on marginal cost pricing – this is the starting point for old-fashioned public-sector economics).

Despite considerable progress under the Expanded Programme of Immunisation, coverage remains low in sub-Saharan Africa and South Asia, having fallen in the former region in the 1990s. For sub-Saharan Africa, coverage increased from 16 per cent in 1980 to 56 per cent in

1990, but then fell ten points to just 46 per cent in 1999.[13] Coverage in South Asia rose steadily from 23 per cent in 1980 to 57 per cent in 1990, remaining stable at around 60 per cent thereafter. Other regions have faired better, achieving rates at or close to 90 per cent by the end of the 1990s. In contrast to other regions, coverage in Eastern Europe fell in the 1980s and early 1990s, but had recovered to 90 per cent by 1999. Prospects for improving coverage now rest with the Global Alliance for Vaccines and Immunisation (GAVI). Whilst the programme covers many of the poorest countries, it is not intended as the sole source of finance. Rather, it is seen as a catalyst for governments to commit their own expenditure, and a complement to bilateral aid funds. However, neither of these sources has traditionally been prioritised towards the needs of the poor.

The Copenhagen Social Summit in 1995 agreed the 20:20 initiative in which 20 per cent of government spending and 20 per cent of aid should go to basic services for the poor, defined as basic health and education, water supply and sanitation. This agreement was not amongst those used to draw up the Millennium Development Goals. However, developing countries ensured that the Millennium Development Goals included Goal 8 concerning global partnership, specifying some goals for their 'partners'. Indicator 33 is the 'proportion of ODA [Official Development Assistance] to basic social services (basic education, primary health care, nutrition, safe water and sanitation)', but there is no quantified target, despite one being readily available from Copenhagen. This fact reflects the unequal nature of the aid 'partnership', in which the side with the power does not bind itself to actual targets. However, the good news is that since data first became available, the share of Development Assistance Committee (DAC) bilateral aid for basic health and education has increased more than eightfold. The bad news is that it was initially less than 0.5 per cent, and the most recent data (for 2000) put it at a paltry 4 per cent.[14]

Donor aid to basic health and education remains pitifully low. But there is at least an upward trend, and the fact that attention is being paid to the 'use' of debt relief funds and that sector programmes are of rising importance does indicate that a genuine change of attitude has occurred at least amongst some donors. But reliance on sector programmes means that government expenditure must be going to the right things, and the evidence here is not encouraging.

This evidence comes from two types of study: benefit incidence and public expenditure tracking (PET) studies. Benefit incidence studies use data on unit costs and use of facilities, taken from household surveys, to estimate the subsidy (public expenditure, less any user payments) to different groups, most usually income quintiles. The limitation of this analysis is that the data usually assume constant unit costs for a given facility level (e.g. health clinic), which is almost certainly not the case, thus imparting a bias which probably understates the skew of resources to the better off. Table 10.6 shows results for selected countries. In all but one case, those in the top quintile are more likely to use all levels of service. They are much more likely to use hospital facilities than are the poor, and hospitals receive far more subsidy per patient than do primary facilities. Thus in all cases the share of public spending on health which benefits the top 20 per cent is greater than that going to the bottom 20 per cent. The rich receive a subsidy twelve times that of the poor in the most extreme case. These results are to a large extent driven by urban bias in service provision.

PET studies analyse how much spending in a sector reaches the grassroots level. There is only one detailed study of health and education, though several others are in the pipeline. The first such study, for Uganda, has the most comprehensive results for education, finding that less than 30 per cent of intended non-salary spending actually reached schools in the early 1990s (Ablo and Reinikka, 1998). The health sector lacked comparable expenditure data, but the authors cite another study which suggested major leakage at the health unit level as staff sell drugs in order to supplement their salaries. In the case of Ghana, Ye and Canagarajah (2002) report that only 20 per cent of non-salary recurrent spending reaches health facilities. Reorienting the spending of social sectors from central ministries to service providers is recommended to address this situation (in some countries, education civil servants have been made into teachers).

To close, it should be repeated that this chapter is not arguing that economic growth is not important to reducing poverty in all its many dimensions. But growth alone is not sufficient, nor is it always necessary.

Table 10.6 Benefit incidence of public spending on health in selected countries

	Quintile shares of:							
	Primary facilities		*Hospital outpatient*		*Hospital in-patient*[a]		*All health*	
	Bottom	*Top*	*Bottom*	*Top*	*Bottom*	*Top*	*Bottom*	*Top*
Côte d'Ivoire (1995)	14	22	8	39	n.a.	n.a.	11	32
Ghana (1992)	10	31	13	35	11	32	12	33
Guinea (1994)	10	36	1	55	n.a.	n.a.	4	48
Kenya (1992)[b]	22	14	13	26	n.a.	n.a.	14	24
Madagascar (1993)	10	29	14	30	n.a.	n.a.	12	30
Tanzania (1992/1993)	18	21	11	37	20	36	17	29
South Africa (1994)	18	10	15	17	n.a.	n.a.	16	17

Source: Castro-Leal *et al.* (1999).

Notes
a Hospital subsidies combine in- and outpatient spending in Côte d'Ivoire, Guinea, Kenya, Madagascar and South Africa.
b Rural only.

Sustainable health services require a strong revenue base, but much can be achieved in the meantime with external support. And some measures, such as promoting breastfeeding, are relatively low cost. Government action can facilitate an improved transmission from growth to poverty reduction. It can do this by ensuring that growth is itself pro-poor. Targeting priority spending is a critical component of any anti-poverty strategy. Of course, most governments claim to target priority spending, so it is important to consider whether this simply has not happened because of lack of capacity.

A government's ability to carry out these actions is thus crucial. At the extreme are collapsed states, the importance of which should not be neglected in any discussion of the Millennium Development Goals. During times of conflict, health services usually collapse. Immunisation rates in refugee camps may be very low, and infant mortality rates as high as 600 per 1,000 live births have been reported in acute emergencies (Roberts *et al.*, 2001: 12). Conflict prevention is thus a critical underpinning for this, and all other, development goals. Other states are functioning but are often believed to lack the capacity to deliver on promises of universal health and education. There are grounds for questioning such judgements. Low-income countries, such as China, Cuba and Vietnam, have put in place effective primary health care. To a lesser extent, Nicaragua and Zimbabwe have also done so in the past. What is perceived as a lack of capacity has often been a mixture of resource misallocation, which is being rectified in response to both internal and external pressures, and the consequent lack of resources at local level.

I would like to end on an optimistic note. Travelling in countries such as Ghana, Malawi and Zambia, countries with supposed weak local capacity, I have been struck by the idealism, commitment and ability of many health and education workers, and of local officials. But unfortunately these people can work only with the resources to hand, so my optimism must be muted by the need to reorient aid and government budgets to meet priority needs. Only if this is done can the Millennium Development Goals on mortality be met.

Acknowledgement

I am indebted to Richard Jolly and Richard Black for useful comments on an earlier draft of this chapter. The usual disclaimer applies.

Notes

1 This is the same debate as that between the World Bank and the United Nations Development Programme (UNDP) during the 1990s (see, for example, Ranis *et al.*, 2000; Ravallion, 1997; White, 1999).
2 Infant, child and under-five mortality are the most commonly used categories.

Any cut-off is of course arbitrary, though demographers argue for having two under-five categories as the cause of death varies by age. The observed rates are sensitive to the cut-off, especially up to about two years, which is one reason why the United Nations Children's Fund (UNICEF) has adopted the under-five measure.

3 The linear nature of the decline is something of a statistical artefact as linear interpolation has been used for some series.

4 Hanmer *et al.* (2002) show that Oman and Saudi Arabia used to be outliers in a scatter plot of infant mortality against income per capita (logged), but are no longer so.

5 Also known as universal coverage of immunisation (UCI), the name used by UNICEF.

6 A similar result is found in the regression reported on pp. 216–217 of this chapter.

7 The 'cold chain' refers to the logistical arrangements to maintain vaccines at the required temperature from the time of production to use in health clinics.

8 Data reported by UNICEF (2002) show that around thirty developing countries have achieved substantial reductions in mortality since the 1960s, leaving some one hundred which have not. The discussion here draws general conclusions from a selection of successful and less successful cases.

9 It is not possible to do justice to the substantial literature on the historical experience of the now developed countries. For further examples, see the papers in Bideau *et al.* (1997) and Schofield *et al.* (1991).

10 It is only approximate as the under-five rate is not the sum of infant and child mortality, but this sum with child mortality adjusted to reflect those not surviving the first year.

11 However, life expectancy, though not under-five mortality, began to decline in the Soviet Union in the 1960s (Cornia and Paniccià, 2000).

12 'Herd immunity' at which the disease should not occur at all is achieved with 95 per cent coverage.

13 Data from the UNICEF Web site: http://www.childinfo.org/eddb/immuni/trends.htm.

14 Data from the DAC Web site: www.oecd.org/dac/statistics (table 19).

References

Ablo, E. and Reinikka, R. (1998) 'Do Budgets Really Matter? Evidence from Public Spending on Education and Health in Uganda', Policy Research Paper 1926, Washington, DC: World Bank.

Bideau, A., Desjardins, B. and Brignoli, H.P. (eds) (1997) *Infant and Child Mortality in the Past*, Oxford: Clarendon Press.

Blazek, J. and Dzúrová, D. (2000) 'The Decline of Mortality in the Czech Republic During the Transition', in Cornia, G.A. and Paniccià, R. (eds) *The Mortality Crisis in Transitional Economies*, Oxford: Oxford University Press.

Caldwell, J.C. (1986) 'Routes to Low Mortality in Poor Countries', *Population and Development Review*, 12: 171–220.

Campbell, C. (2001) 'Mortality Change and the Epidemiological Transition in Beijing, 1644–1990,' in Liu, T-j., Lee, J., Reher, D.S., Saito, O. and Feng, W. (eds) *Asian Population History*, Oxford: Oxford University Press.

Carvalho, S., Perkins, G. and White, H. (2002) *Social Funds: Assessing Effectiveness*, Washington, DC: World Bank, OED.

Castro-Leal, F., Dayton, J., Demery, L. and Mehra, K. (1999) 'Public Social Spending in Africa: Do the Poor Benefit?', *World Bank Research Observer*, 14(1): 49–72, February.

Claeson, M., Bos, E. and Pathmanathan, M. (1999) 'Reducing Child Mortality in India: Keeping Up the Pace' HNP Working Paper, Washington, DC: World Bank.

Cornia, G.A. and Paniccià, R. (eds) (2000) *The Mortality Crisis in Transitional Economies*, Oxford: Oxford University Press.

Filmer, B. and Pritchett, L. (1999) 'The Impact of Public Spending on Health: Does Money Matter?', *Social Science and Medicine*, 49: 1309–1323.

Hanmer, L. and White, H. (1999) *Human Development in Sub Saharan Africa*, The Hague: Institute of Social Studies Advisory Service.

Hanmer, L., Lensink, R. and White, H. (2003 forthcoming) 'Infant and Child Mortality in Developing Countries: Analysing the Data for Robust Determinants', *Journal of Development Studies*, Brighton: IDS, University of Sussex.

Howard, M. and Millard, A. (1997) *Hunger and Shame: Child Malnutrition and Poverty on Mount Kilimanjaro*, London: Routledge.

Jolly, R. (ed.) (2001) *Jim Grant: UNICEF Visionary*, Geneva: UNICEF.

Kaseje, D.C.O. (1992) 'Malaria in Kenya: Prevention, Control and Impact on Mortality', in van de Walle, D., Pison, G. and Sala-Diakanda, M. (eds) *Mortality and Society in Sub-Saharan Africa*, Oxford: Clarendon Press.

McKeown, T. (1976) *The Modern Rise of Population*, London: Edward Arnold.

Mosley, W.H. and Chen, L.C. (1984) 'An Analytical Framework for the Study of Child Survival in Developing Countries', *Population and Development Review*, supplement to vol. 10: 25–45.

Notkola, V. and Siiskonen, H. (2000) *Fertility, Mortality and Migration in Sub-Saharan Africa: The Case of Ovamboland in North Namibia, 1925–90*, Basingstoke, UK: Macmillan.

Pison, G., Hill, K., Cohen, B. and Foote, K. (1995) *Population Dynamics of Senegal*, Washington, DC: National Academy Press.

Preston, S. (1975) 'The Changing Relation Between Mortality and Level of Economic Development', *Population Studies*, 29: 231–248.

—— (1996) 'Population Studies in Mortality', *Population Studies*, 50: 525–536.

Ranis, G., Stewart, F. and Ramirez, A. (2000) 'Economic Growth and Human Development', *World Development*, 28(2): 197–219.

Ravallion, M. (1997) 'Good and Bad Growth: The Human Development Reports', *World Development*, 25(5): 631–638.

Riley, J. (2001) *Rising Life Expectancy: A Global History*, Cambridge: Cambridge University Press.

Roberts, L., Hale, C., Belyakdoumi, F. *et al.* (2001) *Mortality in Eastern Democratic Republic of Congo: Results from Eleven Mortality Surveys*, New York: International Rescue Committee.

Schofield, R., Reher, D. and Bideau, A. (eds) (1991) *The Decline of Mortality in Europe*, Oxford: Clarendon Press.

Shkolnikov, V.M. and Cornia, G.A. (2000) 'Population Crisis and Rising Mortality in Transitional Russia', in Cornia, G.A. and Paniccià, R. (eds) *The Mortality Crisis in Transitional Economies*, Oxford: Oxford University Press.

Skeet, I. (1992) *Oman: Politics and Development*, New York: St Martin's Press.

Tarver, J.D. (1996) *The Demography of Africa*, Westport, CT: Praeger.

UNICEF (2002) *State of the World's Children 2002*, Geneva: UNICEF.

Vögele, J. (1998) *Urban Mortality Change in England and Germany, 1970–1913*, Liverpool: Liverpool University Press.

White, H. (1999) 'Global Poverty Reduction: Are We Heading in the Right Direction?', *Journal of International Development*, 11(4): 503–519.

White, H. with Calandrino, M., Leavy, J., Litchfield, J., Edwards, C. and Amadi, J. (2000) *Poverty in Middle Income Countries*, Report for DFID, Brighton: IDS, University of Sussex.

Woods, R. (2000) *The Demography of Victorian England and Wales*, Cambridge: Cambridge University Press.

Ye, X. and Canagarajah, S. (2002) 'Efficiency of Public Expenditure: Distribution and Beyond', Africa Region Working Paper 31, Washington, DC: World Bank.

11 Towards reproductive health for all?

Hilary Standing

Setting international goals: the rise (and fall) of reproductive health

This chapter differs from others in this part of the book in that it focuses on the broad area of reproductive health, rather than the specific Millennium Development Goal of reducing maternal mortality. This focus reflects two concerns. First, as noted in Chapter 3, data on maternal mortality are amongst the most difficult to pin down in terms of obtaining reliable information with which to analyse global or even country-specific trends. This is reflected in Vandemoortele's discussion of trends on maternal mortality in Chapter 6, where he concludes on the basis of the limited available data that the goal of a three-quarters reduction in maternal mortality is unlikely to be met by 2015.

Second, it also reflects a particular chain of events in the setting of targets for reproductive health. In general, international goals and targets play an important role in focusing attention on key areas of development need and practice. They are also important arenas within which different political agendas are played out. This is particularly well illustrated in the case of reproductive health. Yet the past decade has witnessed two major, but in some ways contrasting, attempts to put the spotlight on reproductive health priorities.

The first of these was the International Conference on Population and Development (ICPD), held in Cairo in 1994 (UNFPA, 1994 and 1999). This produced international agreement on a vision and set of principles for reproductive health and a costed Programme of Action which was adopted by the United Nations (UN) General Assembly (and which is popularly known as the Cairo Agenda). It departed radically from the old-style vertically funded family planning and maternal and child health programmes in emphasising a comprehensive set of sexual and reproductive health needs for both women and men through the life cycle.

The second has been the more focused attempt to identify priority targets and indicators in the area of reproductive health through the International Development Targets and the more recent Millennium

Development Goals. In the International Development Targets, reproductive health was represented both as part of a target on reducing mortality rates, and separately as a restated commitment to the principles of the Cairo Agenda:

- a reduction by two-thirds in the mortality rates for infants and children under five and *reduction by three-quarters in maternal mortality by 2015*; and
- access through the primary health-care system to *reproductive health services for all individuals of appropriate ages*, including safe and reliable family planning methods, as soon as possible and no later than the year 2015.

One of the most significant changes between the Targets and the Goals is in reproductive health. In the Millennium Development Goals, we find that while maternal mortality has become a target in its own right (Table 11.1), the goal of reproductive health for all has disappeared. Reducing the spread of HIV/AIDS has been added as a separate goal, but family planning appears only as an indicator for monitoring the HIV/AIDS targets.[1]

Behind this change lies a tale of continuing political struggle over women's rights to sexual and reproductive health services which meet their needs. Conservative opposition to the Cairo Agenda came from a coalition led by the Vatican, with countries such as Sudan, Libya and Iran as allies. They were joined by fundamentalist Christian groups in North America, which have been particularly instrumental in constraining United States Agency for International Development (USAID) funding for family planning programmes, to ensure that they do not support abortion, however indirectly. USAID is by far the largest bilateral funder of reproductive health-related programmes. With the election of George W. Bush in 2000, the US administration became the powerful new leader of this alliance (Berer, 2001; Girard, 2001).

The writing out of reproductive health from the Millennium Development Goals took place in the UN Secretary General's office under pressure from this US-led alliance and without any wider UN debate. Other early targets of the current US administration have included references to reproductive health in international agreements on commitments to ado-

Table 11.1 Millennium Development Goal for maternal health

Goal: Improve maternal health	Indicators
Reduce by three-quarters, between 1990 and 2015, the maternal mortality ratio.	Maternal mortality ratio Proportion of births attended by skilled health personnel.

lescent health, as well as American funding for UNFPA – supposedly on the grounds that it supports coercive family planning practices in China (Girard, 2001; Jacobson and Mallik, 2002).

There is, therefore, a political tension between these two major international initiatives, both of which many countries simultaneously subscribe to. The dropping of the reproductive health target from the Millennium Development Goals must be viewed with concern after so much international advocacy effort has been expended in pushing reproductive health up the policy agenda.

This tension is also reflected in the structures for monitoring progress in meeting goals and targets. The Cairo Programme of Action is monitored through the UN and has strong formal and informal advocacy constituencies keeping the broad vision alive in international and national arenas.[2] It remains to be seen what range of constituencies emerge in monitoring progress towards the Millennium Development Goals.

The removal of reproductive health as an official Goal has not gone unchallenged.[3] In early 2002 the World Health Assembly passed a very interesting resolution to guide the work of the World Health Organisation (WHO) with regard to achieving the Millennium Development Goals. This was passed with strong support from Latin America, Africa, the European Union and others, and against pressure from US delegates to remove all mention of reproductive health. It urged member states

> to strengthen and expand efforts to meet, in particular, international development goals and targets related to reduction of maternal and child mortality and malnutrition and to improve access to primary health care services, *including reproductive health*, with special attention to the needs of the poor and underserved populations.[4]

This effectively reaffirmed WHO's commitment to the Cairo Agenda and other international resolutions on reproductive health and human rights, and mandated further action on these. It was also a recognition that the targets laid out in the Millennium Development Goals cannot be met unless reproductive health services are available and accessible, and coupled with action on gender disadvantage. However, funding to turn these resolutions into action will be seriously compromised without support from the world's richest nation. There is also the problem of the 'balkanisation' of reproductive health in the Millennium Development Goals which is entailed in splitting it between different goals and targets.[5]

Reproductive health is thus a contested terrain in which are embedded broader ideological struggles over different visions of human rights and needs. It is also a terrain which is particularly susceptible to appropriation by domestic political agendas and to 'unholy' alliances (Berer, 2001) between otherwise unfriendly states.

In the rest of this chapter I will discuss some of the issues raised by both the broad and the narrow commitments to reproductive health in the Cairo Programme of Action and the Millennium Development Goals. I will argue that there are some essential preconditions for making progress in either direction. These relate not only to the willingness of developed countries to implement their financial pledges, but also to the need for systemic improvements in health-care delivery systems in poor countries in particular. This in turn requires attention to the wider context of health sector reforms and how they intersect with the substantive agendas of maternal health, family planning and the range of services which together constitute reproductive health care.

The next section outlines the vision for reproductive health, as effectively set out by the Cairo Agenda. The section after that presents indicators of the present situation in reproductive and maternal health. Two further sections discuss health sector financing issues, and are followed by a section that analyses performance of reproductive health in light of the recent reforms in financing. The likely future of reproductive health, given experience so far, is then examined.

The Cairo Agenda: a comprehensive vision for reproductive health

The concept of reproductive health is now so ubiquitous that it is sometimes difficult to remember that it has quite a recent history in international parlance. It effectively came into being with the commitments made at the 1994 International Conference on Population and Development in Cairo (UNFPA, 1999). Cairo was the most recent of the decadal world population conferences, which had been extremely influential in setting the international tone of the debate about health, population and development.[6] Earlier conferences held in Bucharest and Mexico by and large upheld a majority consensus that population policies meant controlling population growth in developing countries as a way of creating sustainable development.

Whilst not necessarily entailed in the language and resolutions of the earlier conferences, population policy in the 1970s and 1980s translated into narrowly focused and aggressively targeted family planning programmes. The overriding concern was with meeting demographic targets, and major donors funded large-scale population programmes in many developing countries. These programmes were vertical in the sense that they were dedicated to contraceptive service delivery and functionally separate from other health programmes, such as maternal and child health (MCH). They frequently received the lion's share of external funding for basic health services.

Programmes were heavily driven by numerical targets for family planning workers, coupled with incentives for women to use long-term or non-reversible methods of contraception. In a number of programmes this led to a strong bias towards methods such as sterilisation at the expense of reversible methods, concerns about coercion and lack of informed consent, and encouragement to family planning workers to fiddle the books for fear of having their salaries cut if they could not meet their targets (Hartmann, 1995; Sen *et al.*, 1994).

In the 1980s there was considerable disquiet about this approach, and a coalition for change developed across advocacy groups, particularly women's health groups, NGOs and some international agencies (Sen, 1999). Two key demands were articulated: an end to incentive-based family planning targets and methods in favour of a menu approach and informed choice, and a plea for integration of family planning programmes into the framework of primary health care. Behind this lay much broader debates about the causes and consequences of high population growth in poor countries, about human rights in the area of fertility decision-making, and about the need for a stronger developmental approach to population issues, including issues of gender equality.

Cairo was thus a watershed, in that it sealed a paradigm shift that had been gradually taking shape in international and national thinking on population issues (Box 11.1). A broad coalition for change was able to push through at least a rhetorical commitment to a human rights approach to health, social well-being and gender equality. This came together in a new vision of reproductive health and rights.

It is important to note that agreements reached in Cairo with respect to gender and reproductive rights were built upon earlier agreements on women's human rights that had been reached at the UN conference on human rights in 1993 in Vienna. These in turn were reflected in the commitments to gender equality and reproductive health that were reached at the Fourth World Conference on Women, which became known as the Beijing Platform for Action. Further reinforcement of the Cairo agenda on reproductive health and rights came in the macroeconomic agenda of the World Summit on Social Development. This produced the 20:20 agreement on the amount of funding which countries should allocate to the social sector, to be matched by the same commitment from the international community.[7]

Box 11.1 Key moments in the development of the reproductive health approach

1974	World Population Conference, Bucharest
1984	World Population Conference, Mexico City
(1993	UN conference on human rights in Vienna)
1994	**International Conference on Population and Development, Cairo**
1995	Fourth World Conference on Women in Beijing
	World Social Summit on Development, Copenhagen
1999	Cairo (ICPD+5) Review

These various conferences and summits are politically significant in that their agreements become enshrined in UN conventions and resolutions, countries can opt to sign up to them, and international mechanisms are put in place to monitor them. For instance, in 1999 the Cairo +5 review looked at progress with the Cairo Agenda, including a detailed examination of successes and failures in specific countries (Correa and Sen, 1999).

What is the Cairo Agenda?

The Cairo Agenda – or, to give it its official title, the ICPD Programme for Action – produced the following definition of reproductive health:

> *Reproductive health* is the complete physical, mental and social well-being in all matters related to the reproductive system. This implies that people are able to have a satisfying and safe sex life and that they have the capacity to have children and the freedom to decide if and when to do so. Reproductive health care is defined as the constellation of methods, techniques and services that contribute to reproductive health and well-being by preventing and solving reproductive health problems.

We may note here the distancing from demographic objectives and targets. The definition also in part follows closely the wording of the WHO declaration on the concept of health.

It also carries a set of associated rights. Reproductive rights are defined as the rights of couples and individuals to:

* decide freely and responsibly the number and spacing of their children and to have the information, education and means to do so;
* attain the highest standards of sexual and reproductive health; and
* make decisions about reproduction free of discrimination, coercion and violence.

These are matched by a similar set of definitions and rights for sexual health.

Reproductive health may include the following services:

> *Family planning* counselling, information, education, communication and services, *pre-natal care*, education and services; *safe delivery and post-natal care*, especially breastfeeding and women's health care, prevention and treatment for infertility; *abortion care*, including prevention and management of consequences, *treatment* of reproductive tract infections (RTIs), sexually transmitted infections (STIs) and other reproductive health conditions, *information and education* on human

sexuality, reproductive health and responsible parenthood; *referral* for family planning, diagnosis, and treatment for pregnancy complications, delivery and abortion, infertility, RTIs, breast cancer and cancers of the reproductive system, and STIs/HIV/AIDS.

(Cairo Programme of Action, para 7.6)

The Cairo reproductive health vision is based on some key concepts and principles. First, it links sexual and reproductive health to broader human rights for both women and men. This is particularly apparent in the changed language around fertility and contraceptive choice. But it also underpins a shift towards seeing health needs as implying associated rights, such as the right not to die avoidably in childbirth.

Second, it signals a whole-lifespan approach to reproductive health. Still, to a large extent, reproductive health is seen as the aggregate of maternal and child health programmes and family planning for married women of reproductive age only. The lifespan approach takes account of the need to cater for the reproductive health needs of adolescents, unmarried people and people in the post-childbearing years.

Third, there is a focus on both women's and men's roles and responsibilities in securing women's rights and health, particularly in respect of fertility decisions, protection against the risk of sexually transmitted illnesses, and improving maternal health and nutrition. Increasingly, with the HIV/AIDS epidemic and the associated role of other STIs as a co-factor in its spread, the reproductive health agenda has widened further to emphasise men's reproductive and sexual health needs.

Fourth, women's empowerment is seen as an intrinsic aspect of securing their health human rights. Improvements in reproductive health are thus linked to a wider gender equality agenda, including addressing the gender gap in education (see Chapter 9) and empowering women as citizens.

Finally, there is a strong statement of principle on the need for universal availability and accessibility of reproductive health services, including services for underserved groups and minorities such as the poor and adolescents. Related to this is a stress on the quality of services and, particularly, respect for clients regardless of gender, class, ethnic or other differences.

This Agenda represents a considerable achievement for coalition-building at national and international levels. As noted above, it was negotiated in the teeth of considerable resistance from an alliance of religious conservatives from countries in both the North and South. Issues such as abortion (which is a major cause of premature death where legally sanctioned and accessible services are unavailable) and the rights of adolescents to reproductive health services continue to be highly contentious and contested. A number of countries, particularly in the Middle East, have not endorsed the Cairo Agenda. Nevertheless, it moved the debate on population and health decisively in a different direction.

Reproductive and maternal health: how are they faring?

In this section I will look at some of the main status indicators in reproductive health at the start of a new millennium, focusing particularly on
maternal health. This is less easy than may be imagined. Probably the
most reliable figures are on contraceptive prevalence rate, due to the
major efforts of national family planning programmes over the past few
decades. Until recently, reproductive health status indicators have been
poorly defined compared to other areas of epidemiology. Few can be
described as accurate as there are huge problems in data collection and in
availability. What is most difficult to answer is how things have changed
over time. Reliable and appropriately disaggregated time series data are
rarely available. For instance, figures on maternal mortality are difficult to
interpret as much of the increase noted in the recent figures is thought to
be due to better and more accurate reporting.

The Cairo Programme of Action, and subsequently the Beijing Platform of Action agreed at the 1995 World Conference on Women, precipit-
ated considerable efforts to develop appropriate reproductive health
indicators to monitor progress in fulfilling these goals. There has been
something of a tension between the view that countries should select
indicators most appropriate to their needs and capacities to collect data,
and the needs of international agencies to have information for international comparability and monitoring. Consensus on an accepted set of
indicators has thus been elusive, but WHO has used an expert panel
method for identifying a limited number of robust general indicators for
reproductive health in a given setting which can 'stand for' the broader
concept of reproductive health (WHO, 1997).[8]

However, many countries continue to lack the capacity and infrastructure
to collect such data through their existing health information systems.
Much of what we know about reproductive health status therefore relies
upon snapshot surveys carried out by different agencies, often using different methodologies and definitions. The most commonly used global
indicators relevant to reproductive health are the maternal mortality ratio
(MMR) and the contraceptive prevalence rate (CPR).

The maternal mortality ratio figures in both the International Development Targets and the Millennium Development Goals.[9] It is not difficult
to understand why. On average, one woman dies every minute from pregnancy or childbirth. Maternal mortality, like child mortality, provides a
telling proxy for the effects of poverty, inequality and lack of accessible
health services.[10] More than 99 per cent of the estimated 585,000 deaths
annually from pregnancy and childbirth causes occur in developing countries. In developed countries, on the other hand, the risk of dying during
pregnancy or childbirth has declined by fiftyfold over the past seventy
years. Or, to put it another way, the lifetime risk for a woman of dying
from pregnancy- and childbirth-related causes is 1 in 4,000 in Western

Europe and 1 in 48 in developing countries. In some sub-Saharan African countries it is as high as 1 in 9 (Gelband *et al.*, 2001; WHO, 2001a).[11] This reflects both the high level of risk from pregnancy and the high numbers of pregnancies per woman.

The true picture may be even worse than this. Only seventy-eight countries (less than half) routinely record cause of death, and those that do not tend to be the very poorest, where childbearing is the most risky. As experts have noted, MMR estimations should be treated with caution. Routine vital registration data are lacking in many developing countries, and maternal deaths are generally thought to be under-reported for various cultural, definitional and logistical reasons. Indeed, the first global estimates of maternal mortality were not made until the late 1980s. Furthermore, although the global figures are high, maternal deaths are relatively rare events and accurate monitoring requires very large data sets, which are expensive to collect (UNICEF, 1997).

But this is only part of the picture on maternal health. Beneath this stark picture lies another layer of maternal morbidity – illness and disability which does not result in death – and for which we have very little reliable information. However, we know that this affects many more women, often for the rest of their lives (WHO, 1999). Maternal deaths and ill health also have serious consequences for child survival. Maternal death often results in the death of the baby, and surviving children have poorer survival prospects than those with mothers who are alive.

Given the difficulties of getting reliable figures on maternal mortality, trained assistance in childbirth is often used as a proxy for measuring progress in reducing maternal mortality as it provides a measure of access to essential maternal health services (WHO, 2001a). It is now one of the indicators for the Millennium Development Goal on maternal mortality. Simms *et al.* (2001) analysed data on this from Demographic and Health Surveys (DHSs) in twenty-two developing countries. These showed national declines in fifteen of these countries and improvements in only seven of them. The picture is very mixed, with some countries and regions making progress and others lagging or experiencing actual reverses, particularly in sub-Saharan Africa. The impact of HIV/AIDS on health status and on health resources in severely affected countries cannot be overstressed (see Chapter 12).

A similar mixed picture emerges in respect of contraceptive prevalence rates. World-wide, it was estimated that in 1993, 40 per cent of reproductive-age couples still did not have access to modern contraceptive methods. But again, this disguises wide regional variation, as Table 11.2 indicates.

Africa again shows the greatest problems of lack of available, accessible and utilised services. In West Africa the rate of contraceptive use is estimated at only 8 per cent (UNFPA, 2001). This contrasts dramatically with East Asia, where the very high rates of use of modern contraceptives partly reflect historically high levels of compulsion, such as in the one-child policy in China.

Table 11.2 Levels of current contraceptive use by major areas

	Area (%)	*All methods (%)*
World total	62	56
More developed regions	70	59
Least developed countries	60	55
Latin America/Caribbean	69	60
Africa	25	20
Eastern Asia	82	80
South Asia	48	29

Source: Compiled from UN Population Division (1998) and UNFPA (2001).

Prevalence rates are generally rising. In two-thirds of the countries for which trend data are available, prevalence has increased by ten percentage points over the past decade (UN Population Division, 1998). However, there is much that remains unsatisfactory about family planning delivery. Method mix and choice continue to be very constrained in most developing countries, with female sterilisation accounting for nearly 40 per cent of contraceptive use, as compared to 12 per cent in developed countries. Service quality of reproductive health services generally is often of poor technical quality and delivered rudely by inadequately trained, supervised and remunerated staff (Hulton *et al.*, 1998; Simmons and Elias, 1994).

Some of the key causes of this are the collapse of basic health services as a consequence of economic crisis and government failure, endemic conflict and war, and rising levels of HIV/AIDS infection placing intolerable burdens on formal health care. These factors all point to the need to address much larger agendas on poverty, governance and international responsibility in the context of global health crises such as HIV/AIDS.

Who pays for reproductive health?

In the past fifteen years, health sector financing has been a major area of reform in most developing countries. The main shift has been towards a far greater mix of financing sources and mechanisms for cost recovery beyond public finance. There has been a move to much greater reliance on private financing through encouraging greater official private-sector involvement (Kutzin, 1995). The Cairo Programme of Action itself called for a mixed financing strategy for mobilising resources nationally from the private sector, along with the selective use of user fees and other forms of cost recovery.

What is happening internationally?

Cairo produced a set of projections about costs, together with commitments from the international community and national governments. In 1995 the bilateral donor commitment to population assistance was US$1.4 billion, which was US$3.6 billion short of the total bilateral and multilateral commitments for implementing the Cairo Programme of Action by 2000 (Forman and Ghosh, 1999). A total of 73 per cent of this came from just four donors: the USA, the UK, Germany and Japan. It is clear on the basis of this that the 2015 target of US$21.7 billion stands no chance of being met.

Because reproductive health is not a sector but consists of different programmes embedded in a larger health system, it is difficult to plot precisely how much goes to it. But figures from 1990 estimate that 46 per cent of external assistance to health and population sectors went to general health services and 46 per cent to reproductive health. Of this, 42 per cent went to family planning. Safe Motherhood programmes received just 0.2 per cent of total funds. As the Safe Motherhood initiative has been the main international agency response to maternal mortality, this does not give cause for optimism on funding commitments for the Millennium Development Goal (Goodburn and Campbell, 2001).

Overall, grant aid appears to be declining, but international assistance in the form of 'soft' loans from the World Bank and targeting for specific diseases is increasing (Walt *et al.*, 1999). Loan finance favours certain kinds of reform policies in financing – including greater use of the private sector, user charges at point of service and a move away from comprehensive primary health care to basic service packages of selective interventions. Disease targeting tends to favour a vertical approach to health problems.

Most recently, the Commission on Macroeconomics and Health, which was a major international initiative to examine the health situation and needs of poor countries in the context of global poverty reduction targets, argued for an increased international investment in health of US$27 billion per year over the next five years (WHO, 2001b). Health, and particularly the improvement of basic health services for the poor, has come back onto the international agenda, owing to concerns about the potentially destabilising effects of HIV/AIDS and the recognition of the close links between poverty and poor health. It remains to be seen how far those concerns are translated into firm commitments and how much priority is given to reproductive health.

What is happening nationally?

Again, the same difficulty of disaggregation applies, but the general picture on the proportion of national public expenditure going to reproductive health is almost certainly a mixed one. A recent series of country studies on reproductive health financing finds that health and population sector financing had increased in Bangladesh, Egypt and South Africa post-1994 (Forman and Ghosh, 2000). However, it fell in Tanzania and also in Mexico and Indonesia owing to economic crisis. In Tanzania the bulk of earmarked funds are for contraceptive procurement, and in 1996, 98.5 per cent of the country's population and reproductive health expenditures were externally funded by four main donors, leaving little room for national ownership of priorities. Some countries such as South Africa, which are far less dependent on aid, have made efforts to shift resources more towards primary care, which tends to benefit certain kinds of reproductive health interventions.

Some of the very poorest countries are experiencing serious financing problems. I noted the move towards basic service packages in a number of countries. These are an attempt to provide a basic universal minimum of cost-effective health interventions under conditions of financial resource constraints. They are generally favourable to basic reproductive health care as they tend to cover antenatal and obstetric care. However, a recent analysis of health expenditures across forty of the poorest countries, mainly in sub-Saharan Africa, showed average health expenditure per capita of under US$10. This is up to 40 per cent below the level necessary to fund the World Bank-recommended basic service package (Simms *et al.*, 2001).

Such underfunding underlines the importance of the absolute lack of financial resources in some regions. The spending base in most African countries and in some Asian ones is still extremely low. In sub-Saharan Africa, average incomes per capita are now lower than they were in the late 1960s. This problem of low incomes is exacerbated by problems of absorptive capacity for higher levels of external aid in countries where governance and institutional structures are in a poor state.

So, who then is paying for reproductive health care?

In the health sector generally over the past decade there has been a shift towards greater household expenditure on health care through the introduction of user charges in the public sector, increased need to make informal payments to obtain treatment from public facilities, and increased use of private-sector providers (Bloom and Standing, 2001; Kutzin, 1995). This pattern is also present in relation to payment for reproductive health care. Two examples illustrate this.

First, a study in Uganda looked at how households financed health care in poor rural communities (Lucas and Nuwagaba, 1999). These researchers found that many households face difficulties with the multiplicity of demands for cash payments for services, notably in health and education. Women faced particular difficulties as they rarely had access to cash, yet mostly had to take responsibility for both their own and their children's health. At issue was not so much official user charges *per se* but the wide range of informal, illicit payments, which were effectively a user subsidy to underpaid health workers and could be several times the official cost of the service.

Another study looked at the hidden costs of maternity care in Dhaka, Bangladesh (Nahar and Costello, 1998). Utilisation of public maternity facilities is very low in Dhaka compared to other South Asian cities (less than 15 per cent). This is despite the existence of a supposedly free service. The authors examined the actual costs incurred by families in using such facilities. These included informal payments to hospital staff, drugs, and the costs of travel and food expenses. They found that the mean cost for a normal delivery was a quarter of the average monthly household income. The mean cost of a Caesarean operation was almost equivalent to the average monthly income.

Meeting the costs – and improving access and quality

These kinds of findings raise serious issues about how to enable poor people and, particularly, poor women to get access to affordable and competent care. Doing so means looking at the need for cost exemptions for essential interventions and improving the capacity of the very poorest countries to be able to finance these. It means looking at a range of other mechanisms such as community-based and social insurance and medical safety nets for the poorest. It also entails working on the supply side to provide the right kinds of incentives to poorly paid health workers to provide the services they are contracted for. Finally, it also means addressing why people, including the poor, increasingly resort to private-sector services (ranging from for-profit providers, through NGOs, to traditional healers). One of the recurring themes here is that of quality and convenience.

It is important therefore to acknowledge that there is not a one-to-one relationship between the amount of money spent on health care and outcomes of better health. There is considerable variation across countries in the quality of services provided at given levels of health expenditure per capita (Filmer and Pritchett, 1997; Svennson, 1997).

First, provision of effective services is not just a question of resources. Indeed, reproductive health advocates have also questioned whether the funding targets for Cairo were realistic, arguing that better use of existing resources is needed (DeJong, 1999; Petchesky, 2000). Health systems also have to function with a reasonable level of efficiency and some minimum probity. This points to the oft-stated need to improve institutional and government accountability. Generally speaking, the poorer the governance, the worse the services that are provided. Health service delivery on the ground will not function well if drugs and equipment are siphoned off at higher levels, if there is no effective oversight or supervision of health workers, if salaries do not get paid and if officials responsible for these states of affairs are beyond any bureaucratic or civil accountability. Reproductive health services are no exception to this, and making them more effective has also to be part of a wider agenda on governance and accountability.

Second, Cairo drew attention to another broader agenda – that of gender equality and women's empowerment. Analyses of the causes of maternal mortality have drawn attention to the various delays which result in obstetric emergencies turning into obstetric deaths. The first of these delays is in decision-making related to reproductive health behaviour and access to health care at household level. It is important to understand how household and community power structures affect decisions, and how this can lead to delays in seeking treatment, or to denial of care. There are many examples of situations where pregnant women in emergency situations have not been able to get treatment owing to the absence of their husband to give approval in accordance with law or social norms, with tragic outcomes. This again suggests that we have to look to a broader political and advocacy agenda around enabling women to take greater control of decisions which affect their lives (Presser and Sen, 2000).

How has reproductive health fared in the context of health sector reforms?

The Cairo Agenda inaugurated a hard-fought-for, comprehensive concept of reproductive health which went beyond family planning to encompass the lifespan health needs of women and men in relation to all aspects of human reproduction. It was a major achievement in terms of getting international agreement among such a diverse collection of stakeholders. At the same time, over the past decade most countries have been involved in comprehensive reforms of their health sectors in response to the crises and pressures already noted. Much of this process has been driven by donors and international agencies and has entailed, in addition to financing, a wide range of institutional and regulatory reforms. What has happened to reproductive health in this process?

The Cairo Agenda owes its existence and vitality largely to the women's movement and particularly to women's health advocacy groups in both the South and North, which found ways of exploiting political spaces to get progressive policies onto the international agenda. This entailed working through relevant international conventions (e.g. the Convention on the Elimination of All Forms of Discrimination against Women, CEDAW) and pushing through resolutions in international forums such as the Beijing Women's Conference. It enabled women's health groups and NGOs to use the language and (albeit less successfully) the legal apparatus of human rights in advocating for policies. For instance, an issue such as maternal mortality rates in poor countries has been reframed not as a health issue *per se* but as a rights violation.

The rights discourse has both strengths and limitations. It has proved extremely powerful as an international advocacy tool. It has drawn attention to the shocking neglect of even basic health entitlements for many poor people. It opens up the possibility for a greater voice amongst those lacking such entitlements (via demands from 'below' as opposed to need identified and defined from 'above'). Currently its limitations stem from the enormous difficulty of any kind of enforcement. Conventions and resolutions ratified by countries depend on self-regulation and on inter- pretation according to local circumstances. Also, as we have seen, rich countries have not exhibited the commitment to providing resources to poor countries which would make compliance more feasible.

The Cairo Agenda embodies a vision of what should be achieved. It has not proved so easy to translate into practice. From a sectoral point of view, reproductive health has been concerned more with services and how they are delivered. At a broader level, reproductive health advocacy has pio- neered approaches to improving gender inequality as a prerequisite for improved reproductive health. Neither of these has found space in health sector reform programmes. For their part, reproductive health advocates have only recently begun to understand the importance of engaging with health sector reform processes (Standing, 2002).

A considerable gap remains between on-the-ground service delivery issues with which reproductive health is associated, and system-level approaches to health sector reform. There are, for example, a very large number of micro- level initiatives in sexual and reproductive health. There is a lot of good experience, particularly amongst NGOs, of delivering quality services, espe- cially to female clients. But there is very limited experience of, or capacity for, scaling up. Experience of delivering reproductive health services in the comprehensive (i.e. Cairo) sense is very limited and has mostly been con- fined to demonstration projects. Most programmes lack the capacity to deliver integrated services (Mayhew *et al.*, 2000; UNFPA, 1998).

The situation is changing quite slowly. In particular, management and organisational capability needs to improve, and service provision needs to be able to respond more effectively to local priorities. For instance, cervical cancer is currently one of the fastest-growing health problems amongst poor rural women in developing countries, but few if any such countries have facilities and trained staff able to diagnose, refer or treat it. There has also not been much progress on developing programmes on men's reproductive health consistent with the vision of reproductive health for all.

There are thus several reasons for the limited progress in realising the Cairo Agenda. Reproductive health has been framed within a different lan- guage from that of health sector reform. Reproductive health speaks within human rights and women's empowerment discourses, whereas health sector reform is located firmly in the language of management and tech- nical inputs. Whilst the women's health movement has made very good use of the tools of international advocacy, there has not been sufficient dialogue with the national and international agencies driving health sector reform. There is insufficient understanding on both sides as to how good-quality reproductive health services can be expanded in the context of health reforms as they are currently being framed and implemented.

Similarly, reproductive health has been focused on service delivery issues, to the neglect of broader health systems thinking. As Fonn *et al.* (1998) point out, a malfunctioning system cannot work for a woman in labour when it does not work for a man with typhoid either. However, systems issues are quite hard to address. Reproductive health tends to need a visionary approach; it is not a technical area or sector with a budget attached. One problem is where reproductive health, and externally driven programmes like Safe Motherhood, lie in health system terms. Largely based in vertical programmes such as family planning and maternal and child health, its components are often split between different ministries and sectors, producing stakeholder conflicts between different lines of management.

Another problem is the dominant focus in health reforms on the role of the public sector and the neglect of increasing pluralism of health providers. The private sector plays a very significant role in reproductive health service delivery, often in areas where women find it most difficult to access services, such as the provision of abortions. A systems approach to reproductive health itself needs to take a broader view of the concept of a system, going beyond the assumption that needs are wholly or largely met by public-sector provision.

Progress continues to be restricted by problems of data availability. Few data on reproductive health are available disaggregated by age, urban/rural, class/income, religion/culture or ethnicity. Country studies of programme implementation suggest little serious attention by policy-makers. There are no agreed core indicators for monitoring a rights-based approach to women's health, as advocated, for instance, by the Beijing Platform for Action. One advocacy organisation has suggested that wider indicators of women's health status should be developed, such as the degree of gender-based violence (ARROW, 2001). The same organisation also points to the need to develop a monitoring framework for financial indicators which can both differentiate spending on specific services, and monitor spending on comprehensive services from a reproductive health point of view. Some countries, for example Bangladesh, are beginning to develop the capacity to do this through the tool of the Public Expenditure Review (PER) (Sen and Ensor, 2001).

Reproductive health since Cairo: progress and future steps

Despite these limitations, the recent Cairo +5 review process, which examined progress in fifteen countries signed up to the Cairo Programme of Action, noted some promising signs of progress (Correa and Sen, 1999).

First, there is the less-good news: reproductive health programmes remain heavily dependent upon international assistance. In a number of countries, national programmes have simply been renamed as 'reproductive health' programmes but the bulk of resources are still going to family planning. The review notes that reducing maternal mortality requires investments in primary health programmes to be combined with the improvement of referral systems and obstetric assistance. But currently donors are reluctant to fund infrastructure, and structural adjustment requirements have limited domestic investment in facilities and staff.

The findings also indicated that effective improvement of reproductive health services has been very limited, especially in the case of urban poor and rural populations. In many contexts, family planning and maternal and child health programmes continue to be vertically organised and have not established linkages with other programme areas, such as HIV/AIDS or screening for reproductive cancers. Other recurrent obstacles to improving the quality of services in either family planning or reproductive health more broadly are described as the inadequate training, bureaucratic mindset, and gender-insensitive attitude of health managers and providers.

More optimistically, in several countries efforts are being made to overcome the lack of integration between the various components of reproductive health, and greater attention is being given to maternal mortality. For instance, in India, policy-makers, providers and health activists are struggling with the tremendous challenges of turning upside down a long-established vertical and narrow family planning programme. In others, initiatives are being developed to respond to adolescent reproductive health needs. Encouragingly, in all countries examined, policy-makers, NGOs and the media were found to be talking more openly about issues such as gender equality and violence against women (Correa and Sen, 1999).

We have seen that the Cairo Agenda represents a very ambitious and exciting attempt to rethink what is needed to produce good reproductive health for all. We have seen equally that there is a very long way to go. And this in itself has provoked a debate among reproductive health advocates. This broad vision of reproductive health provides a compelling vision to aspire to, but perhaps it is not realistic for all countries, certainly in the time-frame of the Millennium Development Goals (DeJong, 1999; Petchesky, 2000). Where resource and capacity constraints are severe, there are strong arguments for focusing resources on priority populations (e.g. poor rural women) and on key target areas such as maternal health.

Reproductive health is thus likely to remain a flexible construction for the foreseeable future. Some middle-income countries can, and should be expected to, take a more encompassing view and to expend resources accordingly. Others will struggle to manage the most pressing reproductive health problems. An obvious point is the overwhelming impact of HIV/AIDS on epidemiological profiles, health systems and coping strategies in severely affected poor countries. This means that national planners and health advocates need to make their own context-specific assessments of priority reproductive health needs.

Conclusion

In examining reproductive health, this chapter has noted the inherently political nature of targets and goals in international development. The Cairo Agenda and the reproductive health-related Millennium Development Goals represent two different ways of setting international goals. These differences relate to their respective histories. Whereas the Cairo Agenda was advocacy led, the Millennium Development Goals were driven by international bureaucracies. Careful coalition-building enabled the Cairo advocates to drive through a progressive consensus against opposition from some national interests. Such advocacy was absent from the setting of both International Development Targets and Millennium Development Goals. This weakened the capacity of the bureaucracy to withstand pressure from a concerted group of countries and conservative interests, resulting in the dropping of a long-agreed international health goal. Despite this, reproductive health remains a powerful vision which has recently been reaffirmed by the World Health Organisation in its approach to the implementation of the Millennium Development Goals.

In general, this chapter has cautioned pessimism that the targets of Cairo and the Millennium Development Goals can be met within their respective timeframes. Financing of reproductive health is complex and draws from a wide range of sources. International pledges for Cairo have not been met and rich countries do not have a good record of meeting their commitments to development aid. The extremely low levels of resources allocated to the health sector in some of the poorest countries mean that it is not possible to provide even basic universal coverage of essential reproductive health services. Achievements over the past decade have been mixed and not always easy to track, as reliable indicators are lacking and data are missing or unreliable.

From the point of view of the user, national financing strategies increasingly rely on a range of different mechanisms: essential services packages, user charges, insurances and safety nets. These different mechanisms potentially have different impacts on women's capacity in particular to access reproductive health services, and it is important that policy-makers are reminded of this. People are paying more for health services and they are increasingly using the private sector, and this again needs more policy attention than it is currently receiving.

At the same time, the link between greater resources and better health outcomes is not necessarily direct and progressive. Funding needs to be more judiciously targeted. Factors such as poor governance and accountability lead to low-quality, underutilised services. High levels of gender inequality are also major determinants of poor reproductive health outcomes and cannot be tackled by the health sector alone.

I have also argued that the different discourses of reproductive health and health sector reform have contributed to slow progress in providing and improving reproductive health services. There has not been sufficient engagement between the respective protagonists. Yet reforming health systems is a prerequisite for improving reproductive health care and addressing the health-care delivery constraints which contribute to high levels of maternal mortality.

Finally, I have suggested that we need to retain the broad vision of reproductive health embodied in Cairo while attending to and respecting priorities at different levels of developmental capacity. There continues to be a key role for advocacy in keeping reproductive health on international and national agendas. Reproductive health will always carry a political charge as it concerns broad human rights and gender equality issues, yet the narrower targets of the Millennium Development Goals in maternal health, which place specific emphasis on the maternal mortality ratio, will not be achieved without this broader commitment to these issues.

Notes

1 Condom use rate of the contraceptive prevalence rate (CPR).
2 For instance, the 1999 review of progress since the Cairo conference (ICPD+5), which included inputs from international agencies, experts and technical and civil society advocacy organisations.
3 Thanks to Françoise Girard, Senior Program Officer at the International Women's Health Coalition, for providing information on the background to the dropping of the reproductive health target and institutional responses to it.
4 Fifty-Fifth World Health Assembly, agenda item 13.2: WHO's contribution to achievement of the development goals of the United Nations Millennium Declaration, 18 May 2002, WHA55.19.
5 The most recent development is a plan to set up UN task forces to develop strategies for achieving the Millennium Development Goals. Maternal and child mortality will be combined in one and HIV/AIDS will be in another, along with tuberculosis and malaria. Reproductive health advocates are concerned that reproductive health will be lost in this reverticalisation of health priorities.
6 It is estimated that 20,000 delegates from national governments, UN organisations, non-governmental organisations (NGOs) and the media attended this nine-day conference.
7 Developed countries have, however, failed utterly to deliver on the 20:20 commitment.
8 This list contains fifteen indicators, including ones on sexual and men's health, and on infertility.
9 The maternal mortality ratio records deaths per 100,000 live births. For clarification of the difference between ratios and rates, see UNICEF (1997: section 3.1.1).
10 Maternal mortality is generally defined as death while pregnant or within 42 days of termination of pregnancy from any cause related to or aggravated by the pregnancy or its management. However, there are expanded definitions which lead to inconsistency across countries and data sets (Gelband *et al.*, n.d.).
11 The lifetime risk is the cumulative risk of dying over the reproductive period of a woman's life, whereas the MMR is a measure of risk for a woman who is actually pregnant. For further discussion of these measures, see WHO (2001a).

References

Asian-Pacific Resource and Research Centre for Woman (ARROW) (2001) *Advancing the Women's Health Agenda in the Asia-Pacific Region*: http://www.aworc.org/org/arrow/arrow.html.

Berer, M. (2001) 'Images, Reproductive Health and the Collateral Damage to Women of Fundamentalism and War', *Reproductive Health Matters*, 9(18): 68.

Bloom, G. and Standing, H. (2001) 'Pluralism and Marketisation in the Health Sector: Meeting Health Needs in Contexts of Social Change in Low and Middle Income Countries', IDS Working Paper 136, Brighton: Institute of Development Studies.

Correa, S. and Sen, G. (1999) 'Cairo +5: Moving Forward in the Eye of the Storm', *Social Watch No. 3*, ITEM, Montevideo: http://www.dawn.org.fj/publications/index.html.

DeJong, J. (1999) 'The Role and Limitations of the Cairo International Conference on Population and Development', *Social Science and Medicine*, 51: 941–953.

Filmer, D. and Pritchett, L. (1997) 'Child Mortality and Public Spending on Health: How Much Does Money Matter?' unpublished mimeo, Washington, DC: World Bank.

Fonn, S., Makhosazana, X., Tint, K.S. and Conco, S.V. (1998) 'Reproductive Health Services in South Africa: From Rhetoric to Implementation', *Reproductive Health Matters*, 6(11): 22–32.

Forman, S. and Ghosh, R. (1999) 'The Reproductive Health Approach to Population and Development', Paying for Essentials Policy Paper, New York: Center on International Cooperation, New York University.

—— (eds) (2000) *Promoting Reproductive Health: Investing in Health for Development*, Center on International Cooperation, Boulder, CO: Lynne Rienner.

Gelband, H., Liljestrand, J., Nemer, L., Islam, M., Zupan, J. and Jha, P. (2001) 'The Evidence Base for Interventions to Reduce Maternal and Neonatal Mortality in Low and Middle-Income Countries', Commission on Macroeconomics and Health Working Paper Series WG5.

Girard, F. (2001) 'Reproductive Health under Attack at the United Nations' (letter to the editor), *Reproductive Health Matters*, 9(18): 68.

Goodburn, E. and Campbell, O. (2001) 'Reducing Maternal Mortality in the Developing World: Sector Wide Approaches May Be the Key', *British Medical Journal*, 322: 917–920, 14 April.

Hartmann, B. (1995) *Reproductive Rights and Wrongs: The Global Politics of Population Control*, Boston, MA: South End Press.

Hulton, L.A., Matthews, Z. and Stones, R.W. (2000) *A Framework for the Evaluation of Quality of Care in Maternity Services*, Southampton: University of Southampton.

Jacobson, J. and Mallik, R. (2002) *The Far Right, Reproductive Rights and U.S. International Assistance: The Untold Story behind the Headlines*, Washington, DC: Center for Health and Gender Equity (CHANGE).

Kutzin, J. (1995) 'Experience with Organizational and Financing Reform of the Health Sector', Current Concerns SHS Paper 8 (SHS/CC/94.3), Geneva: WHO.

Lucas, H. and Nuwagaba, A. (1999) 'Household Coping Strategies in Response to the Introduction of User Charges for Social Service: A Case Study on Health in Uganda', IDS Working Paper 86, Brighton: Institute of Development Studies.

Mayhew, S.H., Lush, L., Cleland, J. and Walt, G. (2000) 'Implementing the integration of Component Services for Reproductive Health', *Studies in Family Planning*, 31(2): 151–162.

Nahar, S. and Costello, A. (1998) 'The hidden cost of "free" maternity care in Dhaka, Bangladesh', *Health Policy and Planning*, 13(4): 417–422.

Petchesky, R. (2000) 'Reproductive and Sexual Rights: Charting the Course of Transnational Women's NGOs', UNRISD Occasional Paper 8, Geneva: UNRISD.

Presser, H.B. and Sen, G. (2000) *Women's Empowerment and Demographic Process: Moving beyond Cairo*, Oxford: Oxford University Press.

Sen, G.(1999) 'Southern Feminist Perspectives on Population and Reproductive Rights: Continuing Challenges', *Society for International Development* 42(1): 25–28.

Sen, G. with Germain, A. and Chen, L. (eds) (1994) *Population Policies Reconsidered: Health, Empowerment and Rights*, Cambridge, MA: Harvard University Press.

Sen, P.D. and Ensor, T. (2001) 'Public Expenditure Review of the Health and Population Sector Programme', Research Paper 19, Health Economics Unit, Policy Research Unit, Dhaka: Ministry of Health and Family Welfare.

Simmons, R. and Elias, C. (1994) 'The Study of Client–Provider Interactions: A Review of Methodological Issues', *Studies in Family Planning*, 21(1): 1–17.

Simms, C., Rowson, M. and Peattie, S. (2001) *The Bitterest Pill of All: The Collapse of Africa's Health Systems*, London: Save the Children Fund UK.

Standing, H. (2002) 'An Overview of Changing Agendas in Health Sector Reforms', *Reproductive Health Matters*, 10(20): 1–10.

Svennson, J. (1997) 'The Control of Public Policy: Electoral Competition, Polarization and Endogenous Platforms', unprocessed mimeo, Washington, DC: World Bank, November.

United Nations Children's Fund (UNICEF) (1997) *Guidelines for Monitoring the Availability and Use of Obstetric Services*, New York: UNICEF/WHO/UNFPA.

United Nations Fund for Population Activities (UNFPA) (1998a) 'Reorientation of National Family Planning Programmes Towards a Broader Reproductive Health, Including Family Planning and Sexual Health, Approach in East and South East Asia', Occasional Paper Series 5.

—— (1998b) *Levels and Trends of Contraceptive Use as Assessed in 1998: Key Findings*, http://www.un.org/esa/population/pubsarchive/contraceptives1998/contraceptives1998.htm.

—— (1999) *Report of the International Conference on Population and Development*, Cairo, 5–13 September 1994, and ICPD+5, 1999. http://www.unfpa.org/icpd/

—— (2001) *The State of World Population 2001: Monitoring ICPD Goals: Selected Indicators*, http://www.unfpa.org/swp/2001/english/indicators/indicators1.html.

Walt, G., Pavignani, E., Gilson, L. and Buse, K. (1999) 'Health Sector Development: From Aid Co-ordination to Resource Management', *Health Policy and Planning*, 14(3): 207–218.

World Health Organisation (WHO) (1997) *Monitoring Reproductive Health: Selecting a Short List of National and Global Indicators*, WHO/RHT/HRP/97.26, Geneva: WHO.

—— (1999) 'Reduction of Maternal Mortality: A Joint WHO/UNFPA/UNICEF/World Bank Statement', Geneva: WHO.

—— (2001a) *Maternal Mortality in 1995: Estimates Developed by WHO, UNICEF, UNFPA*, WHO/RHR/01.9, Geneva: WHO.

—— (2001b) *Macroeconomics and Health: Investing in Health for Development. Report of the Commission on Macroeconomics and Health*, Geneva: WHO.

12 The global challenge of HIV/AIDS

Ronald Skeldon

The global context of HIV/AIDS

The Joint United Nations Programme on HIV/AIDS (UNAIDS) has estimated that during 2001, 5 million people became newly infected with HIV, the vast majority of them in developing countries. In one single hour, over 500 people are infected with HIV and over 300 people die from AIDS-related diseases. Globally, some 40 million people are estimated to be living with HIV, 28.1 million of them, or 70 per cent of the total, in sub-Saharan Africa. Just 3.8 per cent live in Western Europe and North America combined (Table 12.1). The distribution of new infections in 2001 reflected the total global distribution of HIV infections. Some 3.4

Table 12.1 Global situation of the HIV/AIDS epidemic, December 2001

Region	Adults and children newly infected with HIV (000s)	Adults and children living with HIV/AIDS (millions)	Percentage distribution of column (2)	Adult prevalence rate (percentages)
	(1)	(2)	(3)	(4)
Sub-Saharan Africa	3,400	28.1	70.3	8.4
North Africa and Middle East	80	0.4	1.1	0.2
South and South-East Asia	800	6.1	15.3	0.6
East Asia and Pacific	270	1.0	2.5	0.1
Latin America	130	1.4	3.5	0.5
Caribbean	60	0.4	1.1	2.2
Eastern Europe and Central Asia	250	1.0	2.5	0.5
Western Europe	30	0.6	1.4	0.3
North America	45	0.9	2.4	0.6
Australia and New Zealand	0.5	0.2	0.0	0.1
Total	5,000	40.0	100	1.2

Source: UNAIDS, *AIDS Epidemic Update*, Geneva (2001: 3).

million new infections in the year 2001 were in sub-Saharan Africa, 68 per cent of the total number of new infections. Only 1.5 per cent of those newly infected were to be found in Western Europe and North America. The prevalence rate is about 8.4 per cent in sub-Saharan Africa, compared with 1.2 per cent globally and 0.6 per cent for North America.[1]

The importance of the target is discussed in the next section, and its feasibility, in terms of whether it can be achieved and whether it is likely to be achieved, is the subject of the two subsequent sections respectively.

Does the goal on HIV/AIDS matter?

This chapter presents a critical examination of the Millennium Development Goal for HIV reduction. The Goal itself is to have halted and reversed the spread of HIV/AIDS by 2015, with this Goal replacing an earlier more specific target of a '25 per cent reduction in HIV infection rates among 18–24 year olds in the worst affected countries by 2005 and globally by 2010'. However, before we go on to examine this target, it is important to consider briefly the implications of the current epidemic of HIV/AIDS for the other key development goals dealt with in this volume. Such a review helps to place into context why the target on HIV/AIDS really does matter.

It is already clear that the scope and magnitude of the HIV/AIDS epidemic is putting at least some of these key targets under threat. For example, and most obviously, the target of reducing infant and under-five child mortality by two-thirds by 2015 looks particularly at risk, given the significance of mother-to-child transmission of the HIV virus. According to the UN (2000: 92), 'between one fourth and one third of the children born to HIV-positive women acquire the infection from their mothers'. Child mortality declined in the three sub-Saharan countries for which data are readily available, Cameroon, Kenya and Zambia, during the early 1980s but saw an upturn from about 1986, reaching rates higher, at least in the cases of Kenya and Zambia, than in 1981 (Figure 12.1). In Botswana, under-five mortality in the absence of AIDS would have been 53 deaths per 1,000 live births during the period 1995–2000, whereas it was actually more than double that rate, at 107 child deaths per 1,000 live births (UN, 2000: 93). The same source projects relative increases in under-five mortality for South Africa, Namibia, Kenya, Malawi and Mozambique over the first five years of the twenty-first century. The picture is clear: in the worst-infected areas, child mortality is increasing rather than going down. Even though projected rates will still be lower than those prevailing during the 1950s and 1960s, the possibility of achieving a two-thirds reduction with reference to a 1990 base year is clearly undermined.

Thus AIDS is responsible for the reversal of the long-term mortality decline in several parts of Africa. The incidence of tuberculosis in rural Malawi doubled between 1986 and 1994, largely because HIV-positive persons were

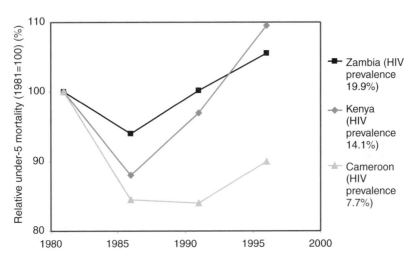

Figure 12.1 Trends in mortality from AIDS amongst children under 5 years old and end-1999 adult prevalence rate, selected African countries, 1981–1996.

Source: Demographic and Health Surveys, Macro International, USA.

seven times more likely to develop the disease than those who were not so infected (UN, 2000: 77–78). Despite the rising mortality and the post-ponement of any progression along the epidemiological transition from infectious diseases to degenerative diseases that has been seen elsewhere, HIV-associated mortality is not yet causing populations to decline, even in the worst-affected countries. It is a case of population growth rates slowing down, which, perversely, can have some macro-level benefits for an economy.

The impact of AIDS-related mortality on life expectancy can indeed be profound, as can be seen in Table 12.2. Life expectancy at age 20 in Botswana in the absence of AIDS would have been 54.6 years during the period 2000–2005. However, with an adult prevalence rate of 22.1 per cent, the estimated life expectancy at age 20 is only 27.6 years. For the ten worst-affected countries, it is estimated that life expectancy at age 20 has been reduced by at least one-third because of the epidemic. Figure 12.2 clearly shows the impact of excess AIDS-related mortality on the age struc-ture of the most deeply affected country, Botswana, based on US Census Bureau projections. In contrast, the worst-affected countries in Asia show a much lower loss of life expectancy in the period 2000–2005 than almost all countries in Africa, though the data from Asian countries nevertheless suggest alarming trends.

As regards the Millennium Development Goals, it is clear that the goal of universal primary education is also under threat as children are

Table 12.2 Impact of AIDS-related mortality on life expectancy at age 20, selected countries, 2000–2005

Country	Adult HIV prevalence	Life expectancy at age 20		Absolute difference	Percentage difference
		With AIDS	Without AIDS		
Botswana	22.1	27.6	54.6	27.0	49.5
Zimbabwe	21.5	28.2	52.0	23.8	45.8
Zambia	16.6	29.2	50.9	21.7	42.6
Namibia	16.1	30.7	49.0	18.3	37.4
Malawi	12.5	34.1	45.0	10.9	24.2
Mozambique	11.9	34.4	49.3	14.9	30.2
South Africa	11.8	33.4	48.4	15.0	31.0
Rwanda	11.2	35.9	53.0	17.1	32.3
Kenya	10.4	30.4	45.8	15.4	33.6
Central African Republic	8.6	37.1	48.5	11.4	23.5
Côte d'Ivoire	8.5	37.2	48.9	11.7	23.9
United Republic of Tanzania	8.2	35.8	47.0	11.2	23.8
Uganda	8.1	36.1	45.7	9.6	21.0
Ethiopia	7.7	36.9	45.4	8.5	18.7
Burundi	7.0	40.8	52.7	11.9	22.6
Togo	6.9	39.2	48.9	9.7	19.8
Lesotho	6.7	36.3	46.5	10.2	21.9
Congo	6.4	39.9	48.7	8.8	18.1
Burkina Faso	6.0	37.6	44.8	7.2	16.1
Haiti	4.1	42.6	48.0	5.4	11.3
Cameroon	4.0	42.8	47.1	4.3	9.1
Dem. Rep. of Congo	3.5	42.3	49.7	7.4	14.9
Nigeria	3.4	41.9	46.5	4.6	9.9
Gabon	3.1	42.5	48.3	5.8	12.0
Liberia	3.0	43.1	47.4	4.3	9.1
Eritrea	2.6	38.4	41.5	3.1	7.5
Sierra Leone	2.6	42.2	45.3	3.1	6.8
Chad	2.2	49.8	53.2	3.4	6.4
Cambodia	2.0	44.4	47.7	3.3	6.9
Thailand	1.8	40.4	43.7	3.3	7.6
Benin	1.8	43.7	46.7	3.0	6.4
Guinea-Bissau	1.7	42.6	46.5	3.9	8.4
India	0.6	51.2	52.2	1.0	1.9
Brazil	0.5	51.9	52.5	0.6	1.1

Source: United Nations, *World Population Prospects: The 1998 Revision*, New York, Department of Economic and Social Affairs, Population Division (2000, volume 3: 93).

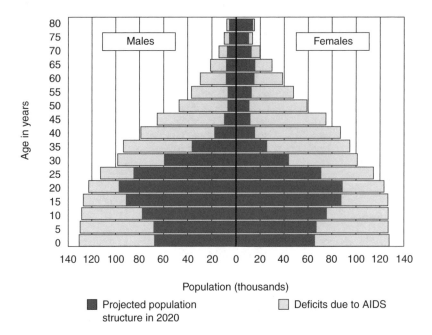

Figure 12.2 Projected population of Botswana in 2020 showing deficits due to AIDS-related deaths by cohort.

Source: United States Census Bureau, *World Population Profile 2000*, Washington, DC, 2001.

withdrawn from schools either to help with the family farm as parents become sick or to care for sick relatives. In Swaziland, for example, school enrolment is reported to have fallen by 36 per cent and girls may have higher drop-out rates than boys, although both sexes are likely to have been profoundly affected (UNAIDS, 2001a: 7).

The overall goal of reducing the proportion of people living in extreme poverty by half between 1990 and 2015 is also under threat in the worst-affected areas. HIV/AIDS is now generally seen as a 'disease of poverty', a disease that afflicts the poor disproportionately. The third report of the UK House of Commons Select Committee on International Development states that 'the fight against HIV/AIDS can be won only through progress in the elimination of poverty'.[2] These are fine words, but the path of the epidemic threatens progress towards reducing poverty. Also, the relationship between poverty and HIV is more complex than is often assumed. Certainly, the epidemic is centred in the poorest region of the world, sub-Saharan Africa, and clearly, too, the lack of physical and human capital militates against the treatment of the disease. However, the HIV epidemic is also intense in the wealthier economies of sub-Saharan Africa, such as South Africa and Botswana, and it also profoundly affects members of wealthier and better-educated groups, who are more able to afford multiple sexual partners. Cultural and societal factors as well as economic deprivation are key to the spread of the epidemic.[3]

Although funeral costs, lost income, and savings and productivity losses are devastating specific household economies and, most specifically, the poorest households,[4] it is much more difficult to calculate the macro-level impact of the epidemic. Two economists, Bloom and Godwin (1997: 3), have argued that there is a 'resounding lack of evidence to support the view that AIDS impedes economic growth'. Botswana, with the world's highest AIDS death rate, also experienced rapid rates of economic growth between 1998 and 2001 averaging 9 per cent per annum, which was one of the highest in the world at that time (IIASA, 2001). Thus high economic growth can occur despite a high prevalence of HIV, although Botswana's economy is relatively small, is dependent on exports and is not reliant upon a large labour supply. The World Bank has projected that in Africa, income growth per capita is likely to be reduced by between 0.1 and 0.4 per cent per annum. GDP in South Africa in 2010 is likely to be 17 per cent lower than it would have been in the absence of AIDS, with the epidemic costing that economy some US$22 billion (Barks-Ruggles, 2001).

However, development is not, or should not be, measured in macro-level indicators alone, and unquestionably the disease is having a profound impact on local economies and households. Thus the HIV/AIDS epidemic is likely to slow, if not reverse, progress towards the attainment of at least some of the targets contained in the Millennium Development Goals themselves, particularly given the fact that many of these targets are essentially goals of human development.

One other contextual issue requires discussion before the actual global target for HIV itself is considered. This is the 'illusion of numbers'. In 1991, projections were made that by the end of the decade 9 million people would be infected in sub-Saharan Africa, with 5 million deaths (UNAIDS, 2000: 7). The actual figures have proved to be three times greater than that estimate. Thus a very big question mark hangs over the quality of the available data and it must be stressed that these data are very 'spongy' indeed – full of holes, with a high degree of variance in the estimates. For example, one of the principal sources of information that is used for virtually every country in estimating infection levels is based upon the number of women attending antenatal clinics. However, if fertility among HIV-positive women is considerably lower than among all women, then the estimates derived from this source may be too low.

Inadequacies in the available data should never be used as an excuse for inaction, and it is necessary to learn to deal with the existing figures with all their weaknesses. Although the quality of our information has almost certainly improved over the past ten years, major areas of uncertainty still remain and a degree of scepticism is always required in any interpretation of the data presented.

Are the international targets for HIV/AIDS achievable?

The goal of halting and reversing the spread of HIV/AIDS by 2015 can be achieved, but it does not go far enough. This statement can be amplified as follows. The headline goal is realistic as, amidst all the gloom in the statistics, there are signs of optimism, or if not of optimism – at least of hope. The number of new infections in sub-Saharan Africa stabilised in 2000 and 2001, after rising inexorably up to 1999. In 2000, new infections in that region were estimated to be 3.8 million, compared with 4 million in 1999 – a small decline, but perhaps a significant one. That decline continued into 2001, when the number of new infections was estimated at 3.4 million, representing a 15 per cent reduction in the number of new infections since 1999. It is useful to consider some of the 'success' stories of the HIV/AIDS epidemic before returning to more sobering situations.

Success stories: Africa

In sub-Saharan Africa, Uganda is seen as one of the few countries that has confronted the epidemic with significant results. Uganda was one of the earliest countries to be affected by the epidemic in sub-Saharan Africa, with infections dating from the early 1980s. It also has been one of the most severely affected countries in the region, with overall prevalence rates reaching 14 per cent in the early 1990s. By 2000, overall prevalence is estimated to have declined to 8 per cent (UNAIDS, 2000: 9). In urban areas, HIV infection among pregnant women attending antenatal clinics has fallen for eight years in a row from 29.5 per cent in 1992 to 11.3 per cent in 2000 (UNAIDS, 2001a: 17). Condom use rose from 7 per cent nationwide since the early 1990s to 50 per cent in rural areas and 85 per cent in urban areas by the late 1990s.

However, just how these figures were derived is not clear. In fact, it is admitted that 'due to weak monitoring, it is not possible to apportion the observed decline between the three factors of abstaining, being faithful to one's partner, and condom use' (UAC, 2000). Also, the prevalence rate appears to have stabilised since 1996 at around 8–10 per cent, still very high by global standards. Hence although Uganda may already have reached the international target of a 25 per cent reduction in prevalence, it has done so from a high base and is still in an unsatisfactory position. A 25 per cent reduction in HIV infection in the worst areas may still leave countries in a very vulnerable position. Nevertheless, progress clearly has been attained in Uganda, a country that ranked 141 out of 162 states in the human development league tables of the United Nations Development Programme (UNDP) in 2001.

In Lusaka, Zambia, HIV prevalence amongst girls aged 15 to 19 who were attending antenatal clinics also declined, from 27 per cent in 1993 to 17 per cent in 1998. In Senegal, success of a different kind gives grounds for hope. Senegal was never one of the sub-Saharan countries to be most severely affected by the epidemic,[5] but significantly, it appears to have been able to take pre-emptive action in order to prevent the disease from taking hold in the first place. The national adult prevalence rate has remained low, at just under 1.8 per cent at the end of 1999.

Success stories: Asia

If the international goals are to be met and to have a significant impact on development at a global level, this must occur in the most populous parts of the world, and particularly China and India. The infection rates of countries in Asia so far do not approach those of sub-Saharan Africa. At the end of 1999 the Asian country with the highest rate of adult infection was Cambodia at just over 4 per cent, followed by Thailand at just over 2 per cent (UNAIDS, 2000). As seen earlier, rates in excess of 10 per cent are common in Africa, with Botswana and Zimbabwe over 20 per cent and Zambia and Namibia over 15 per cent.

In Asia, Thailand is seen to be one of the success stories, with rates of infection dropping through the 1990s. One of the most commonly cited statistics is the marked decline of HIV prevalence amongst 21-year-old military conscripts, which peaked at around 4 per cent in 1993 and has currently fallen to below 1 per cent (Figure 12.3). Infection remains high, however, amongst injecting drug users and commercial sex workers, and

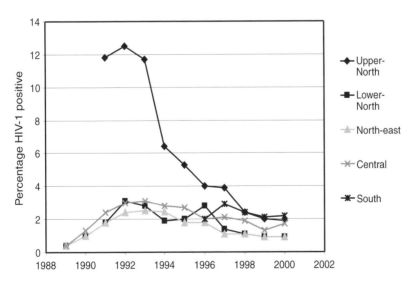

Figure 12.3 HIV-1 seroprevalence among Royal Thai Army conscripts by region, 1989–2000.

Source: Royal Thai Army, Bangkok, 2000.

significant differences remain between urban and rural areas. Sex workers in Bangkok, for example, are estimated to have prevalence rates of only 7 per cent, compared with 20 per cent for sex workers in rural areas.

Reasons for the success stories

These 'successful' countries have certain characteristics in common. They all mounted intensive media campaigns; all raised awareness through education programmes to disseminate information on the way the virus is spread at all levels of society; all actively disseminated condoms throughout the country; most important, however, the governments were willing to confront the epidemic and raise the essentially sexual nature of its transmission to a high profile. Such attitudes, unfortunately, have been all too rare in other countries, and most publicly among senior policy-makers in South Africa.

These success stories conclusively show that people can and do change their behaviour. In Uganda the proportion of girls and boys aged 15 to 19 years who had never had sex rose from 20 per cent in 1990 to 50 per cent in 1995. In Bangkok the number of men frequenting brothels is reported to have halved between 1990 and 1993, with the number of sex-based establishments dropping by about 60 per cent (UNAIDS, 1998). The 100 per cent condom programme has been vigorously implemented in the formal sex sector throughout the country. Using data from Africa, the World Bank has demonstrated the effectiveness of condom use in a population of 500 sex workers, four-fifths of whom were already infected with HIV. Within a year, 10,000 infections could be averted, assuming that condom use can be raised to 80 per cent (World Bank, 1999: box 2.6).

There is, however, no room for complacency in the successful countries. I have argued elsewhere (Skeldon, 2000) that there is evidence to suggest that unsafe practices and high-risk behaviour have moved from the formal sex sector in Thailand to a more informal level – that is, amongst groups of friends or acquaintances at school, college or workplace rather than with professional sex workers in brothels. Also, periodic markets in rural and urban situations or temple fairs are emerging as key nodes, or 'hot spots', in the diffusion of the epidemic in place of the formal brothel or massage parlour environments. There is considerable scope for a second stage in the development of the epidemic.

Are the targets on HIV/AIDS likely to be achieved?

Some countries have shown that infection rates can be reduced in line with the target of a 25 per cent reduction globally by 2010. However, it seems highly unlikely that the majority of countries will follow suit or that the target will be achieved globally, with, as argued earlier, negative consequences for the other Millennium Development Goals. Four often inter-related sets of factors will probably prevent the target from being met: (1) the fact that the epidemic is so recent in many parts of the world; (2) the issue of political commitment; (3) the availability, or otherwise, of money; and (4) geopolitical considerations. Each of these will be considered in turn.

HIV/AIDS as a recent phenomenon

The first clinical evidence for the existence of AIDS dates from just twenty years ago and the area most deeply affected since that time clearly has been sub-Saharan Africa. Over 70 per cent of those living with HIV/AIDS are currently found in that region, which in 2000 accounted for only 10 per cent of the world's population. However, the population of East, South-East and South Asia, at some 3.5 billion people, accounts for almost 58 per cent of the world population. For this reason, at the global level the impact of HIV/AIDS must ultimately be determined by what happens in the most populous region, Asia.

Thus far, the epicentre of the epidemic in Asia has been located in Thailand, specifically in the region known as the 'upper north' in the area north from Chiang Mai into the hill lands bordering Myanmar and Laos. This is an area of relatively sparse population located strategically between the densely populated regions of China to the north and east and South Asia to the west. The fact that the epidemic should have developed in this region is due to a complex combination of factors, of which the following are important:

- These are areas of long-standing trade routes.
- The area has an extensive trade in narcotics, with relatively high local consumption and a high proportion of injecting drug users.
- Cash is readily available from trade in border areas.
- The area has a sex culture in which men and women have been relatively free in the selection of partners.
- Having multiple sequential partners is a much more accepted form of behaviour than in other parts of Thailand.
- Women are sometimes incorporated at a very young age into sex work.

The critical question revolves around what will happen if or when the epidemic takes hold in the densely populated parts of the Indian sub-continent and China. However, it is important to emphasise here that there is no evidence to suggest, one way or the other, that the future path of the epidemic in China or India will follow that of any of the sub-Saharan African countries. However, even if the epidemic follows the path of Thailand, with much lower levels of infection, the resultant human and economic cost will be substantial. The case of Cambodia, one of the poorest countries in its region, just might point to the future direction of the epidemic in East Asia at least. Although Cambodia has the highest adult prevalence rate in Asia, official government figures suggest that the rate has declined from around 4 per cent in 1997 to 2.8 per cent in 2000 (Cambodia, 2001: 110). HIV prevalence amongst pregnant women, too, appears to have declined from 1997 (UNAIDS, 2001a: 15), which again suggests a real trend towards slower growth, even containment, and that the path of the Asian epidemic may be different from that in Africa. Nevertheless, even with lower overall prevalence rates, the human cost will be devastating in the demographic giants of Asia.

In China, at the end of 1999 the number of adults and children living with HIV/AIDS was recorded by UNAIDS at 500,000. This figure seems unrealistically low for a population of 1.3 billion and it is generally accepted that the incidence of the disease is being severely underestimated. Chinese officials had admitted to a figure of 600,000 by June 2001 but by then United Nations officials were talking of 1.5 million infected (Lange, 2001). The same source warns that there could be 20 million infected Chinese by 2010. If that prediction proves to be accurate, it would severely affect any global target for HIV reduction. Reported HIV infections rose by two-thirds in the first six months of 2001 alone (UNAIDS, 2001a: 13). Because of the country's demographic weight, what goes on in China will affect global trends, and if the incidence of infection increases amongst the critical 15–24 years age group, then both the global goal of reversing the spread of the disease, and the target of reducing prevalence rates, are likely to be meaningless without a major pre-emptive programme within China.

A scandal over blood-buying networks in Henan Province, in which villagers were paid US$5 for each blood donation, is estimated to have infected some 100,000 people. Blood was collected to extract the plasma to sell to drug manufacturers and then the pooled blood was re-injected into the villagers so that they could donate more frequently. Needles were shared and infection rates of 43–65 per cent have been reported among blood donors as a result of needle sharing and re-injecting of pooled blood (Lange, 2001). Despite this scandal, the diffusion of the disease is not going to be the result of pooling blood products, sharing needles or drug abuse but through heterosexual contact. The increasing mobility of China's population, with some 100 million undocumented migrants, and an increasing commercial sex sector in the urban areas seem destined to exact a grim toll and one which the government in 2002 finally appeared to be addressing.

The whole issue of population migration and the spread of HIV is extremely complex. There is not necessarily any relationship between the movement of people and the spread of the disease as it is not the movement as such that is the critical variable but the behaviour of the migrants.

Migrants who do not engage in high-risk practices will not spread the disease. However, the movement away from tight-knit kinship and community networks appears to place people in situations where there are higher probabilities for them to engage in such practices. The fact that one of the wealthiest sub-Saharan societies, Botswana, also came to have the highest prevalence of HIV can be attributed greatly to the participation of its population in the circular labour migration to South Africa's mines. It is well established that the disease is spread along truck and trade routes, and the northern Thai epidemic was facilitated by the relatively high mobility of its population. Development, irrespective of whether it is the result of specific plans of action or of gradual evolution, tends to increase the mobility of populations. The rapid rates of growth in Asian economies and the drive for development on the part of most governments can but stimulate further migrations, with significant implications for the spread of HIV/AIDS, and particularly in China and India.[6]

At the end of 2000 it was estimated that in India some 3.86 million people were infected with HIV/AIDS, an overall infection rate of less than 1 per cent. This prevalence rate is again low by African standards but, in terms of absolute numbers, India has more people living with HIV than any country in the world except South Africa (UNAIDS, 2001a: 13). The state with the greatest number of victims is Maharashtra, which is also one of the most prosperous states in India, containing, as it does, the major industrial and commercial city of Mumbai. HIV prevalence among sex workers in that city was estimated to have reached over 70 per cent in 1997 (UNAIDS, 2000: 13). The highest prevalence rates are to be found among the more developed southern states, with HIV having made relatively little inroad so far in the densely populated northern states such as Bengal, or even within that state's megalopolis, Calcutta. In sum, the potential for a rapid spread of the epidemic in the two most populous countries of the world, China and India, seems vast indeed. So, too, is the potential for rapid spread in Indonesia, a country with some 218 million people in 2002 but an adult prevalence rate of just 0.05 per cent at the end of 1999.[7]

The issue of political commitment

Perhaps the most critical set of factors preventing the goal from being met revolves around political commitment or the political recognition of HIV/ AIDS as a major policy issue. There are the 'Three Ds' of HIV/AIDS: Denial, Delay and Do nothing.[8] Many governments are reluctant to accept that HIV/AIDS is a problem. Even if they do accept that it might be a problem, they are reluctant to take action on an issue that touches upon the most intimate aspects of the lives of their citizens. In all the cases of successful intervention discussed earlier, the governments of the respective countries had responded in an open and vigorous way to the spreading epidemic. It is only recently, if a headline in the *Guardian* (London) on 13 November 2001 can be believed, that China 'finally wakes up to AIDS time bomb'. A massive education programme of doctors and health workers throughout the country is planned and anti-AIDS funding will become a separate item in national and provincial budgets.

Other countries are, however, still in the 'denial' or the 'do nothing' stage. Myanmar does not recognise HIV infection as an issue, despite available evidence of a rapid spread in that country. The case of South Africa is still notorious, with President Thabo Mbeki ordering a cut in the AIDS budget as recently as September 2001 based on what a World Health Organization official described as the 'deliberate misinterpretation of old statistics for political ends'. Even in March 2002, Mr Mbeki decried the view that multiple sexual partners or rape might spread the disease as 'demeaning' and 'insulting' (*The Economist*, 11 May 2002). Only an even more recent U-turn in official attitudes towards the disease, largely the result of a court case ruling in favour of the distribution of anti-retrovirals, offers some hope that the official face of South Africa may finally be beginning to confront the enormity of its AIDS problem. As a result of the constitutional court ruling, the government cannot appeal against the high court decision ordering the supply of anti-retrovirals to hospitals, which ultimately may lead to the saving of 30,000 babies a year from infection from their mothers.

Moreover, despite the fact that several of the 'success stories' discussed above were from sub-Saharan Africa, the third report of the UK House of Commons Select Committee on International Development observed that 'The response to the HIV/AIDS epidemic, particularly in Africa, has been a culpable and serious failure in political leadership and governance.'[9] A general consensus appears to be emerging that the only helpful response to the epidemic is bold vision and strong and enlightened leadership. Denying that the epidemic is a problem is counter-productive, and perhaps this political dimension is the greatest global challenge in confronting the diffusion of HIV/AIDS in the twenty-first century.

The availability, or otherwise, of money

Leadership may be the first priority but money and resources are an important secondary need. Expenditure on HIV/AIDS has increased from US$59 million in 1987 to US$293 million in 1998, almost a fivefold increase. The numbers infected with HIV have, however, risen eight and a half times, meaning that expenditure per capita has actually declined.

In April 2001 the Secretary-General of the United Nations (UN), Kofi Annan, called for US$7–10 billion to be spent annually on the epidemic and for a global health fund to be set up for HIV/AIDS. Up to May 2002, just under US$2 billion had been collected and the scope of the fund was broadened to cover both tuberculosis and malaria. The USA, the largest donor, had given US$450 million and the UK some US$200 million. Bill and Melinda Gates had donated US$100 million. To try to put the US$7–10 billion annual commitment into the context of other expenditure, it is worth noting that the US Congress approved US$40 billion to aid recovery efforts in New York City after the events of 11 September 2001, plus an additional US$15 billion to assist the airline industry. Some US$1.2 trillion was lost in stock market investments as a result of financial nervousness following the 11 September attacks.

An annual spending on AIDS of US$7 billion annually would represent more than a 10 per cent increase in total overseas development assistance given by the Organisation for Economic Cooperation and Development (OECD) countries, which seems a somewhat remote possibility. As noted in Chapter 1, in 1970 the UN resolved that development aid should represent 0.7 per cent of gross national product (GNP). However, other than the Scandinavian countries, only the Netherlands and Luxembourg have met this target. The USA manages 0.1 per cent (although it is the second largest donor after Japan in absolute amounts of development assistance). The UK's aid has at least risen in recent years, and in 1999/2000 was at its highest level in real terms since 1976. Even so, the UK's commitment to development expenditure remains at around 0.35 per cent of GNP, or half the UN target.

Geopolitical considerations

One critical issue is the direction that might be taken by the international community after the tragic events of 11 September. As developed nations become increasingly concerned about their own security, and as their attention is turning towards Central Asia, a real danger exists that HIV/ AIDS will be relegated to the back burner and that the worst-affected countries in sub-Saharan Africa will be still further marginalised from the global community and economy. Long before these recent events, sub-Saharan Africa was only tenuously linked to the global economy. Just 1 per cent of foreign direct investment flowed to these countries throughout the mid- to late 1990s. It is not so much a question of whether things can get worse but whether there will be any serious effort to reverse this situation now that the eyes of the world community appear to have shifted to concerns elsewhere.

The geopolitical issue can also be considered from another angle. International peacekeepers have moved to Afghanistan. Parallels can perhaps be sought in Cambodia, which has the highest HIV infection rate in Asia. It is generally acknowledged that the presence of large numbers of foreign troops based in a youthful population that had lost enormous numbers of husbands and fathers was a major factor in the spread of the epidemic in that country. Over 20,000 troops and civil servants of the United Nations Transitional Authority were at one time based in Cambodia, where a significant commercial sex sector thrived on both foreign and local clients (see Caouette, 1998: 15–16). It is estimated that HIV sero-prevalence rates amongst commercial sex workers in 1998 ranged from 25 to 64 per cent, depending upon the region (UNDP, 2000: 7), with national group mean prevalence for direct sex workers in 1999 of 33 per cent (Chantavanich, 2000: 22). Thus if history repeats itself, the introduction of an international peacekeeping force into Afghanistan may contribute to a new AIDS problem. This would once again divert attention from the situation in sub-Saharan Africa as the international community seeks to prevent any increase in infection in a region that has already seen rapidly rising infection rates among Central Asian republics such as Uzbekistan.

Conclusion

Where does this leave the global goal and target for HIV/AIDS? At a global level, the target of reducing HIV prevalence by 25 per cent by 2015 could and should be met. What is likely to act against the target is the spread of the disease into previously little-affected populations, and primarily into Asia. The Asian pattern, however, is unlikely to reach levels currently seen in Africa. More realistically, regional rather than global targets are required. Achieving the global target in some African countries does not go nearly far enough, while it is irrelevant in areas that are only now experiencing the first stages of an epidemic.

The mechanics of the spread of the epidemic are well known. In most areas the people themselves know how the disease is spread. The best practices to introduce in order to contain the disease are also known. Most of all, it is understood that failing to achieve the targets for HIV/AIDS is likely to undermine many of the other Millennium Development Goals. The containment and reversal of the epidemic will be pivotal for the achievement of other dimensions of development. The issue is now primarily one of political will. Perhaps there should be annual targets for the number of governments that seriously confront the epidemic. It can be argued that the HIV/AIDS epidemic has moved firmly onto the political stage, with demographic, economic and even medical aspects being secondary. Targets are now needed in the political arena. Thus the main global challenge of HIV/AIDS is to keep a clear focus on the existing patterns of the epidemic. This might sound trite but the path ahead will not be easy. The future course of the HIV/AIDS epidemic is firmly in the hands of governments and policy-makers.

Notes

1 All figures from UNAIDS (2001a).
2 http://www.parliament.the-stationery-office.co.uk/pa/cm200001/cmselect/cmintdev/354/35405.htm#a1, Executive Summary, p. 1.
3 See, in particular, the work of Caldwell and his associates, with a synopsis in Caldwell (2000).
4 See Knodel *et al.* (2002) for an analysis of the impact of the death through AIDS of adult children on surviving parents in Thailand.
5 Prevalence is lower in West Africa than Eastern and Southern Africa.
6 For a discussion of the general issues of population mobility and HIV/AIDS, see UNAIDS (2001b) and Skeldon (2000), also Chantavanich (2000).
7 See Hugo (2001) for a discussion of information gaps, current knowledge and likely future directions of the epidemic in Indonesia.
8 I am indebted to Steve Kraus of UNAIDS, Bangkok, for this felicitous combination.
9 http://www.parliament.the-stationery-office.co.uk/pa/cm200001/cmselect/cmintdev/354/35405.htm#a1, Executive Summary, p. 9.

References

Barks-Ruggles, E. (2001) 'Meeting the global challenge of HIV/AIDS', Policy Brief 75, Brookings Resources, at http://www.brook.edu/comm/policybriefs/pb075/pb75.htm.

Bloom, D.E. and Godwin, P. (eds) (1997) *The Economics of HIV and AIDS: The Case of South and Southeast Asia*, New Delhi: Oxford University Press.

Caldwell, J.C. (2000) 'Rethinking the African AIDS epidemic', in Caldwell, J.C., Caldwell, P., Orubuloye, I.O. *et al.* (eds) *Towards the Containment of the AIDS Epidemic: Social and Behavioural Research*, Canberra: Australian National University, Health Transition Centre.

Cambodia (2001) *A Situation and Response Analysis of the HIV/AIDS Epidemic in Cambodia*, Phnom Penh: National AIDS Authority.

Caouette, T.M. (1998) *Needs Assessment on Cross-Border Trafficking in Women and Children: The Mekong Sub-Region*, report prepared for the UN Working Group on Trafficking in the Mekong Sub-region, Bangkok.

Chantavanich, S. (2000) *Mobility and HIV/AIDS in the Greater Mekong Subregion*, Bangkok: Asian Development Bank and United Nations Development Programme.

Hugo, G. (2001) *Population Mobility and HIV/AIDS in Indonesia*, Jakarta: International Labour Office.

International Institute for Applied Systems Analysis (IIASA) (2001) 'HIV/AIDS and Development: Are Botswana, Namibia, and Mozambique on Sustainable Paths?', *Options*, Spring: 6–8, International Institute for Applied Systems Analysis.

Knodel, J., Im-em, W., Saengtienchai, C., Vanlandingham, M. and Kespichayawattana, J. (2002) *The Impact of an Adult Child's Death Due to AIDS on Older-Aged Parents: Results from a Direct Interview Survey*, Publication 266. Mahidol University, Institute for Population and Social Research.

Lange, D. (2001) 'A New Vein of Openness', *Far Eastern Economic Review*, 4 October: 58–60.

Skeldon, R. (2000) *Population Mobility and HIV Vulnerability in South East Asia: An Assessment and Analysis*, Bangkok: United Nations Development Programme.

Uganda AIDS Commission (UAC) (2000) *The National Strategic Framework for HIV/AIDS in Uganda, 2000/1 to 2005/6*, Nairobi: UAC.

United Nations (UN) (2000) *World Population Prospects: The 1998 Revision*, New York: Department of Economic and Social Affairs, Population Division.

United Nations Development Programme (UNDP) (2000) *Cambodia HIV Vulnerability Mapping: Highways One and Five*, Bangkok: UNDP.

United Nations Programme on HIV/AIDS (UNAIDS) (1998) *Relationships of HIV and STD Declines in Thailand to Behavioural Change: A Synthesis of Existing Studies*, Geneva: UNAIDS.

—— (2000) *Report on the Global HIV/AIDS Epidemic: June 2000*, Geneva: UNAIDS.

—— (2001a) *AIDS Epidemic Update*, Geneva: UNAIDS.

—— (2001b) *Population Mobility and AIDS*, Geneva: UNAIDS.

World Bank (1999) *Confronting AIDS: Public Priorities in a Global Epidemic*, New York: Oxford University Press.

13 Clean water for all

Richard Jolly

Introduction

Although the Millennium Development Goal for water does not refer to sanitation and hygiene, these other two areas are as important for health and poverty reduction as is safe water. In 2000, some 1.1 billion people lacked access to safe water and 2.4 billion lacked access to adequate sanitation. Allowing for population growth, this means that access to adequate water is needed for an additional 1.5 billion people over the next fifteen years and to adequate sanitation for an additional 2.2 billion. This would represent about a doubling of the numbers who achieved access to safe water over the 1990s and about a trebling of the numbers who got access to adequate sanitation. No global data exist on those with inadequate knowledge of hygiene.

This chapter argues that with political commitment, a clear policy focus and a modest allocation or reallocation of resources, these goals are challenging but achievable. At the time of writing, some seventy developing and transition countries, comprising about half of the population of the developing world, seem to be on track. But another 100 are not: some twenty-five are lagging or far behind while for another seventy-five no data are available, a sign in most cases that the goal is not being taken seriously. In almost all these 100 countries, including most of the poorer and least developed countries, success will require a major acceleration of programme action, much faster than that achieved during the 1990s. Success will also require more focused development assistance, with more attention being given to low-cost water and sanitation activities in peri-urban and rural areas.

Three myths about global goals need to be cast aside: that global goals are never taken seriously; that they focus on the wrong issues; and that global goals imply only top-down action by governments. Success during the water decade of the 1980s and subsequently shows that global goals can help focus and accelerate action, country by country. Moreover, the development of a range of low-cost technologies and their increasing use show what is possible. There are a number of success stories demonstrating advance at a more rapid pace than the international goals require. What is now needed is a co-ordinated international effort of mobilisation and support, followed through at country level, with equal attention to all three goals – of hygiene and sanitation as well as water – to ensure their achievement by 2015.

The Goals for water and for sanitation and hygiene are elaborated in the following two sections. Next, progress towards the targets is examined, and evidence given on the present position of the developing world in terms of access to safe water and sanitation, overall and broken down by region. Then the increase in coverage required to fulfil the future world population's needs is discussed. The chapter then turns to what is needed to achieve the targets: seven key areas of policy required are presented, including social mobilisation, the role of public and private sectors, use of appropriate technologies and pricing strategies, effective monitoring, and the specific role of women in sanitation and hygiene. After this, action for sanitation and hygiene is examined; then, more broadly, a strategy of 'ten commandments' for turning formal goals into action is urged. Finally, the prospects for achieving the targets for water, sanitation and hygiene are examined.

The Millennium Development Goal for water

The seven Millennium Development Goals include one on water: halving the proportion of the world's population without sustainable access to adequate quantities of safe drinking water by 2015. This water goal is important, as a fulfilment of a basic human right, as a step to reducing poverty more generally and as part of a sustainable strategy towards integrated water resource management, globally and in every country.

Access to safe water has been recognised as a human right in a number of international and national conventions – and explicitly in the Declaration of 1977 in Mar del Plata[1] and more recently in Article 24 of the Convention on the Rights of the Child (UNICEF, 1990). Article 24 recognised 'the right of the child to the enjoyment of the highest attainable standard of health ... through the provision of ... clean drinking water, taking into consideration the dangers and risks of environmental pollution' (p. 57).

Though the Millennium Development Declaration and Goals refer only to water, access to adequate sanitation and basic hygiene knowledge are equally important. Indeed, in terms of their contribution to basic health, sanitation and hygiene are arguably more important. Contrary to much public opinion, recent research shows that hand-washing does more for reducing child mortality and the incidence of diarrhoea than the provision of safe water or even basic latrines. For example, in a meta-analysis of some fifteen micro-studies, nine from Asia, three from Africa, two from Latin America and one from the USA over the years 1981–2000, Curtis and Cairncross (2003) estimate that hand-washing on average is associated with a 40 per cent reduction in the risk of infectious intestinal diseases. This leads them to estimate that appropriate hand-washing with soap could save between 0.4 to 1.5 million deaths from these diseases each year – a mean estimate of avoiding almost 1 million deaths per year. Curtis and Cairncross summarise the total number of deaths from infectious intestinal diseases as 4.6 million in 1980, falling to 3.3 million in 1990 and 2.94 million in 1997, whilst they quote the latest World Health Organisation (WHO) estimates as 2.2 million for 2000.

The conclusion to be drawn is not that safe water is unimportant, but that people need access to adequate sanitation and basic hygiene knowledge as well as to safe water. All three contribute to health directly. Yet indirectly, they also contribute to poverty reduction, since reducing the incidence of ill health and disease of children and of adults frees the time of women and men for more productive activities. Access to water and adequate sanitation near the home can also save much of the time and burden of collecting water far away, a cause of many girls being absent from school as well as a heavy chore for children and women involved in daily water collection. Less emphasised is access to improved sanitation and hygiene as a step to ensuring dignity and privacy and, often, security, especially for women and girls.

Goals for sanitation and hygiene

Though goals for sanitation and hygiene were not included in the Millennium Declaration, a major effort was mounted to ensure the inclusion of a sanitation goal in the declaration and plan of action of the World Summit on Sustainable Development at Johannesburg in August and September 2002. Such a goal had already been adopted in several previous international meetings concerned with improving access to water, sanitation and health.[2]

An important step in setting goals for hygiene and sanitation was taken in the 'Vision 21' report presented to the Second World Water Forum at The Hague in 2000. The goal proposed for sanitation was 'by 2015 to reduce by one-half the 1990 proportion of people without access to hygienic sanitation facilities' (WSSCC, 2000b). Meanwhile, for hygiene the report set out several suggested targets for 2015:

- universal public awareness of hygiene;
- 80 per cent of primary schoolchildren educated about hygiene;
- all schools equipped with facilities for sanitation and hand-washing; and
- a reduction in diarrhoeal disease by 50 per cent.

The report's strategy to achieve water, sanitation and hygiene for all by 2025 was more challenging still, envisaging:

- good hygiene practices universally applied;
- all primary schoolchildren educated about hygiene; and
- a reduction in diarrhoeal disease by 80 per cent.

These targets are also summarised in other UN publications (WHO, UNICEF and WSSCC, 2000: 2).

The present position

Table 13.1 summarises the numbers and proportions of the population in developing countries lacking access to water and adequate sanitation in 2000. The figures presented in the table are the result of a world-wide effort by WHO, the United Nations Children's Fund (UNICEF) and the Water Supply and Sanitation Collaboration Council (WSSCC) to assemble data and estimate coverage, based on the latest evidence from as many countries as possible in all regions of the world.

Though there are always problems of data quality and conceptual definition, this latest survey involved a number of improvements over previous efforts to provide global estimates. More countries were involved than in 1990 and a wider range of sources were used, including both assessment questionnaires and household surveys. These were distributed to country offices through WHO country representatives with the support of local UNICEF staff to relevant national agencies. Methodologically, the survey was based on consumer response rather than data from service providers. Even so, the quality of data is still often inadequate. For some countries, including a number of industrial countries, data are totally missing. However, by common consent, the quality and quantity of the data and the estimates are much better than ever before.

Attempts were made in these surveys to apply clear definitions and

Table 13.1 Global water supply and sanitation coverage, 2000

	World population[a] (billions)			Percentage of world population	
	Total	With access	Without access	With access (%)	Without access (%)
Urban water supply	2.8	2.7	0.2	94	6
Rural water supply	3.2	2.3	0.9	71	29
Total water supply	6.1	5.0	1.1	82	18
Urban sanitation	2.8	2.4	0.2	86	14
Rural sanitation	3.2	1.2	2.0	38	62
Total sanitation	6.1	3.6	2.4	60	40

Source: WHO, UNICEF and WSSCC (2000: 8).

Note
a Figures have been rounded to the nearest 100 million.

common standards of access, based on the type of technology in use. Table13.2 shows the classification of technologies, by those considered 'improved' and those 'not improved'. The reasons for a technology to be considered 'not improved' can include limitations on quantity as well as quality, as illustrated by the inclusion of bottled water in the 'not improved' category.

Nonetheless, there are two other dimensions of the adequacy of water and sanitation provision which could not be comprehensively included through lack of data: access by distance to source of water (or sanitation facility), and quality of water (or of upkeep of sanitation facility).

For water, access by distance (or by time taken from household to source) should ideally consider separately differences such as having a water supply inside the house or compound, within 100 metres or less, 100 metres up to 1 kilometre away, and more than 1 kilometre away. In densely populated areas, even finer differences should ideally be taken into account. For quality of water, maximum levels of iron and fluoride as well as dangerous pollutants such as arsenic need to be considered.

For sanitation, some measures of distance and cleanliness also ought to be included. But through lack of data, most of these dimensions have to be ignored in global estimates – though of course they can and should be brought into national and community surveys.

Access to safe water and sanitation by region

Tables 13.3 and 13.4 give the numbers and percentages with and without adequate access to safe water and sanitation by region. In the case of Asia, China and India alone comprised some 2,280 million people in the year

Table 13.2 Water supply and sanitation technologies considered to be 'improved' and those considered to be 'not improved'

Water supply	Sanitation
'Improved technologies'	
Household connection	Connection to a public sewer
Public standpipe	Connection to septic system
Borehole	Pour-flush latrine
Protected dug well	Simple pit latrine
Protected spring	Ventilated improved pit latrine
Rainwater collection	
'Not improved technologies'	
Unprotected well	Service or bucket latrines
Unprotected spring	(where excreta are manually removed)
Vendor-provided water	Public latrines
Bottled water	Open latrine
Tanker truck provision of water	

Source: WHO, UNICEF and WSSCC (2000).

Table 13.3 Coverage of rural, urban and total water supply by region, 2000

	Population[a] (millions)			Percentage	
	Total	With access	Without access	With access (%)	Without access (%)
Rural					
Africa	490	230	260	47	53
Asia	2,330	1,730	600	75	25
Latin America and Caribbean	130	80	50	62	38
Urban					
Africa	300	250	50	85	15
Asia	1,350	1,250	100	93	7
Latin America and Caribbean	390	360	30	93	7
Total					
Africa	780	480	300	62	38
Asia	3,680	2,990	690	81	19
Latin America and Caribbean	520	440	80	85	15

Source: WHO, UNICEF and WSSCC (2000: 8).

Note
a Figures have been rounded to the nearest 100 million.

2000, or over 60 per cent of the region's total population. Thus progress in the Asian region is enormously influenced by performance in these two countries. In this regard, one important caveat needs to be stressed: because the Chinese authorities increased the standard by which they assessed adequacy of sanitation in the 1990s, the gain in coverage by 2000 appears less than would otherwise have been the case.

This point is important in assessing progress in expanding water and sanitation coverage (Table 13.5). Although the data presented in Table 13.5 for 1970 and 1980 are not strictly comparable to those of 1990 and 2000, they are included to give at least an order of magnitude of the progress achieved. The most important conclusion to be drawn is that of the enormous progress made over the past three decades. Over the 1980s, during the years of the 'Decade for Drinking Water and Sanitation', access to safe water more than doubled, whilst access to improved sanitation nearly tripled.

Progress in the 1990s was quantitatively not so large but was still impressive. For example, because of rapid increases in population, the proportions of people with access to water and sanitation inched forward rather than leaped ahead. Nonetheless, by 2000 probably five or six times more people had access to safe water than thirty years before, and four or five times more people had access to adequate sanitation. These are remark-

Table 13.4 Access to rural, urban and total sanitation by region, 2000

	Population[a] (millions)			Percentage	
	Total	With access	Without access	With access (%)	Without access (%)
Rural					
Africa	490	220	270	45	55
Asia	2,330	710	1,620	31	69
Latin America and Caribbean	130	60	570	49	51
Urban					
Africa	300	250	50	84	16
Asia	1,350	1,050	300	78	22
Latin America and Caribbean	390	340	50	87	13
Total					
Africa	780	470	310	60	40
Asia	3,680	1,770	1,910	48	52
Latin America and Caribbean	520	400	120	78	22

Source: WHO, UNICEF and WSSCC (2000: 8).

Note

a Figures have been rounded to the nearest 100 million.

Table 13.5 Estimated coverage of drinking water supply and sanitation in developing countries, 1970, 1980, 1990 and 2000

	Population with access (millions)				Percentage of total population with access			
	1970	1980	1990	2000	1970	1980	1990	2000
Water								
Urban	320	530	1,100	1,480	67	75	95	94
Rural	180	570	1,190	1,480	14	29	66	71
Total	500	1,100	2,300	2,960	29	43	79	82
Sanitation								
Urban	340	370	940	1,370	71	53	82	86
Rural	130	210	600	780	11	13	35	38
Total	470	580	1,540	2,150	27	25	55	60

Sources: 1990 and 2000 – as for Tables 13.1–13.4; 1970 and 1980 – WHO (1981).

able achievements, which cast a positive light on the possibility of expanding coverage much further in the years up to 2015.

Many lessons have been learned nationally and internationally over the past two decades about the actions required to ensure sustained access to water and sanitation of adequate quality. Some of the most important include:

- the importance of ensuring systems for self-sustaining maintenance as opposed to simply installing hand pumps, tube wells and sanitation facilities;
- the need to involve communities in the provision of facilities, their maintenance and their financing;
- the need to ensure empowerment of women in decision-making and action both about new programmes and in the running and maintenance of existing ones;
- the multiplier effects of focusing on primary and secondary schools and schoolchildren, to ensure that schools have adequate sanitation facilities separately for girls and boys and adequate access to safe water.

Schoolchildren can also be agents of change: playing a vital and catalytic role in initiating hygienic behaviour and in spreading new knowledge and practice in their families and their communities.

Future needs

Table 13.6 shows the projections of population growth and their implication for halving the proportion of people without access to water and adequate sanitation by 2015. The figures are large but they are not out of proportion with past achievements except in the areas of urban sanitation and rural water supply. Even in these respects, the major challenges are those in Asia and Africa, not the Middle East or Latin America.

Achieving the goals for water, sanitation and health is neither extremely difficult nor extremely costly. Examples exist in all regions of the world that show how accelerated progress is possible and affordable within the budgetary resources of the country and communities concerned. South Africa, for instance, embarked on a major programme for the provision of safe drinking water in 1994, when the democratic government came to power. Within seven years, by 2001, the new government had halved the

Table 13.6 Additional population required to be covered to meet the 2015 targets for water and sanitation

	Total population (billions)		Coverage (%)		Additional population (billions)
	2000	2015	2000	2015	
Urban water supply	2.8	3.8	94	97	1.0
Rural water supply	3.2	3.3	71	85	0.6
Total water supply	6.1	7.2	82	91	1.6
Urban sanitation	2.8	3.8	86	92	1.1
Rural sanitation	3.2	3.3	38	69	1.1
Total sanitation	6.1	7.2	60	81	2.2

Source: WHO, UNICEF and WSSCC (2000: 32–33, table 5.1).

numbers without safe water, thus achieving the global goal fourteen years ahead of 2015. South Africa now has the goal of achieving safe water for all by 2008. Sanitation progress went more slowly – until the cholera outbreak of 2000; this seemed to act as a wake-up call. South Africa has now increased expenditure and latrine programmes, in one year achieving more than in the previous six years, with the goal of sanitation for all by 2010. South African experience demonstrates the importance of clear political commitment.

Data are also available showing the different rates of progress in expanding access to safe water made over the past few years against the rates required to achieve the Millennium Development Goal for water. This assessment is shown in Table 13.7, which highlights the number of countries that have already achieved the Goal, and how no country, at least of those for which data exist, are moving in the wrong direction.

However, even with positive experience in many countries, barely half of the population of developing countries live today in countries on track to achieve the goal, whilst very few have already achieved it. About a third of the population of the South live in countries lagging far behind. Another 12 per cent live in countries without the data to assess the situation – a sign in most that achieving the goal is not in sight.

Table 13.7 Country progress on halving the proportion of people without sustainable access to safe drinking water by 2015

Number of countries	*Goal achieved*	*On track*	*Lagging*	*Far behind*	*Slipping back*	*No data*
Sub-Saharan Africa	1	9	4	9	0	21
Arab States	0	8	0	3	0	6
East Asia and the Pacific	0	6	1	4	0	8
South Asia	3	4	0	0	0	1
Latin America and the Caribbean	1	21	1	2	0	8
Central and Eastern Europe and the Commonwealth of Independent States	0	8	0	0	0	17
Total number of countries[a]	5	63	7	18	0	75
Percentage of total world population	4	39	5	27	0	10
Percentage of Third World population	5	45	6	32	0	12

Source: UNDP (2002: 25).

Note

a Regions include only Human Development Index countries while the total includes all UN member countries excluding high-income Organisation for Economic Cooperation and Development (OECD) members.

Donor countries have a role to play in supporting action to achieve these three vital goals. But the starting point has to be national action – to recognise the goals as a national priority, to prepare action plans for their achievement, to open opportunities for community action, and to mobilise public awareness and support, especially for sanitation and hygiene.

Seven key areas of policy

Experience over the past two decades underlines seven areas of policy and action which are critical for accelerating country-by-country action towards the achievement of the goals.

First, few developing countries will be able to achieve the goals for hygiene, sanitation or water without widespread social and community action, which in turn requires the mobilisation of populations. To rely on government or the private sector alone in countries of limited resources will require expenditures far beyond the revenues available or the capacity of households and communities to pay. In contrast, approaches based on social mobilisation, in which individual and community action is combined with that of local or central government, can bring into play the additional labour and additional finance to make the goals achievable. These approaches have often been used in many of the countries and states that have seen rapid expansion of water or sanitation facilities. Social mobilisation seems almost the only way in which hygiene education can be expanded to the point where behaviour is influenced on a major scale.

Second, involvement of the private sector will be needed. Several years ago, privatisation in water was seen as the panacea and promoted widely by institutions such as the World Bank. At the time of writing, this has given way to a more pragmatic approach, in the light of experience, especially the failure of some of the early private-sector schemes and the reluctance of the large private-sector water companies to invest further in developing countries. Privatisation of the water system in Buenos Aires, hailed as a great success three or four years ago, is now seen as a disaster.

But the private sector still has an important role to play. In matters of sanitation, and in rural areas more generally, small-scale private entrepreneurs have the skills needed and have often demonstrated a capacity to contribute on an increasing scale. They are often ideal for making the concrete 'slabs' required for simple latrines, for installing local-level water taps and supplies, and occasionally for providing water through drums and bowsers or tankers where these are needed.

Competition is important to ensure that these contributions are made at low cost. In larger towns and cities, the private sector in the form of national and international water companies, if willing, can also play an important role in providing water and sanitation as part of management of major schemes. Here, however, it is important to ensure that the contracts for such companies require them to reach out to the peri-urban areas, especially to poorer communities.

Third, more use of simple, low-cost technologies and approaches is needed. Hand pumps, improved wells, rainwater harvesting, installations using volunteer labour, community maintenance – all these are approaches which are relevant and cost-effective in rural situations, as well as many peri-urban areas. Vision 21 of the Water Supply and Sanitation Collaboration Council (WSSCC) estimated that some US$9 billion per year would be needed between 2000 and 2025 to meet the goals of water and sanitation for all (WSSCC, 2000a: 28). These estimates were based on a cost of US$15 per person for water in rural situations and US$50 in peri-urban areas. For sanitation and hygiene promotion, the average costs were estimated to be US$10 and US$25 per person respectively. These figures were based on a small sample of actual projects and programmes. In contrast, the World Water Commission (2000; see also Global Water Partnership, 2000) estimated that some US$180 billion would be needed each year for ten years to ensure water and sanitation in line with the goals (Global Water Partnership, 2000; World Water Commission, 2000). What explains these enormous differences?

A review of the estimates shows that most of the difference is explained by the much larger estimates in the World Water Commission calculations for urban sanitation and waste disposal. For water, the Commission estimated an additional US$17 billion per year or US$170 billion over ten years compared with US$90 billion for water and sanitation and hygiene in the WSSCC estimates. The difference between these estimates mostly reflects the level of technology implied. The WSSCC estimates focused on the needs of poor people in rural and peri-urban communities. The Commission estimates focused on urban infrastructure, including large-scale technologies.

A fourth key area of policy involves better monitoring, with the results more publicly disseminated. Monitoring is required for efficient management, but also for effective social mobilisation. Monitoring means the development of a regular system of reporting, sufficient to demonstrate progress in a way that can be reported publicly to sustain interest, enthusiasm and political support. Of course, monitoring is also important for administration and efficient budgeting, although experience shows that monitoring for social mobilisation is even more important for sustaining action. Publicising progress in expanding water state by state in India stimulated popular demand and support for water, just as it had in many countries in areas such as child immunisation.

A fifth point is that it is important to set a price policy which is politically acceptable and equitable. Full-cost pricing has become the conventional wisdom, pushed strongly by the World Bank, the International Monetary Fund (IMF) and others working within 'the Washington consensus'. For example, the World Water Commission has stated that full-cost pricing is the single most important policy required to deal with water problems of the twenty-first century (WWC, 2000). In contrast, the Vision 21 report takes a very different position (WSSCC, 2000a). While recognising that issues of pricing are important, Vision 21's approach is pragmatic. It argues that prices must be set in relation to the capacity of different groups to pay and in relation to the overriding commitment to ensure access to water and sanitation for all, in line with international commitments on human rights.

The Dublin Principles, agreed at a major international water meeting in 1991, provided guidelines for integrated water resource management. They emphasised that water needed to be recognised as an economic resource. But the principles neither stated nor implied that full-cost pricing was necessary. The UK government has given a balanced summary of the issues, noting that, 'it is important to continue to recognise water as a social and ecological good as well as an economic good. Indeed, the Dublin conference also recognised that access to clean water and sanitation at an affordable price is a right for all human beings' (DFID, 2001: 32).

In practice, price is an important means to ensure the economical use of a scarce resource and an important means to raise the revenue required for both installing and maintaining water supplies. The same can be said of pricing for sanitation. But simply moving to full-cost charging is too simple. It usually means charging full cost to those who are at present without water or adequate sanitation facilities – and continuing subsidies to those who have long had in-house connections at far below full-cost prices.

In respect of water, a pragmatic approach would start by considering the relative benefits of different levels of charging for the main groups of consumers – those already with access to supplies piped direct to their houses and those relying on community standpipes and other such facilities. Often, those with supplies direct to their own households are both the main users and the ones receiving the greatest level of subsidy. Charging full-cost pricing to this group of consumers holds great potential for generating more resources for the drinking water sector – though, of course, it may involve political difficulties. But according to the WSSCC, this should be the starting point.

For poorer communities, some form of cost recovery is also often desirable, both to generate resources and to encourage efficient use of supplies. But given high levels of poverty and the need to ensure access to water as a human right, systems of cost recovery and resource generation should be judged in relation to capacity to contribute. Often this pragmatic approach may lead to communities being encouraged to provide labour in kind to ensure rapid installation of community supplies by hand pumps and public facilities. Full cost recovery might be adopted for those households wanting to establish connections to their own individual properties. A priority in all cases is to ensure that charging covers maintenance costs, though again successful examples exist of communities providing their own maintenance services. This has proved successful in the Swach project in southern Rajasthan, as well as in Nigeria. Women often prove more reliable in maintaining hand pumps, in part because they are usually the main users, and also because when trained in maintenance they are less likely to move from the community in search of a job elsewhere. This was the logic behind many UNICEF programmes for training women in pump maintenance in Sudan, India and Bangladesh.

The dangers of insisting on full-cost pricing in all situations cannot be stressed too strongly. At its extreme, full-cost pricing is elevated to the level of an unjustified piece of economic ideology, and can also be highly misleading.

A sixth key area of policy concerns the need to ensure the full participation of women in the management and operation of water, sanitation and hygiene programmes. Women are more affected by inadequacies of arrangements in these critical areas and almost always are more motivated to do something to improve the situation. Being the daily drawers and carriers of water, they are also usually the best informed about the inadequacies of the present, and the clearest about what can and should be done. However, very often their voices are not heard and household resources are not theirs to control. Nonetheless, there are increasing examples of how this can be changed if women are empowered to exercise more sanitation control and influence (WSSCC, 2000a, b). In Gujarat in India, in Ethiopia even during the civil war, in Nigeria, Vision 21 gave many examples and built on them. If the goals are to be reached, women's empowerment and control will need to become much more common in water and sanitation than it is at present.

The seventh and final need is for development assistance to be more directly focused on water and sanitation for the poorest. Given the strong donor support for the Millennium Development Goals, one would imagine that donor support for water and sanitation for the poorest would be readily forthcoming. In practice, the bulk of international support goes to urban schemes, at relatively high cost and benefiting the better-off urban communities. Support for water and sanitation schemes in the rural and peri-urban areas forms only a small fraction of the total – probably less than 20 per cent.

This led to the call for '20:20', an agreement first proposed in the *Human Development Report* (UNDP, 1994: 77) with strong support from UNICEF and subsequently endorsed as a recommendation of the World Summit for Social Development in 1995. As discussed elsewhere in this volume, under the 20:20 proposal donors would allocate 20 per cent of their aid for key areas of basic needs – primary education, primary health care, nutrition, family planning and reproductive health care – and low-cost water and sanitation programmes. Developing country governments would allocate a similar 20 per cent of their public expenditures to the same priorities. Calculations showed that these two actions would be sufficient on average to generate the financial resources required to achieve the universal provision in the priority areas within a decade or so.

Some thirty developing countries indicated their willingness to support this approach during the late 1990s – but only two or three donors. Now, with the formal adoption of the Millennium Development Goals, the time seems ripe to renew commitment to this practical measure. But whether or not it is formally adopted, the underlying conclusion still remains. Both donor and developing countries could generate the vast bulk of the resources required to meet the Goals in general – and the goals for water, sanitation and hygiene in particular – by a better allocation of resources already going into these sectors. Donor contributions to water, sanitation and hygiene need to be carefully reviewed in the light of the Millennium Development Goal priorities, and reallocations or additional resources provided to ensure the international support needed, especially for poorer countries committed to achieving the goals.

Action for sanitation and hygiene

As regards sanitation, many low-cost schemes have relied on the sale of concrete 'slabs', around which individual households can build a simple latrine block to whatever standards they choose. One example is the ventilated improved pit latrine (VIP), which is often ideal. The 'VIP' can also be relatively cheap, even though it provides a much higher and better level of service, free of flies and smells. Communities also have developed a range of latrines and simple shower and bathing blocks themselves. Sometimes these are run by the community itself, or sometimes by an individual entrepreneur or the local government. Such blocks can be made available at a relatively low charge, sufficient to cover their maintenance. In the past ten years an increasing number of successful examples have been developed for all these approaches. In India the Sulabh movement led by Dr Bindeshawar Patak has provided toilet facilities for over 10 million people. The twin-pit latrine has been especially successful.

However, sanitation means much more than the provision of latrines with appropriate technologies. Recent years have witnessed the development of many new approaches. Separate latrines for girls and boys in all schools is one critical strategy, the starting point for any serious school messages on hygiene but also a step in mobilising children as agents of change in their homes and villages.

Strategies of '100 per cent sanitation' have proved extraordinarily successful in Bangladesh in motivating whole villages to improve their toilets and waste disposal systems. The approach begins with a village-wide assessment of the whole situation, involving the community and outsiders slowly walking together along a transept across the whole village. Often it is shame at the recognition of the situation that is revealed by villagers and outsiders working together which triggers a collective determination to make changes. It is then left to individual villagers to decide on what they can and will do for their individual homes and plots. No resources are spent in subsidising latrine construction, but rather funds are targeted at supporting the whole process and promoting general awareness of the need for better hygiene (Kar, 2003).

This appears to be a general rule for latrine construction and other forms of household sanitation improvement. It is important to recognise that individuals want to improve their houses, and will do so if low-cost opportunities are available. There is often no need for subsidies. Rather, it is possible to let the market work, with local craftspeople providing the materials and often doing the work. Instead, resources can be channelled into training and motivation, hygiene education and promotion.

The ten commandments for success with goals

Much of the current interest in setting global goals derives from the successful experience of UNICEF in the 1980s and 1990s. In 1985, UNICEF made a formal, major and public commitment to the global pursuit of the goal of universal child immunisation as a critical step to reducing child mortality. Universal child immunisation had already been adopted as a key goal by WHO and UNICEF. However, it was only when UNICEF publicly committed itself to the achievement of this goal by 1990, and mobilised its own staff, resources and reputation to its achievement, that the goal moved to high international profile.

In country after country, major efforts were undertaken to accelerate action and increase coverage. These involved campaigns: mobilisation of churches, mosques, teachers, women's groups and political leaders, as well as health workers, to the goal of reaching in each country at least 80 per cent coverage of immunisation against tuberculosis, measles, polio, diphtheria, tetanus and whooping cough. Contrary to the expectations of many sceptics, by 1990 coverage of these six antigens in developing countries had reached 80 per cent or more on average. Some seventy-two developing countries had individually achieved the goals. These included many countries in Latin America and sub-Saharan Africa, even though the 1980s was economically a lost decade for economic development.

All this is a great example of the power of global goals, provided they are made a priority for a UN agency and are used in a process of national mobilisation at country level. In the case of UNICEF, the achievement of the goals of immunisation in 1990 was used to set a range of other goals for the next decade, which were formally adopted at the World Summit for Children in September 1990. These goals covered ten major areas and seventeen supporting sub-goals.

UNICEF's experience in pursuit of goals was later summarised in a tribute entitled 'The Ten Commandments of Jim Grant's Leadership for Development' (Box 13.1) (Gautam, 2001). These commandments showed

Box 13.1 Jim Grant's ten commandments

1   Articulate your vision for development in terms of inspiring goals.
2   Break down goals into time-bound doable propositions.
3   Demystify techniques and technologies.
4   Generate and sustain political commitment.
5   Mobilise a grand alliance of all social forces.
6   Go to scale.
7   Select your priorities and stick to them.
8   Institute public monitoring and accountability.
9   Ensure relevance to the broad development agenda.
10   Unleash the full potential of the United Nations system.

Source: Jolly (2001).

how formal goals need to be turned into action nationally and globally in ways that mobilise and sustain the interest of people. It requires a political and people-centred process, rather than initiatives of a more technical or administrative nature.

Implementing these ten commandments can help create the enabling environment that in turn can set the stage for accelerating action country by country. Top-down commitment must of course be matched by grass-roots response. Action at both levels is required. When the two are combined, achievement of the global goals becomes possible.

Prospects

Finally, we turn to the future. What are the prospects, at the time of writing in 2002, that the goals will be achieved?

Without doubt, some countries will achieve them. Ten already have achieved the goals for water and another fifty-eight are estimated to be on track. But much could happen, positively or negatively, during the thirteen years before the target date of 2015 is reached. All that one can do today is to offer a conditional forecast of likely future achievements – and a highly conditional forecast at that.

Recall first that there are three important goals, not one – for water, sanitation and hygiene. Recall also that for each there are two quantitative dimensions of achievement: halving the proportion of the total population of developing countries without access and halving the proportion without access within each developing country.

As regards the first, halving the proportion of the total population of developing countries without access, the critical determinant is what happens in China and India. These two countries alone comprise almost half of the total population of developing countries. More important, they comprise an estimated 56 per cent of the total additional population to be reached with safe water and an estimated 64 per cent to be reached with sanitation, if the 2015 goals are to be achieved. If one had to make a forecast today, one would do well to bet that China and India will achieve the water goals on the basis of past experience and achievements.

India is assessed as being on track for achieving the goals for safe water and China, though assessed as lagging (UNDP, 2002), has made considerable advances and has demonstrated remarkable capacity in the past for accelerated action in the social as well as economic sectors. Four of the world's five next most populous countries – Indonesia, Brazil, Pakistan and Bangladesh, but not Nigeria – are also assessed to be 'on track', to judge by their progress over the 1990s (UNDP, 2002: 46–49). If these six countries themselves achieve the water goal, their weight will do much to carry the global average towards the global water goal.

Sanitation presents a less clear picture. China and India have each expanded coverage over the 1990s to reach about an additional 10 per cent of their population (WHO, UNICEF and WSSCC, 2000: 47–48). The size of the backlog means, however, that in each case this is barely a quarter of the distance to go to achieve the target by 2015. Both countries are assessed to be 'far behind' and need about a doubling of their rate of advance to reach the sanitation target. Without this, their weight in the developing country average will make very difficult the achievement of the global sanitation goal. The same four of the five next most populous countries are, however, all judged to be on track to achieve the sanitation goal.

But what about the prospects for goal achievement in other individual countries? This brings us back to the key policy issues mentioned earlier. Using low-cost technologies, the achievement of goals for safe water, sanitation and hygiene are all technically possible with only a modest allocation of additional resources or reallocation of existing ones. And, after all, the goals are modest: only to halve the proportion without access, in countries where half to two-thirds already have access.

Whether the water goal will be achieved in any particular country will, in my assessment, be mostly a matter of three factors:

- *political commitment*, to go to scale and to provide national leadership to make the goal real and meaningful;
- willingness to adopt *participatory approaches* which enable and support local participation and management, especially by women;
- willingness to ensure *adequate resources* for programmes in the rural and peri-urban areas. In the poorest countries, resources will also be required with sustained back-up from donors.

For sanitation and hygiene, the same three factors will be critical. But in addition two others will be important. First, it will be necessary to ensure that the education system gives proper attention to issues of hygiene and sanitation with backing from the national media. Second, support will

need to be obtained from the private sector, especially from soap manufacturers. With such support, the goals for sanitation and hygiene can
readily be achieved in any country.

One final point needs to be made. In most of Asia and Latin America
the above factors cover the main issues. But in the least developed countries, and in most of sub-Saharan Africa, achieving the goals will also
depend on – and be part of – sustained long-run economic development,
of a sort that has not been seen for two or more decades. Civil conflict and
collapse of local administration hinder all aspects of development, including pursuit of the goals for poverty reduction and the goals for safe water,
sanitation and hygiene. The priority problems of Africa are now widely
recognised. The presidents of South Africa, Algeria, Egypt, Nigeria and
Senegal have established the New Partnership for Africa's Development
(NEPAD). The Millennium Development Goals for poverty reduction are
part of this agenda. Whether they are achieved in this continent of such
desperate need will depend on how seriously the goals are taken by the
individual countries and made part of the new partnerships with donor
governments and institutions of the international community.

Notes

1 United Nations (UN) Water Conference held at Mar del Plata, Argentina,
March 1977.
2 See the report of the International Conference on Freshwater held in Bonn,
December 2001 (Germany, 2000). See also WSSCC (2000a).

References

Curtis, V. and Cairncross, S. (2003) 'Effect of Washing Hands With Soap on Diarrhoea Risk in the Community: a Systematic Review,' *The Lancet Infectious Diseases*,
3(5): 275–281.

Department for International Development (DFID) (2001) *Addressing the Water
Crisis: Healthier and More Productive Lives for Poor People*, Strategy Paper, London:
DFID, March.

Gautam, K. (2001) 'Ten Commandments of Jim Grant's Leadership for Development', in Jolly, R. (ed.) *Jim Grant: UNICEF Visionary*, Florence: UNICEF, pp.
137–144.

Germany, 'Federal Ministry for the Environment, Nature Conservation and Nuclear
Safety and the Federal Ministry for Economic Cooperation and Development
(2000) *Water: A Key to Sustainable Development*, report, Bonn: Courir-Druck GmbH.

Global Water Partnership (2000) *Towards Water Security: A Framework for Action*,
Stockholm: Global Water Partnership.

Jolly, R. (ed.) (2001) *Jim Grant: UNICEF Visionary*, New York: UNICEF.

Kar, K. (2003) 'Subsidy or Self Respect? Participatory Total Community Sanitation
in Bangladesh', IDS working paper, WP184, Brighton, Sussex: IDS.

United Nations Children's Fund (UNICEF) (1990) *First Call for Children*, Convention on the Rights of the Child, New York: UNICEF.

14 Achieving sustainability in Africa

James Fairhead

Introduction

This chapter reflects on the form that 'sustainability' takes within the seventh Millennium Development Goal, which is broadly to 'ensure environmental sustainability'. In particular, it considers the linked target, to 'integrate the principles of sustainable development into *country* policies and programmes and reverse the loss of environmental resources'. This Goal and target are themselves adapted from the International Development Target, which envisaged 'the implementation of *national strategies* for sustainable development in all countries by 2005, so as to ensure that current trends in the loss of environmental resources are effectively reversed at both global and national levels by 2015'.

A huge literature has emerged concerning sustainability and development, prompted first by the World Summit at Rio and again in the build-up to the 2002 World Summit on Sustainable Development at Johannesburg, and its outcomes. I do not attempt a review here. Rather, I am concerned to explore how the concept of sustainability is being elaborated around the Millennium Development Goal, and the targets and strategies and programmes to achieve them, considering this particularly in relation to Africa. The main argument is that its elaboration in documentation and initiatives minimises or obscures the way local issues are linked to global forces, whether economic or environmental. Crucial aspects concerning the transnational corporate and global dimensions to current resource uses and their sustainability are rendered marginal, not centre stage, in the focus on *country policies and programmes* of the Millennium Development Goals. In particular, I argue that the impact both of the 'new scramble for Africa' by transnational corporations, and of impending global climate change on African environmental resources, threatens to undermine or override country policies for sustainability.

The Millennium Development Goals do have a Goal concerning global partnership which considers transnational issues, but this neither mentions environmental issues nor balances the potential benefits that corporations can bring for technology-sharing with critical evaluation of their

United Nations Development Programme (UNDP) (1994) *Human Development Report 1994*, New York: Oxford University Press.

—— (2002) *Human Development Report 2002*, New York: Oxford University Press.

Water Supply and Sanitation Collaboration Council (WSSCC) (2000a) *Vision 21: A Shared Vision for Hygiene, Sanitation and Water Supply and A Framework for Action*, Final Report, Geneva: WSSCC.

—— (2000b) *Vision 21: A Shared Vision for Hygiene, Sanitation and Water Supply and a Framework for Action*, Proceedings of the Second World Water Forum, The Hague, 17–22 March 2000, Geneva: WSSCC.

World Health Organisation (WHO) (1981) *Drinking Water and Sanitation 1981–1990: A Way to Health*, Geneva: WHO.

World Health Organisation (WHO), United Nations Children's Fund (UNICEF) and Water Supply and Sanitation Collaboration Council (WSSCC) (2000) *Global Water Supply and Sanitation Assessment 2000*, Report, Geneva: WSSCC.

World Water Commission (2000) *Commission Report: A Water Secure World*, Marseilles: World Water Council.

terms of engagement – and there is no evidence that the rhetoric of partner-ship has translated into more equal international relations (see Chapter 16).

The significance of global economic and environmental forces was highlighted in deliberations and negotiations during the 2002 World Summit on Sustainable Development. It has, for example, been politically difficult for European and American negotiators to consider lifting pro-tectionist trade barriers, and to regulate the problematic conduct of trans-national corporations. It has been politically impossible for American negotiators to deliberate global climate agreements further. It has been easier for the same negotiators to focus on support to local and national conservation and sanitation initiatives in poorer countries, assisted in this by a rhetoric which places the poor centre stage. The focus on 'country programmes' in the International Development Target and the Millen-nium Development Goal reflects the ease with which donor nations of the Organisation for Economic Cooperation and Development (OECD) can involve themselves with sustainability in poorer countries through local and national initiatives there. It also reflects the political difficulty that they face when addressing what I shall argue are the far more important questions of international trade and global climate change.

It should be said, however, that at the World Summit there were attempts among Northern politicians and pressure groups (amongst them the UK leadership) to address environmental sustainability by concentrat-ing on the very problems of global political economy and global climate change. The UK Prime Minister, Tony Blair, for example, made a speech proposing codes to ensure transparency in payments made by trans-national corporations to African governments; payments which have been at the heart of unaccountable government and conflicts in the region. He re-emphasised the importance of global climate change. It is to be hoped that such speeches, and the debate at Johannesburg that signalled their pertinence, might help mark a change in emphasis in approaches to poverty and sustainability, and in the formulation of the Millennium Development Goal.

As it is, however, these international political-economic dimensions to resource use and 'sustainable development' are conspicuously absent from most documentation and strategies linked to the Millennium Devel-opment Goal. Instead, the ways that sustainability is discussed parochialise it. Let us consider the UK Department for International Development's (DFID's) Strategy Paper for achieving the sustainability International Development Target, called *Achieving Sustainability: Poverty Elimination and the Environment.* This document certainly acknowledges that it is the wealthy who cause most environmental degradation. The solutions it pro-poses, however, still seem to lie with the poor: thus to quote the executive summary, 'The main causes of environmental degradation are unsustain-able consumption, particularly of the rich, both in developed and devel-oping countries' (DFID, 2000a: 8) and 'globally, most environmental degradation is caused by the non-poor as the consumption levels of the poor are still low relative to the rich' (ibid.: 12). Yet when actions are discussed to meet International Development Targets, they 'are looked at primarily from a poor country perspective.... Emphasis is placed on working with the poor and on improving often weak and ineffective systems of governance.'

The poor are highlighted because they suffer from degradation, not because they cause it. 'Pro-poor' policy, however, fades into 'working with the poor' rather than with the conditions that lead to poverty. It responds to the supposed cycle of 'poverty and degradation', rather than with the far worse cycle of wealth and the degradation of poor people's resources. The problem is not that these issues are absent, but that they are marginal. Thus the DFID strategy paper acknowledged that a pro-poor focus will involve 'controls on environmentally damaging activities of the non-poor' (ibid.: 26). Yet this is hardly pursued. There is, after all, much less experience in this field to draw on in order to identify best practice. It has long been easier to help the poor than hinder the rich. More significantly, the extent to which this is the local or the international wealthy is not addressed, and neither is the capacity of the wealthy to circumvent such control.

The second pillar of the Millennium Development Goals, or at least of the strategies promoted to date by official development agencies to achieve them, is trade liberalisation. Again, to take the DFID strategy paper as exemplar, trans-boundary concerns *are* raised in relation to globalisation. Yet any potential negative environmental impacts of trade liberalisation are to be addressed by *national* strategies and environmental policies: 'Without the implementation of appropriate environmental policies in all countries, trade liberalisation could lead to environmental damage.' So, it is

> a mistake to argue against further liberalisation on environmental grounds. Marginalising poor countries from the benefits of global trade and investment will not prevent environmental degradation and will alienate developing countries from negotiations on global environmental issues. Rather the challenge of globalisation is that it intensifies the need for better enforcement of appropriate environmental policies at the national level.
>
> (ibid.: 20)

Within this logic, the national strategies of the Millennium Development Goal are proposed as the 'main vehicle for integrating pro-poor economic growth with social improvement and a responsible approach to environmental management' (ibid.: 11; see also DFID, 1997). In the DFID strategy paper there is considerable deliberation over the criteria that could be used to assess whether a country has successfully incorporated considerations of sustainability in its development policies and programmes. Indeed, the UK/DFID input into the 2002 Summit was envisaged as focusing on 'how far countries have effective sustainable development processes in place.'

The emphasis is, however, on poor countries to enforce regulation, rather than on the international financial system. This intensifies the need for 'better enforcement' at a time when there are fewer national financial resources, and, as will become clear, at a time when there is intensified international/multinational interest in African natural resources, and increased financial dependency among African governments on these. The call is for the indebted to regulate the enriched.

Exemplars of success in such regulation should not mislead us. Especially in instances where donors have been willing to support the creation and implementation of regulatory policy, there have been moves towards such regulation. The DFID strategy documents highlight Uganda and Ghana as cases. Yet it can be questioned whether these are replicable exemplars of the way forward. Are they not better understood as 'policy oases' lush on exterior support, or even 'policy mirages' stronger on documentation than implementation, which would be misleading as a basis for sustainable planning?

Moreover, pitting 'national programmes' against the 'forces of globalisation' misses the mutuality between governments of low-income countries (and their elite), transnational corporate finance, and international geopolitical alliances. It is to this issue that I now turn, with a particular focus on sub-Saharan Africa. The next section examines the issue of sustainability in Africa in the context of the international political economy and is followed by a section that discusses global and local causes of climate and environmental damage.

Sustainability and international political economy in Africa

The very same month that the UK published its White Paper *Eliminating World Poverty: Making Globalisation Work for the Poor* (DFID, 2000b), the US National Intelligence Council (NIC) – part of the US Central Intelligence Agency (CIA) – published its own view of global futures in its *Global Trends 2015* (NIC, 2000). This acknowledged straightforwardly that by 2015 – the maturity date for the Millennium Development Goals – 'most African states will miss out on the economic growth engendered elsewhere by globalisation and by scientific and technological advances' (NIC, 2000: 71). This dovetails with the view of many African negotiators expressed at the Johannesburg World Summit when they argued that freeing restrictions on transnational corporate engagement with Africa is leading less to African development through inward investment, than to a more parasitic and exploitative engagement.

The NIC vision for Africa in 2015 is of a catastrophe, reproducing the image of 'hopeless continent' beloved of contemporary journalists (e.g. *The Economist*, 2000). In some contrast to the image of despair, however, the NIC report goes on to predict that Africa will be supplying 25 per cent of North American oil imports by 2015. New oil discoveries in the Democratic Republic of Congo, Uganda, Sierra Leone and Côte d'Ivoire will be adding to the huge reserves to be found in Nigeria, Sudan, Chad, Nigeria, Angola, Gabon, Congo, Equatorial Guinea and others. Despair, however, is maintained, as despite these resources, the Council argues, 'patterns of oil wealth fostering corruption rather than economic development will continue' (NIC, 2000: 73). This is an extraordinary statement. The NIC is happy to affirm this as if African corruption had nothing to do with the strategic interests of the Great Powers, and the commercial interests of their corporations. Nothing could be further from the truth.

Through geological fate, African countries are now known to hold major oil reserves. Several also monopolise global supplies of several strategic minerals such as cobalt and tantalum, on which modern industrial powers have come to depend. The Democratic Republic of Congo (DRC), for example, has 60 per cent of global cobalt reserves (the rest are in Canada and Cuba), and 80 per cent of global tantalum. The heat and electrical properties of tantalum make it a crucial ingredient in capacitors for third-generation mobile phones and other advanced electronics, as well as for jet engines, night vision goggles and fibre optics. Cobalt is a critical ingredient in the superalloys used in air- and land-based turbine engines as well as for rechargeable batteries for cell phones and computers. Moreover, environmental pressures for zero-emission vehicles will massively increase demand for this 'oil of the future'.

As with oil, industrial nations need to secure their supplies, and corporations controlling supplies can profit hugely, so their governments and corporations inevitably work together. African natural resources have long been of strategic significance (Hveem, 1986). This continues. Over the past decade, international security officials have been paying even greater attention to intensified competition over strategic materials, and this has regained centrality in US security planning. Indeed, Klare, writing in *Foreign Affairs*, goes further, arguing that there is now a 'new geography of conflict, a reconfigured cartography in which resource flows rather than political and ideological divisions constitute the major fault lines' (2001: 52).

Strategic resources have now acquired further importance following the attacks on the USA on 11 September 2001. First, Africa's 'non-Islamic oil' has become central to the geopolitics of energy. Second, as former Assistant Secretary of State Susan Rice argued to the US House of Representatives' deliberation on Africa and the war on global terrorism,

> We must recognise that regimes lacking legitimacy and failed states are convenient safe havens as well as breeding grounds for terrorists. If we are serious about our anti-terrorism commitment ... the US

must become more rather than less engaged in the difficult task of peacemaking, peacekeeping and national reconstruction – from the Great Lakes to Sierra Leone, from Liberia to Sudan and Somalia. We must also find effective ways to secure Africa's vast natural resources – its diamonds, cobalt, uranium, oil, timber, coltan, its gold – so they do not provide currency for the world's terrorists.

(Rice, 2001: 12)

New demand for African resources in this second scramble for Africa has not been helping most Africans. For example, Oxfam (2001) reported that poverty and health problems are worse in developing countries that are dependent on oil and mining. They are associated with civil war, military expenditure and with governments that, being financially independent of their populations, cease to become accountable to them (see also Moore, 2000). Many researchers have reiterated the centrality of environmental resources, and more particularly the political-economic conditions of their extraction, to poor governance and conflict (e.g. Auty, 1998; Collier and Hoeffler, 2000, 2001; Nafziger *et al.*, 2000; Reno, 1999). This association has come to be dubbed the 'resource curse' (World Bank, 2002). Geopolitical and commercial rivalry play into national and regional political rivalry, and patterns of social differentiation, so it would be foolish to reduce causality in contemporary conflicts to this (e.g. Mamdani, 1996; Mkandawire, 2002). Nevertheless, it would be equally foolish to ignore it.

The 2003 *World Development Report* pursues this analysis. Speaking of the resource curse, it says:

> The adverse effects are magnified when the natural resource endowment, like petro-chemicals and minerals, are 'lootable' or 'point sourced', meaning that their production and revenue patterns are concentrated [as opposed to 'diffuse']. Coffee and cocoa take on point source characteristics when shipped.
>
> (World Bank, 2002: 149)

Timber, and even 'conservation', can take on such characteristics too when control over resources is granted through state timber concessions or conservation concessions. Of the 45 countries whose growth was not sustained, 'all but 6 are point-source economies. The majority of the countries with point-source natural resources also suffered violent conflict in the 1990s' (ibid.: 149). In cases where this 'curse' has fuelled conflict, the ensuing international response has lobbied for trade embargoes linked to the vocabulary of conflict diamonds, conflict oil, conflict timber, conflict tantalum, and so on. There have been some successes. Conflicts, however, are the more extreme and high-profile manifestations of a corporate and political blight that currently undermines governance and resource-use sustainability in many other countries.

The most documented case of corporate culpability in transforming governance and fuelling conflict is to be found in the DRC. Here, North American, European and Asian corporations have struck deals with governments and rebels; rebel movements themselves have become self-financing through their mining and resource extraction; and neighbouring countries (especially Rwanda and Uganda), allied with rebel movements, have enriched themselves through illegal looting. This has been well documented both by the United Nations (UN) and by assorted non-governmental organisations (NGOs) and academics (e.g. UN, 2001).[1] Assessments suggest that a staggering 2.5 million people have died of this curse in the DRC alone since 1998 (All Party Parliamentary Group, 2001; IRC, 2001).

At the same time, the world's leading mining corporations have supported protagonists in the conflict and profited both from their interests there and indeed, from the increased value of their reserves elsewhere when conflict disrupts Congolese production.

Many of the corporations operating in the DRC and its neighbours have strong political connections. These are hard to research in detail, but some indication of the links can be gauged from the 'revolving door' that sees senior figures in government moving into and out of these corporations. In recent years, for example, Barrick Gold, which has large interests in DRC, has counted three former CIA directors and two former North American presidents in its management (George Bush Snr, Richard Helms, Robert Gates and Brian Mulroney). The Bechtel corporation, which also worked with Congolese rebels, has counted former US Secretary of State George Schultz, alongside Philip Habib and Casper Weinberger, as well as CIA directors William Casey and Richard Helms working for it. The oil company Halliburton, which – together with its subsidiary Brown and Root – has major oil and other interests in the region, had current US Vice President Richard Cheney as its Chief Executive Officer (CEO) until his nomination. Another oil company, Chevron, which is now involved in a US$2bn investment in the DRC, until recently counted Condoleezza Rice as a member of the board. Prior to that, she was Special Assistant to George Bush. Now she has become US National Security Advisor. Corporate expansion in conflict zones has coincided with an explosion in private security firms. The largest private security transnationals not only work closely with the US government, but also are owned by former members of government and the military. The Vinnell Corporation (based in Fairfax, Virginia), for example, is owned by BDM International Inc. and controlled by the Carlyle Group, which counts former CIA deputy director Frank Carlucci and US Secretary of State James Baker among the shareholders. Carlucci was Secretary of Defense under Ronald Reagan and George Bush and, it might be noted, was also former second secretary at the US embassy in the DRC. The nature of corporate and political links can perhaps be gauged well in the work of Cohen and

Woods, a Washington-based lobbying firm. This firm has worked both for mining and security firms seeking contracts and concessions in Africa (such as MPRI in Angola), and for African leaders seeking US political support (such as the late Laurent Kabila). Cohen and Woods is managed by Herman Cohen (former Assistant Secretary of State for Foreign Affairs) and Jim Woods (former Assistant Secretary of State of US Defense).

Liberia provides a contrasting case in which transnational corporations and conservation organisations appear to operate more independently of the political–military–industrial complex. Thus at a time when there has been a UN arms and trade embargo on Liberia, and at a time when the US has been hostile to Liberia, there have have been large external corporate investments in the different resources of the country. United States tele-evangelist Pat Robertson, for example, and his 'Freedom Gold' brokered a deal with the president, Charles Taylor, to prospect in south-eastern Liberia. A friend of the current administration, he has been lobbying for a shift in US policy towards Taylor. Timber concessions have been sold to the 'Oriental Timber Company' and others. Conservation International signed a deal to establish and manage protected area networks covering 1.5 million hectares with a view to establishing 'conservation concessions', inaugurating, perhaps, an era of 'conflict conservation'.[2] Instability is not necessarily fuelled simply by buying arms and paying soldiers, although this is asserted too, and is a powerful image in international lobbying (Global Witness, 2001). It is also fanned by the undermining of citizens' rights, government accountability and the rule of law. Thus the logging operation, for example, drew public criticism concerning the destination of payments, the granting of work permits to foreign workers, disrespect for indigenous rights and resources, non-compensation for damage to property, the exclusion of national regulatory authorities, and the violation of laws and regulations.

After reviewing the role of Western corporations in the unfolding of the current Congo holocaust, Montague argues that 'In order for investment to be used as an effective tool for development, multinationals must understand that massive corporate investments have a negative impact on society in the absence of state stability. Indeed, their financial leverage only exacerbates state instability' (2002: 115).

Environmental resources are fundamental to poor and indebted modern African economies. As I have argued, we see less patterns of governance able to influence management of environmental resources, than the inverse: the transnational dimensions to the management of environmental resources influencing patterns of governance. It is this that modern policy must address. Viewed in this way, it does not become sensible to differentiate between 'renewable' and 'non-renewable' resources.

Indeed, making a strong distinction between renewables and non-renewables has long enabled the transnational dimensions to resource use and sustainability to be downplayed. The focus on renewables, and on their scarcity, leads analysts to explore the causes of conflict in a localised way linked to local use of resources. It is 'population increase' on location that is considered to increase demand for renewable resources and their value, or poverty or social transformation on location that undermines long-term sustainable management. The way international and global economic forces affect governance and resource governance, and thus local environments and resource use, is eclipsed. We lose sight of the way that timber and agribusiness (including cocaine and opium), and the conservation business (including land, rights and resource alienation), affect governance, conflicts and, through this, environmental use and its sustainability. The distinction between renewables and non-renewables has long been ambiguous (encapsulated in analysis of soil or forest 'mining', for example), and from the vantage point of their commercialisation and their relations of commercialisation, their distinction becomes irrelevant. Ignoring the distinction enables us to speak about the way transnational interests in African environments – their diamonds, oil, tantalum, cobalt, timber, cocaine, opium – and biodiversity play into located political economies. It enables other, locally relevant distinctions to get noticed.

Modes of transnational engagement shape, for example, how people in different places understand their 'environment' and 'environmental quality'. For example, it influences whether or not people consider deforestation to be 'degradation', and how views differ. In several locations in West Africa, the return of lands to high forest is considered by many farmers to be degradation. The vast majority of Sierra Leonian, Liberian, Ivorian and Ghanaian forests, after all, have grown over once prosperous places, where cycles of bush fallow have been disrupted following depopulation during the slavery era, and reservation during the colonial one (Fairhead and Leach, 1998). Much of today's Liberian forest did not exist twenty years ago, having grown over war zones. Is the subsequent loss of this forest again 'degradation'? For whom? How does the alienation of rights over heavy timber to state authorities influence these perspectives? How does the alienation of land to reserves, protected areas or conservation concessions influence this? How does the alienation of diamond resources in these areas influence patterns of governance and modes of resource use? How does this alter local engagement with the state, timber companies and conservation organisations?

Whatever the failings of the National Intelligence Council vision for 2015, it does provide a counterpoint with which to escape the utopian and parochial language common to development strategising around sustainability. Yet predictably, despite this contrast, even the NIC, like the Millennium Development Goal and associated strategies, plays down the current problematic international engagement of transnational corporations with African globalisation. International engagement in 2015, the NIC suggests, will increasingly be through 'international organizations and non-state actors of all types: transnational religious institutions, international

like DFID?

nonprofit organizations, international crime syndicates and drug traffickers; foreign mercenaries; and international terrorists seeking safe havens' (NIC, 2000: 73). The operation of transnational corporations is omitted.

Deniability concerning the negative impacts of corporate involvement in environmental resources has been maintained in many ways. First, it is perfectly clear that many of the financial transfers, political support and indeed military interventions are covert in nature, and firm analysis of them does not emerge. Second, accountability is clouded by the complexity of modern corporate structures. Third, major corporations have learned to speak the language of corporate social and environmental responsibility. Belief in the latter will certainly have been shaken by recent corporate and accounting scandals. It remains to be seen whether corporate scandals will reach the African dealings of major corporations. Fourth, blame is easily transferred to the African partners.

In short, approaching issues of sustainable development simply through *national* programmes appears enormously naive. It is in recognition of this corporate co-responsibility for failures in African governance that the philanthropist financier George Soros has recently linked with 'Global Witness' and dozens of other international organisations to lobby for enforced transparency in international corporate financial transfers. Their 'Publish what you pay' initiative would require transnational resource extraction companies to 'publish net taxes, fees, royalties and other payments as a condition for being listed on international stock exchanges and financial markets'.[3] This would facilitate both corporate and government accountability. This approach to sustainability and poverty alleviation is the inverse of that envisaged in the Millennium Development Goal. Action is not to be through *national* programmes, but through calling on the G-7 nations – the world's wealthiest – 'to take leadership and promote transparency over resource revenues worldwide'. It was this (albeit in voluntary rather than regulated guise) that the UK's prime minister, Tony Blair, supported in speeches made around the Johannesburg Summit on Sustainable Development. However, this approach runs up against both the military–industrial complex of contemporary geopolitics as much as the nether world of independent transational entrepreneurs and national 'rent-seekers'. Certainly there would be immense problems in implementation, but it is nevertheless the only way forward. The only caveat that I would add is that it should apply as much to financial transfers for those seeking to control resources as for conservation and transfers relating to extraction.

Concerning 'global and local causes'

A second arena that is marginal to policy documentation on sustainability, poverty and the environment is the impact of Northern industrialisation on African climate and environment. International Development Target strategies make much of the 'many opportunities to meet local environmental priorities while also contributing to global concerns, such as the build up of greenhouse gas emissions in the atmosphere' (DFID, 2000a: 8). Missing, however, is an appreciation of the way global climate changes, with roots in Northern industrialisation, impact on African localities. Whilst it has been easy to dismiss as fanciful, rhetoric arguments that African droughts and famines result from climate changes linked to Northern industrialisation, evidence is now building that the rhetoric lies with the complacent dismissal. Evidence is accumulating rapidly that the wide-scale impact of climate changes on African vegetation and agro-ecology threatens to override many local conservation and development initiatives. Future historians may find such initiatives, whether rooted in participation or exclusion, to have been 'fiddling while Africa burns'. This argument is premised on alarming evidence that has emerged during the past fifteen years that African climates have experienced major fluctuations (at times catastrophic deteriorations) in historical times. African forests appear to be particularly susceptible to global climate fluctuations of the sort associated with global warming.

The sensitivity of African climate and vegetation to global change is indicated by evidence from forest and climate history. For example, archaeological, climate historical and oral evidence combine to suggest that forests in West and Central Africa have responded massively to major climate fluctuations during recent centuries and millennia. In a review, Maley (2002) has concluded that 2,500 years ago a climatic deterioration lasting several centuries led to a catastrophic destruction of central-West African forests, almost halving the current forest range. In recent centuries, forest vegetation has been recovering from this period, and from other less extreme periods of deterioration around 800–1,200 years ago. In Cameroon, more than 1 million hectares of savanna has become forest in this region alone since 1952, whether in the presence or absence of cultivation (Maley, 1999). For equatorial Africa, Vincens *et al.* (1999) suggest that the earlier dry phase appears to have lasted for a very long time, with the start of the current humid phase and recolonisation of forest dating back only to 600–900 years ago.

Preliminary analysis of work conducted by Overpeck and colleagues based on sediment cores and tree remains from Ghana's Lake Bosumtwi indicates that 'Ghana was gripped by a "megadrought" for much of the little Ice Age' (Overpeck pers. comm.). As in Central Africa, West African forests appear to have recovered from this period of climatic deterioration, colonising savannas in recent centuries. The quality of the forest is thus not as 'pristine' or 'biodiverse' as one might expect. As Hawthorne has noted on the basis of tree species distribution, the vast majority of Ghana's forest is effectively a 'scar tissue, a recently assembled group of mainly widespread, well-dispersed species, covering up after some immense disruption of this area and barely infiltrated by rarer species which could occur there' (1996: 138). My own research in Guinea, and more widely in West Africa, indicates that much of what is today classified as the 'forest region' has recently been savanna land (Fairhead and Leach, 1998).

It is thus beginning to appear that African forests have been very sensitive to global climate changes in historical times. The alarming problem is that climatic conditions that led to these African droughts – at least which led to the catastrophic destruction of the Congo forest – appear to be the very conditions predicted for the region by modern climate models linked to human-induced global warming. As Maley (2002) makes clear, if current predictions concerning anthropogenic global warming are accurate, this is likely to have a catastrophic effect on the region's forests. If, as is the case, the key indicator of whether the Millennium Development Goals are met is the 'proportion of land covered by forest', and 'land area protected to maintain biological diversity', these overriding global dimensions to sustainability need to be addressed – indeed, need to have been addressed.

Other recent studies indicate that industrial emissions from North America and Europe may have caused the recent severe droughts that have afflicted the Sahel region of Africa. Industry and power-generation emissions have been creating aerosols that affect cloud formation, altering the temperature of the Earth's surface. In climate modelling, temperature change causes the Earth's surface in the north to cool relative to the south, appearing to drive the tropical rain belt southwards and causing droughts in the Sahel.

As we gain more knowledge about global climate relations and history, we shall be made increasingly aware of these underlying dimensions to sustainability. Future phases of desiccation associated with forest fires and future droughts might well be attributable more to greenhouse-gas and other emissions from industrialised countries than to land users in West Africa. It will appear, however, from attention to proximate causes that 'Africans are responsible'. This should not, however, deflect attention to underlying causality and responsibility. Attention to the impact of global climate change on African environments, and especially its threats on the Congo forest, puts in its place the fanfare that accompanied the recent announcement at Johannesburg by an interagency partnership to 'save the Congo forest' through located interventions.

The other lesson from African climate history is that it undermines the idea of stability and predictability that has infused many interpretations of 'sustainability'. This poses some problem for the expansion of 'results'- or 'target'-based planning of international development and the Millennium Development Goals into the field of environmental sustainability, when the results of social interventions are measured simply in relation to environmental qualities. The focus should be less on getting institutions right, as if there were a single solution, than on questions of power, political economy and the processes shaping the evolution of institutions of resource governance. Equally, the focus should be less on 'stabilising the forest' than on flexible adaptation in response to non-equilibrial ecological and economic environments (Leach *et al.*, 2002).

Conclusions

The aim of this chapter has been to indicate a central deficiency in the Millennium Development Goal concerning sustainability. The 'country programmes and policies' which are its linchpin may well be necessary, but they will be by no means sufficient. Clearly there is a huge importance to national policies which I have not explored in this chapter. Yet national policies themselves must be contextualised within international strategies that respond realistically to the way the global political economy currently shapes resource use and its governance, and to strategies that address global climate change. Otherwise it will become increasingly apparent that the focus on national strategies is a comfortable ideological device promulgated by OECD countries and donors which has the effect of transferring responsibility for current patterns of unsustainability to African countries.

Several international organisations, including the OECD, have already developed linked initiatives to address this. The OECD countries have, for example, ratified a 'Convention on combating bribery of foreign public officials in international business transactions'. This entered into force in 1999 but awaits effective implementation (OECD, 2002). Many donors have also allied themselves in anti-corruption initiatives, such as the European Union anti-corruption resource centre and the World Bank anti-corruption initiative, having 'identified corruption as the single greatest obstacle to economic and social development'.[4] These initiatives could have provided the foundation for a Millennium Development Goal and more concerted action on corruption. Yet this has not happened, and this chapter has raised issues which help to explain why. The 'publish what you pay' initiative is the single most important initiative to have emerged in the field of development and sustainability in the past fifty years. Attempts to craft governance for sustainability without it may be doomed to failure.

Debates concerning sustainability at the Johannesburg conference also went well beyond the narrow remit of the Millennium Development Goal – and indeed beyond its narrow indicators. This was exemplified in the speech of the British prime minister, Tony Blair, highlighting the central issues of transparency of financial transfers and global climate change.

As it is, the prospect, at present, is that Africa's oil (and other environmental resources) will undermine sustainability twice over: their extraction leading to problems in governance and accountability so fundamental to any policy of sustainability, and their use leading to major problems of global climate change.

Notes

1 See also the addenda to this UN report, and NGO reports posted at http://www.globalpolicy.org/security/issues/kongidx.htm.
2 See the official agreement, http://www.liberiaemb.org/vol1.6.pdf.
3 http://www.globalwitness.org/text/campaigns/oil.
4 See www.u4.no and http://www1.worldbank.org/publicsector/anticorrupt, respectively.

References

All Party Parliamentary Group (2001) All Party Parliamentary Group on the Great Lakes and Genocide Prevention, at www.appggreatlakes.org/downloads/report_2001.pdf.
Auty, R.M. (1998) *Resource Abundance and Economic Development: Improving the Performance of Resource-Rich Countries,* Research for Action 44, UNU/WIDER, Studies in Development Economics, New York: Oxford University Press.
Collier, P. and Hoeffler, A. (2000) 'On the Incidence of Civil War in Africa', *Journal of Conflict Resolution,* 46(1): 13–28.
—— (2001) *Greed and Grievance in Civil War,* World Bank.
Department for International Development (DFID) (1997) *Eliminating World Poverty, a Challenge for the 21st Century,* London: DFID.
—— (2000a) *Achieving Sustainability: Poverty Elimination and the Environment,* London: DFID.
—— (2000b) *Eliminating World Poverty: Making Globalisation Work for the Poor,* White Paper on International Development, London: DFID.
Economist, The (2000) 'The Hopeless Continent and The Heart of the Matter', 13 May.
Fairhead, J. and Leach, M. (1998) *Reframing Deforestation,* London: Routledge.
Global Witness (2001) *Taylor-Made: The Pivotal Role of Liberia's Forests in Regional Conflict,* 2nd edition report, September, at http://www.globalwitness.org/text/campaigns/forests/liberia/reports.html.
Hawthorne, W. (1996) 'Holes and the Sums of Parts in Ghanaian Forest: Regeneration, Scale and Sustainable Use', *Proceedings of the Royal Society of Edinburgh,* 104B: 75–176.
Hveem, H. (1986) 'Minerals as a Factor in Strategic Policy and Action', in Westing, A. (ed.) *Global Resources and International Conflict: Environmental Factors in Strategic Policy and Action,* Oxford: Oxford University Press, pp. 55–84.
IRC (2001) Mortality Study Eastern D.R. Congo, at http://www.theirc.org/what/index.cfm?fa=show&topicID=86&wwwID=440.
Klare, M. (2001) 'The New Geography of Conflict', *Foreign Affairs,* June 2001.
Leach, M., Fairhead, J. and Amanor, K. (eds) (2002) 'Science and the Policy Process: Perspectives from the Forest', *IDS Bulletin,* 33(1).
Maley, J. (1999) 'L'Expansion du palmier à huile (*Elaeis guineensis*) en Afrique

Centrale au cours des trois dernier millénaires: nouvelles données et interpréta-
tions', in Bahuchet, S., Bley, D. and Pagezy, H. (eds) *L'Homme et la forêt tropicale*,
Paris: Bergier, pp. 237–254.

—— (2002) 'A Catastrophic Destruction of African Forests about 2500 Years Ago
Still Exerts a Major Influence on Present Vegetation Formations', *IDS Bulletin*,
33(1): 1–12.

Mamdani, M. (2001) *When Victims Become Killers: Colonialism, Nativism, and the Genocide in Rwanda*, Princeton, NJ: Princeton University Press.

Mkandawire, T. (2002) 'Post-colonial Rebel Movements in Africa', *Journal of
Modern African Studies*, 40(2), 181–216.

Montague, D. (2002) 'Stolen Goods: Coltan and Conflict in the Democratic
Republic of Congo', *SAIS Review*, 22(1) (Winter/Spring): 103–118.

Moore, M. (2000) 'Political Underdevelopment', paper presented at the Tenth
Anniversary Conference of the Development Studies Institute, London School
of Economics, London, 7–8 September.

Nafziger, W., Stewart, F. and Vayrynen, R. (eds) (2000) *The Economic Causes of
Complex Humanitarian Emergencies*, Oxford: Oxford University Press.

National Intelligence Council (NIC) (2000) *Global Trends 2015: A Dialogue about the
Future with Nongovernmental Experts*, NIC 2000, at http://www.cia.gov/nic/pubs/
2015_files/2015htm.

Organisation for Economic Cooperation and Development (OECD) (2002) Report
by the Committee on International Investment and Multinational Enterprises:
*Implementation of the Convention on Combating Bribery of Foreign Public Officials in
International Business Transactions and the 1997 Recommendation*, OECD 2002 (date
declassified), Paris: Directorate for financial, fiscal and enterprise affairs, at
http://www.oecd.org/pdf/M00029000/M00029509.pdf.

Oxfam (2001) *Extractive Sectors and the Poor*, Boston: Oxfam America, at
http://www.oxfamamerica.org/pdfs/eireport.pdf

Reno, W. (1999) *Warlord Politics and African States*, Boulder, CO: Lynne Rienner.

Rice, S. (2001) Submission to 'Africa and the war on global terrorism', Hearing
before US House of Representatives, Committee on Social Relations (Subcom-
mittee on Africa), 107th Congress, 1st Session (no. 107–46), 15 November.

UN (2001) *UN Report of the Panel of Experts on the Illegal Exploitation of Natural
Resources and Other Forms of Wealth of the Democratic Republic of the Congo*, 12 April,
at http://www.globalpolicy.org/security/issues/kongidx.htm.

Vincens, A., Elenga, H., Reynaud-Farrera, I. *et al.* (1999) 'Forest Response to
Climate Changes in Atlantic Equatorial Africa During the last 4000 Years BP and
Inheritance on the Modern Landscapes', *Journal of Biogeography*, 26: 879–885.

World Bank (2002) *World Development Report 2003*, Washington, DC: World Bank.

15 Building a global partnership for development?

Peter Clarke

Introduction

The history of development programmes in recent decades has been characterised by steadily increasing use of conditioned aid to influence recipient government policy. Concerns about project and programme failure have served to justify conditionality in ever-wider policy areas. At the same time, concern has been growing that the sustainability of policy reform depends on the degree of local political will behind reform, and that conditionality tends to have a negative impact on so-called 'ownership'. This has led to widespread demands for a change in North–South aid relationships away from coercive conditionality and towards more equal 'partnership' to such an extent that the policy statements of most major multilateral and bilateral donors now centre around this concept. The Millennium Development Goal of building a 'global partnership for development' represents one example of this increased emphasis on partnership, with targets encompassing a more open, rule-based, predictable and non-discriminatory trading and financial system, a commitment to good governance, increased levels of development assistance, measures that address the problems of debt, provision of access to essential drugs and new technologies, and specific attention to the needs of young people, in the least developed countries as well as landlocked and small island states.

The rhetoric of partnership includes a shift away from the traditional government-to-government power structure in the aid relationship, expanding policy and aid management processes to encompass the private sector and civil society in both North and South. That there are tensions and ambiguities about the interests served by such partnership is evident from questions surrounding the legitimacy of non-governmental organisations (NGOs) as representatives of 'the poor' and, for some, by the mere fact that the private sector is also seen as a partner striving for the common goal of 'development'. However, the discussion here focuses on the problems surrounding relationships between donor and recipient governments. Does the discourse of 'partnership' indicate a fundamental move to more equal relationships between North and South, or instead mask ever wider and deeper infiltration of development power relations in the South? Moreover, what forms of resistance to these interventions can be detected, and to what extent can development agencies or individual actors challenge existing power relations?

In this chapter, I address these questions through an examination of the partnership discourse of the UK government's Department for International Development (DFID). The chapter first seeks to locate DFID policy in the broader context of the partnership discourse in development, before examining the discourse of partnership in DFID policy documents from 1997 to 2001. A key critique of the discourse of partnership is that it represents a 'political technology' (Foucault, 1978: 86; Shore and Wright, 1997: 4) that functions to break down boundaries limiting the global penetration of power, rather than an attainable relationship between North and South. Yet there remains scope for Southern actors to contest and work within this discourse, through complex negotiations over the course and meaning of development at a local level.   *partnership – resistance?*

Partnership discourses in development

The use of the term 'partnership' to prescribe the appropriate relationship between international aid donors and recipients has spread remarkably in the past few years and achieved a central place in the policy documents of all major multilateral and bilateral donors, as well as in the Millennium Development Goals themselves (German and Randel, 2000). The notion of a partnership for development dates back at least to the Pearson Commission, set up in 1968 by the World Bank in the context of concern about the limited impact of 'twenty years of development assistance' (Pearson, 1969: vii), and its report was entitled *Partners in Development*. The objective of development assistance[1] at that time was defined in a limited and straightforward way as 'self-sustaining economic growth' (ibid.: 130). Partnership was represented as a new kind of development relationship that would avoid 'friction, waste of energy, and mutual irritation', while maintaining 'clear and accepted channels' for 'advice, consultation and persuasion' (ibid.: 127). The precise objective of development made it possible to satisfy the 'natural' interest of aid providers in the use of their resources, while avoiding donor monitoring of the whole of social policy in developing countries, by defining two indicators of progress: 'adequate and sustained increases in the ratio of domestic savings to national income and in the ratio of exports to imports' (ibid.: 132), simultaneously taking appropriate account of factors outside the country's control. Since partnership implies mutuality, relations between donors and recipients were to be 'based on an informal understanding expressing the reciprocal rights and obligations' (ibid.: 127). From the beginning, partnership relationships were to be supported by improved donor coordination, and the 'donor community' would accept its responsibility to guarantee predictable and long-term performance-related aid flows. But also from the start, doubts were expressed in the South about the credibility of the proposals:

> Unfortunately, the concept of a genuine partnership in development somehow lacks credibility. There has never been any real sense of equality between donors and recipients even when they attend the same consortium meetings and sit around the same table in many other forums. . . . The donors have parliaments and public opinion which reign so supreme that a mere reference to them should silence all criticism, whereas the recipients should obviously be able to manipulate at will their parliaments and public opinion in the interest of appropriate development policies. A mere equality of opportunity in engaging in dialogue cannot establish parity in decision-making. Nor can the platonic world of knowledge as a sufficient basis for right conduct be easily summoned into existence.
>
> (Patel, 1971: 305)

A significant early application of the partnership concept was the Lomé Convention, signed in 1975 between the European Economic Community and the African, Caribbean and Pacific (ACP) countries. The approach differed from the Pearson proposals by replacing the informal agreement between partners with a formal contract. Maxwell and Riddell (1998: 260) argue that this formal definition of mutual commitments and procedures for redress is essential for symmetrical accountability in partnership, but consider that the initial European Union (EU) model was too inflexible and failed to permit response to political and policy changes.

The partnership discourse began to dominate mainstream policy in the 1990s following discussions in the Development Assistance Committee (DAC) of the Organisation for Economic Cooperation and Development (OECD). The Committee's 1995 statement *Development Partnerships in the New Global Context* was followed by the more detailed 1996 report which set out the International Development Targets. Comparison of these reports with the partnership proposals of the Pearson Commission report shows important similarities, but also substantial differences. There is continuing emphasis on donor co-ordination and the clear definition of mutual responsibilities (OECD, 1996: 2). On the other hand, the OECD gives increased attention to 'coherence between aid policies and other policies which impact on developing countries'. Whereas the earlier report defines a clear and narrow aim for development assistance and closely circumscribes the recipient policy areas for donor concern, the 1996 document explicitly refers to a change of conception to encompass a 'much broader range of aims' (ibid.: 13). Thus in addition to proposing the adoption of the International Development Targets, there is a simultaneous emphasis on 'locally owned development strategies'.

Since 1996 the discourse of partnership has achieved a place at the centre of development policy, and in the presentation of a wide range of new policy instruments (German and Randel, 2000: 19). In the UK, a new Labour government was elected in 1997, and introduced a new development policy centred around 'partnership'. The newly established Department for International Development published the first White Paper on development since 1975, and this, alongside documentation of the new policy in other official publications and the writings of leading officials, offers an excellent opportunity to analyse the discourse of partnership as it is conceived by a major aid donor.

Partnership in DFID policy discourse

The first DFID White Paper dedicated twenty-eight of its eighty pages to a section entitled 'Building partnerships' (DFID, 1997: 22–49), and almost every imaginable institutional divide is to be crossed by this type of relationship: public–private, civil society–state, North–South, and so on. However, the argument here concentrates on relationships between DFID as a Northern government donor agency, and Southern recipients, which are mainly governments.

How is the new type of relationship justified, and how is it characterised? Partnerships are represented as an alternative to 'old conditionalities' (DFID, 1997: 37) and are described as 'putting developing countries in the lead, devising and taking forward their own development strategies' (DFID, 2000a: 91). The justification for a less coercive relation is fundamentally instrumental (ibid.: 92), as 'over-prescriptive aid conditionality has a poor track record in persuading governments to reform their policies'. A subsequent account goes on to state that 'recipient governments have learnt to play the game. They may have no real commitment to the conditions which they sign up to' (DFID, 2001: 28). According to the then Chief Economist of DFID, Andrew Goudie,

> Most fundamental to the partnership approach is the perception that, without the full political support of developing country partner governments, any efforts to eliminate poverty in those countries will be seriously constrained. . . . Strategies and policies to eliminate poverty need fundamentally to be designed and initiated by the government itself. . . . Partnership seeks to build on existing political will within partner countries and provide support to expand and generate a broader constituency.
>
> (Goudie, 1998a: 171)

This political will is considered necessary for sustainable policy reform and is argued to be dependent on creating policy 'ownership' (e.g. DFID,

2001: 10) in the Southern government. This concept is especially problematic and will be further discussed below.

Since conditionality has proved incapable of achieving policy ownership, this is instead to be achieved primarily through partner selection. DFID's partnership policy is based on more focused aid to priority countries, selected on the basis of their need and their commitment to poverty elimination, as expressed in 'sensible policies' (DFID, 1997: 38). This selectivity is not limited to defining a threshold for aid, but is also applied to determine the depth and duration of partnerships. Goudie argues that 'partnership ... necessarily carries with it the implications of a degree of selectivity in the manner in which we work with partner governments' (1998a: 171). The problems of applying selectivity in practice have been discussed by White (2001: 1063).

The partnership approach is associated in DFID policy with a broad range of policy changes. In the following summary, the most characteristic changes are isolated for the purposes of discussion, although there are important links between them.

Comprehensive interventions

The partnership approach is associated with 'reducing support for stand-alone projects' (DFID, 2000a: 93), which are characterised as 'isolated and poorly integrated actions' (Goudie, 1998a: 170). Instead, development interventions are to become increasingly comprehensive and long term, with 'increasing support for sector-wide reforms' (DFID, 2000a: 93), or even 'the economy as a whole' (DFID, 1997: 38).

Donor co-ordination

Coherence is also to be served by donor co-ordination. According to the DFID 2000 White Paper, 'we have worked hard to promote greater harmonisation among development agencies' (2000a: 93). The reduction of the administrative burden on developing country governments is argued to justify 'working with the international community to strengthen joint working including providing resources through common funding mechanisms' (DFID, 2000a: 44). Goudie suggests additional benefits in terms of more coherent policy influence:

> [We] should look for a consistency between our bilateral response and the multilateral response – it clearly makes little sense for our programme and, for example, a Bank/Fund ESAF [enhanced structural adjustment facility]/structural adjustment programme to be moving along different tracks and sending conflicting and confusing signals to government about our multi-sided partnerships.
>
> (Goudie, 1998b: 9)

Comprehensive policy concern

The comprehensive nature of donor policy interventions is matched by similarly comprehensive policy concern, as shown in the selection criteria for prospective partners, spelt out in the 1997 White Paper:

> We would expect partner governments to: have a commitment to the principles of the agreed international development targets and be pursuing policies designed to achieve these and other UN targets which they have agreed; be committed to pro-poor economic growth and conservation of the environment, and be pursuing appropriate policies; wish to engage with us and with the donor community to this end; pursue policies which promote responsive and accountable government, recognising that governments have obligations to all their people; promote the enjoyment of civil, cultural, economic, political and social rights; and which encourage transparency and bear down on corruption in the conduct of both the public service and the business sector.
>
> (DFID, 1997: 39)

In this way, relationships move away from conditionality focused on 'certain very specific measures and actions' (Goudie, 1998a: 173), to partnerships in which 'we have both a necessary and legitimate interest in a potentially vast range of partner country affairs' (Goudie, 1998b: 3). This is consistent with a substantial broadening in the development agenda since the Pearson Commission report – it is argued to be no longer possible to limit intervention to a single objective, nor monitoring to a few indicators.

Means of legitimising policy prescriptions

The broadening development agenda creates an equally growing challenge to justify the legitimacy of a vast range of policy prescriptions. As the above quotation suggests, DFID policy documents consistently construct this array as a taken-for-granted international policy consensus. On a few occasions the attribution is more explicit – for example, when referring to 'the almost universal consensus that has developed since the end of the Cold War in favour of democracy and on creating an enabling environment for a liberalised economy' (DFID, 2001: 9). Descriptions of the policy consensus present two kinds of problems. Some reduce a series of highly contestable and complex issues to repeated keywords (Shore and Wright, 1997: 18) such as 'democracy', 'participation' and 'sustainability'. Others refer to highly specific and fashionable solutions through expressions such as 'effective and efficient public sector management'. In both cases the specifications are subject to widely different interpretations. The assumption of consensus also ignores the experience that even among donors, policy prescriptions have shown a tendency for drastic change every decade.

Means of legitimising intervention

Closely related to the issue of legitimising policy prescriptions is the need to legitimise external intervention in recipient government policy, especially at the comprehensive level proposed. This is constructed in various ways – first, with reference to the responsibility of DFID to taxpayers and Parliament, and the justification given to them for international aid.[2] As Goudie explains,

> The Secretary of State for DFID is . . . bound to account to Parliament in a formal sense . . . for the effectiveness and efficiency of the manner in which she deploys her scarce resources . . . to address legitimate concerns of her own UK constituencies. . . . We should, therefore, be under no illusions that the developmental concerns of the UK constituency play a key role in driving departmental concerns and . . . we have both a necessary and legitimate interest in a potentially vast range of partner country affairs.
>
> (1998b: 3)

A further contribution to legitimation is made by reference to the International Development Targets (DFID, 1997: 39). A similar and more comprehensive basis is provided by reference to 'universal human rights'. Goudie explicitly addresses the issue of 'the legitimacy of the interest of the external community in the governance of any other country' (1998b: 2), and starts from the foundation of the Universal Declaration of Human Rights, which, he argues, is 'perhaps, the best example of an international acceptance of this legitimacy'. Despite concern about the lack of universal agreement about the boundaries of acceptable interference, he believes that 'certainly in the governance field, and particularly the human rights field, external interest is broadly accepted'.[3] A final contribution to legitimise intervention is based on the contract implicit in the aid partnership:

> Once a partner government has explicitly decided to enter into a form of partnership with an external interest, and where the external party – as is the case with the Department for International Development – has established a programme of development assistance that entails the transfer of resources in some form, then the legitimacy of the external interest will take on a greater intensity.
>
> (Goudie, 1998b: 2–3)

Mechanisms for recipient compliance

Even within the partnership framework, some mechanism is still required to achieve recipient compliance with policy prescriptions. The documents sometimes slip back into a language of direct conditionality: 'international support is conditional on economic, social and environmental policies which will systematically reduce poverty' (DFID, 2000a: 91), but there are other formulations more characteristic of the partnership approach. A first requirement is some mechanism of policy monitoring, and this is facilitated by donor coordination, associated with International Monetary Fund (IMF) surveillance (DFID, 1997: 71) and such mechanisms as donor consultative group meetings (German and Randel, 2000: 20). Second, rewards and sanctions are required, and a well-differentiated range of these is proposed within the framework of partnership. The rewards are articulated through partner selectivity, since this is not limited to entry conditions but also promises a graded scale of aid intensity and duration, according to policy compliance. The access to resources and flexibility in their use are to depend on 'the confidence we have in [partner governments'] policies and actions' (DFID, 1997: 40). Sanctions are also maintained within partnership, with the threat of partial withdrawal when policies begin to deviate. Thus Goudie argues that 'we shall need to reconsider the scale and nature of ... partnerships if the commitment of partner governments continues to cause concern' (1998b: 8). The 1997 White Paper defines appropriate measures where the government policies of a poor country fail to win approval:

> Where poor countries are ruled by governments with no commitment to helping the poor realise their human rights, we will help – where we can do so – through alternative channels. These will include institutions of civil society, voluntary agencies and local government.
>
> (DFID, 1997: 39–40)

This alternative may be viewed with concern by Southern governments, since in many countries civil society organisations are platforms for opposition politicians. Goudie acknowledges difficulties, but reluctantly lays them aside:

> We should be deeply uneasy about working with civil society if it is somehow to the exclusion of government or as a substitute for a government or it acts to displace government. At times, we may need to live with this unease while we work to build government partnerships.
>
> (1998b: 9)

More extreme policy deviations are seen to justify more extreme sanctions:

Where there are large-scale violations of international humanitarian law and crimes against humanity, and where the government in question is unable or unwilling to halt the atrocities, the UK believes that the international community should take action. . . . Once all non-violent measures have been exhausted, it may, in exceptional circumstances, be necessary and appropriate to use force to achieve the humanitarian purpose.

(DFID, 2000a: 102)

Consistency of UK government policy

DFID responds to the criticism of development and aid discourses that they construct a boundary around certain relations with developing countries defined as 'development interventions', or certain transfers defined as 'aid', leaving other areas of Northern government policy 'free' to pursue self-interest in a way that causes substantial prejudice to developing-country interests and to net transfers. Its 1997 White Paper dedicates a substantial section to these issues, under the title 'Consistency of policies' (DFID, 1997: 50–76).[4] The argument is made as follows:

[T]here is a complex web of environmental, trade, investment, agricultural, political, defence, security and financial issues which affect relations with developing countries. . . . To have a real impact on poverty we must ensure the maximum consistency between all these different policies as they affect the developing world. Otherwise, there is a risk that they will undermine development, and development assistance will only partly make up for the damage done.

(ibid.: 50)

The White Paper commits DFID to 'ensure that the full range of Government policies affecting developing countries . . . takes account of our sustainable development objective'.

Partnership as political technology

How do the characteristics of the partnership approach described in the previous section interact with the expressed aspiration for more equal relations between donor and recipient? Renaming them as partners does not change the condition of donor and recipient, and arguably the dependence of the latter on the flow of resources from the former will tend to dominate the relationship. Attempts to ignore this power relation are, with the best will in the world, likely to run up against the expressed 'legitimate' donor needs to demonstrate timely results of their spending to their parliaments and taxpayers. As Helleiner (2000) argues, agencies are pushed to undermine local control by varied and entrenched forces: their own procedural and accounting requirements, cross-country priorities, demands to spend budgets, as well as career interests. The tendency seems to be that rather than diminishing, these pressures are currently increasing, with a growing emphasis on measurable aid impact and rigorous programme auditing.

In this context, the move from limited project interventions to much less bounded actions supporting substantial policy areas over the long term in whole national territories similarly opens up this much larger space/time to donor personnel and interference, in parallel with (legitimate) comprehensive donor concern with virtually the whole of recipient government policy.[5]

Donor co-ordination has the effect of closing Southern governments' options to diversify their foreign co-operation portfolio, further tightening their policy straitjacket. This is exacerbated by the increasing costs of non-compliance due to the potential impact of sanctions by a co-ordinated international community, right up to the extreme of the 'just war'.

The policy prescriptions themselves are also problematic. Influences on international consensus are unlikely to be equal, even in forums such as the United Nations (UN) where each member has a relatively equal voice. It could be argued that if Southern governments had played a greater role in the development of international targets and the Millennium Development Goals, other issues – such as Northern trade protectionism and debt – might well have been included earlier, giving them more weight and clearer objectives.

Similarly, the supposed benefits of a coherent UK government policy in relation to developing countries[6] – breaking down the artificial boundaries between policy areas – disappear when faced with the realities of power.[7] DFID does not set the agenda for other government departments; the objectives of the Department of Trade and Industry, the Foreign Office or the Ministry of Defence might still be expected to predominate, despite significant increases in DFID funding.[8]

This review of the impact of the policy reforms associated with 'partnership' shows how the pursuit of coherence, comprehensiveness, co-ordination and consistency itself consistently promotes a breaking down of boundaries: between limited project intervention or conditionalities and broader policy areas, between different donor programmes, between Northern development policy and other policy areas. As the boundaries are opened, power may flow more freely (and at lower cost) into every last corner.

How can the discourse of partnership and ownership be understood if its practice is really so contradictory? The extent of the contradictions is shown by an example of World Bank pressure on Mozambique to remove protection of a key industry. According to a Mozambique official, the World Bank told us we must say this is our policy and stop saying it is imposed by the World Bank ... now we must lie to get World Bank approval. And we will. But we remain totally opposed to a policy that will destroy our cashew industry.

(Hanlon, cited in White and Dijkstra, 2002)

Helleiner (2000: 85) quotes a donor representative during a recent study of aid relationships as remarking that 'ownership exists when they do what we want them to do but they do so voluntarily'. In this sense, the concept of 'ownership' can be seen as part of an attempt to represent a political problem as a technicality,[9] and its use seems to refer less to a reality than to an illusion that must be constructed precisely because true policy ownership is absent. When recipient governments respond to aid conditions with façade compliance, donors resolve to seek out governments that share their policy perspectives, and apply a test for ownership. In this way, ownership adds a further criterion to the burden of (effective) conditionality, to the extent that it seeks to appropriate the agency of aid recipients. Recipients, as well as complying with policy conditions, are even compelled to be convincing about *wanting* to comply.[10] The costs of domination through coercion are reduced inasmuch as the recipient government internalises the agenda of power. Nevertheless, the stick of IMF disapproval (or, ultimately, military intervention) and the carrot of flexible aid transfers remain in place. In this view, the discourses of partnership and ownership are revealed as examples of policies as 'political technologies' concealing an ever wider and deeper penetration of power (Foucault, 1978: 86; Shore and Wright, 1997).

The development policy narrative (Apthorpe, 1996: 8; Roe, 1991) described thus far, with its emphasis on coherence, comprehensiveness, co-ordination and consistency, suggests the construction of a monolith, but are there no cracks in the edifice? Must any counter-narrative be so monolithic? The remainder of this chapter explores this question, and whether these cracks allow a place for human agency and resistance to dominant conceptions of 'partnership', in an attempt to move beyond the definition of human actors as instruments of development and/or its victims. As Leach and Fairhead (2000: 36) warn, 'subsuming bureaucratic practice into discourse absolves the actors involved of consciousness, intentionality and responsibility'. How can agency be given a place? An alternative view of the same issues as are addressed by this chapter is presented by Chambers *et al.* (2001: 3). Their analysis of partnership also points to the contradiction between its rhetoric and its practice, but focuses on the responsibility of development professionals, arguing that 'personal behaviour and attitudes are pivotal in helping or hindering change, and directly influence wider norms and relationships'. The argument follows Chambers's earlier publications (e.g. 1997), in which he argues for a personal transformation of development professionals, who are charged with a reversal of power relationships, to release the agency of the poor. However, by focusing on the role of the 'developers' as the problem, they paradoxically become the basis for the solution, and their agency assumes an exaggerated importance. If neither analysis achieves a balanced view of agency, how is the dilemma to be approached?

If attention is turned away from the abstraction of policy documents and towards specific situated arenas of development practice, the picture changes substantially, suggesting that the wood may have obscured our view of the trees. Leach and Fairhead (2000: 36) point to the value of actor-oriented sociology as an approach to these issues. As Arce and Long argue,

> [W]hereas discourse scholars ... give priority to understanding how Western science and development models enrol, discipline and transform forms of knowledge rooted in other cultural traditions, actor-oriented research focuses upon the 'diverse and discontinuous configurations of knowledge' ... that we encounter in specific development arenas.
>
> (Arce and Long, 2000: 24)

This approach shows how external interventions 'enter the existing life-worlds of the individuals and social groups affected, and in this way are mediated and transformed by these same actors and structures' in the contexts of their own projects and strategies (Long, 1992: 20). The implication is that interpretations of the diversity of actor behaviour by development professionals as compliance or resistance are based on their own narrow and self-important perspective: actors are simply getting on with their own particular projects, and development may or may not create opportunities or obstacles for them (cf. Crewe and Harrison, 1998: 1, 159).

Viewed in this way, aid relationships take on a more differentiated character. The division between aid donors and recipients becomes hard to sustain in specific development arenas – aid flows through many hands so that even DFID is a recipient of funds (from the UK government budget), while a Southern community group may also be a donor in relation to households or individual members. Agency staff may be dependent on recipients through their need to disburse funds on time. As Foucault argues, the pervasiveness of power is matched by the resistance it encounters everywhere (1980: 142). The UK Secretary of State for Development, in campaigning to defend a boundary between commercial and development interests and to abolish the tying of aid, may be viewed as having been resisting, as may a development bureaucrat who subverts established procedures in order to permit local institutions to work at their own pace, or an NGO which refuses project funding rather than accept donor conditions.

Conclusion

A discourse of 'partnership' forms the core of the last Millennium Development Goal, and has taken centre stage in the development policy of DFID and other major multilateral and bilateral donors. The analysis of key statements of DFID associated with this policy, in the context of unequal power relations between donor and recipient, shows that far from moving towards more equal relations, these measures can be viewed as constituting a 'political technology', breaking down boundaries that limit the global infiltration of power. The discourses of partnership and ownership can in this sense be seen as attempts to mask an ever wider and deeper penetration of development power relations in the South.

This 'political technology' and its associated discursive structure should not be viewed as monolithic, converting human actors into victims or instruments of development. But care should equally be taken to avoid exaggerating agency and grounding solutions exclusively in the personal transformation of development professionals. Actor-centred approaches to the analysis of local development arenas suggest a more differentiated picture of development relationships, in which clear divisions between donors and recipients break down, and both power and resistance can be detected in complex dynamic interactions.

The analysis of this chapter gives only a partial view of the meaning of a 'Global Partnership for Development', as it is limited to policy documents and does not engage with the relations of partnership in everyday practice. As Sivaramakrishnan and Agrawal (1999: 21) argue, 'development is most fruitfully studied at the several loci of its practice, and in the multiple genres of its enactment'. Just as a 'macro' analysis, such as this, tends to give an oversimplified picture, a 'micro' study may see only complexity and differentiation. Further analysis of these issues would therefore benefit from an endeavour to combine the two levels. How would a more balanced analysis of development relationships look, one which might contribute to a clearer understanding of relationships between the power of discursive structure and individual agency?

Harrison's study of the complexity of power relations in a Zambian aquaculture project suggests how this may be done. Her multi-sited ethnography (Food and Agriculture Organisation (FAO) Rome, Harare and Luapula Province, Zambia) looks at 'the ways in which ... "local" concepts of development and modernity are adopted and internalised' and analyses 'the extent to which the supposed cohesion of the development bureaucracy is in fact real or illusory' (Harrison, 1995: 6). She argues that it is necessary to go beyond a sharp and simple division between 'us' and 'them' towards 'a fuller exploration of how the boundaries between one apparent category of social actors and another are bridged, transformed and shifted'. The study rejects the assumption that 'developers always develop while local people resist' (ibid.: 266). A picture emerges of complex negotiations of interests and a multiplicity of competing interpretations of development. A fuller assessment of whether a 'Global Partnership for Development' might ever be possible would surely depend on similarly nuanced analysis of how development targets are reinterpreted and mobilised at a local level.

Notes

1 The gradual move from development 'assistance' to 'cooperation' implies an increasingly active role for donors.
2 The DFID 2000 White Paper states this in terms of both justice and self-interest: 'The policies set out in this White Paper ... will increase social justice. They are also in the UK's self-interest because they will contribute to a more stable and prosperous world at a time when no country can be isolated from global developments' (DFID, 2000a: 104).
3 This application of human rights instruments is consistent with the considerable importance given by DFID to 'a rights-based approach to development' (DFID, 2000b).
4 See also the Development Assistance Committee statement 'Development Partnerships in the New Global Context' (OECD, 1995: 2): 'Other policies need to be coherent with development goals.'
5 Helleiner demonstrates the absurd level of detail of policy intervention by citing the example of World Bank insistence on the privatisation of the dog-sniffing service at the airport in Jamaica (2000: 83).
6 The supposed benefits of policy 'coherence' are also questioned by Duffield (2002), who concentrates on its impact on the work of humanitarian agencies.
7 In a parallel way, NGOs are increasingly entering into broader 'partnerships' with donors, which give them improved access to resources, but become an opportunity for increasing donor control of their development policies.
8 If DFID manages sometimes to defend 'developmental' criteria in UK government policy, this may perhaps be to the credit of the Secretary of State – which raises issues of the role of agency and resistance, discussed later in this section.
9 cf. Shore and Wright (1997: 8): '[P]olicies appear to be mere instruments for promoting efficiency and effectiveness. This masking of the political under the cloak of neutrality is a key feature of modern power.'
10 Interestingly, for the purposes of the donor it is sufficient that the recipient government believes itself in control, while for the recipient it is sufficient if the donor believes in its shared policy conviction.

References

Apthorpe, R. (1996) 'Reading Development Policy and Policy Analysis: On Framing, Naming, Numbering and Coding', in Apthorpe, R. and Gasper, D. (eds) *Arguing Development Policy: Frames and Discourses*, London: Frank Cass.
Arce, A. and Long, N. (2000) 'Reconfiguring Modernity and Development from an Anthropological Perspective', in Arce, A. and Long, N. (eds) *Anthropology, Development and Modernities: Exploring Discourses, Counter-tendencies and Violence*, London: Routledge.
Chambers, R. (1997) *Whose Reality Counts? Putting the First Last*, London: Intermediate Technology Publications.
Chambers, R., Pettit, J. and Scott-Villiers, P. (2001) 'The New Dynamics of Aid:

Power, Procedures and Relationships', IDS Policy Briefing 15, Brighton: Institute of Development Studies.

Crewe, E. and Harrison, E. (1998) *Whose Development? An Ethnography of Aid*, London: Zed Books.

Department for International Development (DFID) (1997) *Eliminating World Poverty: A Challenge for the 21st Century*, White Paper on International Development, London: The Stationery Office and at www.dfid.gov.uk/Pubs/files/whitepaper1997.pdf.

—— (2000a) *Eliminating World Poverty: Making Globalisation Work for the Poor*, White Paper on International Development, London: The Stationery Office, and at www.dfid.gov.uk/Pubs/files/whitepaper2000.pdf.

—— (2000b) *Realising Human Rights for Poor People: Strategies for Achieving the International Development Targets*, London: DFID, at www.dfid.gov.uk/Pubs/files/tsp_human.pdf.

—— (2001) *Making Government Work for Poor People: Building State Capability*, London: DFID, www.dfid.gov.uk/Pubs/files/tsp_government.pdf.

Duffield, M. (2002) 'Politics vs. Aid?', *Insights: Development Research*, 39: 1–2, ID21, Brighton: Institute of Development Studies.

Foucault, M. (1978) *The History of Sexuality*, Harmondsworth, UK: Penguin.

—— (1980) *Power/Knowledge: Selected Interviews and Other Writings*, Brighton: Harvester Wheatsheaf.

German, T. and Randel, J. (2000) *Some Notes on Conditionality and Ownership*, Reality of Aid, at http://www.devinit.org/jpdfs/jdipaper.pdf.

Goudie, A. (1998a) 'Eliminating World Poverty: A Challenge for the 21st Century. An Overview of the 1997 White Paper on International Development', *Journal of International Development*, 10: 167–183.

——(1998b) 'Is a Good Government Agenda Practical? An Approach to Governance', talk given at Overseas Development Institute, 25 March, at www.odi.org.uk/speeches/goudie.html.

Harrison, E. (1995) 'Big Fish and Small Ponds: Aquaculture Development from the FAO, Rome, to Luapula Province, Zambia', D.Phil. thesis, Brighton: University of Sussex.

Helleiner, G. (2000) 'External Conditionality, Local Ownership, and Development', in Freedman, J. (ed.) *Transforming Development: Foreign Aid for a Changing World*, Toronto: University of Toronto Press.

Leach, M. and Fairhead, J. (2000) 'Fashioned Forest Paths, Occluded Histories? International Environmental Analysis in West African Locales', *Development and Change*, 31: 35–59.

Long, N. (1992) 'From Paradigm Lost to Paradigm Regained? The Case for an Actor-Oriented Sociology of Development', in Long, N. and Long, A. (eds) *Battlefields of Knowledge: The Interlocking of Theory and Practice in Social Research and Development*, London: Routledge, pp. 16–43.

Maxwell, S. and Riddell, R. (1998) 'Conditionality or Contract: Perspectives on Partnership for Development', *Journal of International Development*, 10: 257–268.

Organisation for Economic Cooperation and Development (OECD) (1995) *Development Partnerships in the New Global Context*, Paris: Development Assistance Committee, at www1.oecd.org/dac/pdf/dpngce.pdf.

—— (1996) *Shaping the 21st Century: The Contribution of Development Co-operation*, Paris: Development Assistance Committee, at www1.oecd.org/dac/pdf/stc.pdf.

Patel, I.G. (1971) 'Aid Relationship for the Seventies', in Ward, B., Runnalls, J.D. and D'Anjou, L. (eds) *The Widening Gap: Development in the 70s*, New York: Columbia University Press, pp. 295–311.

Pearson, L.B. (1969) *Partners in Development: Report of the Commission on International Development (IBRD)*, London: Pall Mall Press.

Roe, E. (1991) 'Development Narratives', *World Development*, 19(4): 287–300.

Shore, C. and Wright, S. (1997) 'Policy: A New Field of Anthropology', in Shore, C. and Wright, S. (eds) *Anthropology of Policy: Critical Perspectives on Governance and Power*, London: Routledge, pp. 3–39.

Sivaramakrishnan, K. and Agrawal, A. (1999) 'Regional Modernities in Stories and Practices of Development', paper presented at South Asia Anthropology Group Conference, School of Oriental and African Studies, University of London.

White, H. (2001) 'Will the New Aid Agenda Help Promote Poverty Reduction?', *Journal of International Development*, 13: 1057–1070.

White, H. and Dijkstra, G. (2002) *Beyond Conditionality: Programme Aid and Development*, London: Routledge.

16 Aid, trade and debt

How equal is the global partnership?

Kevin Watkins and Juliana Amadi

Introduction

Sixty years ago, the Marshall Plan laid the foundations for the social and economic recovery of Europe after the Second World War. It was motivated by the view that prosperity and security in one part of the world could not be protected if mass poverty and hunger reigned elsewhere. Political leaders of the day also had the vision to act accordingly.

The contrast with today is striking. While governments in the developed world seldom miss an opportunity to offer rhetorical commitments on poverty alleviation, they have collectively cut aid budgets to their lowest-ever levels in real terms, failed to dismantle the trade barriers facing developing countries, and implemented 'debt relief' programmes which leave poor countries with levels of external debt that are inconsistent with the financing requirements for achieving the Millennium Development Goals.

There are other important differences between the role of development assistance under the Marshall Plan and international co-operation today (White, 1999). The Marshall Plan was administered by the Organisation for European Economic Co-operation (OEEC), the forerunner of today's Organisation for Economic Cooperation and Development (OECD). Receipt of Marshall Aid was based on national plans subject to scrutiny by OEEC, with no special status accorded to the United States by virtue of its position as donor. By contrast, developed countries have retained the upper hand in their dealings with developing countries. Aid management functions fall under the OECD body the Development Assistance Committee (DAC), despite attempts of the more representative UN body, the United Nations Conference on Trade and Development (UNCTAD), to play this role. Attempts to create a large grant-giving aid body within the UN in the early 1960s (the Special United Nations Fund for Economic Development, SUNFED) failed, donor countries instead favouring the creation of the International Development Association (IDA) within the World Bank – an agency whose voting structure is based on economic strength rather than the one country, one vote principle of the UN. Today the World Bank and the International Monetary Fund (IMF) act as 'gatekeepers' to bilateral aid, with donors insisting on compliance with their loan conditions as a requirement for transferring aid. In short, developing countries are very much the junior partners in the development assistance contract.

The language of Goal 8 of the Millennium Development Goals, which is 'to develop a global partnership for development', sounds like a break with the recent past. But does the reality of actions in the main areas identified under Goal 8 – notably aid, trade and debt – match up to the rhetoric? This chapter argues that the global partnership is far from equal. Developed countries retain the upper hand, and are taking inadequate steps toward fulfilling the commitments implied by their adoption of the Millennium Development Goals. The next section begins by arguing that Goal 8 is not taken as seriously by developed countries and development agencies as are the other goals. Then, in the three following sections, attention is turned to the three areas in which targets have been set in relation to Goal 8 – on aid, trade and debt. Finally, we outline actions that are necessary for the Millennium Development Goals to be achieved – actions broadly related to aid, debt relief and international trade.

Last amongst equals: Goal 8 and the Millennium Development Goals

The International Development Goals proposed in the 1996 OECD document *Shaping the 21st Century* set out targets to be achieved by developing countries, with no mention of the supporting actions required by developed countries to help these goals be fulfilled. As Fairhead argues in this volume (Chapter 14), it is inappropriate to focus on strategies by poor countries when the goal is to attain environmental sustainability. Yet feasible strategies for poverty reduction more generally also depend on international conditions – hence the importance of a set of goals for actions to ensure that poor countries, and the poor people within them, benefit from globalisation through increased access to financial resources, markets and technology. Strategies to close the huge gaps in health, education and living standards between rich and poor will otherwise fail.

Whilst the first seven Millennium Development Goals are mutually reinforcing and are directed at reducing poverty in all its forms, Goal 8 is about the mobilisation of the financial resources and other actions required to attain the first seven Goals: specifically, the elimination of trade barriers to developing country exports, debt relief for heavily indebted poor countries (HIPCs), additional financial assistance for the poorest developing countries, and ensuring access to technology, including pharmaceutical products. In a broad sense, Goal 8 is about creating an international enabling environment in which national development strategies can succeed.

The term 'global partnership for development' implies a partnership in the fight against poverty: partnership in the aid relationship, trade relationship and debt-relief relationship between donor governments and developing countries. Simply put, the bargain on offer can be summarised as follows: commit to poverty reduction and good governance, and in return expect more development finance and greater flexibility in the use of resources (Maxwell and Riddell, 1998). Though the philosophy is nothing new, it marks an important shift in approaches to development. It is based on the proposition that development is as much about autonomy, self-determination and self-respect as it is about income growth. Yet admirable as the principle of a new partnership with developing country governments committed to poverty alleviation and good governance might be, translating principle into action is difficult. Genuine participation implies joint ownership, with mutual rights and obligations. It involves a greater degree of formal reciprocity than currently appears to be on offer from the industrialised world. It also implies a contractual relationship, with procedures for redress in the case of default.

Behind the rhetoric, Goal 8 has an inferior status to that of the other Development Goals. Moreover, this is an area where the gap between commitments and action is exceptionally large, even by the normal standards of development discourse.

First, it is notable that the indicators selected for Goal 8, unlike those for the other seven Goals, do not include any time-bound commitments. This is the case even though there are long-standing targets that could be used. For example, there is no target for aid listed amongst the targets, let alone, say, 'achieve aid as 0.7 per cent of gross national product (GNP) by 2010' or to meet the promise made at the 1995 Copenhagen Social Summit under the '20:20' initiative that 20 per cent of aid should be for basic services. Second, the same effort is not put into producing reports on progress for these indicators as for the others. Neither the World Bank nor the OECD Web sites for the Millennium Development Goals report these indicators, whereas they do report indicators for the other seven Goals. This is the case despite the fact that some of the data, such as aid as a percentage of GNP and the debt service ratio, are readily available from World Bank and OECD sources.

Moreover, industrialised countries are already back-tracking on their commitments. Aid commitments are but one illustration. At Monterrey in 2002, governments reaffirmed their commitments to achieving the Millennium Development Goals. They also reaffirmed that developing countries would need to supplement domestic resources in order to achieve the Goals since most have limited sources of capital available to them and are unable to attract substantial private-sector investment. The Monterrey meeting also provided what many see as a last chance to mobilise the necessary financial resources needed. Yet despite the international commitment to achieving the Millennium Development Goals, donors refused to pledge the necessary additional aid resources.

Since the terrorist attack of 11 September 2001, many governments have spoken of the link between a peaceful global order, inequality and poverty. Governments from the industrialised world have embarked on a war against the evils of terrorism. But they have yet to commit themselves seriously to the war against the evils of mass poverty, disease and illiteracy. This failure to act will reinforce inequalities between rich and poor countries. It also calls into question the willingness of industrialised countries to support inclusive forms of globalisation, or partnership for that matter. While flows of private capital to poor countries are increasing, those countries with the most entrenched poverty are being bypassed. Without increased development finance, they face an increasingly marginalised future.

On current trends, the 2015 Millennium Development Goals will not be achieved in many parts of the world. Numerous countries are off track and the gap between the required rate of progress and actual outcomes is in some cases widening. According to the United Nations Development Programme (UNDP), thirty-three countries, accounting for more than one-quarter of the world's people, will not achieve even half of the Millennium Development Goals. Sub-Saharan Africa faces particularly acute problems. Twenty-three of the countries that are off track are located in the region, and another eleven lack sufficient data to make an assessment. The share of people in the region living on less than US$1 a day was the same at the end of the 1990s as at the start, at around 47 per cent (UNDP, 2002). Nothing more powerfully illustrates the human costs of failing to meet the Millennium Development Goals than child mortality trends. The number of additional child deaths that will occur as a result of the gap between the target rate for achieving the Millennium Development Goals and current trends represents a cumulative total of around 56 million deaths. By 2015, sub-Saharan Africa will account for around 55 per cent of total child deaths, compared with around 30 per cent in 2000 (Oxfam calculations based on UNICEF, 2002).

Fortunately, trend is not destiny. All these outcomes and the loss of potential and suffering associated with them are avoidable. According to Oxfam, an additional US$100 billion a year in aid would be enough to realise the Millennium Development Goals and honour the commitment to the world's poor (Oxfam, 2002b). For many countries, debt relief could play a critical role in filling financing gaps. At the same time, measures to strengthen the links between trade and poverty reduction could provide a powerful catalyst for human development. But without the political will that is needed to make these changes possible, there is a real danger that the Millennium Development Goals will be missed by a wide margin. Northern governments face a choice. They can continue their current policy of using UN summits to deliver a large volume of rhetoric on poverty reduction, devoid of any financing commitments. Or they can commit themselves to the investments in poverty reduction, health and education that could transform the lives of poor people, creating the foundation for shared prosperity.

Global trends in aid

A first target as part of the Millennium Development Goal to develop a global partnership is to address the special needs of the least developed countries, in part by more generous Official Development Assistance (ODA) for countries committed to poverty reduction. There has been a restatement of the pledge to raise aid to a target level of 0.7 per cent of GNP, last reiterated at the Rio de Janeiro Earth Summit in *Agenda 21*, the programme for action that set out policies for combating poverty and improving living standards. Since Rio, aid as a percentage of GNP has declined substantially, reaching its lowest level of 0.22 per cent in 1997 (OECD, 2001). Having increased in the last two years of the 1990s, ODA as a percentage of GNP again fell back to 0.22 per cent in 2000. Only five donor countries – Denmark, the Netherlands, Sweden, Norway and Luxembourg – have managed to meet the UN target of 0.7 per cent or increase their aid as a percentage of GNP. Sixteen Development Assistance Committee (DAC) donors – including Italy, France and Japan – have been cutting aid, while most G-7 donors have allowed their aid as a percentage of GNP to decline over the past ten years. The USA, Canada, Germany and Italy are allowing aid contributions to stagnate at exceptionally low levels. Even as the Financing for Development Summit approached, G-7 donors allowed their aid to fall by 3 per cent in real terms between 1999 and 2000. On average, the G-7 countries – Canada, France, Germany, Italy, Japan, the UK and the USA – in 2000 gave just 0.19 per cent of GNP in aid – even lower than their 0.21 per cent figure for 1999.

Several DAC members – Canada, Greece, Ireland, Switzerland and the UK – have targets for increasing aid. But these commitments must be seen in their proper context. The UK, the largest donor committed to increases, has been making substantial progress. But even so, if current targets are achieved, UK aid as a percentage of GNP will still be significantly below the level achieved when a Labour government last left office in 1979. Canadian aid is unlikely to rise above 0.33 per cent – far below the level maintained from 1970 to the mid-1990s. Sweden plans to reach 0.81 per cent of GNP in 2003, but it does not have a timetabled commitment to return to the previous level of 1 per cent of GNP achieved in both 1982 and 1992. Even the weak proposals tabled for Monterrey by the European Commission (EC), which called for a target of 0.33 per cent by 2006, were accepted by member states only after much prevarication. So while planned increases are welcome, there is a clear record of DAC governments failing to deliver on commitments, and many of the commitments are in any case to reach levels lower than those achieved at earlier dates.

Perhaps the bleakest picture is the fact that five of the G-7 donors – the USA, Italy, Germany, France and Japan – show no real signs of reversing the declines that have occurred in their aid. More generally, the record of even some of the strongest performers, including the UK, falls short of what is required to achieve the Millennium Development Goals. In the case of the USA, the Bush administration did announce on the eve of the Finance for Development conference in Monterrey a 50 per cent increase in aid by 2006 – representing resources of around US$5 billion a year. However, this still leaves the USA rooted at the foot of the donor league table. Moreover, the Bush administration has chosen to administer the funds on a unilateral basis through a Millennium Challenge Account, with aid eligibility governed by a wide range of economic reform criteria. This is making it more, rather than less, difficult to allocate resources to where they are most needed.

If we look at the long-term trend in aid, the 0.7 per cent target is now far removed from actual trends. Through the 1980s, donors maintained aid at around half the UN 0.7 per cent GNP target; even a decade ago, aid as a percentage of GNP was stable at 0.33 per cent. But any optimism that the end of the Cold War would result in a new world order in which the fight against poverty was prioritised quickly evaporated, with aid declining sharply to an all-time low of just 0.22 per cent of the combined GNP of DAC countries. Optimism that a post-11 September world would result in a stronger commitment to reduce poverty must be seen against this background.

More worrying is the fact that the countries most dependent on aid have suffered major losses. In 2000 only half of all aid went to low-income economies with an income per capita of less than US$700. The other half went to middle-income economies, where income per capita ranged from US$700 to US$9,000. Real aid per capita fell from US$34 to US$20 in sub-Saharan Africa in the second half of the 1990s, and halved in South Asia over the same period (White, 2002).

Some of the deepest cuts have fallen in areas that have the most potential to reduce poverty. For instance, at the end of the 1990s aid flows directed towards agriculture were running at one-third of their level in the late 1980s (IFAD, 2001). This is despite the fact that rural communities account for the overwhelming bulk of global poverty, and despite the pressing need for public investment in infrastructure, marketing and extension services.

Trade

A second general goal on partnership focuses on trade, calling for further development of an open, rule-based, predictable, non-discriminatory trading and financial system. This includes a commitment to good governance, development, and poverty reduction – both nationally and internationally. This is important, since international trade as one of the motors for globalisation is far more important than aid in defining poverty reduction. As a source of economic growth, it has never been more important for global prosperity, yet the benefits of trade are distributed unequally. While some developing countries – notably in East Asia – have tapped into the benefits of globalisation, others are being left behind.

At an international level, a variety of forces are at play, systematically skewing the benefits of trade towards rich countries, perpetuating a highly unequal pattern of globalisation in the process. Protectionist trade policies targeted at Southern exports, the disposal by rich countries of heavily subsidised agricultural surpluses on world markets and poorly designed IMF–World Bank trade liberalisation programmes all play a part. More broadly, the 'rules-based' system enshrined in the World Trade Organisation (WTO) is facing a crisis of legitimacy. There is a gathering perception in the developing world that many of the rules reflect blatant hypocrisy and double standards on the part of industrialised countries. Viewed from the developing world, the WTO is reinforcing a system that leaves countries representing four-fifths of the world's population with less than one-fifth of world exports.

Since the Uruguay Round of world trade talks concluded in 1996, promises have been in steady supply. Industrialised countries pledged to phase out protection against imports of textiles and garments, to scale down agricultural subsidies and to remove trade barriers against the poorest of countries. They made commitments to ensure that WTO rules on intellectual property and investment do not undermine development prospects. They also promised technical assistance to enhance the capacity of developing countries to participate in the WTO and trade. In practice, however, the attempts of industrialised countries to open up the markets of developing countries through reduced tariffs, allowing trade in services and protecting intellectual property, have not been matched by reciprocal behaviour where the actions would adversely affect pressure groups in developed countries.

Market access

The trend in the past thirty years has been towards increased openness in international trade. With the advent of structural adjustment in the early 1980s, developing countries have been strongly encouraged to open their markets. In addition to ensuring that developing-country markets are open to exports from developed countries,[1] the Uruguay Round introduced new concerns of particular interest to industrialised countries, in particular trade in services and protecting intellectual property rights. At the same time, little progress has been made on areas of most interest to developing countries: dismantling state support for agricultural production in developed countries and removing distortions in the global footwear and garments market.

Improved access to industrialised-country markets would help create employment opportunities in developing countries and achieve a fairer distribution of global wealth. In this respect, trade is far more important than aid. According to Oxfam (2002a), every 0.7 per cent increase in exports by developing countries generates as much income as they receive each year in aid. But increased market shares require increased access to markets.

Since the mid-1980s, South Asia, Latin America, East Asia and sub-Saharan Africa have all halved average tariffs. Industrialised countries have responded by maintaining exceptionally high trade barriers. These protectionist barriers are costing developing countries approximately US$100 billion per annum – twice the amount they receive in aid (Oxfam, 2002a). Far from supporting poor countries, industrialised countries are actively discriminating against them. Again, according to Oxfam (ibid.):

- For manufactured goods, tariffs on developing country exports to industrialised countries are on average four times higher than those facing the exports of industrialised countries.
- High tariff and non-tariff barriers are concentrated in areas of special interest to developing countries, such as agriculture and labour-intensive goods.
- Between them, the USA and the European Union (EU) have launched 234 anti-dumping cases against developing countries since the end of the Uruguay Round trade talks in 1994.

In the 1994 Uruguay Round, the Agreement on Textiles and Clothing (ATC) was seen as a step in the right direction. It provided a commitment by industrialised countries to phase out quotas on textiles and garments in four stages by 2005. Developing countries account respectively for 50 per cent and 70 per cent of these export categories. Despite this agreement, the vast majority of quotas are still in place. Industrialised countries have found ways to comply with the letter of the ATC while comprehensively violating its spirit, for example by back-loading liberalisation and 'liberalising' goods not previously subject to quotas. Consequently, developing countries continue to face excessive trade barriers in textiles and garments:

- The EU and the USA should have phased out over 70 per cent of the quota restrictions. In reality, the EU has removed one-third of the quotas on goods subject to restriction, and the USA one-tenth (International Textile and Clothing Bureau, 2002).
- The average industrialised country tariff on textiles and clothing imports from developing countries is 11 per cent – three times higher

than the average tariff on imports from industrialised countries. Tariffs will remain in excess of 10 per cent even after the Multi-Fibre Agreement (MFA) phase-out.

These measures are having devastating effects on developing countries. Textiles and clothing account for 10 per cent of total developing-country exports; South Asia alone is estimated to lose around US$2 billion per year as a result of trade barriers erected by industrialised countries. More broadly, the World Bank estimates that industrial country restrictions on trade in textiles and garments have prevented the creation of well over 20 million jobs in developing countries (IMF and World Bank, 2002). In many countries, these jobs would have been taken by women workers. Notwithstanding important problems relating to labour rights, health and safety conditions and wage discrimination, many of these jobs would have created an escape route from rural poverty, while at the same time providing vulnerable populations with income for health and education spending.

The failure of industrialised countries to match trade reforms has played a determining role in the failure of trade reform in developing countries to deliver anticipated benefits. This unbalanced liberalisation is denying poor countries the opportunity to share in the benefits of globalisation.

Set against the limited trade liberalisation undertaken by Northern governments, many developing countries have dramatically lowered tariff and non-tariff barriers. This has been encouraged under IMF–World Bank loan conditions, which frequently require rapid trade liberalisation. One effect of the intervention of the Bretton Woods agencies in this area has been to reinforce the asymmetric pattern of liberalisation outlined above: in contrast to commitments undertaken at the WTO, Northern governments do not have to reciprocate unilateral liberalisation carried out by developing countries under IMF–World Bank programmes. There is also evidence that poorly designed and weakly sequenced liberalisation programmes have undermined the livelihoods of the poor, reducing the contribution of trade to poverty reduction. In the case of Haiti, rapid liberalisation of the rice sector resulted in the country being flooded with heavily subsidised US rice, with damaging consequences for rural poverty (Oxfam, 2002a: chapter 5).

The IMF and World Bank attempt to justify their role in promoting trade liberalisation by citing econometric evidence purporting to show that more open economies achieve more rapid growth and poverty reduction. However, the evidence itself is at best contentious – and at worst a sophisticated irrelevance. By using trade:GDP ratios to measure openness, the World Bank has diverted attention from more important indicators of trade policy, including the speed and depth of liberalisation. Many of the most successful developing countries in terms of reaping the benefits of integration into global markets – such as China, Vietnam and Mauritius – have combined rising trade:GDP ratios with relatively high levels of protection and a slow pace of liberalisation. There are no blueprints for success, but this raises questions over the liberalisation blueprint advocated by the IMF and World Bank.

Agricultural policy

Agricultural trade has a major bearing on poverty reduction efforts. Approximately three-quarters of the poorest people in developing countries live in rural areas. Their livelihoods are affected both by export opportunities and by competition from imports. Subsidies in industrialised countries exclude poor countries from world markets. They also result in unfair competition in local markets, since smallholder farmers cannot compete on price with subsidised exports.

Declared to be the start of a new era in which the withdrawal of subsidies in industrialised countries would open new opportunities for poor countries, the Uruguay Round agreement on agriculture was heralded as a triumph for resolve and political will. In fact, the new era has yet to start. The agreement committed industrialised countries to subsidy and tariff reductions of 36 per cent. The action, however, has been minimal. By choosing a reference period (1986–1988) of very low world prices and high subsidisation as a yardstick for cuts, industrialised countries have been able to avoid meaningful reductions. As a result, there has been no real decline in agricultural protection.

While the headline figures point to subsidy cuts, these have been achieved through a reclassification exercise. Income transfers have continued but are classified as 'support payments' rather than subsidies. Annual emergency payments to US farmers, permissible under the WTO, have grown rapidly. The net effect has been to create the appearance of subsidy cuts while allowing past practices to continue.

- At the end of the 1990s, subsidies accounted for almost 40 per cent of the value of OECD agricultural output – the same as in 1986–1988.
- The average tariff imposed by industrialised countries on agricultural goods from developing countries is close to 20 per cent, almost five times higher than the average tariff on all goods.
- Tariff peaks for commodities such as groundnuts in the USA, and meat and dairy products in the EU, exceed 100 per cent.
- Processed food products attract tariffs at least as high as those on unprocessed products, and usually higher.
- In the cotton sector, US farmers produced a level of output valued at US$3 billion in world price terms, but received US$3.9 billion in subsidies.

These barriers represent a major obstacle to trade for developing countries seeking to break into export markets, and are estimated to cost them approximately US$20 billion per year. Developing countries also lose from the price-depressing effects of rich-country exports in third markets. For example, West African cotton farmers are estimated to have sustained foreign exchange losses in excess of US$200 million in 2001 as a direct result of US cotton subsidies.[2]

The continuation of export subsidisation has been equally damaging. Agriculture is the only area in the WTO where the practice of dumping, or the sale of exports at prices below the cost of production, is institutionalised as an acceptable practice. Of the twenty-five countries that reserved the right to use export subsidies under the Agreement on Agriculture, twenty-three were industrialised countries. Between them, these countries account for 93 per cent of the US$21 billion of export subsidies in the base period (Konandreas, 2002).

Oxfam's verdict on the Agreement on Agriculture is that it was designed to let industrialised countries continue with essentially the same policies. The Agreement has introduced minimal restraints, notably by creating a so-called Green Box arrangement under which certain forms of direct payments to farmers provided by the EU and the USA are not counted as trade-distorting subsidies. Imbalances in the agreement highlight the way in which the WTO framework has been subordinated by rich countries to the vested interests of large farmers and powerful lobbies in the agribusiness sector.

A better deal for the least-developed developing countries

At the 1996 Singapore Ministerial Conference, governments agreed to a 'Plan of Action, including provisions for ... duty free access aimed at improving the overall capacity of Least Developed Countries to respond to opportunities provided by the international trading system' (WTO, 1997). During the 2001 third UN developing country conference, industrialised nations failed to act on this commitment. As in other areas, there has been no real progress towards policies that might help the poorest countries capture larger shares of the benefits from trade.

The forty-nine countries classified by the UN as least developed countries (LDCs) are the poorest in the world. Around half of their population – some 300 million people – live below the poverty line. Collectively they account for less than 1 per cent of world trade. Yet several years after the Uruguay Round, their exports continue to face stringent protectionist barriers in industrialised countries:

- In the USA and Canada, only around one-tenth of all tariffs are above 5 per cent. Yet in both countries, approximately half of all LDC exports face tariffs higher than this.

- Imports into industrialised countries from LDCs are twice as likely to face tariffs in excess of 15 per cent as imports from other industrialised countries.
- Trade barriers are highest in sectors where LDCs have a potential comparative advantage. Restrictions are particularly high for sugar exports to the EU and clothing and footwear exports to the USA and Canada.

According to the World Bank, eliminating duties and quotas on LDC exports would generate US$2.5 billion in additional export earnings (Hoekman *et al.*, 2001). These are very large, static losses for countries facing extreme foreign exchange constraints. Even so, they understate the dynamic losses associated with lost opportunities for investment and growth. These losses translate into large-scale losses of employment opportunities and income for vulnerable populations, denying them a stake in the potential benefits of trade. In some countries, such as Canada and the USA, trade barriers against LDC imports cost more than is given in aid, demonstrating how bad trade policies can seriously undermine development assistance.

To its credit, the EU attempted to act on the commitment to improve market access for LDCs. Its 'Everything but Arms' (EBA) proposal called for the removal of all tariffs and quotas on LDC imports. However, the proposal adopted by governments was substantially watered down. Following intensive lobbying by farmers and agribusiness, liberalisation of trade in key products such as rice and sugar – the very products which offered the largest potential foreign exchange gains for LDCs – was postponed.

Special action for Africa

The special problems facing sub-Saharan Africa have consistently been acknowledged by developed nations. At the Lyon G-7 summit in 1996 they launched a New Global Partnership for Development, with a special focus on Africa. At the Okinawa summit, developed countries agreed to give HIPCs and other low-income developing countries a stake in world trade and to improve access for these countries to international markets. Similar pledges were made at the end of the Uruguay Round of world trade talks and in the Doha Development Agenda. Once again their performance has been less impressive than the rhetoric.

The challenge facing Africa is immense. It has 12 per cent of the world's population, but accounts for less than 1 per cent of exports – one-quarter of the share it enjoyed in the 1970s. Africa is the only region in which the incidence of poverty has increased during the 1990s. More than citizens in any other part of the developing world, Africans are being bypassed by the benefits of globalisation.

Industrialised countries have failed to act on their pledge to improve market access. Unrestricted access to industrialised countries would generate an additional US$2.5 billion in non-oil export earning – a rise of 14 per cent. Several initiatives have been launched ostensibly aimed at improving Africa's trade prospects. The US Africa Growth and Opportunity Act provides in theory for duty-free and quota-free access in textiles and garments. The EU's 'Everything but Arms' proposal provides similar concessions for a far wider group of products. However, generosity in each case is highly circumscribed. In the case of the USA, unrestricted duty- and quota-free access is open only to products using American yarn. Similarly, the EU modified its original 'Everything but Arms' proposal in the light of lobbying by agro-industries. Both sugar and rice are now subject to a far slower pace of liberalisation. On one estimate, Mozambique is losing around US$80 million a year because of lost export opportunities in sugar (Oxfam, 2002d).

But the problems facing Africa go beyond market access. The slump in global commodity prices has had a devastating impact on the region, causing economic collapse and large increases in poverty. Oxfam interviews with coffee farmers in Tanzania indicate that many are taking their children out of school in the face of a 50 per cent decline over three years in the price they receive for coffee. Primary commodities account for three-quarters of Africa's exports. Without concerted international effort to address the causes of low commodity prices, which are rooted in chronic over-supply, there is little prospect of Africa reversing its decline in world export shares (Oxfam, 2002a: chapter 6).

The proposal to establish an International Trade Organisation (ITO) in 1948, alongside the IMF and World Bank, included an objective to secure 'commodity prices as are fair to consumers and provide a reasonable return to producers'. Fifty-three years later, this promise has yet to be fulfilled. The issue of commodities has been kept off the WTO agenda, in stark contrast to the issues of concern to industrialised countries, such as investment or intellectual property.

Global patent rules that safeguard public health in poor countries

The application of the Trade-Related Aspects of Intellectual Property Rights (TRIPS) agreement to pharmaceutical products was one of the most controversial parts of the Uruguay Round agreement. The agreement established for the first time a global intellectual property regime enforceable through trade sanctions. That regime included a minimum twenty-year period of patent protection (Lanjouw and Cockburn, 2001; Oxfam, 2001a).

Developing-country governments raised concerns about the potential effect of more stringent patent protection on the affordability of vital medicines to the poor, and on development more generally. These concerns were partially reflected in provisions (Article 31) allowing for compulsory licences to override patent claims on public health grounds by authorising local production. The agreement also included a provision allowing countries to import a patented drug from another country if the patent holder was charging a higher price domestically – the so-called parallel importing provision. However, neither of these loopholes addressed the fundamental tensions in the agreement. In particular, they failed to address the rights of countries lacking a strong generic industry and therefore capable of producing cheaper versions of patented drugs. They also opened the door to extensive litigation on the part of companies seeking to restrict parallel importing rights. The weakness, from a public health standpoint, of the original agreement rapidly became apparent.

In South Africa, thirty-nine drugs companies began a court action to prevent the South African government from importing cheap generic copies of patented HIV/AIDS drugs. This case was followed by the US decision to take Brazil to a WTO dispute panel (see Oxfam, 2001b; Watkins, 2001). Once again, the aim of the complaint, subsequently withdrawn in the face of public protest, was to prevent Brazil from producing generic copies of vital drugs. The potential inflation in drugs prices related to more stringent patent protection is part of a broader problem. In a given year, 14 million people in developing countries will die from infectious diseases. Many factors contribute to this distressing figure, including poverty, weak health infrastructure, inadequate access to water and sanitation, and poor policies. But many of the deaths could be prevented if people could afford basic medicines. The TRIPS agreement poses an acute threat because it will raise the cost of medication. Patented medicines frequently cost more than ten times the price of generic equivalents. And for poor people, price differences of this scale can be a matter of life and death. The counter-case, argued by bodies representing the pharmaceuticals industry, is that patents are vital to create incentives for research into diseases affecting the poor. That such research is desperately needed is not in doubt. In its second White Paper on international development, the UK government pointed out that 90 per cent of drugs research is on diseases affecting 10 per cent of the world's population (DFID, 2000). It proposed to support research into drugs of use to the poor by guaranteeing the purchase of these products. The problem with seeking to create market incentives through the patent system is that the very basis of the incentive – namely, higher prices – has the effect of excluding the poor from markets.

Despite acknowledging the difficult public health issues raised by patenting, industrialised governments have supported the efforts of transnational pharmaceutical corporations to enforce the most stringent interpretation of the TRIPS agreement. The USA in particular has used the threat of bilateral trade sanctions to demand that the patent claims of US companies be enforced. Countries such as India, Argentina, the Dominican Republic, Brazil, Vietnam and Thailand have all been threatened under the 'Special 301' provision of US trade law. This contrasts in stark fashion with actions in industrialised countries.

Industrialised countries are guilty not just of threatening the health of vulnerable people in developing countries, but of extreme double standards. The US and Canadian governments have shown themselves willing to threaten to override patents at home when faced with bio-terrorist threats to their own citizens. Although no compulsory licences for patented antibiotics were eventually issued, the threat of purchasing low-cost generics was successfully used to bargain down prices. The application of one set of rules when North American public health is threatened, and another for the health crisis in poor countries, is unacceptable. Whatever the future threat posed by anthrax, the number of casualties that prompted the change in approach to patents pales into insignificance against the deaths associated with HIV/AIDS, which claims 2 million lives each year in Africa alone. Moreover, the budget constraints of Northern governments are far less severe than those of developing countries.

When trade ministers met at the WTO summit in Doha, in November 2001, they finally adopted a 'public health declaration' specifying that patents would not be allowed to take precedence over public health claims. Since then, there has been a protracted deadlock over the most appropriate measures for translating this commitment into action, not least because of the requirement that it reflects the provisions of the original agreement. Several developing countries have argued that in countries lacking a strong generic drugs industry, governments should be allowed to issue a 'compulsory licence' to override patent claims, and that generic manufacturers elsewhere should be automatically entitled to export to that country. This approach has been resisted by the USA, which wants each case to be considered separately on its merits, and by the global pharmaceuticals industry.

Aid and technical assistance to developing countries

At the end of the Uruguay Round, industrialised countries promised technical assistance to developing countries to help them meet the costs of implementing the Uruguay Round agreements, and to enhance their ability to participate in the WTO. Less developed countries were promised special treatment, but there is a huge gap between this promise and the actual disbursement of funds.

For many developing countries, the cost of implementing the Uruguay Round agreements is prohibitive, and places a huge burden on limited human resource capacities. It will cost Tanzania US$10 million to meet WTO customs evaluation standards, for example. The cost of drafting and enforcing new laws on intellectual property in Bangladesh is estimated at more than US$1 million per annum. Despite this, at the end of the 1990s the WTO budget for technical assistance was only US\$500,000, sufficient to meet less than one-fifth of the requests made for technical assistance.

The Integrated Framework to provide technical assistance to developing countries, launched in 1996, has an even more abysmal record. By the end of the 1990s it had failed, and was relaunched in 2002. To date, industrialised countries have provided US\$7 million to undertake a 'needs assessment' in a small group of pilot countries. There are no concrete funding commitments for the future to address the priorities that emerge.

Failure to provide adequate technical assistance is reflected in the huge imbalances in negotiating strength and institutional capacity at the WTO:

- The average developing-country trade mission at the WTO has three people, compared with seven for developed countries. Even a large country like Bangladesh has only one representative.
- Of the thirty-eight African countries in the WTO, fifteen have no resident delegate; four maintain only one-person offices.
- On average, there are forty-six delegate meetings per week in the WTO. There are complex negotiations across large areas of industrial, agricultural, investment and services policy that have profound implications for human development. Yet many of the world's poorest countries lack the capacity to monitor, let alone influence, the direction of these negotiations.

Industrialised countries also promised action to help developing countries acquire a greater share of the benefits of international trade. Financial and technical assistance is crucial to help them take advantage of new market opportunities. In particular, developing countries need support to address the constraints in producing goods for export, such as inadequate infrastructure and limited technical facilities and skills to add value to domestic produce and ensure that goods meet quality and other export standards.

Will the WTO help create the conditions for sustained growth and poverty reduction in developing countries?

The Doha Round of trade talks has been dubbed the 'development round' – and there is much encouraging rhetoric for developing countries. The document adopted by trade ministers at Doha acknowledged that 'There is need for positive efforts designed to ensure that developing countries ... secure a share in the growth in international trade commensurate with the needs of their economic development' (WTO, 2002). Industrialised countries claim that nothing in the WTO will hamper the ability of developing countries to achieve this goal. This is untrue: WTO agreements restrict governments from introducing policies that might enable their countries to reap the benefits of integration into the global economy.

Under the Uruguay Round agreement, developing countries lost the right to implement many of the policies that had been central to East Asia's success. These included the selective protection of domestic industries, targeted subsidies for domestic firms, restrictions on foreign investors, the copying of patented technologies, and requirements on foreign investors to link with the local economy.

The TRIPS agreement is a particular concern. Meanwhile, the WTO Trade-Related Investment Measures (TRIMs) agreement, concluded in 1994, poses similar problems. It severely restricts the right of governments to impose 'local content requirements' – an obligation to source inputs from local industry – on foreign investors. Countries such as South Korea and Taiwan used this local content rule extensively to build dynamic linkages between the export sector and domestic firms. Today, these two countries account for over one-third of medium- and high-technology exports from developing countries. Unlike countries such as Mexico, they have succeeded in entering dynamic new markets on the basis of domestic innovation and enterprise – and they capture a larger share of the value of their exports as a result. Yet the policies behind their success have been outlawed through the WTO.

The General Agreement on Trade in Services (GATS) is another area of concern. Negotiations in this area cover not just financial and technical services, but also utilities such as electricity, water and education. To date, the effects have been minimal. However, powerful corporate lobbies, led by the Coalition of Service Industries, and strongly supported by both the EU and the USA, are seeking to advance an agenda for radical liberalisation. In principle, developing countries could gain from some aspects of service market liberalisation, especially in areas such as software and construction. However, firms in developing countries are ill-equipped to compete with transnational corporation service providers in areas such as finance and insurance.

There is a real danger that these WTO agreements will lock developing countries into a subordinate position in the global trading system, leaving them unable to upgrade their exports. Instead of supporting the development of East Asian-style dynamic export growth, the WTO is promoting Mexican-style dependency on investment by transnational corporations, weak linkages between the export sector and the domestic economy, and low wages.

Debt relief

A third broad Goal on global partnership concerns debt relief. Unsustainable debt presents a huge barrier to progress in the fight against poverty (Oxfam, 2002e). Debt repayments by some of the poorest countries in the world are diverting the necessary resources required for development financing. The Heavily Indebted Poor Country Initiative, announced in

1996, was to eliminate debt as an obstacle to poverty reduction. In 1999 the HIPC Initiative was reformed. The new Enhanced HIPC initiative provided for earlier and deeper debt relief, and sought to establish a close link between debt relief and poverty reduction. However, the level of debt repayment after the Enhanced HIPC initiative debt relief remains far too high, undermining the necessary investment needed to accelerate poverty reduction.

The HIPC Initiative has already freed up resources from debt servicing for twenty-six low-income countries, enabling pro-poor expenditure and some progress towards the Millennium Development Goals (IMF and IDA, 2002). Preliminary analysis of the HIPC Initiative's achievements shows that in some countries debt relief has resulted in demonstrable social and economic gains (World Bank, 2001a). For 2001–2003, the HIPC Initiative reduces the average debt service paid by HIPC graduates by about one-third. Among these countries, social expenditures are expected to increase in 2000–2003 from the levels in 1998–1999. Where countries have had resources freed up from debt, the proceeds have resulted in some new development programmes and economic progress, such as a free immunisation programme for children in Mozambique; the abolition of user fees for primary education in Uganda, Malawi and Tanzania, and in rural areas of Benin; and planned increases in spending on HIV/AIDS prevention in Mali, Mozambique and Senegal. Moreover, the requirement to engage in a consultation process in designing Poverty Reduction Strategy Papers (PRSPs) has helped to increase the potential for people to influence national resource allocation processes.

But the HIPC Initiative stops short of what is needed. Although the examples demonstrate that debt relief can generate additional resources that contribute to furthering human development, the socio-economic gains are by no means universal and, where they exist, they are limited and precarious. Worse, the development gains made with the small additional resources provided by the Enhanced HIPC Initiative may be swept away without additional financing. HIPC countries, like all low-income countries, continue to face development challenges such as the spread of HIV/AIDS, low literacy levels and poor nutrition, and they face them equipped with scarce and highly vulnerable domestic resources. Given the fragile social and economic conditions prevalent in HIPCs, the benefits derived from limited amounts of debt relief are likely to be small or easily reversed.

For example, in almost all HIPCs, private-sector flows will not make up for chronic resource deficits. The marginalisation of the African continent from global trade is equivalent to a loss of 21 per cent of regional GDP, or US$68 billion per annum. For Africa in 2001, after adjusting for inflation, non-fuel commodity prices are at one-half the annual average value for the period 1970–1981. The World Bank and IMF estimate that eight to ten of the HIPCs most affected by the slump in commodity prices will have higher debt:export ratios by completion point than the 150 per cent target set by the HIPC Initiative itself. Instead, the HIPCs continue to rely on external official assistance, particularly in the form of grants, to fund their domestic spending and balance of payments gaps. Despite optimistic projections in decision-point documents, new HIPCs are not receiving the levels of external finance anticipated that will in turn help them to achieve the Millennium Development Goals.

Levels of debt relief

Under the Enhanced HIPC Initiative, debtors receive debt relief under a two-phase process. After complying with an IMF programme and demonstrating progress towards the development of a PRSP, they reach a decision point. At this stage, calculations are made of the level of debt reduction needed for them to reach sustainability, defined in terms of a range of threshold indicators. The (net present) value of debt stock is measured against exports of goods and services. If the ratio of debt to exports is greater than 150 per cent after the full application of the traditional debt-relief mechanism, the country's debt is considered unsustainable. It then qualifies for interim debt-service relief to reduce the level below the threshold. Provided that it continues to comply with the IMF programme and finalises a comprehensive PRSP, it can then graduate to completion point and receive debt-stock relief. The arrangement is intended to provide a permanent exit from unsustainable debt.

Four countries – Bolivia, Uganda, Tanzania and Mozambique – have so far reached completion point. Another twenty-two are receiving interim debt relief, having reached decision point. IMF and World Bank staff reports invariably express the level of debt relief provided in terms of long-term changes in debt stock, or debt:service rates. For example, the April 2001 review noted that nominal debt relief for the twenty-six countries covered amount to US$40 billion (and US$25 billion in net present value terms) (IMF and World Bank, 2001a). For the same group of countries, the average annual debt servicing as a percentage of exports for 2001–2005 was projected to fall by almost one-third from the 1998–1999 level. In a similar vein, debt service relative to government revenue is projected to fall from an average of 24 per cent a year to 13 per cent over the same reference period. Viewed in the context of strategies for mobilising financial resources for poverty reduction, this represents a huge drain on public finances:

- Out of twenty HIPCs at decision point, Mali, Niger, Sierra Leone and Zambia will have annual debt payments due in 2003–2005 which will be higher than their annual debt service paid in 1998–2000.
- Five countries (Ethiopia, Guinea-Bissau, Honduras, Nicaragua and Uganda) will be paying as much in debt service payments as before the HIPC Initiative.

- In six countries, annual debt service will be reduced by a modest US$15 million in 2003–2005.
- The medium- to long-term projections on debt servicing are also alarming: Senegal's debt service jumps by 61 per cent in 2004 and Honduras's by 93 per cent.

Savings measured in terms of the gap between projected debt servicing pre- and post-Enhanced HIPC Initiative (much of which would not have been paid in any case) have limited relevance when it comes to real current spending capacity. Similarly, nominal debt stock figures provide some insights into financial sustainability, but offer little information about budget resources. Since it is these resources that dictate what governments are able to finance, the sustainability of debt should be assessed against budget criteria, as well as foreign exchange ratios.

Debt and government revenue

The current system of debt relief, the Enhanced HIPC Initiative, is not working effectively. When it is measured against domestic resource mobilisation, its shortcomings are painfully apparent. The problem is that debt repayments continue to absorb a large share of the limited revenue base available to governments. If sustainability is measured against the criteria of financing for human development, the debt burdens of many countries – especially those at the centre of HIV/AIDS crisis – are unsustainable. Consequently, some countries will soon be left with unsustainable debts once again. Not only are some HIPCs spending more on debt relief, they are overshooting the World Bank and IMF's own definitions of debt sustainability.

Of the twenty-six countries receiving Enhanced HIPC debt relief in 2002, half of them are still spending an average of 15 per cent or more of government revenue on debt repayments. Only two of the twenty-six HIPCs currently receiving debt relief have debt-service repayments equivalent to less than one-half of total spending on health. While several HIPCs now spend less than 10 per cent of revenue on debt servicing, the repayments are crowding out vital public investment in health, education and other areas. Thirteen of the twenty-six countries receiving debt relief are still spending more on debt than on public health. These are some of the worst cases:

- Zambia and Malawi have amongst the highest HIV/AIDS prevalence rates in the world. But while Zambia has almost 1 million people affected, the country is spending 30 per cent more on debt than on health. Malawi's health budget is equivalent to its debt servicing. These are countries in which HIV/AIDS is driving an increase in child mortality.

- In Cameroon, HIV prevalence rates have passed 5 per cent. Debt repayments amount to three and a half times the spending on health.
- Zambia, Mali, Niger and The Gambia, amongst other countries, all spend more on debt than on education.
- Several countries – including Cameroon, Sierra Leone and Mauritania – spend more than twice as much on debt as on education.

Unfortunately, the tensions between debt servicing and financing for basic services are not untypical. Even HIPC countries that have benefited from significant debt relief face an acute mismatch between the claims of creditors and the resources allocated to investment in basic public services:

- For every $1 that Mali spends on health, $1.60 is transferred to creditors.
- Niger, with the highest child mortality in the world, continues to spend more on debt servicing than public health even after debt relief.
- Sierra Leone, with one of the world's highest maternal mortality rates, will spend 2.5 times more on debt servicing than on health in 2002 on current projections.

Debt repayment obligations inevitably clash with efforts to help finance development strategies called for under UN targets. For instance, the national strategic plan for HIV/AIDS developed by the government of Malawi plans to allocate around US$24 million annually of domestic resources. Yet its capacity to undertake these investments is being compromised not just by a disastrous famine, but also by a debt-service profile that resulted in transfers to creditors of US$57 million in 2002.

Heavily indebted countries in West Africa face acute problems. National adult HIV/AIDS prevalence rates have already passed 5 per cent in several countries, reaching 7 per cent in Burkina Faso. Even countries with relatively low debt-service:revenue ratios face debt-related financing constraints. In Burkina Faso the financing provisions for the national AIDS strategy amount to approximately one-half of the amount that every woman, child and man in Burkina Faso currently transfers to external creditors.

The finance and service delivery challenge facing HIPC governments is of daunting proportions. When the human and financial implications of HIV/AIDS are considered, the inadequacy of the Enhanced HIPC Initiative is as apparent as the gap between rhetoric on development and action (or more accurately, their inaction) on development financing. According to the Commission of Macroeconomics and Health, governments of low-income countries need to increase spending on health by 1.6 per cent of GNP a year to 2015 (based on 2002 costs) in order to move towards universal coverage (WHO, 2001). Current spending on debt servicing after Enhanced HIPC Initiative debt relief amounts on average to 3 per cent of GDP. In other words, the additional health spending could be financed to a significant degree by a transfer of resources from external creditors to domestic service providers.

The mirage of debt sustainability

There is a misconception over the time at which countries achieve debt sustainability, defined by the World Bank and the IMF as a 150 per cent debt:exports ratio. Board papers assert that debt sustainability will be achieved on reaching completion point, and explicitly act on the assumption that debt relief will be 'delivered unconditionally'. But rather than occurring immediately, the debt relief is implemented over as long as thirty- to forty-year periods, depending on the relief method chosen.

As a result of the slide in commodity prices, some countries are already overshooting the World Bank- and IMF-defined threshold of debt sustainability. The international financial institutions' response of supplementing the HIPC Initiative with a 'one-off' post-completion point 'topping-up' facility is little guarantee that the Initiative's graduates will be in a position to sustain their debt-servicing liabilities in the short term, let alone meet the promise of a 'robust exit from unsustainable debts'. Uganda, the first HIPC graduate, currently has debts of over 200 per cent of the debt: exports ratio. This will be the third time Uganda has exceeded its debt sustainability after reaching completion points. The March 2002 Completion Point Board paper for Burkina Faso concludes with the expectation that after receiving its 'topping up', the country may achieve debt sustainability by the year 2016! However, contrary to most preceding definitions (net present value to exports) of debt sustainability produced by the World Bank and IMF, it asserts that 'debt sustainability is not endangered' because there is sufficient liquidity to cover debt servicing. This is the first time, and against the agreed rules, that the World Bank and IMF have changed definitions of debt sustainability to include liquidity as the operative criterion.

World Bank and IMF projections and estimates for future growth, investment rates and financial inflows have been systematically over-optimistic and bear no relation to rates achieved in the past. The use of wholly unrealistic assumptions about the future financial and economic performance of HIPCs is bound to lead to unrealistic debt sustainability analysis and countries overshooting their sustainability thresholds.

Amongst the multiple difficulties faced by HIPCs is their extreme vulnerability to external shocks. In particular, their high concentration of exports on few commodities leaves them acutely sensitive to external shocks in commodity prices and climatic conditions. The current criterion of the net present value of debt to exports for debt sustainability analysis therefore has a limited use. Because of its reliance on the narrow and highly volatile variable of export earnings as a means of calculating future debt sustainability, it is the key failing of the HIPC Initiative. Also, exports alone do not reflect the resources available to HIPC governments for poverty reduction expenditures. It would be quite possible, under the current criteria, for a country's debts to be considered sustainable from the point of view of external viability while that country has insufficient resources to meet even the most basic poverty reduction expenditures. For most HIPCs, exports are therefore an unreliable predictor of medium-term and, for some, even short-term debt sustainability.

Effective debt relief could help by releasing the resources needed for a concerted assault on poverty. The financial implications of HIV/AIDS for the attainment of the Millennium Development Goals point to a wider need to reassess the adequacy of the HIPC Initiative. Changing that picture for the better in the face of the challenge posed by the epidemic will require unprecedented commitment to resource mobilisation. If governments are serious about achieving agreed human development targets, they need to assess – or reassess – the costs of doing so in the light of the HIV/AIDS epidemic. And creditors need to balance their claims against the financing needs of debtor countries.

Notwithstanding a US$1 billion 'top-up' at the Kananaskis G8 summit, developed countries have consistently failed to respond to the inadequacies of the Enhanced HIPC Initiative. No attempt has been made to revise debt sustainability indicators in the light of the financing requirements for addressing the HIV/AIDS crisis and achieving the Millennium Development Goals. Meanwhile, many countries are being forced back into acute debt unsustainability by a protracted decline in commodity prices, weak aid flows and wildly over-optimistic export growth projections by IMF and World Bank staff.

Actions required to achieve the Millennium Development Goals

More than additional financing will be required if the Millennium Development Goals are to be met and a genuinely equal global partnership achieved. Improvements in the delivering and quality of service are a precondition for progress. Money is not the only input that matters – or even the most important one. However, many of the poorest countries lack the domestic financial resources needed to achieve the 2015 targets. Moreover, there is now a credibility gap between the rhetoric of the industrialised countries, the World Bank and IMF, and the reality of development financing. Action needs to be taken in relation to aid, trade and debt for the Millennium Development Goals to be reached.

Financing the gap

Various estimates have been made of the costs of achieving the Millennium Development Goals. The World Bank suggests an indicative range of US$40–60 billion in additional aid for the next fifteen years. Whilst it is difficult to calculate exactly how much money is needed, the estimates made are, in Oxfam's view, significant understatements of the resources needed. This is because the World Bank's estimates understate the cost of achieving the Millennium Development Goal for health, and associated investments in water and sanitation. According to Oxfam, the real cost of achieving the Millennium Development Goals by 2015 will be approximately US$100 billion extra per year (Oxfam, 2002b).

The headline figure is large, but affordable. Had donors met their pledge to spend 0.7 per cent of GNP on aid, they would now be spending an extra US$114 billion. The financing requirements for achieving the 0.7 per cent target are modest in relation to government expenditure. The average increase in government spending required for the G-7 countries would be around 1.4 per cent. Instead, they have cut their aid budgets.

The cost of this investment in human development has to be assessed against the potential benefits, both human and economic. According to the Commission on Macroeconomics and Health, aid investment equivalent to 0.1 per cent of the GNP of industrialised countries could avert 8 million deaths a year by 2015 (WHO, 2001). Using extremely conservative estimates, the Commission suggests that the increased wealth generated by improved health would represent three times the costs of increased health spending by rich and poor countries.

Just as the different aspects of deprivation are mutually reinforcing, so are the benefits to human development. For instance, each additional year of education is associated with an increase in output of around 9 per cent among smallholder farmers, with the adoption of new technologies. Improvements in girls' education are intimately related to better health, especially for children. Comparative research across countries has found that each additional year of maternal education reduces child mortality by around 8 per cent. Improved health is also one of the requirements for improved learning.

The uncertainty that continues to surround debates on financing for Millennium Development Goals highlights the need for all developing countries to work with donors in developing reliable national estimates. This exercise should be a central part of the process for preparing Poverty Reduction Strategy Papers (PRSPs). The financing requirements should be reflected both in government financial frameworks and in IMF/World Bank programmes. More immediately, and notwithstanding current donor reluctance to increase aid, it is important that the UN and World Bank avoid tailoring figures to suit the preferences of industrialised countries.

Whatever the precise costs of achieving the Millennium Development

Goals, two things are clear. First, while there is scope for additional financing through resource mobilisation in least developed countries (LDCs), through improved efficiency, greater equality and enhanced revenue collection, poverty imposes financial constraints. The Millennium Development Goals will not be achieved without a major and sustained increase in aid spending. Second, increased aid will not be enough. Past experience shows that political commitment on the part of aid recipients is vital. Building health and education systems that are responsive to the needs of the poor, and reprioritising public spending to emphasise poverty reduction, are the keys to success.

Developed countries should set a five-year time-frame for achieving the 0.7 per cent aid target. This would generate US$130 billion a year in additional financing by 2007 – sufficient not just to achieve the Millennium Development Goals, but also to sustain a broader campaign against poverty. The costs of that campaign would amount to an annual increase in government expenditure of 0.2 per cent over five years for countries such as the UK and Germany, and 0.3 per cent a year for the USA. The cost of success in the war against poverty is modest when compared with other priorities adopted by governments:

- The US$11 billion annual increase in spending required for the USA represents around one-quarter of the increase in military spending scheduled for 2003, and one-seventh of the tax cuts for the period 2002–2014.
- The EU could reach the 0.7 per cent target if it were to increase aid by an amount equivalent to the subsidies provided under the Common Agricultural Policy (US$35 billion).

Enhancing the Enhanced HIPC Initiative

The HIPC Initiative marked an important step forward in addressing the debt problems of low-income countries. It provided for the first time an integrated framework for dealing with all categories of debt, and it set limits on creditor demands linked to a notion of sustainability. The Enhanced HIPC Initiative provided for earlier, deeper and broader debt reduction. But it has not gone far enough. The Initiative is teetering on the brink of failure in its central objective, namely, the provision of a credible guarantee that countries entering it will be provided with a once-and-for-all exit from unsustainable debt.

As a debt-relief strategy, the benefits of the Initiative are being eroded by wider pressures and mismanagement. This is doubly unfortunate, since there is evidence that it is contributing in a powerful way to poverty reduction efforts across a wide range of countries. Five interacting problems are contributing to this outcome: (1) failure to prioritise the government revenue: debt service ratio in assessing sustainability; (2) failure to factor in low and unstable commodity prices; (3) persistent over-estimation of export growth prospects by the IMF; (4) insufficient and uncertain debt-relief provision prior to completion; and (5) inadequate flows of aid.

From the outset, levels of debt relief have been dictated by what creditors deem affordable, rather than by the needs of debtors. Moreover, the criteria for determining levels of debt relief reflect a narrowly defined financial perspective, focused on foreign exchange indicators. No attempt has been made to develop debt sustainability indicators that reflect the financing requirements for achieving poverty reduction goals. The inadequate weight attached to the proportion of government revenue allocated to debt servicing reflects this bias. Another problem has been the central role of the IMF in managing the Enhanced HIPC Initiative. Assessments of country performance by IMF staff that are often at best weakly related to poverty reduction considerations have resulted in delayed disbursement of debt relief, introducing high levels of uncertainty into the framework.

Current responses to the problems posed by the Enhanced HIPC Initiative betray a short-sighted piecemeal approach. Successive meetings of G7 finance ministers have witnessed repeated wrangles over financing 'top-ups' to compensate for adverse commodity price trends – and for the reckless projections of export performance developed by IMF staff. No attempt has been made to confront the more fundamental challenge of integrating debt relief into a coherent resource mobilisation strategy for realising the Millennium Development Goals.

What is needed is a bold new strategy, which should include the following elements:

Assessing the financing implications of HIV/AIDS

The financial assessments of the implications of HIV/AIDS in HIPCs should inform evaluations of debt sustainability and levels of debt relief provided. As part of the PRSP process, all countries should cost their national AIDS plans, identify the financing gaps that could be filled through debt relief and other measures, and ensure that financing provisions are reflected in national budgets and medium-term expenditure frameworks.

Deepening debt relief

Current debt sustainability indicators suffer from two problems: they are tangentially related to resource mobilisation for poverty reduction goals, and they are not sufficiently generous. An upper ceiling of 5 per cent should be set on the proportion of government revenue allocated to debt servicing. Such a limit would have mobilised an additional US$1.6 billion in the 26 countries currently receiving Enhanced HIPC debt relief. While this implies real costs for creditors, these costs represent less than 3 per cent of existing aid flows. The human costs of continuing with business as usual are beyond estimation.

Broadening debt relief

There is a strong case for broadening debt relief in response to the threat posed by HIV/AIDS and wider poverty reduction challenges. For instance, both Kenya and Angola have been deemed 'sustainable debt' cases under the existing framework, and Nigeria is not covered. The limitations of the HIPC Initiative have been further exposed by crises in the private capital market. Indonesia – the world's fourth most populous country – has been allocating more than one-fifth of government revenue to debt servicing since the 1997 financial crisis, rising to over one-third in some years. No effective debt-relief mechanisms exist (despite the fact that Indonesia has a lower income per capita than Honduras, which is eligible for HIPC debt relief). This has hampered social and economic recovery. It has also undermined efforts to curtail HIV/AIDS. After more than a decade with negligible rates of HIV, the country is now seeing infection rates increase rapidly. There is an urgent need for the international community to look beyond the confines of the HIPC Initiative to provide effective protection from the claims of private capital market creditors, including negotiated debt write-offs and standstill agreements.

Recruiting new gatekeepers

The IMF and the World Bank, with the former first among equals, remain the gatekeepers to entry into the HIPC Initiative, and the arbiters of compliance with conditions during the interim debt-relief period. There is little evidence that the IMF in particular prioritises approaches to public spending aimed at achieving poverty reduction goals. This suggests a strong case for the involvement of other agencies, including specialised UN bodies.

Strengthening and democratising Poverty Reduction Strategy Papers

Most PRSPs provide little more than cursory treatment of the links between HIV/AIDS and poverty, and few set out clear estimates of the resource implications of responding to the crisis. Such estimates would help to clarify debt relief and aid needs. More generally, there is a need for a renewed emphasis on costing poverty reduction goals, and on creating effective public expenditure management systems. Civil society could – and should – make an important contribution to debates on the use of debt relief to support HIV/AIDS strategies and wider poverty reduction efforts.

Implementing an 'Education for All' action plan

Increased public investment in education is urgently needed in HIPC countries, both to absorb the costs associated with HIV/AIDS, and to support effective preventive work. In April 2002, finance and development ministers from rich countries finally agreed to support an action plan aimed at getting all children into school by 2015. Implementation will require US$4 billion a year, but no financing deal has yet been agreed. This should be seen as a key element in the HIV/AIDS strategy.

Trade

In the area of trade, hypocrisy and double standards have characterised the behaviour of industrialised countries towards the poor. Such behaviour has not only undermined the efforts of developing countries to reap the rewards of trade for development, but has also undermined the credibility of the multilateral trading system. To ensure a genuine partnership in development in addition to the attainment of the Millennium Development Goals, the cycle of broken promises must end. Otherwise, the Millennium Development Goals will join a growing list of failed development strategies.

In the area of developing countries' access to open markets, industrialised nations need to ensure that average tariffs for imports from developing countries are no higher than tariffs on imports from developed countries. Tariffs in areas like agriculture and labour-intensive manufactured goods that are of special interest to developing countries must be scaled down. A moratorium on anti-dumping actions against developing countries must be declared. In terms of market access for textiles and garments, industrialised countries should catch up within a year with the schedule for phasing out the MFA quotas. They should eliminate tariffs and quotas on all textile and garment exports from developing countries by January 2004.

In the area of reduced agricultural protectionism, a comprehensive ban on all agricultural export subsidies must be introduced in all industrialised countries. The rights of developing countries to protect their agricultural systems for food security reasons have to be acknowledged. The structure of agricultural support to promote social and environmental objectives, including a transition to less intensive agriculture, must be re-geared. Developed countries must substantially reduce tariffs against developing-country agricultural exports, including processed food products.

A better deal for the least-developed developing countries requires industrialised countries to agree to provide duty-free and quota-free access to all products exported from the least-developed developing countries.

In terms of special action for Africa, the New Partnership for Africa's Development (NEPAD) provides an important opportunity to strengthen

Africa's capacity to benefit from trade. Industrialised countries should support it by substantially improving market access for all products exported from sub-Saharan Africa. They should also convene an international conference to explore strategies for tackling the crisis in commodity markets.

The system of global patent rules that safeguards public health in poor countries – the TRIPS agreement – needs to be reviewed. The social and development objectives of TRIPS should be paramount. Each provision of TRIPS should be interpreted in this light. Health obligations should take precedence over intellectual property rights. Nothing in the TRIPS agreement should prevent countries from adopting measures to protect public health. Governments should have an absolute right to introduce compulsory licences in order to meet pressing public health needs, and to import patented drugs from the cheapest source. They should agree to an in-depth review of the agreement from a health and development perspective, with a view to amending it in this light. The length and scope of pharmaceutical patents should also be reduced.

In the area of aid and technical assistance, industrialised countries must increase substantially the funding of trade-related technical assistance and capacity-building to improve the participation of developing countries in the WTO, and their ability to take advantage of new market opportunities.

For the WTO to help create conditions for sustained growth and poverty reduction in developing countries, future meetings need to focus on areas of priority concerns to developing countries. The WTO can do this by providing meaningful special and differential treatment for developing countries by extending transition periods for developing and least developed countries to comply with TRIPS, in line with their achievement of health and development milestones. Industrialised countries have to give developing nations more flexibility in areas such as protection for infant industries and regulation for foreign investment. There also needs to be a review of the implications of TRIPS for access to technology by developing countries.

Notes

1 However, developing country tariff barriers are on average higher than those of developed countries. Developing country exports generally face higher barriers in entering other developing countries than they do developed ones (World Bank, 2001b).
2 This is based on data provided by the International Cotton Advisory Committee. For a detailed analysis of the structure of US protectionism in cotton, see Oxfam (2002c).

References

DFID (2000) *Realising Human Rights for Poor People: Strategies for Achieving the International Development Targets*, London: Department for International Development.

Hoekman, B., Ng, F. and Olarreaga, M. (2001) *Tariff Peaks in the Quad and Least Developed Country Exports*, Development Research Group, World Bank, February, at http://www.worldbank.org/research/trade/pdf/peak.pdf.

International Fund for Agricultural Development (IFAD) (2001) *Rural Poverty Report 2001*, Rome: IFAD.

International Monetary Fund (IMF) and International Development Agency (IDA) (2002) *Financial Impact of the HIPC Initiative: First 26 Country Cases*, July 2002.

International Monetary Fund (IMF) and World Bank (2001) 'HIPC Progress Report', mimeo, April, Washington, DC: World Bank.

International Monetary Fund (IMF) and World Bank (2002) 'Market Access for Developing Countries – Selected Issues', paper prepared by staff of the IMF/World Bank, 26 September.

International Textile and Clothing Bureau (2002) 'Agreement on Textiles and Clothing: Where It Stands', mimeo, April, Geneva: ITCB.

Konandreas P. (2002) 'Agriculture and agricultural policies in the developing countries ten years after the Uruguay Round Agreement on Agriculture', mimeo. Paper presented to conference on agricultural policy reform and the WTO: where are we heading? Capri (Italy), June 24–26.

Lanjouw, J. and Cockburn, I. (2001) 'New Pills for Poor People? Empirical Evidence after the GATT, *World Development*, 29(2), 265–289.

Maxwell, S. and Riddell, R. (1998) 'Conditionality or Contract: Perspectives on Partnership for Development', *Journal of International Development*, 10(2): 257–268.

Organisation for Economic Cooperation and Development (OECD) (1996) *Shaping the Twenty-First Century*, Paris: OECD.

—— (2001) *Development Co-operation Report*, Paris: OECD.

Oxfam (2001a) 'Patent Injustice: How World Trade Rules Threaten the Health of Poor People', Oxfam Briefing Paper, 02/01, Oxford: Oxfam.

——(2001b) 'Drugs Companies versus Brazil: the Threat to Public Health', Oxfam Briefing Paper, Oxford: Oxfam.

—— (2002a) 'Rigged Rules and Double Standards: Trade, Globalisation and the Fight Against Poverty', Oxfam Make Trade Fair Briefing Paper, Oxford: Oxfam.

—— (2002b) 'Last Chance in Monterrey: Meeting the Challenge of Poverty Reduction', Oxfam Briefing Paper 17, Oxford: Oxfam.

—— (2002c) 'Cultivating Poverty – The Impact of US Cotton Subsidies on Africa', Make Trade Fair Briefing Paper 30, Oxford: Oxfam.

—— (2002d) 'The Great EU Sugar Scam: How Europe's Sugar Regime is Devastating Livelihoods in the Developing World', Oxfam Briefing Paper 27, Oxford: Oxfam.

—— (2002e) 'Debt Relief and the HIV/AIDS Crisis in Africa: Does the Heavily Indebted Poor Countries (HIPC) Initiative Go Far Enough?', Briefing Paper 25, Oxford: Oxfam.

United Nations Children's Fund (UNICEF) (2002) *State of the World's Children*, New York: UNICEF.

United Nations Development Programme (UNDP) (2002) *Human Development Report*, New York: UNDP.

Watkins, K. (2001) 'Pharmaceutical Patents', in Bircham, E. and Charlton, J. (eds) *Anti-capitalism*, Sydney: Bookmarks.

White, H. (1999) 'Foreign Aid', in *Encyclopaedia of Political Economy*, London: Routledge.

—— (2002) 'Long Run Trends and Recent Developments in Official Assistance from Donor Countries', paper prepared for WIDER conference on external finance, August 2002, Helsinki.

World Bank (2001a) *Financial Impact of the HIPC Initiative: First 23 Country Cases*, June 2001, http://www.una.dk/ffd/Godk_int_org/Financial_Impact_end_June.pdf.

—— (2001b) *Globalization, Growth, and Poverty: Building an Inclusive World Economy*, New York: OUP for the World Bank.

World Health Organisation (WHO) (2001) *Macroeconomics and Health: Investing in Health for Economic Development*. Report of the Commission on Macroeconomics and Health, Geneva.

World Trade Organisation (WTO) (1997) Comprehensive and integrated WTO plan of action for the Least-Developed countries, adopted on 13 December 1996, at http://www.wto.org/english/tratop_e/devel_e/action_plan.htm.

—— (2002) *The Road to Doha and Beyond: A Road Map for Successfully Concluding the Doha Development Round*, at http://www.wto.org/english/res_e/booksp_e/roadtodoha_e.pdf.

Index